GEOGRAPHIES OF REGULATION

In the nineteenth century, British authorities at home and abroad attempted to regulate prostitution in order to combat the spread of venereal diseases. Philip Howell examines in detail four sites of such regulated prostitution – Liverpool, Cambridge, Gibraltar and Hong Kong – and considers the similarities as well as the differences between colonial and metropolitan practices. Placing these sites within their local, regional and global contexts, the author argues that the British administration of commercial sexuality was deeper and more extensive than conventionally portrayed. The book challenges our understanding of what constitutes colonial regulation and also confronts imperial historiographies in which projects are simply translated from metropolis to periphery. By emphasizing both particular sites of regulated prostitution, and their place in the British imperial world, this book contributes not only to histories of gender and sexuality, but also to the revision of British imperial history.

PHILIP HOWELL is Senior Lecturer in the Department of Geography, Cambridge University, and a Fellow of Emmanuel College, Cambridge.

Cambridge Studies in Historical Geography 43

Series editors
ALAN R. H. BAKER, RICHARD DENNIS, DERYCK HOLDSWORTH

Cambridge Studies in Historical Geography encourages exploration of the philosophies, methodologies and techniques of historical geography and publishes the results of new research within all branches of the subject. It endeavours to secure the marriage of traditional scholarship with innovative approaches to problems and to sources, aiming in this way to provide a focus for the discipline and to contribute towards its development. The series is an international forum for publication in historical geography which also promotes contact with workers in cognate disciplines.

For a full list of titles in the series, please go to: www.cambridge.org/historicalgeography

GEOGRAPHIES OF REGULATION

Policing Prostitution in Nineteenth-Century Britain and the Empire

PHILIP HOWELL

CAMBRIDGE UNIVERSITY PRESS
Cambridge, New York, Melbourne, Madrid, Cape Town, Singapore,
São Paulo, Delhi

Cambridge University Press
The Edinburgh Building, Cambridge CB2 8RU, UK

Published in the United States of America by Cambridge University Press, New York

www.cambridge.org
Information on this title: www.cambridge.org/9780521853651

© Philip Howell 2009

This publication is in copyright. Subject to statutory exception
and to the provisions of relevant collective licensing agreements,
no reproduction of any part may take place without
the written permission of Cambridge University Press.

First published 2009

Printed in the United Kingdom at the University Press, Cambridge

A catalogue record for this publication is available from the British Library

Library of Congress Cataloguing in Publication data
Howell, Philip, 1965–
 Geographies of regulation: policing prostitution in nineteenth-century
 Britain and the Empire / Philip Howell.
  p. cm. (Cambridge studies in historical geography 43)
 Includes bibliographical references and index.
 ISBN 978-0-521-85365-1 (hardback) 1. Prostitution–Great Britain–History–
 19th century. 2. Prostitution–Great Britain–Colonies–History–19th century.
 I. Title.
 HQ185.A5.H68 2009
 363.4′40917124109034–dc22   2009020684

ISBN 978-0-521-85365-1 hardback

Cambridge University Press has no responsibility for the persistence or
accuracy of URLs for external or third-party internet websites referred to
in this publication, and does not guarantee that any content on such
websites is, or will remain, accurate or appropriate.

Contents

	List of figures	*page* vi
	List of tables	viii
	Preface and acknowledgements	ix
1	Introduction: Britain and the historical geography of regulationism	1
2	Partial legislation and privileged places: the Contagious Diseases Acts	28
3	Liverpool, localisation and the municipal regulation of prostitution in Britain	76
4	A private Contagious Diseases Act: prostitution and the proctorial system in Victorian Cambridge	113
5	Sexuality, sovereignty and space: colonial law and the making of prostitute subjects in Gibraltar and the British Mediterranean	152
6	Race and the regulation of prostitution in Hong Kong and the overseas empire	188
7	Conclusions: mapping the politics of regulation	229
	Sources and bibliography	252
	Index	288

Figures

0.1	Plan of Spinning House, Cambridge	*page* x
1.1	Commemorative stained glass portrait of Josephine Butler, All Saints' Church, Jesus Lane, Cambridge	13
2.1	Subjected districts under the Contagious Diseases Acts	29
2.2	The administrative structure of the Contagious Diseases Acts of 1864, 1866 and 1869	40
2.3	Women registered under the Contagious Diseases Acts, 1870	48
2.4	Members of the Association for Promoting the Extension of the Contagious Diseases Acts, 1870	57
2.5	Memorial from members of the medical profession in support of the Contagious Diseases Acts, 1872	58
2.6	Local secretaries and correspondents of the Ladies' National Association for the Repeal of the Contagious Diseases Acts, 1873	59
2.7	Petition for repeal of the Contagious Diseases Acts, 1878	60
3.1	Offences for drunkenness in England and Wales per 100,000 population, 1892	84
3.2	Prostitution offences in England and Wales in proportion to the female population aged 15–40, 1871	85
3.3	Brothel districts in Liverpool, c.1890	100
3.4	Blandford Street, Liverpool, c.1890	101
3.5	'Drabs and duchesses': Liverpool Chief Constable Nott-Bower attacked for picking on working-class women	109
4.1	Two views of the Spinning House, St Andrew's Street, Cambridge, c.1890	118
4.2	'A curious group of buildings in Cambridge': the Spinning House in the local landscape of morality	119
4.3	Brothels and suspected houses in Victorian Cambridge	123
4.4	Residences of women arrested in Cambridge by the proctors, 1840 and 1850	124

4.5	Locations of streetwalking and soliciting offences in Cambridge, 1823–94	125
4.6	Arrests of suspected prostitutes in Cambridge, 1823–94, and Oxford, 1822–53	136
4.7	Geographical origin of arrested women in Cambridge, 1823–94	138
5.1	Plan of Gibraltar in the late nineteenth century	163
5.2	Location of brothels in Gibraltar, 1868–1921	178
6.1	Recognised and licensed brothels in central Hong Kong, 1853–78	202
6.2	Prosecutions under Hong Kong Contagious Diseases Ordinances, 1859–77	203
6.3	Sir John Pope Hennessy and family, 1889	205
6.4	Licensed brothels in central Hong Kong, 1879	213
6.5	Unlicensed brothels in central Hong Kong, 1872	214
6.6	Reported classes of licensed brothels in central Hong Kong, 1879	216

Tables

2.1	Recorded dates of commencement of operations in subjected districts under the Contagious Diseases Acts	*page* 44
2.2	Lock hospital provision for the subjected districts under the Contagious Diseases Acts up to 1870	45
2.3	Statistics for stations under the Contagious Diseases Acts, 1870	47
2.4	Statistics of venereal infection of men in stations under or not under the Contagious Diseases Acts, 1867–72	52
4.1	Occupations of parents of women arrested by Cambridge proctors as suspected prostitutes, 1823–94, by employment classification	139
5.1	Residence and status of sex workers in Gibraltar, 1868–1921	175
5.2	Ages of sex workers in Gibraltar by residence and status, 1868–1921	177

Preface and acknowledgements

They're not so unimportant, the places we live in. They aren't only the framework for our actions, they involve themselves in the actions, they change the scenery; and not infrequently, when we say 'circumstances', what we really mean is a particular place which never became interested in us.   Christa Wolf, *The Quest for Christa T.*

My old department office looks down onto Downing Place. Not very much more than a hundred years ago, if the same vantage point had existed, the view would have included the backyard of the Spinning House, the University's private prison, where women suspected of being common prostitutes were locked up and compelled to undergo inspection for signs of venereal disease. Today it is the noises associated with laboratory animals that carry, but back then it might have been the sounds of commotion from incarcerated women. Every day, I pass not only the location of the Spinning House, but also those of other Victorian disciplinary institutions: the former police station, the old town gaol, and the servants' training institute set up by University clergymen, part of whose mission was to divert wayward girls from a career of prostitution. Crossing like this into what was once known as 'Barnwell' is far from the journey that it was in the nineteenth century, but the social divisions that helped to authorise the policing of prostitution can be faintly felt even so. It does not take that great a feat of the imagination to imagine the geographies of regulation that once existed, and the circumstances that Christa Wolf's narrator sees as reducing individuals more or less to anonymity even as they dominate and structure their lives.

This book does indeed primarily concern the contours of power and control in particular places, rather than, say, the practices of prostitution or the experiences of sex workers. I have tried nonetheless, even and especially when the archives offered little in terms of the nature and texture of people's lives, to remember those who inhabited these landscapes of regulation. My route out of the heart of town, down Mill Road, skirts the cemetery where the fifteen-year-old sex worker Emma Rolfe, the victim of a brutal murder, is buried, and whose headstone I chanced upon years ago. It was always salutary to remember that Emma Rolfe was more than a name in a register, though what we know of most other women

x *Preface and acknowledgements*

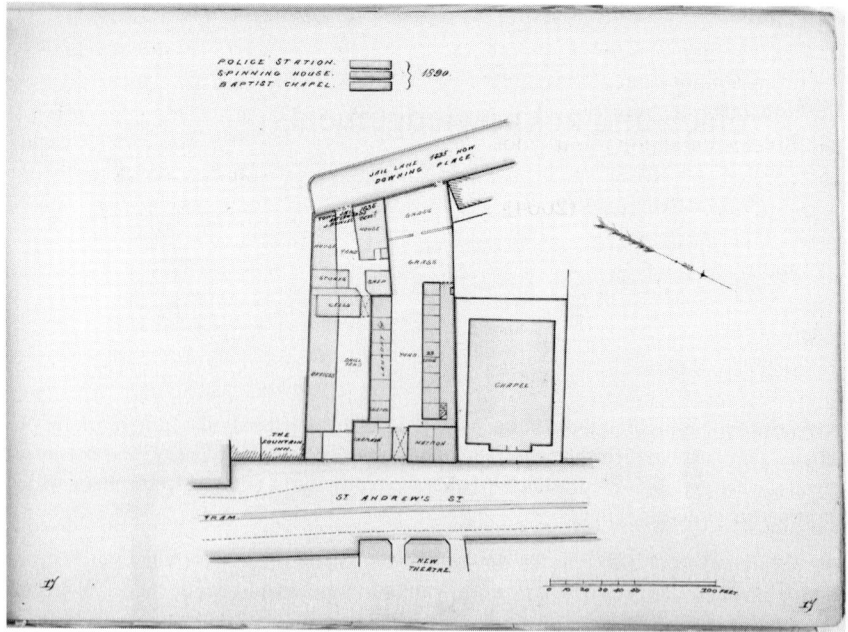

Figure 0.1 Plan of Spinning House, Cambridge. Source: Cambridge University Library MS. Plans. a.1(17).

in her situation is limited largely to what was recorded in the bureaucracy of regulation. And, whilst she clearly cannot stand in for all those who participated in the business of sex, the characterisation of sex workers as, or only as, victims being politically problematic, she remains all the same a reminder of how dangerous 'sex work' can be. Whether it is appropriate to use words like 'sex worker' to describe women like her is also debatable, and it might be worth pointing out that I have generally avoided contemporary terminology in this book. I have instead tended to switch between terms such as 'prostitute', 'prostituted woman', 'prostitute woman', and (very occasionally) 'sex worker', if only to acknowledge the terminological, conceptual and political difficulties involved in any writing on this topic. Whilst this book is not intended as a contribution to current controversies, I might hereby enter a plea that the complexity and diversity of 'Victorian' approaches to policing 'prostitution' be recognised, and not reduced as it so often is to a caricature of repressive moralism.

It is a very long time since I began researching this topic, and it is a surprise to me, if perhaps not to others, quite how long this book has taken to write. Partly, and inevitably given the nature of modern academic life, this is because research typically has to be directed at the relative immediacy of journal publication. I am accordingly grateful to the editors of a number of journals, and to my co-authors, for permission to use material that was published first in the form of the following papers: 'A private Contagious Diseases Act: prostitution and public space in Victorian Cambridge', *Journal of Historical Geography* 26 (2000), 376–402; (with David Lambert) 'John Pope Hennessy and the translation of "slavery" between late nineteenth-century Barbados and Hong Kong', *History Workshop Journal*, 55 (2003), 1–24; 'Race, space and the regulation of prostitution in colonial Hong Kong', *Urban History*, 31 (2004), 229–48; 'Sexuality, sovereignty and space: law, government and the geography of prostitution in colonial Gibraltar', *Social History*, 29 (2004), 444–64; (with David Beckingham and Francesca Moore) 'Managed zones for sex workers in Liverpool: contemporary proposals, Victorian parallels', *Transactions of the Institute of British Geographers*, 33 (2008), 233–50.

Partly too, the equally immediate needs of teaching have taken their toll, though I am at the same time extremely glad to have had the opportunity to have shared this research with several generations of undergraduates, particularly those taking my specialist projects and papers. I have benefited from their comments and questions more than I have usually let on. This is also an opportunity to acknowledge the contribution of a number of students and one-time students who have become colleagues and friends. David Lambert, with whom I have collaborated in researching the imperial career of Sir John Pope Hennessy, has been one of the most important, and it has been a pleasure to watch the progress of his career. Another is Stephen Legg, who has, in addition to sharing his ideas and expertise, well above the call of duty and friendship, cajoled, reprimanded and generally encouraged, all at the right times. Rory Gallagher and Andy Tucker, who have worked on the geographies of contemporary sexuality, have also been invaluable to talk to and argue with. One of my own graduate students, Jong-Geun Kim, has been of great service in discussing another imperial regime of regulated prostitution. But it has probably been my other current graduates who have been the greatest help. It has been a real privilege to supervise Francesca Moore and David Beckingham, and I can record their contribution here without needing to say much more than that I have learned a great deal with them and from them, and that I would not have missed it for the world. Of course, I am responsible for any errors and flaws that exist.

My colleagues in the Geography Department at Cambridge, past and present, have been enormously important to me, even though, as I suppose that I have been independent to a fault, they may not immediately recognise it. Alan Baker, Mark Billinge, Robin Glasscock and Derek Gregory were my earliest guides and inspirations. Subsequently, Jim Duncan, Nancy Duncan, Gerry Kearns, David Nally and Richard Smith demonstrated that academic clusters were useful well beyond the needs of administrative convenience. Others whom I have studied with in and at Cambridge include Sarah Bendall, Iain Black, Andrew Crowhurst, Felix Driver, Miles Ogborn and Chris Philo, who have all given me further help and support. I would like to single out Miles Ogborn, to whose work on the Contagious Diseases Acts I am indebted; I am very grateful indeed to draw upon some of his work here. Others whose research has been close and cognate are

Satish Kumar, whom I met at a point when this research was starting, and who has been a great academic companion ever since; Richard Phillips, who has always provided a more comprehensive analysis of the regulation of sexuality and its historical geography; and – above all perhaps – Philippa Levine, who has set the bar stratospherically high but who has also been unfailingly generous, characteristically interdisciplinary, always encouraging. I have also benefited from talking to and corresponding with Caroline Bressey, Michael Brown, Paul Deslandes, Richard Dennis, Julia Laite, Paul Laxton and Alan Lester. Additional help, large and small, has come from Maeve Bent, Lynn Hollen Lees, Jonathan Parry, Maria Paschalidi, and Chris Whitton. Maria Paschalidi and her family offered me astonishing hospitality as well as help in Corfu, and Ingrid de Smet and Hugo Tucker provided the same service, a long time ago now, in Oxford. Other friends, for whose intellectual and social support I give heartfelt thanks, include Stuart Basten, Millie Glennon, Nic Higgins and Estelle Levin.

I received a small but important grant from HSBC, administered by the Royal Geographical Society with the Institute of British Geographers, which I gratefully acknowledge, in addition to financial support from the Department of Geography, the University of Cambridge and Emmanuel College. At the Drawing Office in the Department of Geography, Ian Agnew, Owen Tucker and, in particular, Philip Stickler, gave me great help in drawing up most of the maps and graphs in this book, too often requested woefully late. The staff, fellows and the Master of Emmanuel have also provided a wonderful academic home for me, with, amongst other notable advantages, probably the best computing office in the world. The archivists, librarians and record keepers with whom I have worked have been uniformly helpful and well informed, and sincere thanks are proffered to them all. Chris Jakes of the Cambridgeshire Collection, Denis Beiso and Tom Finlayson in Gibraltar, Kate McNichol at the Merseyside Police Information Management and Disclosure Department in Liverpool, and Simon Bailey at the Bodleian in Oxford have been particularly helpful. I am also grateful to the Oxford University proctors for permission to use material from the university archives, specifically the 'Black Book'. The same goes for material from Cambridge University Library, the Cambridgeshire Collection of the Cambridgeshire Library Services, Liverpool Central Library and the Royal Geographical Society. It is a further pleasure to acknowledge the efforts of my successive editors at Cambridge University Press – first Richard Fisher, who commissioned the book, and, secondly, Michael Watson, who took over responsibility for it. I am also very grateful to Helen Waterhouse for overseeing the production progress so ably and patiently.

Finally, and most importantly, I owe everything to my parents and family and to my wife, Elizabeth Mozzillo, for their continuing support. This book is scant enough reward for their love and forbearance, but it was always written with gratitude to them in mind.

1

Introduction: Britain and the historical geography of regulationism

The regulation of prostitution was one of the key components in the British imperial state's attempt to manage the sexual lives of its citizens and subjects in the modern era. In parts of Britain and in many of its colonies a series of measures were introduced to try to reorder sexual relations between female prostitutes and their clients. These policies were most clearly elaborated in the second half of the nineteenth century, though they had their origins earlier, and many continued until the early decades of the twentieth. They were not in force everywhere or at the same time, and characteristically appeared in different forms in different places, to different degrees of stringency. Some were codified in 'contagious diseases' statutes or ordinances, explicitly designed to combat the spread of sexually transmitted infection, whilst others remained informal regimes, patchwork and piecemeal combinations of powers, though likewise directed at the control of disease and disorder. By exercising control over prostitutes' lives, their residences, movements and activities, a more regularised and structured market for commercial sex might be produced, one that was more amenable to police and medical supervision. This was the theory.

This book considers the development of these powers, practices and policies, these so-called 'regulationist' attempts to bring prostitution or sex work under the management of central and local authorities. It recognises that the British regulation of prostitution took the form of a series of discrete sites and spaces of power, and argues that these were inseparable from the global reach of the imperial enterprise. Regulation of prostitution was manifested in distinctive landscapes, local geographies of managed sexuality and characteristic micro-tactics of spatial control and surveillance. Beyond this, however, British prostitution regulation partook of the grand strategies of imperial rule and the politics of national self-definition. Not only was the regulation of prostitution a form of local spatial policing of sexuality, it was also inscribed in the geopolitics of the imperial state at the global scale. For all that it took the form of local, situated regimes, often extremely distant and differentiated from each other, this British tradition of regulated sexuality can only be understood fully in relation to the wider imperial network in which the home country and its colonial dependencies were enmeshed.

This study looks in detail at four key instances of both domestic and colonial forms of prostitution regulation. I want to show in the central chapters of this book how the government of prostitution was worked out as a politics of place – not as the imposition of some abstract disciplinary or regulatory power, but as a localised intervention in the economy of sex, a strategy above all of *containment*, one that both attended to and was disturbed by the particularities of the places into and onto which it was projected. These four regulationist regimes – in the towns of Liverpool and Cambridge, in the fortress of Gibraltar, and in the colony of Hong Kong – are portrayed here as geographies rather than geometries of power, topographies rather than topologies. Understanding them requires detailed attention to the complexities of the locality, to what Mariana Valverde describes as the 'actually existing, often unsystematic assemblages of technologies and rationalities' comprising the practice of governance; which is also to say, as the geographer Stephen Legg has neatly expressed it, that 'places are the *excess* of space'.[1] This is an argument about particular regimes of sexual policing. All the same, the specific sites under review here are not intended as isolated examples, as case studies. These instances of regulation are placed in relation to other places and regions, and considered in their regional and political contexts, so that they make claims beyond their local histories and geographies. I want to present them in fact, altogether, as the products of a singular imperial culture, rather than as merely the creations of circumstance and locality. Most importantly, I argue that, whether 'at home' or 'abroad', 'domestic' or 'colonial', for all the very large differences between individual regimes, these measures followed in the end the same logic. They were derived from the same principles and assumptions, the same kinds of biases and blindspots about gender and sexuality, class and race, much the same view of the world. Though hitherto marginalised and misunderstood, not least by the tendency to separate 'metropolitan' from 'colonial' regimes, these projections of power amount to a distinctive and significant imperial enterprise. In attending to the historical geography of a neglected regulationist project, this book aims to contribute to our understanding of one of the distinctive 'rhythms of rule and sexual management' in which the British were engaged during the high imperial era.[2]

Regulation, regulationism and the modern state

This introductory chapter makes the case for the importance of these British practices, particularly insofar as these are characteristically sidelined next to the

---

[1] M. Valverde, '"Despotism" and ethical liberal governance', *Economy and Society*, 25 (1996), 357–72, p. 358, S. Legg, *Spaces of colonialism: Delhi's urban governmentalities* (Oxford, 2007), p. 16.

[2] See A. L. Stoler, 'Carnal knowledge and imperial power: gender, race, and morality in colonial Asia', in R. N. Lancaster and M. di Leonardo (eds.), *The gender/sexuality reader: culture, history, political economy* (London, 1997), p. 30.

more prominent example of France and its legacy to the continent of Europe of a 'French system' of prostitution regulation. I argue that the British tradition of regulationism should be recognised, and reassessed, principally in terms of its military and imperial rationale and in the connections and tensions between the domestic and the colonial spheres. It would be well to begin with a discussion of the nature of *regulationism*, however, and of its history and geography, since this is a necessary preliminary to the argument that the British experience, particularly in its interwoven domestic, colonial and imperial manifestations, has been overlooked. I should note straightaway that this study concerns the 'regulation' of prostitution in both its formal sense and in the looser, more general sense of management. Although it has become common to talk of the regulation of sexuality, and of moral regulation, the term means specific things when used in the context of policing prostitution or sex work. Here, *regulation* and *regulationism* refer to the measures introduced at various times, in various places, to control the perceived dangers of uncontrolled female prostitution – principally, public disorder and the propagation of sexually transmitted diseases. Unregulated commercial sexuality seemed to threaten – and this was an incomplete, indiscriminate, ill-defined series of fears – to promote public nuisance, to endanger the respectable, to tempt the innocent and waylay the unwary, and to facilitate the spread of venereal infection from the vicious to the virtuous. One characteristic response to these threats has been the attempt to 'regulate' sex work, by bringing it under the supervision of the authorities and their appointed agents. In this way, prostitution might be tolerated but tamed, its worst excesses prevented, its utility to society and the state maximised. Sex might be structured, dangerous sexualities policed. In short, prostitution might be governed.

The essentials of this modern strategy for the policing of commercial sexuality are clear enough. Formally, *regulationism* meant the inscription of known, and thus 'tolerated', prostitutes into a police register, their regular medical inspection for signs of communicable venereal disease, and if necessary their commitment to special 'lock' hospitals or equivalents until such time that they were considered as no longer posing an epidemiological threat. This approach can be summed up as the combination of *identification, inspection* and *incarceration*.[3] In addition, however, we may specify a small number of practices that have played a role in both pre-modern and modern forms of regulationism, including the explicit licensing of sex workers, the licensing and inspection of brothels and other houses of prostitution in which registered prostitutes were to be restricted, the formal or informal zoning of vice districts, and the formation of a dedicated morals police to enforce the administrative regulations and to repress unregulated prostitution as far as possible. In some countries, such as in much of nineteenth- and early twentieth-century France, more or less the

---

[3] See L. Bernstein, *Sonia's daughters: prostitutes and their regulation in imperial Russia* (Berkeley, 1995).

full panoply of regulationist measures was more or less generally installed; in other places, such as the British garrison towns under the Victorian Contagious Diseases Acts, only the more modest agenda was realised. Whether in restricted or extended form, however, these regimes can all fairly be called regulationist.

It is important, however, to go on to insist that there is no *absolute* boundary between 'regulationist' and 'non-regulationist' systems. An essential part of my argument in this book is that regulationism – particularly *British* regulationism – has taken many forms, some of them more strict, rigid, official and explicit than others. Regulationism was not wholly distinct, as a science, as a medical project, as a policy and practice; the label of regulationism was instead part of a contested political discourse, denied by some, affirmed by others. This is an index of regulationism's protean qualities, its existence as a palette of tactics and techniques for bringing prostitution under the sway of government. We may at the very least recognise varieties of regulationist practice. My preference here is to define regulationism in a somewhat less formal and restrictive sense, and in the simplest terms as those systems 'which, no matter what the legal framework, effectively tolerate and contain prostitution within limits usually defined by police or other regulatory bodies'.[4] In treating the various policing regimes in the places covered by this book as 'regulationist' in this more expansive definition I want to argue that the geneaological map of British regulationism be extended, and thus the nature and complexity of the British experience of regulation be appreciated as rather deeper and more substantial than is usually allowed.

A further justification is needed when considering the distinctive *modernity* of the nineteenth- and early twentieth-century regulationist regimes that are considered here. Tracing the historical geography of regulationism remains parlous, and always vulnerable to the charge of ahistoricism, particularly where the name and nature of 'prostitution' is debatable, and where concepts of 'sexuality', 'society' and the 'state' may be considered at times blatant anachronisms. Some may worry about *any* attempt at analytical categorisation, preferring to attend to the contours of discourse alone. We can surely take our reservations too far in this regard, however. Whilst, as the medieval historian Ruth Karras observes, we would be ill advised to try to import the preferred contemporary term 'sex work' to the world, say, of the European *meretrices*, she elsewhere equally rightly rejects the *a priori* argument that concepts like 'sexuality' are in similar fashion impossible in the pre-modern world.[5] By extension, I think, it would be a mistake to insist, again in an *a priori* fashion, that we can trace no connections across cultures and across the centuries, no points of comparison

---

[4] F. M. Boyle, S. Glennon, J. M. Najman, *et al.*, *The sex industry: a survey of sex workers in Queensland, Australia* (Aldershot, 1997), p. 12.

[5] See R. M. Karras, 'Women's labours: reproduction and sex work in medieval Europe', *Journal of Women's History*, 15 (2004), 153–8, and R. M. Karras, *Sexuality in medieval Europe: doing unto others* (London, 2005).

and classification. In this case, whether or not the nature of 'prostitution' itself is strictly comparable, there are good reasons for thinking that some pre-modern regimes at least share certain significant assumptions, ideological correlates, with the more recent forms of regulationism.

All attempts to manage prostitution are predicated for instance on the belief that it may be neither repressed nor suppressed; the accepted inevitability of commercial sex is assumed in virtually all systems of regulation. So we can find much the same kind of statement about the 'necessity' of prostitution in European antiquity and in the Middle Ages as we find in the most self-consciously enlightened and 'modern' theorists of the nineteenth century onwards. For example, the great French hygienist and the most prominent promoter of modern regulationism, Alexandre Parent-Duchâtelet, famously likened the management of prostitution to the operation of municipal sewers, in a direct and explicit endorsement of the views of St Augustine, St Paul and others. In this view, prostitution was a necessary evil, 'an indispensable excremental phenomenon that protects the social body from disease'.[6] The regulation of prostitution could be portrayed accordingly as an unpleasant but necessary civic duty, one that protected societies and communities from worse physical and moral pollution. This view might be elaborated as an endorsement of prostitutes and their work, particularly in the face of fears about sodomy and the other darkly perceived dangers of unlicensed male sexuality. Ideas such as these have their close correlates in more modern times.

These regimes also patently took their cue from common attitudes towards gender and sexuality. Whilst modes of sexual categorisation are clearly not stable, and some have argued that they have changed very abruptly, there are nevertheless deeply embedded ideas and practices surrounding gender roles and what was considered natural and appropriate for men and women.[7] And, since the putative separation of sex from gender in modern times, debatable in itself, can hardly be found at all in pre-modern societies, persistent ideas about who men and women *are* necessarily meant persistent ideas about what we would now call, without a great deal of hesitation, 'sexuality'. It would be foolish to generalise too far about all of the ages before the modern, even within the cultures of the West, but we can say without undue hazard that the sexually active single woman was almost always, almost everywhere, regarded with suspicion – typically equated with the 'prostitute', in fact – in a manner that was simply not comparable to the treatment of men. We need to avoid the idea of an eternal double standard, supposedly central to an essentially unchanging patriarchal or phallocentric culture, but women – not just prostitute women – were still far more likely to be the subject

---

[6] A. Corbin, *Women for hire: prostitution and sexuality in France after 1850* (Cambridge, MA, 1990), p. 4.

[7] For transformations in ideas about sex and sexuality, see most famously M. Foucault, *The history of sexuality, volume I: an introduction* (New York, 1980), and T. Laqueur, *Making sex: body and gender from the Greeks to Freud* (Cambridge, MA, 1990).

of control than men. There are also long-term continuities in the treatment and construction of ideas about women and venereal disease, and an inglorious misogynistic tradition in which women themselves were characteristically portrayed as abnormal, deformed or diseased: 'it was taken for granted that women were principally responsible for the spread of disease and that it was by controlling the liberty of such women, by branding them either physically or metaphorically that the disease would cease to be a problem.'[8] Such tenacious ideas about sex and gender thus provided a good part of the justification for the regulation of prostitution. It is hardly surprising that regulationism as a strategy has typically involved the surveillance and supervision of prostitute women, not their clients, nor their male equivalents.

It follows that we should not be too quick to read the advent of modernity as a radical discontinuity. Elements of this culture remained remarkably robust, including variants of this sexual and gender double standard. Even so, recognisably *modern* forms of regulationism in the West, emerging from the later eighteenth and early nineteenth centuries, did exhibit a number of largely new features, which allow us to separate them from the pre-Reformation era of licensed brothels and the last great flowering of regulationist zeal in Europe before the modern age. There are three, interrelated, elements that are particularly worthy of emphasis: the relationship of regulationism to the development of the modern *state*, its recourse to the authority of medical and social *science*, and the role of *war and empire* in promoting regulationist regimes.

We can readily agree, first, on 'the enduring power of the state as the author and executor of regulation', as an historian of prostitution regulation in imperial Russia has it.[9] But we should go further by insisting on the pre-eminent importance of the modern, reformed and *enlightened* state rather than, say, its earlier, absolutist counterparts. As Isabel Hull has most systematically demonstrated in a study of the German polities, the modern attempt to regulate prostitution developed alongside a demarcation of state from civil society, achieved in part through the constitution of a rationale of sexual citizenship.[10] This was 'enlightened', but neither 'liberal' nor 'democratic' in the ideological, self-congratulatory sense: rather it translated and transmuted class and gender privileges into a newly rationalised framework for understanding and policing sexual behaviour. It became possible, for instance, to advance the regulation of prostitution as the responsibility of the state precisely because of the dangers that sexuality posed to the newly discovered realm of civil society. We can argue that modern prostitution regulation is a product of this 'enlightened' separation in political terrain of state from society, public from private, male from female.

---

[8] M. Spongberg, *Feminizing venereal disease: the body of the prostitute in nineteenth-century medical discourse* (New York, 1997), p. 1.
[9] Bernstein, *Sonia's daughters*, p. 9.
[10] I. V. Hull, *Sexuality, state, and civil society in Germany, 1700–1815* (Ithaca, 1996).

The precise nature of the relationship of prostitution regulation to the constitution of the modern liberal state, with its institutionalisation of rights and freedoms, and its endorsement of a particular norm of sexual citizenship is fraught with controversy. But the historical coincidence between the emergence, or re-emergence, of regulationism and the birth of the modern state remains of the first importance, particularly given the priority of France in its historical geography. The forms of the modern state, as Michel Foucault once commented in an entirely conventional aside, were Napoleonic in origin, and to be considered quite distinct from the police states of absolutist Europe.[11] Modern France has also been described as regulationism's 'home country', and indeed said to have created the 'ideal form' of regulationist regimes.[12] This is certainly a simplification, for brothels in France had long been licensed under the *ancien régime*, and associated policies extended as late as 1778. The full development of what tellingly became known throughout Europe as the 'French system' of regulated prostitution – *reglémentation* to give it its technical title – was nevertheless a product of the early nineteenth century, the era of Revolution and reform, the era of Napoleon and of republican imperialism. Having swept away the old regime, the French Revolution promptly dispensed with all of the existing regulations concerning prostitution; but the practice of registering prostitutes and inspecting them for signs of disease was quietly taken up again at the municipal level and in the absence of central direction.[13] Regulationism continued to prosper from this point on, and, by the early nineteenth century, suspected women in Paris, the heart of the system, were required by a dedicated morals police to attend the Bureau Sanitaire for inspection, and, if found to be in a condition that threatened their clients with infection, consigned to the hospital of Saint-Lazare. It is this 'French system' that became exemplary for regulationist practice worldwide, being spread, copied and adapted in the nineteenth century in the rest of continental Europe, and indeed far beyond. We can find variants in Belgium, Denmark, Italy, Germany, Russia, Portugal, Spain, Sweden and Switzerland, and in Argentina and Mexico, to give just two non-European examples. These regimes form the most striking attempts in the modern era to formally regulate the commerce in sex. There remains some dispute as to the legal basis for these regimes, and their relation to the Code Napoléon, but it is fair to say that a new era for regulated sexuality was established, with the systems of licensed brothels,

---

[11] M. Foucault, 'Space, knowledge, and power', in P. Rabinow (ed.), *The Foucault reader* (London, 1991), pp. 241–2.
[12] Corbin, *Women for hire*, p. ix; P. Baldwin, *Contagion and the state: 1830–1930* (Cambridge, 1999), p. 369.
[13] S. P. Conner, 'Politics, prostitution and the pox in Revolutionary Paris, 1789–1799', *Journal of Social History*, 22 (1989), 713–34, and 'Public virtue and public women: prostitution in Revolutionary Paris, 1793–1794', *Eighteenth-Century Studies*, 28 (1994), 221–40.

the networks of venereal dispensaries, the establishment of *police des moeurs*. The 'French system', with its example to other nations, shows particularly clearly how the regulation of prostitution, along with other attempts to manage sexuality, flourished under the development of modern state forms. In this understanding, France was the originator of a revolution in the policing of sexuality: 'By the middle of the nineteenth century', writes Kristin Luker with pardonable exaggeration, 'virtually all European states had moved the regulation of family life and its alternatives – prostitution, fornication, adultery, and "deviant" sexual practices – out of the control of church courts and under the aegis of secular state control of one kind or another.'[14]

The second distinctive element in modern regulationist regimes is their legitimation by modern scientific authority. As Peter Baldwin puts it, 'Regulationists ... regarded their position as the expression of modern, rational, hygienic principles, the application of enlightened public health measures to a devastating scourge.'[15] Modern regulationism found its vocation in the struggle to contain the ravages of venereal diseases, and syphilis in particular. By controlling prostitution – that is, by controlling prostitute women – it might be possible to limit the transmission of this uniquely virulent and unpleasant disease. As the etiological understanding of syphilis developed, it became possible to identify periods of greatest contagiousness; and if women in such a condition could be taken out of sexual circulation, then the ravages of venereal disease might be hindered if not entirely halted. The developing authority of medical science has thus been an equally important theme in the emergence of modern regulationist practice. Kathryn Norberg puts it very succinctly: 'The prostitute now belonged to the physicians, and public policy would henceforth treat her as a biological problem ... The foundations of nineteenth-century regulation were in place: mercenary sex had become a medical problem and syphilis an object of state policy.'[16]

Syphilis had existed for centuries, however, long before the development of nineteenth-century regulationist regimes. The scientific rationale for regulationism cannot be understood with reference to the revolutions in experimental and clinical science alone, nor its history rehearsed simply as a pragmatic medical response to the emergence of a unique epidemiological threat. It is most closely related to the development of sciences of society and statecraft, and in response to the challenges of modern, urban, industrial civilisations. The intellectual and practical lineage for regulationism lies in the successive developments of medical police, state medicine and the public health movement – all related to the

---

[14] K. Luker, 'Sex, social hygiene, and the state: the double-edged sword of social reform', *Theory and Society*, 27 (1998), 601–34, p. 602.
[15] Baldwin, *Contagion and the state*, p. 362.
[16] K. Norberg, 'From courtesan to prostitute: mercenary sex and venereal disease, 1730–1802', in L. E. Merians (ed.), *The secret malady: venereal disease in eighteenth-century Britain and France* (Lexington, 1996), pp. 44–5.

emergence of the theory and practice of state authority described above.[17] It was not physical disease that was the focus, therefore, so much as the identification of the need for social hygiene. To put it another way, it was necessary for the conception and practice of government to be modernised before regulationism could exist. Regulationism, like similar medical projects, is dependent upon the elaboration of a 'biopolitics' in which population, health and productivity are incorporated as key governmental concerns because of their threat to a newly delineated social body.[18]

As a policy – rather than as a series of unsystematic and dubiously legal practices – regulation thus required a theory of society and of the role of the state in promoting the health and welfare of the population. It needed a modern rationale, and it arguably found it not in the Napoleonic era but in the early years of the July Monarchy, in the work of the great French theorist of regulationism, Parent-Duchâtelet, whose work has already been noted. Though there had been pioneering analyses in the eighteenth century, it was not until 1836 and the publication of Parent's *De la prostitution dans la ville de Paris* that a self-consciously scientific case for regulation was made, backed up by statistical analysis, empirical research and the rest of the apparatus of an infant social science.[19] For Parent, as we have seen, prostitution was inevitable, if not quite outside history. It could not be wished away; it needed to be tackled from the point of view of public hygiene rather than be the subject of an empty moralism. Parent's investigations were designed to separate the truth of prostitution from the chaff of prejudice and rhetoric. His is not, however, a study of the market for sex, for male clients are absent from his analysis, and we may cast doubt upon his 'scientific' objectivity; his work is better seen as a taxonomy and anthropology of the female prostitute. By studying the records of thousands of women registered with the French police, and supplementing this with interviews and personal observation, Parent concluded to his satisfaction that prostitutes were a class apart. His is a collective portrait of women 'differing as much in their morals, their tastes, and their habits from the society of their compatriots, as the latter differ from the nations of another hemisphere'.[20] At the same time, however, these women are shown to have emerged from the world of deracinated workingwomen, *femmes isolées*, all

---

[17] For medical police, see G. Rosen, *From medical police to social medicine: essays on the history of health care* (New York, 1974); for public health, D. Porter, *Health, civilization and the state: a history of public health from ancient to modern times* (London, 1999), pp. 52–4.

[18] The best discussion of biopolitics is in M. Foucault, *'Society must be defended': lectures at the Collège de France 1975–1976* (New York, 2003), pp. 239–63.

[19] A. J. B. Parent-Duchâtelet, *De la prostitution dans la ville de Paris* (Paris, 1836). See A. Corbin, Prèsentation, Alexandre Parent-Duchâtelet, *La prostitution à Paris au XIXe siècle* (Paris, 1981).

[20] Quoted in Corbin, *Women for hire*, p. 5.

of whom had the potential to become prostitutes, whether by prior disposition or unfortunate circumstance. The problem as Parent posed it was one of the social *environment*, the lack of order, providence and discipline that it passed on to the female working poor. These are presented, as Joan Scott puts it, as 'lives lived outside regulated contexts': '*Femmes isolées* represented the domain of poverty, a world of turbulent sexuality, subversive independence, and dangerous insubordination.'[21]

It followed, in the tidy logic of regulationism, that the solution to prostitution is as profoundly spatial as is the problem. If the latter is posed as that of unrestricted, unregulated sexuality, the answer is the installation of discipline and regulation through the means of enclosure and surveillance. The wider theme of moral regulation also directs prostitution towards spaces of confinement and discipline, typically by limiting commercial sexuality to specific, usually marginal, sites. Yet this kind of moral policing reaches its most explicit form in regulationist regimes, where the principles of enclosure and containment are most carefully elaborated. Alain Corbin, in describing the nineteenth-century French system, argues that 'The first task of regulation is to bring the prostitute out of the foul darkness and rescue her from the clandestine swarming of vice, in order to drive her back into an enclosed space, under the purifying light of power.'[22] The female prostitute must be made visible to the authorities, if at the same time kept hidden from respectable society. She must be removed from the threateningly opaque milieux of the working classes and installed in strictly monitored locales – meaning not just the official brothels but also other disciplinary institutions such as reformatories, hospitals and prisons. In this way, by confronting the problem of the prostitute's social and geographical mobility head on, she could be controlled and disciplined. This injunction to *discipline* the prostitute only becomes more urgent when responsibility for the transmission of venereal diseases was added to the list of her crimes, her capacity for moral contagion complemented by the physical threat of syphilis and the other venereals.

Thus the concern for social order may be ultimately restated as one for social hygiene, and a prophylactic quarantine added to the older strategies of combating disorder. There are ready associations here for the social and critical theorist of modernity. In a Weberian sense, it is certainly possible to suggest that this kind of regulation of commercial sexuality, in ambition and practice, exemplifies 'the tendency for ever larger spheres of social life and institutions to be brought under a unified and coherent system of rationalization and administration'.[23] Most

---

[21] J. W. Scott, *Gender and the politics of history*, revised edition (New York, 1999), p. 147.

[22] A. Corbin, 'Commercial sexuality in nineteenth-century France: a system of images and regulations', *Representations*, 14 (1986), 209–19, p. 215.

[23] R. Cooter and S. Sturdy, 'Of war, medicine and modernity: introduction', in R. Cooter, M. Harrison and S. Sturdy (eds.), *War, medicine and modernity* (Stroud, 1998), p. 6.

compellingly, however, it is Foucault's analysis of the deployment of surveillance technologies within a developing disciplinary society that is immediately applicable to the project of regulation; and many historians have made the connection. Regulationism may be seen as part of a disciplinary modernity reliant on spatial technologies of surveillance and police or state regulation. Its characteristic 'political geography of containment' is exemplified not just by the structures of confinement put in place by a range of authorities; the enclosed world of regulation refers too to the panoptic surveillance of registered prostitutes, and indeed, at a certain level, of all women's behaviour.[24] In this sense we can see the production of prostitutional space in the service not just of the state but also of a disciplinary society constructed on the principle of panoptic surveillance: 'The desire for panopticism ... finds expression in a quasi-obsessional way in regulationism', and that regulationism was 'a tireless effort to discipline the prostitute, the ideal being the creation of a category of "enclosed" prostitutes'.[25]

War, imperialism and regulation

In all of these respects, it is indeed France that clearly took the lead, providing the iconic form of modern regulationist policing of commercial sexuality. There is a third distinctive element in modern regulationism, however, one that is rather less readily acknowledged, and which has important implications for our understanding of its historical geography. This is the link between regulationism and the modern *imperial* state, particularly insofar as the regulation of prostitution has been prosecuted through a military rationale, in response to the accidents and exigencies of war and dominated by the demands of national and imperial security. Although links are increasingly made between regulation and modern imperialism, with a recent proliferation of studies of the *colonial* regulation of prostitution, there has been less attention to the role of imperial regimes of regulated sexuality 'at home' as well as abroad. Similarly, whilst there has been an acknowledgement of the role of the military and war in the formation of the modern state, with important studies of regulationism from the perspective of the military and in times of military crisis, the integration of military and imperial perspectives is rare.[26] In fact, the major exceptions are the studies

---

[24] P. Levine, 'Consistent contradictions: prostitution and protective labour legislation in nineteenth-century England', *Social History*, 19 (1994), 17–35, p. 29.

[25] Corbin, *Women for hire*, p. 9. For the analysis of disciplinary society, see M. Foucault, *Discipline and punish: the birth of the prison* (New York, 1979).

[26] Though see L. Bland, 'In the name of protection: the policing of women in the First World War', in J. Brophy and C. Smart (eds.), *Women-in-law: explorations in law, family and sexuality* (London, 1985); P. Levine, 'Battle colors: race, sex, and colonial soldiery in World War I', *Journal of Women's History*, 9 (1998), 104–30; L. D. H. Sauerteig, 'Sex, medicine and morality during the First World War', in R. Cooter, M. Harrison

of the regulation of prostitution in Nazi Germany, whose military, expansionist and racial ambitions may fairly be termed imperial, and by the Japanese imperial state, both at home and in its colonial possessions.[27] These studies are, however, somewhat marginalised in the historiography, exceptional in the stark authoritarianism of their military polities. Julia Roos has argued for instance that in their extremism and brutality Nazi policies in Germany 'shed the traditional confines of earlier forms of regulationism'.[28]

If, however, we proceed from the perspective that military and imperial considerations were central rather than marginal both to the modern state and to its reliance on scientific authority, the nature of modern regulationism becomes much clearer. Far from being of limited importance – warped to the demands of fascism for instance – the military-imperial aspects of prostitution regulation are readily apparent, and indeed right from its very beginnings. For regulation is not only the characteristic product of the enlightened, reformed Napoleonic state, with its endorsements of democracy and the Rights of Man, but also of a bureaucratic militarisation, a mass mobilisation of men in the age of citizen armies. Regulationism was shaped in the military forge of modernity, the Napoleonic system being directly stimulated by the demands of the army, and the spread of regulationist regimes following swiftly in the wake of the Napoleonic military machine. In Hamburg, for example, a strict regulationism was established following the Napoleonic invasion, complementing the indigenous forms of imperial Germany; and the same was true for other places inside and outside Europe.[29] In its paradigmatic form, then, the 'French system' of regulationism was both republican and imperial, civil and military.

A wider recognition of the military basis for this system of regulated sexuality – *'drilled* and *housed* and *barracked* vice', as the great English anti-regulationist campaigner Josephine Butler (Figure 1.1) put it – is overdue.[30] In a general sense the genealogy of discipline requires a more detailed analysis of the military

---

and S. Sturdy (eds.), *War, medicine and modernity* (Stroud, 1998); J. Smart, 'Sex, the state and the "scarlet scourge": gender, citizenship and venereal disease regulation in Australia during the Great War', *Women's History Review*, 7 (1998), 5–35.

[27] J. Roos, 'Backlash against prostitutes' rights: origins and dynamics of Nazi prostitution policies', *Journal of the History of Sexuality*, 11 (2002), 67–94, A. F. Timm, 'Sex with a purpose: prostitution, venereal disease, and militarized masculinity', in Dagmar Herzog (ed.), *Sexuality and German fascism* (New York, 2005); S. Garon, 'The world's oldest debate? Prostitution and the state in imperial Japan, 1900–1945', *American Historical Review*, 98 (1993), 710–32.

[28] Roos, 'Backlash', p. 94.

[29] R. J. Evans, 'Prostitution, state and society in imperial Germany', *Past and Present*, 70 (1976), 106–29.

[30] J. E. Butler, *The principles of the abolitionists* (London, 1885), reprinted in J. Jordan (ed.), *Josephine Butler and the prostitution campaigns: diseases of the body politic, volume II: the Ladies' appeal and protest* (London, 2003), p. 114.

Figure 1.1 Commemorative stained glass portrait of Josephine Butler, All Saints' Church, Jesus Lane, Cambridge. Photograph: author.

contribution to modernity. Roger Cooter and Steve Sturdy have rightly reminded us of Weber's observation that 'the discipline of the army gives birth to all discipline'.[31] Studies of Foucault's 'bellicose history' have also recently begun to attend to the 'military dream of society' that for him heralded 'the birth of meticulous military and political tactics by which the control of bodies and individual forces was exercised within states'.[32] Foucault's apparent inversion of Clausewitz, to the effect that politics is war by other means, points to an unexcavated archaeology of war and the military. If much of this work remains to be accomplished, military history reintegrated within cultural history, a number of relevant features of the modern condition and constitution are worth indicating here. The construction of a military model of masculinity is at stake here. The glamour of the military, together with its denigration of civil society and its romanticisation of the soldier, may be noted as formidable contributors to the modern gender order, with all of their implications for the study of sexuality. At the same time, the militarisation of modern society is distinctive, apparent in a number of different

[31] Cooter and Sturdy, 'Of war, medicine and modernity', p. 3.
[32] Foucault, *Discipline and punish*, pp. 144, 168, 169; on war and the 'war-machine' see also p. 211.

forms, such as the tendency for civil and military spheres to blur, and the overlap between the welfare and the warfare state. The spread of medical discipline from the military to the civilian sphere is emblematic, for instance, of a modernity characterised by 'the civilianization of medicine in war and its militarization during peacetime'.[33] Regulationism's medical rationale certainly points directly to the sociological twinning of modernity and war noted by Philip Lawrence as a distinguishing feature of Enlightenment European culture.[34]

Now it may be, with regard to prostitution regulation, that *Britain* is the best example of this kind of military modernity. As I have noted, the championing of France as the 'home country' of regulationism, and the historical geographical narrative of its export of regulationism to the rest of the continent of Europe and beyond, all tend to relegate *British* practices to the margins. In the conventional view, Britain is the 'odd land out', to use Peter Baldwin's magisterial but misleading phrase.[35] Certainly Britain never got round to regulating prostitution in most civilian areas. London never saw tolerated prostitution in the way that Paris did. Nor did it have its own Parent-Duchâtelet, the nearest equivalent being the venereologist William Acton, a disciple of the French hygienist, but one whose authority was far more ambiguous and disputed.[36] The closest that Britain came to continental regulationism was the well-known experiment with the Contagious Diseases (or CD) Acts from 1864 to 1886, described by Frank Mort as, for Britain, 'the single most important legislative intervention addressing sexuality throughout the nineteenth century'.[37] Yet this lasted only twenty or so years, in around a score of military stations marginal to the great population centres of Britain: this is a record that looks distinctly paltry compared to the experience of a century and a half, with Paris at its hub, that the French record describes. All in all, modern Britain seems at best half-hearted in its commitment to regulationism. This would, however, be to miss the significance of the wider British experience with prostitution regulation. Concentration on the role of regulation of prostitution in civil society, within domestic regimes, and within continental Europe has taken attention away from the development of regulationist systems as part of the military operations of imperial states. If the role of the military is emphasised, then the specifically military rationale for the CD Acts becomes of much greater importance. Lesley Hall has rightly noted in this regard that the CD Acts amounted to a militarisation of prostitution, within a

---

[33] Cooter and Sturdy, 'Of war, medicine and modernity', p. 7.
[34] P. K. Lawrence, *Modernity and war: the creed of absolute violence* (Basingstoke, 1997).
[35] Baldwin, *Contagion and the state*, p. 371.
[36] For a recent assessment, see I. Crozier, 'William Acton and the history of sexuality: the medical and professional context', *Journal of Victorian Culture*, 5 (2000), 1–27.
[37] F. Mort, *Dangerous sexualities: medico-moral politics in England since 1830* (London, 1987), p. 68.

cultural context in which the boundary separating civil and military life was being increasingly eroded:

> The Contagious Diseases Acts ... seem to have been attempting to create an equivalent cadre of women to supply the sexual needs of these men regarded as outcasts from decent society: almost, one might say, a *cordon sanitaire* protecting society at large... The women affected by the CD Acts were presumed, like soldiers, to be volunteers, but subject, through practising their trade in a garrison or naval town, to militaristic rigours of discipline.[38]

The Acts were certainly directly stimulated by the British disasters in the Crimea, and arose out of concerns about the prevalence of disease amongst the rank and file. It should be noted that calls for army reform were a consequence not only of the new sanitary science but also of changes in the prestige of the military and more positive reassessments of its role in the national life; in 1860, *The Times* remarked, for instance, with a new and notable sense of satisfaction, that England was 'at heart a military nation'.[39] Rather than being marginal, the concerns of the military – and of national security – were central to what has variously been called the warfare, garrison or military-fiscal state. Moreover, the recourse to regulationist policies in conditions of wartime suggests what we might take to be the latency or dormancy of British regulationist ambitions. We can note that during the two World Wars fears about security quickly saw the reintroduction in Britain of measures to police common women's sexuality and to compel them to submit to medical examination. As we shall also see, there are some overlooked examples of regulationist and quasi-regulationist practice at home that deserve reassessment, indicative as they are of a wider commitment to regulating commercial sexuality than is usually accepted. These histories and geographies together give the lie to the notion that outside of the brief heyday of the CD Acts there was no British attempt to manage prostitution.

Most important, however, is the recognition that the British experience of regulationism was dominated not just by military but also by imperial concerns. As Philippa Levine points out, 'Britain's military needs were seen, in many respects, as coterminous with Britain's role as an imperial power.'[40] It was not just the Crimea that stimulated contagious diseases laws; the imperial setbacks represented by the 1857 rebellion in India also served to emphasise the

---

[38] L. Hall, '"War always brings it on": war, STDs, the military and the civil population in Britain, 1850–1950', in *Comparative perspectives on the history of sexually transmitted diseases, volume I, being proceedings of a conference held on 26–28 April 1996* (Institute of Commonwealth Studies, University of London, 1996), p. 2.

[39] *The Times*, 25 June 1860, cited in J. Parry, *The politics of patriotism: English Liberalism, national identity and Europe, 1830–1886* (Cambridge, 2006), p. 238.

[40] P. Levine, *Prostitution, race, and politics: policing venereal disease in the British Empire* (London, 2003), p. 57. She is careful to argue, however, that military and imperial are not synonymous.

importance of the sexual health of the forces.[41] In any event, regulationist measures in several British colonies date from at least the early nineteenth century, long predating the CD Acts, and lasting until the first decades of the twentieth, long after the demise of the 'domestic' legislation. These were more formal and typically more stringent – in fact, more like the French and continental systems in their explicit licensing of brothels and prostitutes. Their existence suggests that, where the British military and political authorities felt that the security of imperial power was threatened, it was willing to suspend the panoply of liberal rights, particularly where colonised and/or non-white populations were concerned. Studies of the British colonial regulation of prostitution suggest that, whilst the health of the armed forces was held to be paramount, the willingness to extend measures to the civilian population more widely was routinely sanctioned. In short, the British experiment with regulation was 'preeminently an imperial system devised by the military-medico establishment to protect the soldiers of the empire'.[42]

The British experience of prostitution regulation is by these measures just as long lasting as continental European forms, and at least as extensive geographically. If we acknowledge in this way the military and imperial character of British regulationism we can perhaps perceive a separate tradition and career from that of France and the French system, very different but no less important. This is the argument of this study.

Empire, sexuality and space

The regulation of prostitution is only one part of a much wider regulation of sexuality in which the British imperial authorities invested, and which has become the focus of a large and ever-growing body of research in recent years. Ronald Hyam's once provocative claim that 'sexual dynamics crucially underpinned the whole operation of the British Empire' has long since been confirmed.[43] Scholars from a range of disciplines have demonstrated beyond doubt that sex was 'a key site of imperial fear, concern and action'.[44] They have, however, generally refused and refuted Hyam's preoccupation with sex as act and opportunity for British men in the colonised world. The problems with this pioneering reading, with its deliberate demarcation of sex from gender, its strident masculinism, and its tendentious conclusion that sex was an act of racial reconciliation, are evident

[41] D. M. Peers, 'Imperial vice: sex, drink and the health of British troops in North Indian cantonments, 1800–1858', in D. Killingray and D. Omissi (eds.), *Guardians of empire: the armed forces of the colonial powers c.1700–1964* (Manchester, 1999).
[42] R. Hyam, *Empire and sexuality: the British experience* (Manchester, 1990), pp. 63–4.
[43] *Ibid.*, p. 1.
[44] P. Levine, 'Sexuality and empire', in C. Hall and S. O. Rose (eds.), *At home with the empire: metropolitan culture and the imperial world* (Cambridge, 2006), p. 123.

enough and do not need to be rehearsed in detail here. More pertinent to the present enquiry, however, is Hyam's *centrifugal* model of sexual politics: in his view, a sexual culture developed in what is significantly called 'the British home base' was *exported* via colonial expansion to the wider British world. There it encountered problems and opportunities, and was changed and adapted to suit colonial conditions, only to be confronted with a wave of prudery and prejudice, again emanating from the metropolis, in the form of the distinctive 'social purity' politics of the later nineteenth century.

Quite apart from the rehashing of some of the staler stereotypes of 'Victorian' sexuality, it is the basic model of the historical geography of British sexuality that is at fault here. Most obviously, there is simply no consideration of the ways in which the metropolitan and colonial worlds of sexuality helped to constitute each other, not only through the pointed contrasts between British and non-British cultures, important as these were, but also in the parallels that were sometimes advanced between them. A number of critics have shown how inseparable metropolitan sexualities were from the reality and cultural representation of sexuality in the colonised world.[45] We may note at once the effort – the collective cultural work – expended to distinguish 'domestic' ideals of gender, sexuality and morality from those of the kinds of societies the British encountered or imagined in their imperial adventure. Philippa Levine remarks that sexuality was 'a deep measure for the British of colonial otherness', and we can add of course, at the risk of redundancy, that it was therefore a measure for Britishness itself.[46] The contrast between passion and reason was one calibration, for instance, of how far racially distinct subject peoples fell from the highest ideals of a Christian, civilised society; their ascribed sexual proclivities were clearly used to reinforce the idea of a virtuous and normal British sexual culture.

We must be careful, however, not simply to focus on the role of the sexually differentiated colonial 'Other' for the delineation of a homogeneous domestic British sexuality. We should also recognise the instability of this process of definition, and the potential to make connections between sexualities 'at home' and 'abroad'. The morals of the metropolitan lower classes were, to give one example, commonly represented and understood as having more in common with those of the savage and the heathen than with their bourgeois betters. In noting that prostitute women were portrayed as '"white negroes" occupying anachronistic space', Anne McClintock has shown how the 'impossible edges of modernity' stretch from the colonial bazaar to the metropolitan brothel, making connections between the domestic and the imperial worlds rather than simply making use of

---

[45] For example: Levine, 'Sexuality and empire'; A. McClintock, *Imperial leather: race, gender and sexuality in the colonial contest* (London, 1995), A. L. Stoler, *Race and the education of desire: Foucault's History of Sexuality and the colonial order of things* (Durham, 1996).

[46] Levine, 'Sexuality and empire', p. 125.

the contrast between self and other.[47] In another important commentary, Inderpal Grewal's study of the discursive contrast between English 'home' and Eastern 'harem' demonstrates how certain qualities of the East were nevertheless understood to parallel metropolitan phenomena: the make-up of the 'painted' prostitute of the London streets, for example, signifying the kinds of opacity associated with the harem and its oriental inhabitants.[48] In a contentious *Westminster Review* article titled 'The Western Harem' (1884), if we may continue this theme, the author's focus is on both *exotic* forms of corruption and the hypocrisy of its *domestic* equivalent, '[t]he results', that is, 'upon national stamina and *morale* of the Oriental attitude towards one-half of the human race, of the respect for purity in a section of the women because it is expedient (the principle of the harem), instead of the respect for purity in every human being because it differentiates us from the brutes, because it is wholesome and righteous, because it is beautiful, rational and divine'.[49] In more or less the same register, by asserting that prostitution in the metropolis was a form of sexual *slavery* having more in common with the morally degraded cultures of the non-Western world, it was possible to redraw the distinction between home and away without collapsing it entirely. Once more we have the emphasis on domestic virtue, only for the home/away distinction to be undercut by the invocation of a differentiated metropolis and its abject inhabitants.

There was more going on then than simply the elaboration of metropolitan/colonial differences. The domestic and the colonial can never be the markers of completely distinct sexual cultures. It is the differentiation of sexual roles and characters that cut across and complicate the etymology of coloniser and colonised that is striking. If this is a matter of the formation of sexual identity, these are multiply fractured and inherently unstable. The spatiality of discourses of sexuality did not produce coherent sexual selves, assigned to fixed and stable territories, but rather a proliferation of dangerous sexualities, both internal and external to the nation, operating across and beyond the moral boundaries of empire. Even if there has inevitably been more written about the faraway colonial other, at the expense of European states' internal colonial subjects, it is the combined projection and retrojection of sexual knowledges, their extroversion and turning in on themselves, that is distinctive about the modern, imperial sexual order. There was no domestic sexuality completely distinct from an imperial or colonial one, no original or essential sexual culture, and no one-way transference from metropolis to margins, or indeed the other way round. A distinctively British sexuality might be better thought as a series of sexualities mapped out across this imperial

---

[47] McClintock, *Imperial leather*, pp. 56, 72.

[48] I. Grewal, *Home and harem: nation, gender, empire, and the cultures of travel* (London, 1996), p. 27.

[49] *'The Western Harem'. Reprinted from the 'Westminster Review', July 1884* (London, 1885).

field, dispersed and differentiated into sites and spaces that folded into each other rather than being held rigidly apart. Sexuality was not something to be exported, but always already 'an effect of empire, a category built and shaped by imperial concerns, never stable, always in danger of breaking out of its confines, ever to be watched and guarded'.[50] As a form of knowledge it was a map of dangerous sexualities, not just at the immediate and immediately sexualised 'contact zones' of imperial encounter in the wider world, but also in the heart of the Empire, within the supposedly self-confined metropolitan society itself.[51]

These are important arguments for this particular study, since I want to resist the temptation simply to confront or compare 'metropolitan' with 'colonial' sexualities, and to assume that their construction and regulation was distinctively different. The tendency within histories of prostitution regulation has been to examine the domestic and the colonial quite separately. Philippa Levine's landmark study of prostitution and contagious diseases ordinances in four British colonies – India, Hong Kong, the Straits Settlements and Queensland, Australia – makes the persuasive case for instance that regulationist policies in these colonies were less circumscribed and more extreme and explicit than anything to be found in Britain.[52] Race, above all, helped to structure the regulation of commercial sexuality in the colonies – not in the same way, certainly, but in ways that find little comparison with domestic practices. Levine's four sites together portray a *colonial* regulation of sexuality that is decisively different from the *metropolitan* culture and polity. Despite the emphasis on the local framing of such policies, it is the rule of colonial difference – to use Partha Chatterjee's axiom – that is reiterated.[53] Richard Phillips, too, in his ambitious study of the politics of regulation and resistance across the British Empire, focuses on a series of non-metropolitan sites in India, Africa and Australia, and their interaction with activists, authorities and institutions in the metropolis.[54] Pointing to three main areas of legislation that dominated imperial sexuality politics in the later nineteenth century: laws around the age at which women and girls could consent to sex, the prohibition and legal penalties directed at men who engaged in sex with other men, and the acts and ordinances that regulated prostitution, Phillips argues that these 'sites of sexuality politics were mutually connected, generating and patterning geographies of sexuality politics', a form of cognitive mapping inseparable from the geopolitics of imperialism.[55] This is a pioneering work

---

[50] Levine, *Prostitution, race, and politics*, p. 141.
[51] Mort, *Dangerous sexualities*; M. L. Pratt, *Imperial eyes: studies in travel writing and transculturation* (London, 1992).
[52] Levine, *Prostitution, race, and politics*.
[53] P. Chatterjee, *The nation and its fragments: colonial and postcolonial histories* (New Delhi, 1993).
[54] R. Phillips, *Sex, politics and empire: a postcolonial geography* (Manchester, 2006).
[55] *Ibid.*, p. 10.

in the historical geography of the politics of sexuality, and convincing in his complaints about Eurocentric and metropolitan bias, but the attention to non-metropolitan sites nevertheless reinforces the distinction between the British metropolis and the colonies, without enquiring further into the nature of that distinction and the ways in which projects of sexual regulation were imagined both through and across that divide.

In this book, by contrast, I am concerned with problematising 'the place of empire', for unsettling the metropolitan/colonial distinction.[56] My preference for 'imperial' rather than 'colonial' should be immediately acknowledged. One of my aims here is to avoid equating the two, and also to avoid essentialising the supposedly distinct worlds of 'home' and 'abroad'. The regulation of prostitution in Britain and the rest of the Empire was, I argue, part of the same project, home or away. This is not to play down the real and inevitable differences between the operation of local regulationist regimes, or the equally important differences between the domestic and the non-domestic realms, but these are not reducible to any *fundamental* distinction between the 'metropolitan' and the 'colonial'. This study follows instead the well-known injunction of the 'new imperial history' to treat the metropolitan and the colonial worlds under a single conceptual aegis.[57] This axiom, still more addressed in the breach than in the promise, is the right response to the limitations of earlier research paradigms that failed fully to engage with the ways in which the domestic arena was profoundly altered by the experience of empire. Instead of holding the metropolitan and the colonial to be distinctively different spaces with their own completely separate characteristics, 'we should see the construction of spatial relations within the colonised setting as being simultaneous with the construction of different but related sets of relations in the home setting'.[58]

Where then should we look for 'the place of empire', both in our specific purpose and in our more general orientation? One answer is to turn to the *local*, as Gregory Mann has recently advised, in a plea that location be more than just a handy and trendy post-colonial metaphor, 'a plea that the specificities of particular *places* be brought to the fore, not only to ground research empirically but also to disaggregate and cast new light upon colonial and postcolonial circumstances'.[59] Imperial histories certainly need a sense of place, and there is an important intersection

---

[56] C. Hall and S. O. Rose, 'Introduction: being at home with the Empire', in C. Hall and S. O. Rose (eds.), *At home with the empire: metropolitan culture and the imperial world* (Cambridge, 2006).

[57] See F. Cooper and A. L. Stoler, 'Between metropole and colony: rethinking a research agenda', in F. Cooper and A. L. Stoler (eds.), *Tensions of empire: colonial cultures in a bourgeois world* (Berkeley, 1997).

[58] S. Mills, *Gender and colonial space* (Manchester, 2005), pp. 27–8.

[59] G. Mann, 'Locating colonial history: between France and West Africa', *American Historical Review*, 110 (2005), 409–34, p. 410, emphasis in original.

between the prioritisation of detailed local analysis and varieties of anti-structuralist, anti-foundationalist theory that takes it away from the charge of 'mere' empiricism. In some of the reserved and reticent epistemologies that have followed the Foucauldian example, for instance, we have a model for historical work that chimes with the geographer's attention to place and particularity. In this book, I deliberately turn to studies of particular localities, not as representative or purportedly typical 'case studies', nor as the aggregative elements for a comparative analysis; I choose to see these studies rather as *instances*, unapologetically partial, of the regulation of prostitution. British prostitution regulation was pursued in particular places, sites and landscapes, the logic of regulationism there producing distinctive local regimes of managed sexuality. That the British Empire itself, by necessity and by design, forwarded its projects of governance in and through the localities, and that this aspect of colonial or imperial 'governmentality' was of a piece with the culture and values of British political society, only reinforces the importance of studying regulation through research into circumscribed and particular imperial sites. There was no single blueprint, then, no ideal type or Platonic form of prostitution regulation, only located and localised practices that were sometimes regarded as models and promoted as precedents on the wider stage.

Yet the place of empire cannot be restricted to these locales. The historical geography of empire is not the aggregate history of colonial spaces. It is not just that empire was to be found 'at home' as well as in these avowedly colonial sites, as we now know. Nor is it the fact, equally important, that the range of colonial sites is rather more extensive and disparate than is typically acknowledged, though this is one reason why in this book I have turned to one less obviously 'colonial' site as well as to a more familiar regime. It is also the case, as Mann recognises, that '[t]he linked questions of scale and locality are unresolved'; and that we need as a result to consider 'the integration of disparate sites and discursive maneuvers into a larger, more encompassing analytical framework that is at once localized and supra-local'.[60] Better then – necessary even – to conceive of an 'imperial network' in which the metropolis was connected to a series of imperial (rather than 'colonial') sites, and all these sites of empire to each other.[61] This is a potentially very powerful way of understanding not only the way the British Empire worked, such as in its governance or 'governmentality', but also its very nature – its ideological or discursive dimensions, its relations with settlers and subject peoples, its challenges and its failures. The need to consider the connections between imperial sites is an accepted in this study: as Ronald Hyam observed, 'The empire was as much a system of prostitution networks as it was (in Kipling's famous phrase) a web of submarine cables.'[62]

[60] *Ibid.*, pp. 412, 434.
[61] See D. Lambert and A. Lester (eds.), *Colonial lives across the British Empire: imperial careering in the long nineteenth century* (Cambridge, 2006).
[62] Hyam, *Empire and sexuality*, p. 212.

Despite their avowed intention, however, proponents of the metaphors of 'networks' or 'webs' run a certain risk of reinforcing the coherence and centralised character of empire, so it is worth emphasising the fact that this perspective, whilst not playing down the power of the metropole, acknowledges multiple sources of power and multiple lines of affiliation, not simply those that run from the metropole to the colonies. The British Empire lacked the solidity that the universalist fantasies of its apologists, past and present, imagine. As Levine has succinctly put it, if empire and metropole were not separate sites, 'empire itself was not a single site'.[63] Or, with apologies to the historical sociologist Michael Mann, we might say that empires are far messier than our theories about them.[64] We should be directed by the conception of a 'networked' Empire to the contingent and the conjunctural, to the ephemeral and the fleeting, to the temporary and transitory, as much as to the unified, centralised and coherent. The powers, projects and practices that constituted the attempts to regulate sex work were unevenly distributed and differentiated, fractured and unstable. They were codified in diverse forms, some more formal than others. That they were products of the British 'imperial network', however, is difficult to deny. Piecemeal exercises of power at a local level as they were, they were linked together in the imperial network, constituting a distinctive approach to what were conceived as the problem of managing sexuality in the imperium. By returning this experience to its specific history and geography, to the 'tangibleness of space' and the 'particularities of conceptions of time' this book aims to address the historical and geographical singularity of this distinctive imperial project.[65]

Outline of chapters

This book is organised as a cumulative argument about the extensiveness and distinctiveness of British regulationism. Chapter 2 reviews the domestic Contagious Diseases (or CD) Acts not only because they are the most prominent and by far the most studied legislation for the policing of prostitution in Victorian Britain, but also because they are wrongly taken to be the beginning and the end, the be-all and the end-all, of British regulationism. This chapter offers a critical appraisal of this conventional view. It situates the Acts in their historical and historiographical context, and provides a general overview of their origins and operation, forming a necessary index to the regulation of prostitution examined elsewhere, and particularly in the substantive chapters that follow. Unlike many accounts of the CD Acts, however, I focus on their practical rather than symbolic qualities, and most consistently on the spatial and geographical dimensions of

---

[63] Levine, *Prostitution, race, and politics*, p. 4.
[64] M. Mann, *The sources of social power, volume 1: a history of power from the beginning to AD 1760* (Cambridge, 1986), p. 4.
[65] F. Cooper, *Colonialism in question: theory, knowledge, history* (Berkeley, 2005), p. 126.

the legislation. At one level, this is a matter of paying due attention to the scope and nature of their operations – where and how the Acts were instituted, and their impact at a local level. The emphasis is also, however, on the restricted nature of the Acts, their partiality and provisionality, their incoherence, inconsistency, and to some extent their dysfunctionality. The actual policing that was instituted varied widely from station to station, and was always far more contingent and arbitrary than the passing of the primary legislation suggests. The intention here is therefore to challenge some of the lingering preconceptions about the homogeneity and consistency of the regulationist regime that the CD Acts introduced during the period of their operation, and thus to begin the task of pointing out the *heterogeneity* of the strategies adopted in Britain for policing sexuality throughout the nineteenth century. In moving away from a diachronic emphasis on a short period of formal regulationism to a synchronic one on the persistent variety of policing measures in Britain, the priority of the CD Acts is questioned and a much longer and more geographically extensive experience of managing prostitution is proposed. It also needs to be recognised that regulation 'at home' was already *imperial*, in that the Acts drew heavily upon colonial experiences, and took in three stations in the colony or quasi-colony of Ireland. This is one more indication of the ways in which the supposedly singular 'metropolis' was in fact geographically fractured. Another is the political geography of regulation, whose contours are outlined in the discussion of the struggles between advocates of regulation and their 'repeal' or 'abolitionist' opponents. Ultimately, this chapter portrays the 'domestic' policing of sexuality, and its politics, as characteristically complex and geographically uneven.

Chapter 3 continues this theme, with regard to other forms of the policing of prostitution in the mainland of Britain, beyond the territories of the CD Acts, focusing on the city of Liverpool. As this chapter points out, late-nineteenth-century Liverpool was seen as one of the nearest regimes in mainland Britain, outside the remit of the Acts, to explicit regulationism, and it was repeatedly associated with their more formal management of prostitution. Again, the unevenness of the domestic legislative map is the focus, and particularly the role of the municipalities in forwarding policing policy. As this chapter argues, Liverpool became the model for one municipal type of proactive policing, revolving around the tolerance of known brothels in particular districts of the city. The policy of containment or 'localisation' was the touchstone of this form of management, falling short of formal regulationism in some respects, but incontrovertibly following its logic, and repeatedly associated in the popular and political mind with explicitly regulationist regimes. The immediate contrast was with Glasgow and Manchester, and with a set of policies that attempted to repress prostitution through the aggressive use and strict enforcement of existing legislation and the co-operation of purity and vigilance groups. Municipal autonomy could only go so far, however, and Liverpool's policing strategy was forced in the end to conform to the political standards of the era following the repeal of the CD Acts, but the city's example of municipal regulation still shows how variegated was the Victorian policy map. This in itself cautions against overassertive assessments of a 'Victorian' morality and sexual culture. The principal intention in this chapter is to direct attention away from the notion of a single, ideal type of regulationism, to focus on the range of policing practices that existed in the metropolis and on the discursive map in which these were politically situated.

A further domestic example is given in Chapter 4, this time much more straightforwardly regulationist, though quite neglected in the historiography. In Cambridge, the authorities of the University implemented a regulationist regime of long standing, stretching back to privileges first granted in the Middle Ages but reinstalled in the modern era as a measure to protect the sexual health of its undergraduates. Under this 'proctorial' system – named after the University's appointed agents of discipline – the University authorities managed prostitution through a strategy of careful tolerance in one part of the town, and repression of street prostitution in the other. It combined this with a system for the compulsory inspection of prostitute women, and their prophylactic detention if found to be diseased. The effects of this regime for women of the town and for women who made a career out of prostitution are examined in detail, as is the sexual activity of the male undergraduates who were their presumptive clients. Some consideration of the counterpart system in Oxford is also considered, particularly for the light that this sheds on undergraduate male sexuality. It is particularly notable, however, that the proctorial system in the University towns helped to pave the way for the Contagious Diseases Acts and the campaign for their extension, because they represented a viable precedent for regulating prostitution amongst the civilian population, one that was for its supporters remarkably successful in policing social hygiene; this domestic exemplar of regulationism fulfilled the same function as did some colonial regimes. This chapter considers the political significance of these statutes, and the tying of their fortunes to the fate of the national legislation. Ultimately, and unfortunately for advocates of regulation, the Universities' clear endorsement of gender and class privileges made it politically vulnerable to the opponents of the CD Acts. These 'repealers' or 'abolitionists' made common cause with local parties in characterising the Cambridge system as a medieval anachronism, incompatible with the moral tenor of the modern age. The campaign against regulation in Cambridge and Oxford was bound up, this chapter concludes, with the simultaneous critiques of University life and standards. Educational reform and moral reformation were twin themes in the political critique of Oxford and Cambridge in the second half of the nineteenth century, and the regulation not of prostitute women but of upper-class men was increasingly the focus of concern.

Chapter 5 extends the coverage of British regulationism to a third, again thoroughly neglected, example: the colony and fortress of Gibraltar. Put into the context of the British experience of regulated prostitution in the Mediterranean, including Malta and the Ionian Islands, this study of Gibraltar shows the importance, practically and politically, of these often overlooked regulationist regimes in the near Empire. Typically disregarded, both from analyses of colonialism that ignore the near colonies of the Mediterranean, and from histories of regulationism, because it never had explicit contagious diseases legislation, Gibraltar nevertheless shows how unspecific but effective forms of regulationism could be constructed in colonial settings. As in Liverpool and Cambridge, the lack of formal legislation in no way precluded the enactment of regulationist regimes, nor their political recognition as such. As the repealer Josephine Butler noted, 'there is no special Act applying to Gibraltar, but none the less is the system carried out there with a brutality of logic which could hardly be exceeded'.[66] In this case, the formal powers of the governor of the fortress to expel non-resident foreigners provided the means by which medical inspection might be compelled. In Gibraltar, the residence and naturalisation status of prostitute women formed the basis for their licensing and toleration, and allowed the authorities to pressure such women to live in houses within an informal brothel district. Here, fears about venereal health overlapped with those concerning the health, numbers and political orientation of the civilian population of the colony; effectively, the politics of prostitution were those of sovereignty and citizenship in a colonial setting. Chapter 5 is thus a study of colonial law and informal regulation, and this chapter demonstrates how closely allied were the operations of law and disciplinary power.

In Chapter 6, the fullest workings of the colonial regulation of prostitution are explored with regard to Hong Kong, drawing especially on the fact that this was '[t]he only Colony in which the practical working and effects of the system have been the subject of official inquiry'.[67] Here, the landscape of racialised sexuality constructed by regulationist policing is readily apparent, racial and cultural difference being written into the structure of the market for commercial sex. The role that space played in the government of prostitution is fulsomely acknowledged in this chapter, which carefully maps out the geography of brothel prostitution, and corrects some previous assessments, both substantive and theoretical. Although the attempt to regulate prostitution by segregating women and brothel houses intended for European clients from those patronised by Chinese men clearly indicates the racialisation of colonial sexuality in Hong Kong, the specifics of this policy, and the implications for the social geography of prostitution, were worked out via a discursive emphasis on the discretionary limits of colonial power. Rather than see this management of sexuality as an indication of colonial ambition, however, I portray it as an expression of a colonial governmentality

---

[66] J. E. Butler, *The revival and extension of the abolitionist cause: a letter to the members of the Ladies' National Association* (London, 1887), reprinted in I. Sharp (ed.), *Josephine Butler and the prostitution campaigns: diseases of the body politic, volume V: the Queen's daughters in India* (London, 2003), p. 27.

[67] *Ibid.*, p. 28.

based upon a discursive recognition of Chinese racial and cultural difference. In this explicitly limited intervention into the colonial sexual economy, prostitution regulation was promoted as a wise acknowledgement of cultural and political realities, even to the extent that the regulation of prostitution itself was seen as a Chinese political institution necessarily followed by the British administration. This chapter, like its predecessors, also focuses on the role of the politics of prostitution in representing local regimes on a wider stage. In this case, Hong Kong became a battleground for the repeal movement, particularly as a result of the engaged sympathies of the eccentric governor, Sir John Pope Hennessy. Pope Hennessy played a central role in embroiling Hong Kong in debates over the existence of female 'slavery', making the racial nature of regulated prostitution in the colony a touchstone for the humanitarian conscience. At the same time, the issue of slavery became more problematic where the exploitation of the subject races by the colonial powers could not be mobilised. By concluding this chapter with the difficulties in which Pope Hennessy found himself, I indicate the boundaries of rule not only of colonial government but also of a liberal imperial humanitarianism.

The final argument of this study further develops this theme. Whilst the struggle between regulationist advocates and their repeal opponents has been well recognised, the imperial dimension of this politics has only relatively recently come into focus, especially through the lens of the new imperial and post-colonial histories. In the conclusion of this book, an attempt is made to place this politics, considering the geographical imaginations appealed to by regulationists and repealers, and also in our own assessments. I argue that the proponents of repeal constructed a politically effective map of state-recognised vice, an imperial system that connected sites of regulated prostitution both in Britain and in its colonial possessions, and that their focus, consistent with the liberal tradition to which most belonged, remained on the geopolitics of nation and empire. This did not match our contemporary stress on the categories of the 'metropolitan' and the 'colonial', however, and I argue that it is easy as a result to misread with hindsight the geopolitics of imperial liberalism. This is particularly true with regard to the importance of 'race' and the putative rule of racial difference in colonial regimes. For, whilst the *practical* regulation of prostitution in many of the British colonial possessions – like Hong Kong – was indeed clearly racialised, dependent on and constructing clear racial divides, the *politics* of the repeal movement largely shied away from confronting the starkest implications of imperial rule over its subjected races. Instead, the political commitments of the opponents of regulation typically centred on the British nation conceived of as both part of and separate from its empire, and invoking a national imperial mission compatible with humanitarian and liberal sentiments. Whilst their political work demonstrated the installation of regulationism in British imperial authority, theirs was, I suggest, a politics of *displacement* that prevented them from connecting the illegitimacy of the sexual double standard to the illegitimacy of empire. It was left to others to condemn the regulation of prostitution as a distinctive, characteristic product of British imperial arrogance. These conclusions thus consider the geographical imaginations in which and through which the politics of British prostitution regulation was articulated, and the successes and failures of the anti-regulationist critique of imperial sexual exploitation. For, whilst repealers expunged regulationist ordinances from the statute books, they also effectively removed the experience of regulating prostitution from the political imagination of Britishness itself.

2

Partial legislation and privileged places: the Contagious Diseases Acts

The first of the Contagious Diseases (CD) Acts was passed in 1864, as an exceptional and temporary measure intended to protect the health of soldiers and sailors in eight garrison and dockyard towns in England (Aldershot, Chatham, Colchester, Plymouth/Devonport, Portsmouth, Sheerness, Shorncliffe and Woolwich) together with three in Ireland (Cork, the Curragh army camp in County Kildare, and Queenstown). Under this Act (27 & 28 Vict., c. 85), women who were identified by police and magistrates as 'common prostitutes' could be subjected to medical examination and, if found to be suffering from contagious venereal disease, detained for up to three months. A replacement Act followed in 1866 (29 Vict., c. 35), adding Windsor to the schedule, extending the territory policed to a radius of five miles beyond the scheduled districts, and increasing the maximum period of sanitary detention to six months. In this Act, which introduced periodical medical examination for the first time, local magistrates' powers were eroded, their authority being increasingly replaced by government-appointed visiting surgeons in dedicated 'lock' hospitals or wards. There was a minor amendment in 1868 (31 & 32 Vict., c. 80), but the third CD Act proper, in 1869 (32 & 33 Vict., c. 96), continued these trends, adding Canterbury, Dover, Gravesend, Maidstone, Southampton and Winchester, taking in the likes of Dartmouth, Deal and Greenwich, extending supervision to ten miles around these towns, and allowing women to be detained for up to nine months.[1] By 1869, a complex administrative structure was authorised that allowed women in these 'subjected districts' to be registered as prostitutes, and required them under pain of criminal prosecution to present themselves for regular medical examination followed, if necessary, by sanitary detention (Figure 2.1).

---

[1] This amendment closed up a loophole and brought Ireland into line with the English legislation. Though minor, this Act indicates the specificity of the Irish situation, and many repealers chose to refer to the *four* CD Acts rather than the more conventionally cited three.

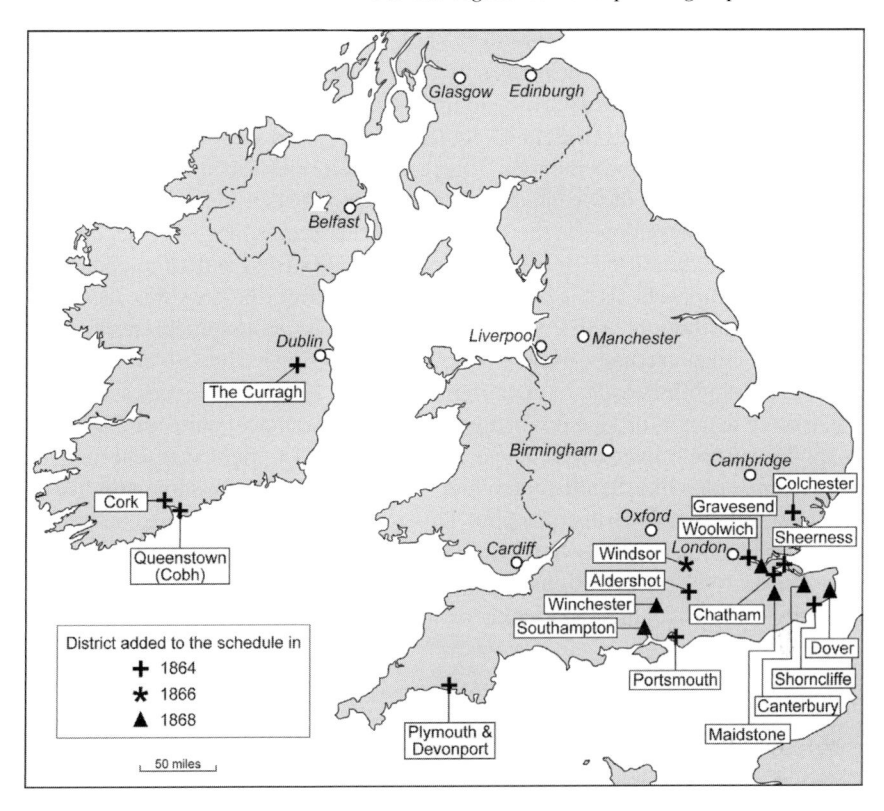

Figure 2.1 Subjected districts under the Contagious Diseases Acts

The three key elements of identification, inspection and incarceration clearly align this legislation with other attempts to combat venereal disease by regulating prostitution. Though the promoters of the CD Acts were always at pains to distance themselves from continental regimes, they are recognisable as regulationist both in principle and in practice. Compared to the continent this management of commercial sexuality was certainly modest. The CD Acts operated only in the specified districts, which never included London or any of the large industrial cities or seaports. They applied almost exclusively to military stations rather than civilian towns, Southampton being the notable exception, and this only because of its proximity to the troops at Portsmouth. Prostitutes and brothels were never explicitly licensed, nor was a dedicated morals police ever established. Like their continental cousins, though, the Acts were clearly associated with the growing authority of the central state and with an increasing willingness to intervene in sexual relations in the name of public health. They represented a significant development in the policing of prostitution in the British Isles, particularly as women could be arrested and detained, under threat of criminal punishment, merely on *suspicion* of prostituting themselves.

Since the regulationist nature of the Contagious Diseases Acts has been widely accepted, and since a great deal has now been written about them, there is inevitably a sense of apology in returning to the theme. Precisely because the Acts *are* so prominent in histories of British regulationism, this chapter provides an overview of their origins and operation, together with a brief account of the equally significant opposition they generated. It draws special attention, however, as few previous studies have done, to the *geography* of the Acts, which has been notably neglected or marginalised, or simply ignored.[2] Some casual and all too common references to the Acts, as for instance their constituting 'the laws that regulated Victorian prostitution', misleadingly overlook their geographical restrictions altogether.[3] Other accounts, usually popular but sometimes with academic pretensions, are straightforwardly in error. Nils Ringdal's recent and remarkably unreconstructed account of global prostitution has it for instance, quite wrongly, that '[n]ew laws were implemented between 1864 and 1867 to fight venereal disease, first in port cities like Southampton and Plymouth, later in London, and finally throughout the whole British Empire. This series of statutes came to be known as the Contagious Diseases Act.'[4] Given these abundant sources of confusion, it is necessary to begin our discussion of British regulationism by mapping out, as carefully as possible, the historical geography of the CD Acts.

Origins

The 1864 'Act for the Prevention of Contagious Diseases' arrived on the statute books largely unheralded and 'without that salutary and beneficial purification which discussion and opposition supplied', as Home Secretary Henry Bruce subsequently put it.[5] The bill passed the House of Commons late in session, with little discussion or dissent, its apparently innocuous title aligning it with rather less contentious veterinary measures also occupying Parliamentary attention. The suspiciously covert manner in which the legislation was introduced – 'like a thief in the night', 'in hot haste and in secrecy at the midnight hour', as the repealers charged – suggests that its promoters appreciated perfectly well the measure's

---

[2] The most notable exception to this neglect is Miles Ogborn, and I gratefully acknowledge my debt to his work: see M. J. Ogborn, 'Discipline, government and law: the response to crime, poverty and prostitution in nineteenth century Portsmouth' (PhD, University of Cambridge, 1990), M. Ogborn, 'Law and discipline in nineteenth century English state formation: the Contagious Diseases Acts of 1864, 1866 and 1869', *Journal of Historical Sociology*, 6 (1993), 28–55.

[3] D. E. Nord, '"Vitiated air": the polluted city and female sexuality in *Dombey and Son* and *Bleak House*', in A. H. Miller and J. E. Adams (eds.), *Sexualities in Victorian Britain* (Bloomington, 1996), pp. 38–69, p. 39.

[4] N. Ringdal, *Love for sale: a global history of prostitution* (London, 2004), p. 263.

[5] *Hansard*, 209:334, 13 February 1872.

potential for controversy.[6] From the point of view of such critics, every effort was made to mislead the public about a major legislative change with vital social, moral and political implications. Another repealer saw it as 'a law foisted in under a title calculated to blind, and virtually passed in secret, so far as the nation was concerned, though passed by the representatives of that nation'.[7] Even contemporary defenders of the Acts could not and did not defend the secrecy of their introduction. From a somewhat different angle, this might all be attributed to carelessness rather than to conspiracy. Many years later, for instance, on the eve of their repeal, Gladstone could claim that the Acts had arrived 'almost without the knowledge of anyone'.[8] Like the acquisition of the Empire, it could be maintained that the Contagious Diseases Acts were passed in a fit of absence of mind.

This narrative was always misleading, however. Paul McHugh notes that the idea that legislation was simply smuggled through Parliament was in the end a convenient political fiction for repealers and repentant regulationists alike. The introduction and passing of the Acts was in truth rather more contentious and public than these subsequent justifications suggest. In committee, if not in the debating chamber, the 1864 bill was subjected to searching questions, some offensive clauses being removed and some significant amendments made. There were those, moreover, outside Parliament, who perfectly well understood the implications of the legislation, and who vigorously opposed it in principle. Florence Nightingale registered early and vociferous objection to the progress of the legislation, noting that, whilst regulation had been repeatedly urged for places like the army town of Aldershot, this was incompatible with British traditions:

In civil life at home, it is supposed inconsistent with individual liberty to put down bad places of resort, and to prevent open temptations to profligacy; while, in certain continental states, it is *not* supposed against liberty or morals to make prostitution as little disagreeable as possible – viz., by 'regulating' it, to avert the consequences of this vice, leaving all the temptations just as they were.[9]

It is safer to argue that few MPs initially recognised, or were willing to recognise, objections to the tenor of the legislation, and were mollified, or were willing to be mollified, by the promoters of the Acts, who argued that these were necessary and pragmatic proposals, hedged around with constitutional protections, and of a completely different nature to continental practices. Significantly, the Acts were

---

[6] J. Stansfeld, *Substance of the speeches of the Rt Hon. James Stansfeld, MP, on the Contagious Diseases Acts* (London, 1875), p. 6, J. E. Butler, *Our Christianity tested by the Irish question* (London, 1887), p. 4.

[7] W. Arthur, *Hush or speak out? A word upon the question of the hour* (London, 1885), cited by P. McHugh, *Prostitution and Victorian social reform* (London, 1980), pp. 38–9.

[8] McHugh, *Prostitution and Victorian social reform* (London, 1980), p. 42.

[9] F. Nightingale, *Army sanitary administration and its reform under the late Lord Herbert* (London, 1862), emphasis in original.

presented as local and specific legislation, not a dramatic change in policy by the state.

Nor were the Acts introduced from out of the blue. If a shadow of surreptitiousness remains in terms of the principal legislation, they were clearly the result of a sustained, long-term campaign for legislative change. From the perspective of the general debate on the 'social evil', the regulation of prostitution had been discreetly canvassed for a number of years. In 1868, *The Lancet* could look back with evident satisfaction on the advantages of a free press working in harmony with a proactive government to promote the benefits of venereal diseases legislation: 'The people have been "educated" by members of our profession, and by various papers, to the requisite extent.'[10] William Acton's contribution has already been noted, though it is important to emphasise the reticence of his call for regulation in the 1857 edition of *Prostitution*, before the Acts, as opposed to the more often cited advocacy of the 1870 version.[11] Less well known, though arguably just as important, was the aggressive promotion of medical police by the likes of Henry Wyldebore Rumsey. From the perspective of an increasingly proactive public health movement, Rumsey's approval of continental European systems, and his call for 'a judicious centralization, aided by local enterprise' at home, explicitly recommended the registration and regulation of prostitutes. In terms that are virtually identical with those of later proponents of the Contagious Diseases Acts, Rumsey wrote as early as 1856 that:

So long as a class of women live by the wages of prostitution, they should be considered as offenders against society and public morality, whom it is proper to place under surveillance; and this involves systematic inspection and control, both of which are of great importance, not only for the prevention of diseases, of which this unfortunate class are the propagators, but for the diminution and detection of other crimes of which they are often the abettors.[12]

Many of those who claimed expertise in social and medical reform had long been persuaded by the cause of regulation, and we do need to invoke the role of a medical profession growing in authority and flexing its muscles in its calls for a more hygienically proactive state. It is no surprise that *The Lancet*, again in its role as the voice of the medical establishment, immediately welcomed the Acts with open arms: 'we are persuaded, repeatedly and energetically to call upon Government to arm science with the social powers necessary to destroy this

[10] *The Lancet*, 25 July 1868, p. 118.
[11] W. Acton, *Prostitution, considered in its moral, social & sanitary aspects, in London and other large cities. With proposals for the mitigation and prevention of its attendant evils* (London, 1857); W. Acton, *Prostitution, considered in its moral, social, and sanitary aspects, in London and other large cities and garrison towns. With proposals for the control and prevention of its attendant evils*, reprint of 2nd edition, 1870 (London, 1972).
[12] H. W. Rumsey, *Essays on state medicine* (London, 1856), pp. 29, 58.

spreading cancer of civilization.'[13] Still, regulationists did not hold a monopoly over progressive, scientific or medical thought. The profession was not unanimous in its support for regulationism or for the associated public health programme. John Simon, for instance, a strong proponent of state medicine but also a fervent 'Christian moralist', was lukewarm about many of the arguments for extending the Acts, and came to be regarded by regulationists as something of an apostate; John Birkbeck Nevins, the prominent Liverpudlian opponent of the Acts, was also originally in their favour. It is an error to think of the Acts as merely adjuncts to the growing authority of the medical profession and the public health movement, and flowing straightforwardly from them. Mid-Victorian sanitary science simply did not speak with one voice.

It is better therefore to focus on the immediate and specific backing of the Acts. In this regard, we should see contagious diseases legislation being most forcefully promoted by the British military. The way was being deliberately prepared for the Acts at least as early as 1860, with the publication of the important pamphlet *Soldiers and the social evil*, ostensibly the private contribution of 'a chaplain to the forces', but surely forwarded by the military to test the temper of the times. Although characteristically careful to abjure the 'Continental system', this letter made the critical call for '*partial* legislation': that is, for an experiment restricted to specific military sites rather than being universal in its application.[14] The problem was the level of venereal disease amongst the ranks, where, in estimate after estimate, an alarming incidence of disease was recorded. In 1859, for instance, the Army Medical Department stated that for every 1,000 men there were 422 hospitalisations for venereal disease; in 1862, the army reported that 33 per cent of the home-based forces were currently infected with disease.[15] In the early 1860s, between seven and nine days per man were estimated to have been lost every year, each man staying on average twenty-four days in hospital. The cost every year to the navy alone was £20,000 in the first half of the 1860s.[16] These terrible statistics were fundamental to the argument for regulation that culminated in the passing of the CD Acts.

The periodic reports on the health of the army and navy, parading this information, eventually led to the committee of enquiry that sat in 1862, under the chairmanship of Samuel Whitbread. Judith Walkowitz and others have noted that this committee was partly the creation, if not exactly the creature, of Florence

[13] 'Venereal disease in the Army and Navy', *The Lancet*, 19 March 1864, p. 329.
[14] *Soldiers and the social evil. A letter addressed by permission to the Right Hon. Sidney Herbert, MD, Secretary of State for War, by a chaplain to the forces* (London, 1860).
[15] M. Trustram, *Women of the regiment: marriage and the Victorian army* (Cambridge, 1984), p. 157; E. M. Spiers, *The late Victorian army 1868–1902* (Manchester, 1992), p. 143.
[16] B. Hill, 'Statistical results of the Contagious Diseases Acts', *Journal of the Statistical Society of London*, 33 (1870), 463–85, pp. 476, 479.

Nightingale, and it was in no sense a rubberstamping exercise for regulationism.[17] It concluded indeed that the evidence for the success of continental and colonial systems of regulation was at best incomplete, and doubted that the forms of coercion involved could ever be introduced at home. The committee recommended instead the encouragement of voluntary admission in new lock hospitals, improvements to sanitary and leisure facilities for soldiers and sailors, and the greater use of existing powers by local authorities to crack down on prostitution in the garrison towns. These recommendations gave regulation a public airing, but came down heavily against its basic principles. Some of the dissenting arguments of Sir John Liddell, director general of the naval medical department, were influential nevertheless, and the effect of the report was to goad the regulationists on rather than to confound their arguments. Though a signatory to the report's conclusions, Liddell remained convinced of the necessity for compulsory examination. He stressed both the seriousness of the problem, and also the changing climate of public opinion making the question of sanitary surveillance and detention an immediate one:

> as a good deal of right feeling is now stirring on the subject of the social evil, which is forcing itself on the attention of the country, the time seems very favourable for trying to get the Legislature to place these women under the immediate surveillance of the police, and to commit them compulsorily, when diseased, to Lock wards prepared for their cure.[18]

Furthermore, discussion of the problem of disease in the ranks could not be confined to the military reports. Just as Liddell suggested, the question of the 'social evil' was very much in the public mind, and with it the problem of syphilis for the population at large. Throughout the 1860s, its devastating effects were regularly rehearsed through the correspondence pages of journals and newspapers.[19] To take just one contribution as more or less representative:

> When fever or cholera occur we look to our drains and whitewash our houses; vessels on board of which certain diseases may have appeared are placed in quarantine, often to the great personal inconvenience and detriment of the people on board, none of whom have been accountable for having become themselves infected, or being within range of infection. Persons on account of mental disorders, for which they are themselves in no way to blame, are, if considered to be dangerous to the public, removed and carefully excluded during the time that their attack of illness may continue; but yet, strange to say, an evil which is far more general in its prevalence than any of these is permitted to prevail to an extent unknown in any other country than the United Kingdom.[20]

---

[17] J. R. Walkowitz, *Prostitution and Victorian society: women, class, and the state* (Cambridge, 1980), p. 75.

[18] *Report of the committee upon venereal disease in the Army and Navy* [1863], NA WO 33/12/188, p. 5.

[19] See, for example, 'The great evil of garrisons', *The Times*, 12 November 1860, p. 8; 'Universities and garrison towns', *The Times*, 5 December 1860, p. 9; *The Times*, 31 August 1863, p. 10; 'Health of the British Army', *The Times*, 31 October 1863, p. 6.

[20] C. A., 'Vice and disease in garrison towns', *The Times*, 23 April 1862, p. 11.

This correspondent noted in passing a recent public meeting of residents of Aldershot in support of regulationist measures, and essayed the hope that other towns in which bodies of the military were stationed might follow the example it provided. This Aldershot meeting had defended the town and its garrison against the calumnies of those who drew attention to 'the flagrant disgrace and scandal' of a town supposedly dominated by brothel-keepers and publicans.[21] The town's indignant residents were quick to praise the military authorities, and more or less commended the good order of 'the tribe of camp followers and those other evils which were inseparable from such an establishment'; but there were also resolutions to do more to manage the latter. As the mover of the first resolution successfully argued:

As to the women who infested the neighbourhood, experience showed that it was impossible to get rid of them in a garrison town; but he hoped that something might be done, by bringing them under better control, to mitigate as much as possible the evils – both moral and physical – arising from indiscriminate intercourse.[22]

By the following year, advocates of regulation were bolder still, one navy correspondent writing that there was but one sure way of alleviating the evil of prostitution and its consequences in the garrison towns: 'to give the magistrates and police power in naval ports and garrison towns to cause any known immoral women to be medically inspected, sent to hospital, and retained there till cured.'[23] Regulationist solutions, in the very restricted form of 'partial legislation' applicable to particular military stations, were clearly being widely and publicly canvassed in the years leading up to the passing of the first CD Act. In August 1863, *The Times* itself came down on the side of management, essaying an editorial call for regulation, albeit one so discreet that it could not bring itself even to use the word 'venereal', referring instead to the alarming proportion of soldiers and sailors invalided at any one time by sickness 'created by acts of their own'.[24] The paper's leader conceded that anything resembling continental practice 'would be certain to offend feelings which we shall not call prejudices', and that 'We could hardly tolerate recognition, still less registration, in such a case, nor is a country in which an agitation can be got up against licensed drinking-houses likely to connive at an extension of licences to worse resorts than taverns.'[25] Nevertheless, the limited medical intervention that was again called for prompted, as it was surely meant to, further public discussion of the principle of regulating prostitution. Another prominent correspondent, possibly a member of the India Office, noted dutifully that, whilst '[t]he English public would not, *as yet*, bear with the legislative sanitary restrictions on this trade exercised on the Continent, to the undoubted diminution of the more loathsome consequences of the evil, – the

---

[21] 'The soldier at Aldershott [sic]', *The Times*, 7 April 1862, p. 12.
[22] 'Indignation meeting at Aldershott', *The Times*, 15 April 1862, p. 12; see also 'The morality of Aldershott', *The Times*, 23 April 1862, p. 11.
[23] R. Coote, letter, *The Times*, 31 August 1863, p. 10.
[24] *The Times*, 19 August 1863, p. 8.   [25] *Ibid.*

evident restraint of its most revolting public intrusion', a system of registration in the military stations would be a practicable improvement.[26] Once the subject was installed like this in the public sphere, whatever discretion remained was increasingly flimsy. Though careful still to avoid the accusation of encouraging licence, this same correspondent came ultimately, despite these reservations, to a direct recommendation of the 'continental' or 'foreign system':

> I say, better even to resort to the full Continental system than rest content as we are. I see less to deplore in recognizing – sanctioning, if you will, after a sort, what we cannot wholly be without, than in allowing this moral plague to assault openly all society.[27]

It is impossible to prove conclusively that these contributions were part of a deliberate and concerted campaign. What is important to note is the specifically *military* rationale that was made for British regulation. Many correspondents drew on their own experience of life in the military stations, noting the efforts made at improving the moral code of the armed forces, but insisting that the surveillance and compulsory detention of prostitute women was a necessity for army reform. It is also the tradition of military medicine that is most directly involved in the promotion of the Acts. Instead of Acton and Greg, or Rumsey and Chadwick, we might best turn to individuals like James Bird, one time surgeon of the European General Hospital at Bombay and Physician General to the Bombay Army. In 1854, contemporaneous with Rumsey's publications on state medicine, Bird had argued for a system of medical police, the importance of preventive medicine being brought home to him by his time in India. Aligning syphilis and gonorrhoea with other contagious diseases 'which are propagated from one individual to another, by the generation of a subtle excreted matter, capable of exciting like affections in others', Bird went on to hope that 'though such has hitherto been little cultivated in England, I trust the time is not far distant when it will be systematized and taught in our schools as much as other departments. To the army medical officer, if not of greater, it is at least of equal importance with other departments.'[28]

The prior *colonial* expertise of men like Bird who pressed for the introduction of 'domestic' legislation should also be heavily underlined. The advocacy of preventive medicine and medical police, drawing not just upon military but also imperial experience, deserves far more credit for the institution of domestic contagious diseases legislation than it has hitherto received. Whilst the majority of historians have chosen to see the military interest in sexual regulation as dominated by concerns raised by and after the Crimean War, it would be better

---

[26] *The Times*, 22 August 1863, p. 6, emphasis in original. See also 28 August 1863, p. 5, and 4 September 1863, p. 8. McHugh, *Prostitution and Victorian social reform*, p. 36.
[27] *The Times*, 4 September 1863, p. 8.
[28] J. Bird, *The laws of epidemic and contagious diseases and the importance of preventive medicine: an introductory address to the Epidemiological Society* (London, 1854), pp. 11, 31–2.

to point to a rather longer history of anxiety over the threat posed by venereal disease to British security, a history that is inextricable from Britain's colonial presence. The army and navy reports that stated the case for regulation also made particular mention of colonial systems that were thought to be *already* proving the worth and the workability of stringent medical policing. Malta, Gibraltar and the Ionian Islands were specially cited, as were Hong Kong and the stations in British India. In the years leading up to 1864, public advocates of regulation routinely pointed to these colonial precedents. The author of *Soldiers and the social evil* thus referred *alternately* to the 'continental' and 'Maltese' systems.[29] It was said of such systems of medical inspection that '[t]his has been tried in the British dominions at Malta, Hongkong, and, I believe, Gibraltar, with entire success'.[30] *The Times* offered this further opinion:

> That such measures can be made efficacious we know from the example of a colony where the temporary suspension of a restrictive and successful law was immediately followed by a return to the evil which had provoked the enactment. We may not be able to reproduce such legislation at home, but we may do something, and few persons after perusing the foregoing statistics will deny that something should be done.[31]

The immediate origins of the CD Acts can thus be traced to responses to concerns raised by the British armed forces, concerns that drew upon military experience in the service of British imperialism. Advocates of the domestic regulation of prostitution conscientiously cited the favourable results of measures enacted in the colonies, and suggested these as both precedent and example for British legislation. As the regulationist William Morgan peremptorily put it:

> This enforced isolation of DISEASED PERSONS we have now mentioned extends to those gallant men who are kept for the protection of the State both by sea and land; and it is fervently to be hoped that the time will come when these beneficent Acts will throw their protective powers over the whole of England and her far-distant and extensive colonies.[32]

Surgeon Major Thomas Atchinson, in making the same point, also segued straightforwardly from the military metaphor of struggle against disease to the practical example of the military forces to the nation as a whole:

> if we first prevent by wholesome legislation, and then attempt the cure by expulsion of our enemy, (who, in most cases, should never have entered), see how simplified is our duty to our neighbour, and to posterity.

---

[29] See H. Ware, 'The recruitment, regulation and role of prostitution in Britain from the middle of the nineteenth century to the present day' (PhD, University of London, 1969), p. 166.
[30] *The Times*, 31 August 1863, p. 10.   [31] *The Times*, 19 August 1863, p. 8.
[32] W. Morgan, *Contagious diseases: their history, anatomy, pathology, and treatment, with comments on the Contagious Diseases Acts* (London, 1877), p. 182.

In other places the beneficial working of the Contagious Diseases Acts has been most apparent; our fleets and armies have already reaped the benefit. Why should the same boon be denied to our civil population?[33]

The Acts thus had an indelibly imperial caste from their very conception. They should never be taken merely as 'domestic' legislation, for they took shape in an imperial context and they were constantly and consistently related to Britain's imperial dependencies. The public health historian F. B. Smith was quite right to note – for all his later impassioned defence of their medical benefits – that '[t]he Contagious Diseases Acts are an ominous indication of what determined doctors, economics, military men and illiberal politicians could achieve when they combined for the health of the Empire'.[34]

Operation

The operation of the Acts was also far more complex than many overviews allow. Whilst the specific precepts of the three major CD Acts have usually been passed over with little comment, it is essential to recognise the elaborate and cumbersome nature of the legislation. The three CD Acts were constructed from a range of medical, legal, military, political and philanthropic institutions whose workings cannot be reduced to any simple formula of disciplinary power, still less conjured up from the abstractions of sanitary discourse or medico-moral ideology. Each Act was really a kind of *assemblage*, partly grounded in well-thought-out sanitary principles but equally as much the result of pragmatic manoeuvres designed to satisfy this range of interests. Each was thus no more or less than a 'workable system of regulation'.[35]

In detail, the initial Act, which was originally intended to be in force for three years only, allowed the Admiralty and the Secretary of State for War to oversee arrangements for the policing of prostitution and the treatment of venereal disease in its eleven localities. It authorised the military to appoint an Inspector of Hospitals whose task was to certify accommodation for venereal patients. It stipulated that only after a hospital was certified, and on the condition of it being no more than fifty miles from its intended district, could women believed to be prostitutes and believed to be suffering from venereal disease be directed to attend there for medical examination. This could only take place, moreover, when information to this effect was laid before a Justice of the Peace, either by a superintendent or inspector of police (local constabulary or plain-clothes Metropolitan policemen) or by an authorised medical practitioner. Women served with a notice to attend the hospital were able to submit themselves voluntarily for examination,

---

[33] T. Atchison, *Letters to 'The Times' on small-pox encampments. And a word on the Contagious Diseases Acts* (London, 1871), p. 13.
[34] F. B. Smith, *The people's health, 1830–1910* (London, 1990), p. 418.
[35] Ogborn, 'Discipline, government and law', p. 223.

but the police were also authorised to apprehend anyone served with a warrant and to convey her to the hospital. Once there, inspection had to be carried out within a twenty-four-hour period, but, if a woman was then found to be diseased, she could be detained at the hospital, again on the order of a magistrate, for up to three months. The penalty for refusal to submit to examination, or detention, or indeed for any infringement of hospital regulations, was summary punishment of up to one month's imprisonment for a first offence, two months' imprisonment otherwise. In addition to these regulations, the Act allowed the imposition of penalties on owners, occupiers, managers or assistants of any residence of women believed to be common prostitutes suffering from venereal disease; the options for the magistrates in this case were a fine of up to £10, or a sentence of three months, with or without hard labour.

There are several features of this initial legislation that deserve emphasis, indicating both its careful drafting and its unwieldy architecture. There was, first of all, the distinctive combination of local and national agencies, with the external authority of the Inspector of Hospitals matched by the local powers of the magistracy, the operations of police and doctors falling somewhere between the two. The Metropolitan Police, answerable formally to the Home Office, was to combine with the local constabulary in the surveillance and compulsion of prostitute women, whilst local medical practitioners were to work, similarly, hand in hand with the medical officers of the centrally certified hospitals. This structure of government was not particularly unusual in itself, but the historical geographer Miles Ogborn has rightly drawn attention to the fact that the familiar rationale of medical policing – the sanitary principle – was supplemented, and partially compromised, by the legal discourses and practices whose operation was relatively autonomous.[36] Ogborn has also usefully modelled the complex operation of the different actors within this 1864 legislation, in doing so drawing attention to the tensions inherent in the regimes it instituted (Figure 2.2a).

We can go further by noting that the bureaucratic geography of the 1864 Act is correspondingly complex. The fifty-mile rule for the provision of certified hospitals establishing a limit to the distance a woman might reasonably be transported for purposes of examination is straightforward enough, but the geographical specification of the subjected districts is rather less so. The 1864 Act, as with the other CD Acts, was restricted to particular localities, but the specified districts could not form anything remotely like a seamless administrative web. The districts were not all based on the same established boundaries, nor unlike the Poor Law did they install a completely different administrative map. Instead, the various CD Acts cobbled together territories using combinations of urban and rural parishes, tithings, townships, municipal boroughs and urban improvement districts. Some of the more self-contained districts like Aldershot or Colchester had clear enough political boundaries, distinct islands

---

[36] Ogborn, 'Law and discipline', p. 41.

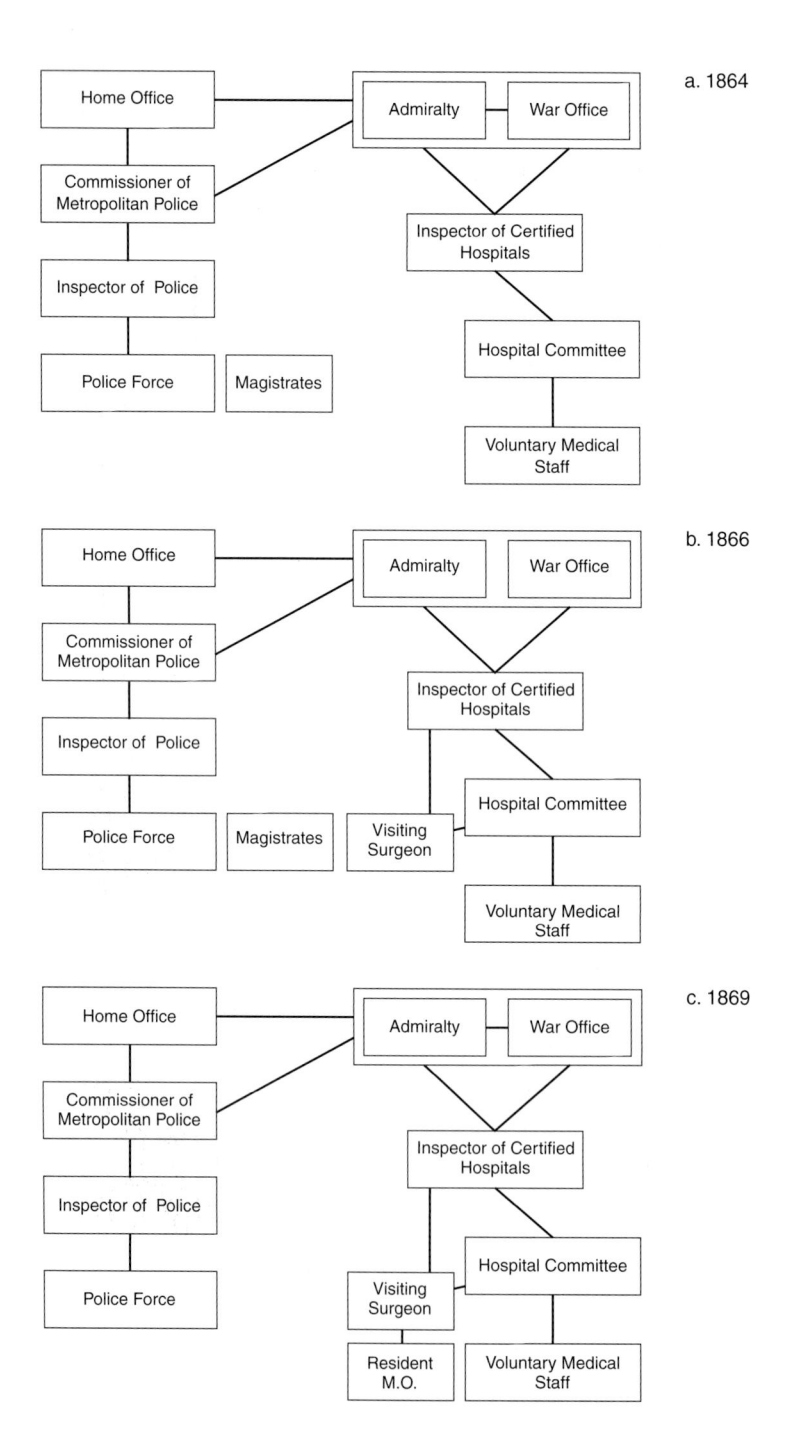

Figure 2.2 The administrative structure of the Contagious Diseases Acts of 1864, 1866 and 1869. Source: Ogborn, *Discipline, government and law*, pp. 225, 232.

of regulationist authority; some, like the Kent towns, form instead a kind of administrative archipelago.

It should be noted, moreover, that in the 1864 legislation there was no system of regular medical inspection, which qualifies its strict regulationist credentials without meaning that there was no element of coercion. Subsequent apologists like Robert Lawson, an Inspector General of Hospitals, could write that the 1864 Act 'merely provided for the treatment of such persons who applied voluntarily to have the advantage of it, or who were specially reported to a magistrate, and, while undergoing this, they were at liberty to leave the hospital, whether cured or not'.[37] But to claim that the system was a voluntary one, as it was only put in force against women suspected of being diseased, no register or periodical examination being kept, or because once admitted women were not strictly compelled to remain in hospital, was disingenuous in the extreme. All the same, this was an administrative system that was less systematically coercive than that introduced by the subsequent Acts of 1866 and 1869.

The later Acts did move closer to the kinds of regulation attempted and imposed in other countries, and particularly on the continent. In 1866, following the repeal of the earlier statute, a new law began the periodical inspection of prostitutes – not just women suspected of suffering from disease, but, necessarily, all women suspected of being prostitutes. From a medical perspective, concerned to reduce the incidence of venereal disease, the 1864 Act had clearly been remarkably ineffective: information about prostitute women was unsystematically produced and unreliable; women residing outside of the subjected districts but working as prostitutes within them could escape attention; the division of authority between justices and doctors meant that it was difficult to compel women to remain in hospital until deemed 'cured'; without a systematic registration and inspection, infectious women too easily slipped through the administrative net. The 1866 Act repealed the earlier legislation, and made periodical inspection the cornerstone of the system: where information on oath was laid by a superintendent of police that he had good reason to believe that a woman was a common prostitute permanently or temporarily resident in the district, the magistrate could order the women to be subject to a periodical medical examination for any period not exceeding one year. Though this reproduced the role of the Justice of the Peace, the nature and machinery of periodic examination meant that the role of doctors in certifying women as diseased and thus liable to detention was significantly increased. Since, in the majority of cases, women volunteered, or were volunteered, to submit themselves for examination, the role of the magistrates' bench was inevitably restricted. Moreover, once a woman had been initially registered for a year and ordered to attend hospital examination (or

---

[37] R. Lawson, 'The operation of the Contagious Diseases Acts among the troops in the United Kingdom, and men of the Royal Navy on the Home Station, from their introduction in 1864 to their ultimate repeal in 1884', *Journal of the Royal Statistical Society*, 54 (1891), 31–69, p. 31.

where women had applied voluntarily for periodical examination), subsequent detention could bypass the bench altogether and be authorised by 'visiting surgeons'. These were medical officers appointed by the Secretary of State for War, adding another layer of central state authority. The power of the magistrate was effectively replaced in this legislation, doctors being able to order the arrest of women who failed to present themselves at the hospital, to order their detention beyond the initial limit of three months (up to a maximum of six), to transfer women from one hospital to another, and to remove them from the examination altogether. The magistracy could be called upon where a woman could prove that she was no longer a prostitute and that she should be removed from the register, but even so this meant that the legal system was invoked only for the entrances and the exits of women from the system. There were some additional clauses to mollify critics of the principle of regulation – the Act doubled the penalties for harbouring prostitutes, for instance, and required facilities for the moral and religious instruction of women at the hospitals – but essentially this was a pronounced *medicalisation* of the system (Figure 2.2b), bringing it closer to the more stringent regulationist regimes in force on the continent, and in the British colonies.

There were some further changes to the geography of the 1866 Act. The stipulation that hospitals should be close to the subjected districts was deemed unnecessary, and dropped. The authority of the legislation was extended, adding Windsor to those places administered under the 1864 Act, but also tightening up the territory of the subjected districts, adding a few tithings and hamlets here and there, altering and extending the districts of Chatham and Colchester, and realigning Plymouth and Devonport by exchanging parish boundaries for those of the municipal and parliamentary boroughs. Most importantly, information could be presented against women living within five miles of the limits of the districts under the schedule, if they had been suspected of working as prostitutes within the districts, within the previous fortnight. This clause was inserted to take in women who would otherwise escape the surveillance of the police; even so, the Woolwich district was specifically exempted because of its proximity to the capital.

The introduction of periodical examination was the key element, and the final CD Act made no significant changes in this respect (Figure 2.2c). The Act of 1869 stipulated that a woman might be detained for up to five days before examination, and added a series of clauses that extended and tightened the spatial policing of prostitution. In addition to the new districts under the schedule (Canterbury, Dover, Gravesend, Maidstone, Southampton and Winchester), there were some major extensions to Plymouth and Devonport, Colchester, Shorncliffe and Woolwich, bringing in sometimes non-contiguous places like Dartmouth, Deal and Folkestone, Deptford and Greenwich. Jurisdiction was also extended to ten miles of the limits of the subjected districts, taking in women with no settled place of abode who had prostituted themselves within the districts, and also women who had been outside of the limits for the purposes of prostitution with men resident within the limits.

If the legislation was complex, however, so was the actual implementation of the CD Acts. Even a cursory examination of the practical operations and effects of the Acts disturbs any suggestion that they constituted a smoothly functioning system of social hygiene. For a start, the enactment of the legislation was tardy, partial and compromised (Table 2.1). The 1864 Act was only passed in July of that year, and its requirements for certification of appropriate hospitals meant that it could not be introduced overnight. Of the eight English stations, only Portsmouth seems to have been in a position to bring the Act immediately into force, and that only in the last few weeks of the year. Plymouth and Devonport, Sheerness, and Chatham, all followed suit, according to later reports, within a few months, but it appears that in half of the English districts the 1864 Act was never operational at all. The Irish subjected districts were probably no better able to institute the Act, though there is no official notice of the commencement of operations; lock hospitals in Cork and the Curragh appear only to have been established in 1869, for instance, despite much debate on their desirability.[38] According to the Liverpool regulationist surgeon Frederick Lowndes, there were only ever in fact nine government lock hospitals during the entire operation of the CD Acts – in Aldershot, Chatham, Colchester, Cork, Devonport, Kildare, London, Portsmouth and Shorncliffe – between them with only 626 beds.[39] Lowndes may well have underestimated the number of lock wards and hospitals, and Table 2.2 may be regarded as more reliable if far from definitive as a guide to the provision of hospitals in the early years of the Acts. But, whatever the exact details, the initial record of hospital provision was clearly far from satisfactory.

The towns where the CD Acts were introduced and administered were, moreover, very varied – all of them military garrisons, of course, or near to them in the case of Southampton, but otherwise with different situations and political complexions. To a greater extent than has been recognised, it was the localities themselves that shaped the nature of their specific regulationist regimes. The combination of central state and local authority – as we have seen, a distinct feature of contagious diseases legislation – inevitably meant that the Acts operated in different ways in different places. By far the most important, at least in

---

[38] C. Costello, *A most delightful station: the British Army on the Curragh of Kildare, Ireland, 1855–1922* (Cork, 1996), p. 163, M. Luddy, *Women and philanthropy in nineteenth-century Ireland* (Cambridge, 1995), p. 137, M. Luddy, '"Abandoned women and bad characters": prostitution in nineteenth-century Ireland', *Women's History Review*, 6 (1997), 485–503, p. 488, M. Luddy, *Prostitution and Irish society, 1800–1940* (Cambridge, 2007), p. 140.

[39] F. W. Lowndes, *Lock hospitals and lock wards in general hospitals* (London, 1882), p. 27.

Table 2.1 *Recorded dates of commencement of operations in subjected districts under the Contagious Diseases Acts*[a]

Schedule	Subjected district	Operations commenced according to Royal Commission	Operations commenced according to Army Medical Reports	Register reported as first taken
1864/1866	Portsmouth	3 December 1864	8 October 1866	February 1869
1864/1866	Plymouth/Devonport	1 April 1865	10 October 1866	January 1869
1864/1866	Sheerness	9 June 1865	6 November 1866	February 1869
1864/1866	Chatham	12 June 1865	6 November 1866	January 1869
1864/1866	Woolwich	14 November 1866	6 November 1866	February 1869
1864/1866	Aldershot	12 April 1867	12 April 1867	February 1869
1866	Windsor	1 April 1868	1 April 1868	February 1869
1864/1866	Shorncliffe	27 July 1868	24 or 27 July 1868	February 1869
1864/1866	Colchester	27 January 1869	27 January 1869	January 1869
1864/1866	Cork	n.d.	June 1869 (1868?)	n.d.
1864/1866	Curragh	n.d.	6 December 1869	n.d.
1864/1866	Queenstown	n.d.	n.d.	n.d.
[added to Woolwich, 1869]	Greenwich	2 or 6 January 1870	n.d.	January 1870
1869	Winchester	6 January 1870	6 January 1870	January 1870
1869	Dover	19 January 1870	19 January 1870	January 1870
1869	Canterbury	21 January 1870	21 January or 5 February 1870	January 1870
[added to Shorncliffe, 1869]	Deal	5 February 1870	n.d.	February 1870
1869	Maidstone	15 January or 15 February 1870	15 January 1870	February 1870
1869	Gravesend	17 January or 17 February 1870	n.d.	February 1870
1869	Southampton	27 or 28 May 1870	n.d.	May 1870

[a] See *Report of Royal Commission upon the administration and operation of the Contagious Diseases Acts* [1871], P.P. 1871 (C.408) XIX.1., p. 797, and J. Stansfeld, 'On the validity of the annual government statistics of the operation of the Contagious Diseases Acts', *Journal of the Statistical Society of London*, 39 (1876), 540–72, p. 553. Inconsistencies are indicated in the table.

Table 2.2 *Lock hospital provision for the subjected districts under the Contagious Diseases Acts up to 1870*[a]

	Hospital accommodation	Date hospital opened	Period of accommodation for venereal patients under CD Acts
Portsmouth	Royal Portsmouth, Portsea; Gosport Hospital	3 December 1864	December 1864–December 1870
Plymouth/Devonport	Royal Albert, Devonport	1 April 1865	April 1865–December 1870
Sheerness	St Bartholomew's, Rochester; London Lock Hospital; Chatham Lock Hospital	12 June 1865; 13 November 1866; 11 February 1870	June 1865–March 1870; March 1867–March 1870; February–December 1870
Chatham	St Bartholomew's, Rochester; London Lock Hospital; Chatham Lock Hospital	12 June 1865; 13 November 1866; 11 February 1870	June 1865–March 1870; March 1867–March 1870; February–December 1870
Woolwich	London Lock Hospital	13 November 1866	November 1866–December 1870
Aldershot	London Lock Hospital; Aldershot Lock Hospital	13 November 1866; 28 June 1867	April–June 1867; June 1867–December 1870
Windsor	London Lock Hospital; Aldershot Lock Hospital	13 November 1866; 28 June 1867	June 1867–February 1870; February–December 1870
Shorncliffe	Shorncliffe Lock Hospital	27 July 1868	July 1868–December 1870
Colchester	Colchester Lock Hospital	27 February 1869	February 1869–December 1870
Greenwich	London Lock Hospital	13 November 1866	January–December 1870
Winchester	Aldershot Lock Hospital	28 June 1867	January–December 1870
Dover	Shorncliffe Lock Hospital	27 July 1868	January–December 1870
Canterbury	London Lock Hospital; Chatham Lock Hospital	13 November 1866; 11 February 1870	January–March 1870; March–December 1870

Table 2.2 (cont.)

	Hospital accommodation	Date hospital opened	Period of accommodation for venereal patients under CD Acts
Deal	Shorncliffe Lock Hospital	27 July 1868	January–December 1870
Maidstone	Chatham Lock Hospital	11 February 1870	February–December 1870
Gravesend	Chatham Lock Hospital	11 February 1870	February–December 1870
Southampton	Royal Portsmouth, Portsea; Gosport Hospital	3 December 1864	May–December 1870

[a] *Report of Royal Commission upon the administration and operation of the Contagious Diseases Acts* [1871], p. 796.

England, were the pre-eminent military stations of Portsmouth and Plymouth, the latter including Devonport, with the district eventually being extended to include Dartmouth to the east. Below these in importance, in terms of the registration and inspection of women, came Aldershot, Woolwich and Greenwich (always special cases because of their proximity to the capital), and the Chatham district, which may be taken to include Gravesend and arguably the more isolated Sheerness. The seven largest subjected districts accounted for the vast majority of the women registered and inspected under the Acts. In the statistics for 1870, the other eight English stations (that is, Canterbury, Colchester, Dover, Maidstone, Shorncliffe/Deal, Southampton, Winchester and Windsor) provided between 15 and 20 per cent of the registered women, brothels, known prostitutes, and examinations carried out by the visiting surgeons (see Table 2.3, Figure 2.3). In most of these places, the average number of women on the register during that year was well below one hundred – distinctly minor compared to the larger stations, let alone to the continental systems of regulation. Figures were not provided for the Irish stations, but the Curragh probably compares with Aldershot in terms of numbers of men and numbers of registered prostitutes, whilst Cork appears to have had about 300 registered women in 1869, and half that number the following year, which would put it on a par with a garrison town such as Chatham.[40]

[40] Costello, *A most delightful station*, p. 173, notes that there were perhaps 500 in 1865, but with a normal summer figure of 100; *Select committee on the administration and operation of the Contagious Diseases Acts* [1881], P.P. 1881 (351) VIII.193, evidence of Osborne Morgan, 6220–6221.

Table 2.3 Statistics for stations under the Contagious Diseases Acts, 1870[a]

	Total, soldiers, sailors, marines	Average no. of women on register	No. of women registered	Common women, before Acts	Women remaining on register	Brothels, end of 1870	No. of examinations made by visiting surgeon
Aldershot	12,551	326	1,021	266	239	35	6,961
Canterbury	700	41	123	42	42	15	478
Chatham	4,346	316	942	220	281	65	5,672
Colchester	1,686	84	219	158	74	12	1,672
Cork	n.d.	n.d.	n.d.	n.d.	n.d.	n.d.	n.d.
Curragh	n.d.	n.d.	n.d.	n.d.	n.d.	n.d.	n.d.
Deal	1,157	22	52	26	15	7	371
Dover	2,394	102	204	92	95	21	1,654
Gravesend	516	59	129	47	40	12	1,016
Greenwich	n.d.	145	269	151	141	22	2,773
Maidstone	299	45	91	58	40	7	697
Plymouth/ Devonport	10,124	612	2,621	1,770	557	121	10,393
Portsmouth	13,252	661	2,034	1,355	590	195	11,633
Queenstown	n.d.	n.d.	n.d.	n.d.	n.d.	n.d.	n.d.
Sheerness	1,908	56	292	73	59	24	883
Shorncliffe	2,200	53	262	70	46	6	901
Southampton	426	159	219	154	155	42	1,125
Winchester	546	54	159	76	49	10	1,202
Windsor	1,126	43	170	54	30	0	642
Woolwich	5,866	199	881	240	197	47	4,297

[a] From *Report of Royal Commission upon the administration and operation of the Contagious Diseases Acts* [1871].

48 *Partial legislation and privileged places*

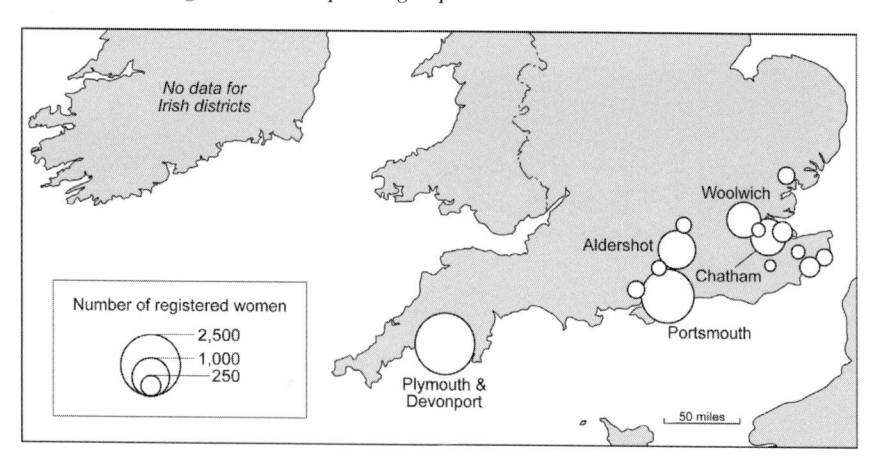

Figure 2.3 Women registered under the Contagious Diseases Acts, 1870. From *Report of Royal Commission upon the administration and operation of the Contagious Diseases Acts* (1871).

Just as important, however, were the differences in political complexion between the subjected districts, between stations where government influence was strong, and those where civic society and civil authority acted as more of a counterweight. In most of the military towns, dependent as they were upon government patronage and the commercial opportunities on offer from the presence of the garrisons, there was relatively little tension between civilians and soldiery, and a united front was presented in regards to the management of prostitution. Aldershot, for instance, was a town that had sprung up quickly around its garrison, a very large camp of over 10,000 men; the two or three hundred 'common prostitutes' there were characterised as particularly degraded. These camp followers, sourced in large part from London and Ireland, were described in 1867 as living in holes in the sandbanks, in drains and in other squalor.[41] Despite this wretchedness, however, a marked improvement under the Acts was repeatedly asserted, and there was no evident friction between the respectable inhabitants and the garrison's commanders. We have already noted that, before the introduction of the CD Acts, under the earlier charge of fostering degradation and immorality, public opinion in Aldershot quickly rallied round to defend the town's reputation. After the Acts were implemented, an even more complimentary portrayal of the camp was painted by pro-regulationists, such as William Acton's encomium to

[41] J. R. Walkowitz and D. J. Walkowitz, '"We are not beasts of the field": prostitution and the poor in Plymouth and Southampton under the Contagious Diseases Acts', *Feminist Studies*, 1 (1973), 73–106, pp. 73, 76. See also B. Hill, 'Illustrations of the workings of the Contagious Diseases Act. III – Aldershot, Winchester, and Windsor', *British Medical Journal*, 1 February 1868, p. 94.

the absolute 'propriety of conduct' of the prostitutes to whom he was directed by the police.[42] In such government towns – and the same might be said of Windsor, Portsmouth and Plymouth – opposition to the Acts was very low, or effectively marginalised by a union of interests and sympathies. In Cork, too, there was apparently very little resistance to the Acts. Their introduction was welcomed by many of the Catholic clergy, one of whom praised their operation as 'the most judicious, the most humane, and the most merciful that could possibly be'.[43] The Bishop of Cork, though unwilling to express a direct opinion on the Acts, was said to be satisfied with the greater opportunities it afforded for women's reclamation and reformation; apparently the Acts allowed priests to be more active in finding abandoned women in their lodgings and in the hospital.[44] The condition of the streets was also supposed to be much improved by the agency of the Acts; the notorious behaviour of the city's prostitutes was said to be a thing of the past, under the surveillance and through the co-operation of police and priests.[45] This was a familiar refrain in most of the subjected districts, and one of the reasons that the Acts were so well supported by the respectable classes. In the three towns of Chatham, Rochester and Strood, Berkeley Hill painted a very similar picture:

> The morals of the lower classes are extremely vicious; and, though now a crying disgrace in this respect, public decency has been greatly improved since the Act has been enforced. The frightful abandonment to all kinds of foul debauchery is now lessened. The lowest haunts of vice are regularly visited by the police; and thus the worst excesses of vice are prevented. The material condition and the moral feeling of the women are greatly raised. The police, in gaining the intimate acquaintance with the women necessary for carrying out the Act, have become, in a certain sense, their friends and protectors from the tyranny and brutality of the beershop- and brothel-owners, who, as a class, are most loathsome. To these girls the police inspector is often able to give a word of advice, to persuade them to communicate with their friends; and, should a desire for reformation really exist in them, which, however, is rarely a lasting one, the girls' better feelings can be appealed to with more chance of success in the quiet wards of an hospital than in their degrading haunts and among their rude, vicious companions.[46]

In this way, even if we take much of this as rhetoric rather than reality, tangible local gains in public order could be set against abstract points of moral principle, turning all but the most fervent in favour of regulation.

---

[42] Acton, *Prostitution*, 2nd edition, pp. 56–8.
[43] *Report from the select committee on Contagious Diseases Acts* [1882], evidence of Rev. Canon Hegarty, 11038.
[44] *Select committee on the administration and operation of the Contagious Diseases Acts* [1881], evidence of Rev. Reed, 6180.
[45] *Ibid.*, 6199, 6200, 6202. See Luddy, *Prostitution and Irish society*, p. 145.
[46] B. Hill, 'Illustrations of the working of the Contagious Diseases Act, I – Chatham and Portsmouth', *British Medical Journal*, 28 December 1867, 583–5, p. 584.

Any notion of general approval of the Acts in the subjected districts is misleading, however. Not all of the stations were quite so pliant and placid as this picture of the Chatham district. Judith and Daniel Walkowitz make a pointed contrast between Plymouth and Southampton, for instance. Whereas Plymouth – dominated by the military, with one-third of the male population in military service – was consistently held up to be a model or 'pattern' station, and the focus of regulationist propaganda, Southampton was a commercial port with a civil population. The exception within the ranks of the subjected districts, it only found itself with a regulationist regime because of the fear that women from the town were making their way to the neighbouring Portsmouth for purposes of prostitution. Under these circumstances, with so much less in the way of government influence, it is not surprising that a significant repeal agitation was prosecuted, led by ministers, magistrates and other representatives of the middle-class, but abetted by members of the working class, labour aristocrats and radicals alike.[47] Even in government towns such as those in the Chatham district, the seeming lack of opposition to the Acts in the subjected districts must be severely qualified. Whilst the town of Chatham was solidly behind the administration of regulation, the neighbouring 'non-militarised' city of Rochester provided numerous repealers, and an agitation against the Acts was maintained throughout the period.[48] In Colchester, too, an energetic political agitation was mobilised against the Acts. In these towns, though the presence of the military was strong, opposition to the Acts was not only possible but prominent.

Before we come to the opposition movement proper, however, it is well to consider the effects of the Acts in terms of the public health concerns that were their main justification. Here, again, we may note the importance of the geographical differentiation between and beyond the regulated districts, at least as a political issue. For one of the most contentious points in the argument over the efficacy of the Acts in reducing venereal infection was the statistical comparison between regulated and unregulated districts. Supporters of the Acts regularly trotted out this contrast, comparing for instance fourteen of the larger subjected districts (namely, Devonport and Plymouth, Portsmouth, Chatham and Sheerness, Woolwich, Aldershot, Windsor, Shorncliffe, Colchester, Winchester, Dover, Canterbury, Maidstone, Cork and Curragh (no Gravesend, Southampton or Queenstown)) with fourteen places drawn from the ranks of major ports, industrial centres, and towns with significant military personnel (the Isle of Wight, London, Warley, Hounslow, Pembroke Dock, Sheffield, Manchester, Preston, Edinburgh, Fermoy, Limerick, Athlone, Dublin and Belfast).[49] This geographical comparison seems to have first

---

[47] Walkowitz, *Prostitution and Victorian society*, p. 168.

[48] B. Joyce, *The Chatham scandal: a history of Medway's prostitution in the late 19th century* (Rochester, 1999), pp. 97–8.

[49] J. B. Nevins, *The health of the Navy. An analysis of the official report for 1876, and of the special return relating to five ports under and five ports not under the Contagious*

appeared in the army medical report of 1871, but was seized upon subsequently by supporters of the Acts. In the regulationist view, this comparison conclusively demonstrated the wisdom of the legislation. Dr Archibald Jacob noted for instance that the daily loss from venereal disease in the fourteen subjected stations from 1860 to 1863, *before* the Acts, was 24.01 per thousand, whilst in the unregulated stations it was 19.75; but, in the period 1870–3, with the Acts in force, the daily loss in the fourteen districts of 11.31 per thousand should be set against the control group's 13.73.[50] But the inference, as the repealer Dr J. Birkbeck Nevins recognised, was that *all* these places were for all intents and purposes *identical* to each other in terms of public health conditions, except for the fact that one set was subject to medical regulation, and the other not. Not only did this comparison neglect the very uneven introduction of the Acts, it also ignored the immense differences between these districts, whether regulated or not: 'the ratio of disease has been so widely different in different stations, as to make it impossible to compare them together' is how Nevins put it.[51] The fundamental comparison between places labelled 'Under the Acts' and 'Not under them' was thus for him, and for other opponents of the state regulation of prostitution, impossible. Nevins argued that 'there is no common ground between the two sets of stations upon which they can be compared, except the presence of the Acts in one case and their absence in the other; and the incongruity is evident of classing London and Pembroke Dock together as *not* under the Act, and comparing them with Aldershot and its 12,000 soldiers, and Maidstone with its barely 500, as under them.'[52] He went on to note that 'The Army Reports themselves have always recognized the necessity for dividing these places into several different classes for other sanitary purposes, viz.: "Dock Yards," "Seaports," "Camps," "Large Manufacturing Towns," "London," "Dublin," &c. But for the purpose of shewing the effect of the CD Acts, they are put together into just two classes, "under" and "not under," regardless of the essential differences between them in every other respect.'[53]

Comparing the relative position of the fourteen stations under and the fourteen stations not under the Acts, the average ratio of men infected with primary venereal sores was not a very convincing argument in favour of the utility of the Acts in any event (see Table 2.4). There appears from this comparison to be little connection between the presence or absence of the Acts and the amount of disease, and thus we might agree with the repealers that 'It is to other causes that we must look for an explanation of the difference between different ports and stations, and not to the presence or absence of this legislation.'[54] James Stansfeld similarly noted

Diseases Acts, which was ordered to be laid before the House of Commons, on the 4th July, 1877 (London, 1878).
[50] A. H. Jacob, 'The working of the Contagious Diseases Acts', *The Medical Press and Circular*, 96 (1886), 445–8, p. 448.
[51] Nevins, *The health of the Navy*, p. 32.
[52] Ibid., p. 16.   [53] Ibid.   [54] Ibid., p. 18.

Table 2.4 *Statistics of venereal infection of men in stations under or not under the Contagious Diseases Acts, 1867–72*[a]

	Average ratio per 1,000	Average ratio per 1,000
1. Pembroke Dock	Not under Acts	34.0
2. Athlone	ditto	43.0
London (Household Cavalry) 9 yrs	ditto	48.0
3. Chatham and Sheerness	Under Acts	56.0
4. Shorncliffe	ditto	57.0
5. Woolwich	ditto	58.0
6. Belfast	Not under Acts	63.0
7. Devonport and Plymouth	Under Acts	64.0
8. Cork	ditto	65.0
9. Portsmouth	ditto	66.0
10. Edinburgh	Not under Acts	66.6
11. Winchester	Under Acts	67.3
12. Warley	Not under Acts	67.5
13. Fermoy	ditto	68.3
14. Aldershot	Under Acts	68.8
15. Curragh	ditto	69.6
16. Dover	ditto	71.0
17. Hounslow	Not under Acts	79.3
18. Isle of Wight	ditto	79.6
19. Canterbury	Under Acts	85.0
20. Windsor	ditto	88.0
21. Colchester	ditto	90.0
22. Limerick	Not under Acts	96.0
23. Maidstone	Under Acts	110.0
24. Preston	Not under Acts	111.0
25. Manchester	ditto	118.0
26. Sheffield	ditto	119.0
27. Dublin	ditto	159.0
28. London (Foot Guards), 9 yrs	ditto	162.0

[a] Nevins, *The health of the Navy*, pp. 17–18; these figures, from 1867 to 1872 inclusive, are taken from the report on the health of the Army for 1873.

'the great and often sudden variations in disease at some stations, variations which point to the operation of other causes than the existence of Contagious Diseases Acts'.[55] Though the efficacy of the Acts in controlling disease remains contested, it is well to contrast the humility of this view with the hubris evident in the equivalent propaganda coming from the regulationist lobby. The repealers' arguments

[55] Stansfeld, 'On the validity of the annual government statistics', p. 552.

are in fact the only ones that consider, however crudely, the social and economic, and even political, differences between stations that bedevil any assessment of the effects of the Acts.[56] One contemporary statistician has recently argued that the Acts were carefully assessed by use of a control group, evidence for what he calls 'a controlled experimental design for the introduction of a criminal justice measure'.[57] But this is quite wrong: whilst comparative statistics were indeed used to justify the Acts, this assessment completely overstates the degree of sophistication in their design, and neglects the arguments amongst statistical commentators over the appropriateness of these geographical comparisons. As exercises in comparative statistics go, it is the repealers' contributions, not the regulationists' spurious 'control' group, which seem with hindsight more persuasive.

However we look at the venereal statistics, the record can at best be considered inconclusive. A few historians have accepted the statistics with little or no reservation, but most are far less sanguine. Even the most aggressive critics of the repeal movement have accepted that the Acts were probably ineffective in combating syphilis and the other venereals.[58] The historian Edward Spiers considers the statistics extremely doubtful, and suggests that any reductions in rates of venereal disease may be owing to a decline in virulence, to higher public standards of sanitation, or to greater provision of recreational facilities in the barracks.[59] This might be taken as support for Nevins' contention that the most important distinction was all along that between *military* towns (seaports, camps, dockyards and arsenals) and others, with fluctuations in the rate of venereal infection, seen before the Acts were introduced, the result of 'some controlling influence in operation in what may be called the military towns, which is not so effective in the non-military towns'.[60] It may simply be that the statistics revealed little more than the greater attention given to sanitary discipline in the military, whether this be in the subjected districts or outside them. The package of measures designed to improve the health of the soldiers and sailors in the garrison towns may have helped to check the operation of venereal disease, but, in themselves, the Acts should be considered a failure.

[56] Thus consider the Nevins circular cited by Stansfeld, 'On the validity of the annual government statistics', p. 557, in which towns were grouped into the following classes: the Metropolis (London); Metropolitan Towns (Dublin, Edinburgh); Agricultural (Exeter, Ipswich, etc.); Cathedral (York, Norwich, etc.); Hardware (Birmingham, Sheffield, etc.); Manufacturing (Manchester, Paisley, etc.); Pottery (Leek, Staffordshire); Public Schools (Rugby); Universities (Cambridge, Oxford).
[57] D. Spiegelhalter, 'The Contagious Diseases Acts: a controlled experiment in criminal justice', *Significance*, 1 (2004), 88–9, p. 89.
[58] F. B. Smith, 'The Contagious Diseases Acts reconsidered', *Social History of Medicine*, 3 (1990), 197–215, pp. 213–15.
[59] Spiers, *The late Victorian army*, p. 144.
[60] J. B. Nevins, *Statement of the grounds upon which the Contagious Diseases' Acts are opposed* (London, 1874), p. 36.

Opposition

This is a judgement made only in hindsight, of course. In the early years of the Acts, long before anything like a considered analysis could be made, there was a significant body of opinion that held that they *were* working, that they had already brought major improvements to the health of the armed forces and to the general public in the subjected districts. The extension of the Acts to the rest of the country, and to the general civilian population, was quickly canvassed. The repealer Joseph Edmondson was surely right to state that the Acts were all along intended to be only a prelude to a national scheme, 'and not a more local affair, applicable to certain naval and military districts, as is sometimes ingeniously, if not ingenuously, stated'.[61] The gradual expansion of the territory under authority of the three CD Acts provided some precedent for extension, as did the presence of military personnel in towns and garrisons not under the Acts. The logic of regulationism, if we may continue to call it that, always pointed in that direction, the free movement of 'diseased' women from areas not under police and medical supervision being a standing rebuke to the operation of the legislation; this was indeed the reason for including the civilian town and commercial port of Southampton under the 1869 schedule. *The Lancet* expressed this logic by pointing to the inherent weaknesses of *partial* legislation: 'As it is at present, we are endeavouring to grapple with a large and wide-spread evil by attacking it in detail at some isolated outposts. There could be no more expensive or inefficient method of procedure.'[62] And, at a more theoretical level, the French physician Alex Vintras noted the necessity of extending the Acts to the civilian population: 'Now that the work of repression has begun, it cannot be stopped; these measures must become general; there cannot be *privileged* towns.'[63]

For the Acts to be extended to Great Britain as a whole, however, a non-military rationale would have to be made. The existence of similar social conditions, encouraging the spread of venereal disease, such as could be found in the major seaports, was a compelling argument, albeit still a specific one. The advantage of emphasising the universal benefits of regulationist legislation, of promoting the Acts as an answer to the general problems associated with the 'social evil', is clear. Particularly important in this regard was the claim that the Acts were beneficial to the prostituted women themselves, helping many of them move out of the business of prostitution and on to more respectable employment, and to

---

[61] J. Edmondson, *The moral forces which defeat the hygienic regulation of social vice* (London, 1882), reprinted in I. Sharp (ed.), *Josephine Butler and the prostitution campaigns: diseases of the body politic, volume I: the moral reclaimability of prostitutes* (London, 2003), p. 157.

[62] *The Lancet*, 8 February 1868, p. 205.

[63] A. Vintras, *On the repressive measures adopted in Paris compared with the uncontrolled prostitution of London and New York* (London, 1867), p. 76, emphasis in original.

the general public, with brothels being reduced in number and the general tone of the streets much improved. The necessity of combining the sanitary argument with one that emphasised in greater measure moral and social improvement is evident, and the Association for Promoting the Extension of the Contagious Diseases Acts, founded as early as 1866, consistently took the line that the Acts were successful not only from the point of view of military principles but also regarding these wider concerns. They were said to help rather than victimise the confirmed prostitute – '[m]ost of them regard its regulations as the natural order of their lives, they have never known of different arrangements, and would sorely feel any interruption to its working' – as well as protecting the wayward and vulnerable who might be drawn into prostitution – '[t]he Acts reach all alike, and render all accessible to benevolent persons anxious for their reformation, and by passing *all* the sick, evil and well-disposed, through a salutary ordeal, check the downward progress of the young and giddy, and revive good feelings even in those too weak of purpose to quit without assistance their vicious life when restored to liberty.'[64] Whilst it is clear that these benefits were incidental to the principal purpose of combating the spread of disease, they took on particular importance when civilian regulation was considered. There is no need to doubt the sincerity of this view, this alliance between coercive policing and moral reform that Walkowitz has termed 'repressive humanitarianism', not exactly free from misogyny and class prejudice, but convinced and even self-satisfied in its commitment to a practical philanthropy.[65]

However, in moving away from the military rationale that had justified the exceptional, partial and limited nature of the Acts, extensionists inevitably had to confront directly the broader legal, moral and social questions that they raised. Critical, as ever, was the necessity of distancing any British legislation from the abhorred French and continental systems: the Acts aimed 'simply at secluding women who follow the *trade* of prostitution when they become diseased, and so prevent them doing mischief to the community'.[66] This was no novelty either, it was argued, no alien import, as sanitary principles had long been established, and no new powers were given to the police, who already had ample statutory power to arrest women for solicitation.[67] Nor could such legislation be called oppressive to women, for it was only applicable to those who had chosen a way of life injurious to others as well as themselves: 'No woman need be a prostitute unless she chooses, but that if she deliberately adopts such

---

[64] Association for Promoting the Extension of the Contagious Diseases Act, 1866, to the Civil Population of the United Kingdom, *1st Report* (London, 1868), p. 14, and *3rd Report* (London, 1870), p. 49.
[65] Walkowitz, *Prostitution and Victorian society*, p. 85.
[66] Association for Promoting the Extension of the Contagious Diseases Act, *3rd Report*, p. 43.
[67] See also C. W. S. Deakin, *The Contagious Diseases Acts* (London, 1872).

a mode of gaining her living, the imminent risk which she incurs of contracting a serious contagious disease renders her so dangerous to the community as to justify state interference to prevent her doing mischief to others.'[68] In arguments like these comes across more of the repression than the humanitarianism, perhaps, and the statements of impartiality ring rather hollow when pushed to their logical extremes:

> It is only among the female sex that we find a considerable number of persons openly gaining a livelihood by the practice of prostitution as a trade. When any considerable number of men can be found letting themselves out for hire in the same way, there will of course be the same reason for subjecting them to supervision and sanitary legislation.[69]

Nevertheless, the leading extensionists were genuinely concerned by the extent of venereal disease amongst the civilian as well as the military population, and the conditions that promoted its propagation. The surgeon Berkeley Hill's visit to the various haunts of prostitutes in London convinced him that the most wretched and destitute would positively welcome the benefits of stringent sanitary regulations, whilst even their more prosperous sisters would raise but little opposition.[70] The tone of apologists for regulation hardened in later years, when confronted with an implacable opposition levelling accusations of brutality, but even then it never lost its air of wounded surprise that its essential humanitarianism and sound sense were not properly recognised: 'Certain women are, under certain circumstances, dangerous to the health of the community, and it is proposed to seclude them while the danger exists. That is all!'[71]

The extensionist movement was a campaigning pressure group, not the metropolitan medical and male conspiracy that opponents of regulation sometimes suggested. It had an Establishment constituency, certainly, with prominent patrons drawn from the professional and political classes. Amongst its four hundred or so members could be found distinguished surgeons, doctors, deans and dukes, viscounts and vice-chancellors. The Association developed branches in the provinces, and in Ireland, but this was still largely a southern English, and London-based movement (Figures 2.4, 2.5), a pattern that reflects both the geography of the CD Acts and the established concentrations of power and authority, and which contrasts so markedly with the strongholds of their opponents in the industrial north (Figures 2.6, 2.7). Nevertheless, to characterise extension as an elitist, metropolitan, medical movement is probably too simple. The

---

[68] Association for Promoting the Extension of the Contagious Diseases Act, *3rd Report*, p. 29.
[69] *Ibid.*, p. 40.
[70] Berkeley Hill, 'Illustrations of the workings of the Contagious Diseases Act. IV. The venereal disease among prostitutes of London', *British Medical Journal*, 23 May 1868, pp. 505–6.
[71] *The Lancet*, 23 October 1869, p. 598.

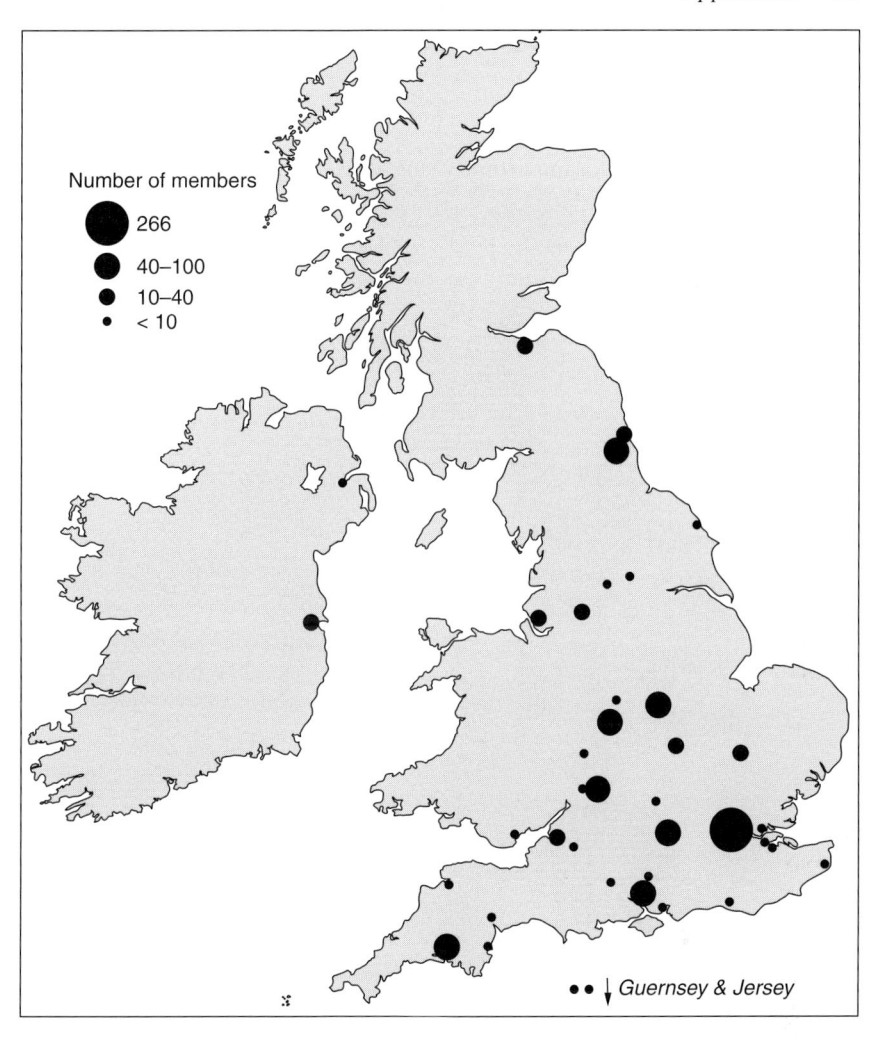

Figure 2.4 Members of the Association for Promoting the Extension of the Contagious Diseases Acts, 1870. Source: Third Annual Report.

Association was a coalition of diverse and not necessarily consistent interests, accurately described by Bertrand Taithe as 'a somewhat loose coalition of clubs united in the promoting and soon the defence of a sanitary-moral measure'.[72] *The Lancet* reported that the most eminent members of the medical profession

---

[72] B. O. Taithe, 'From danger to scandal: debating sexuality in Victorian England: the Contagious Diseases Acts (1864–1869) and the morbid landscape of Victorian Britain' (PhD, University of Manchester, 1992), pp. 62–9, 75.

58 *Partial legislation and privileged places*

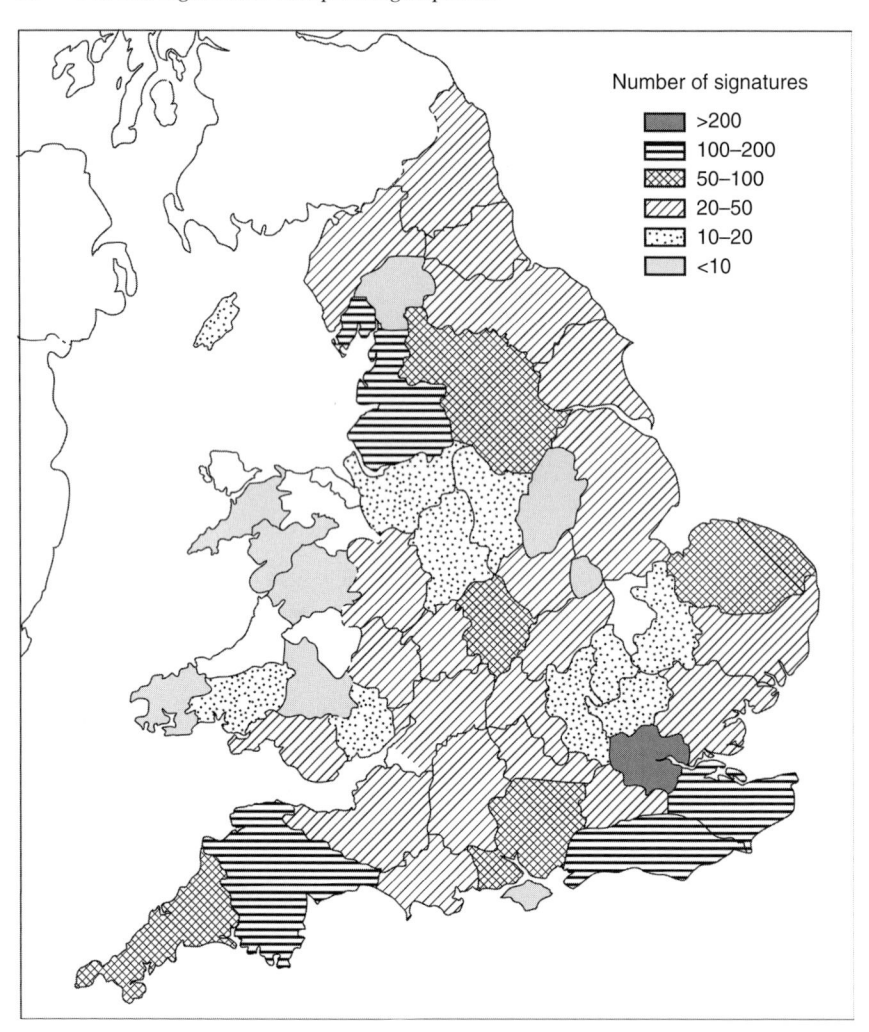

Figure 2.5 Memorial from members of the medical profession in support of the Contagious Diseases Acts, 1872. Source: P.P. 1872 [80] XLVII.489 and P.P. 1872 [245] XLVII.495.

were committed to regulation, and that the 'healthier and – if we may so say – manlier tone of feeling' extended to 'bishops, lawyers, the heads of our universities, peers, church people and dissenters, Jews and gentiles'.[73] But this was pure propaganda. The medical men who were the most stringent advocates of regulation were venereologists, never the most fashionable or high-status branch of the profession, and, as in the case of Acton, not exactly with an unassailable

[73] *The Lancet*, 24 April 1869, p. 573.

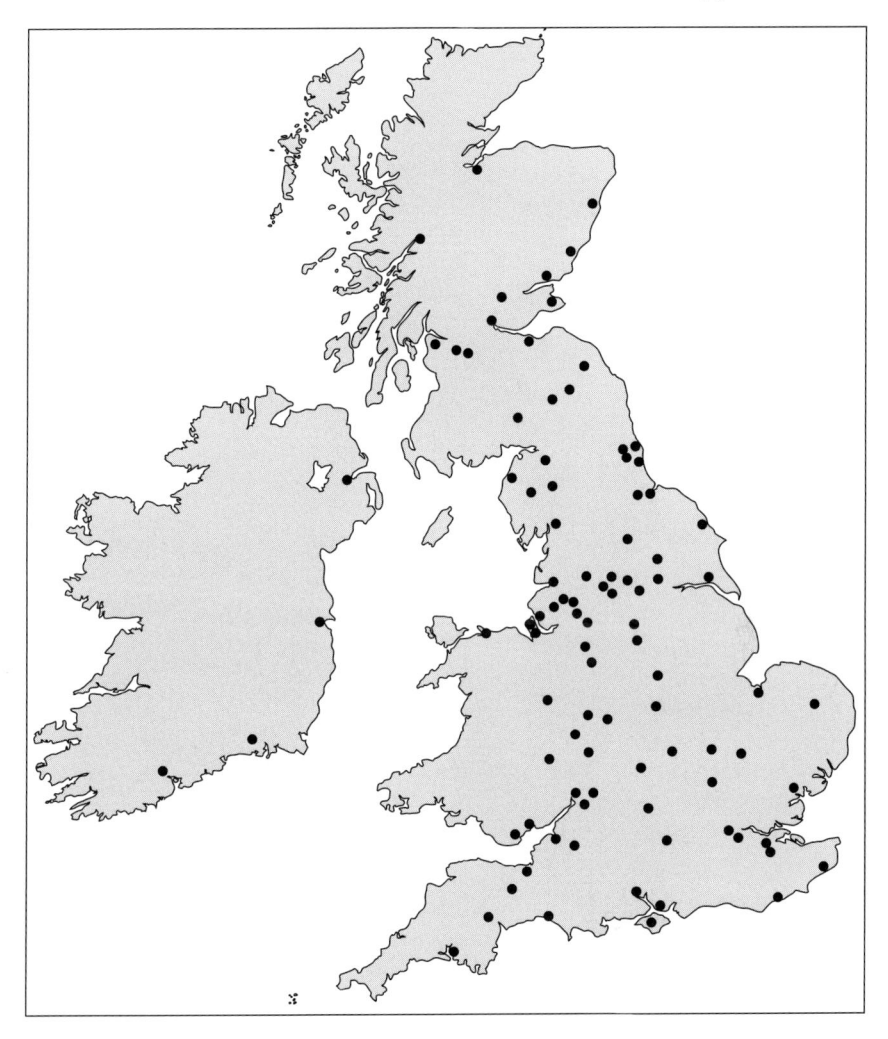

Figure 2.6 Local secretaries and correspondents of the Ladies' National Association for the Repeal of the Contagious Diseases Acts, 1873. Source: Fourth Annual Report.

reputation. Many shared these men's aspirations to sanitary science and state medicine, but in 1869 medics still made up only one-quarter of the signatories to the Association, and the medical profession as a whole was more divided on the issue of regulation than it can appear.

The perspective of moral science that they espoused differs in any case from the views of those for whom the military rationale of national security remained of paramount importance. If not quite living up to the debauched reputation that their radical critics promoted, aristocratic supporters of the Acts and their

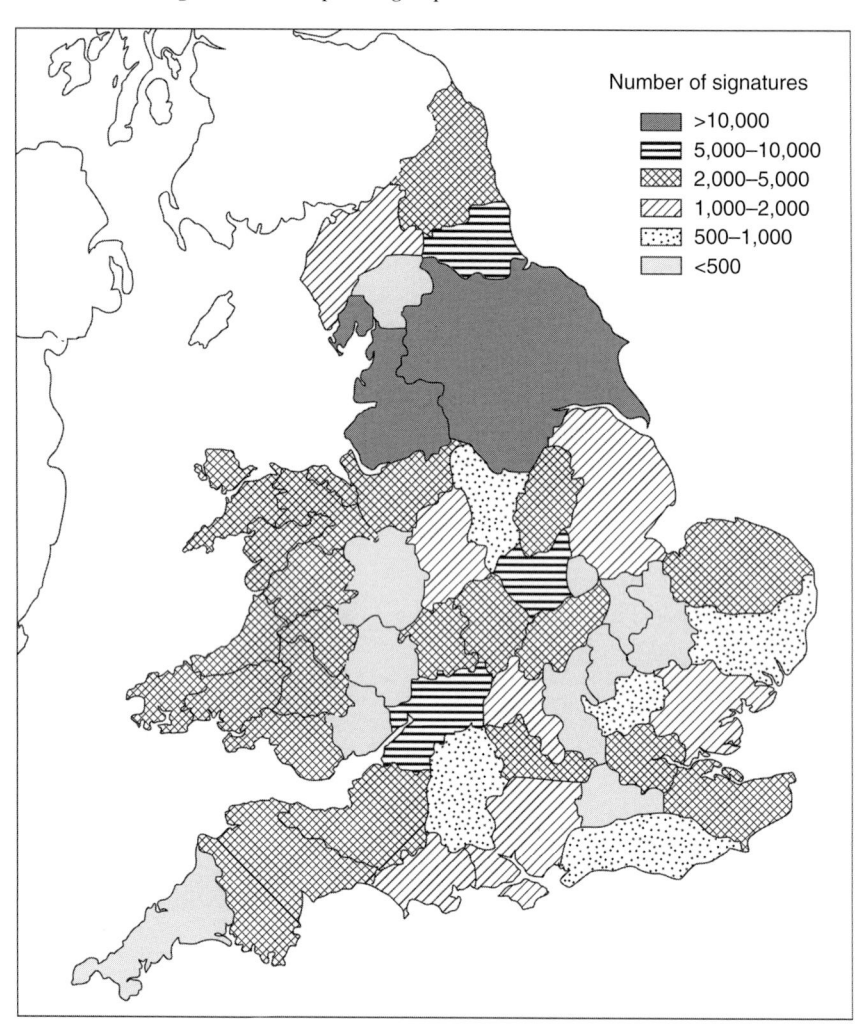

Figure 2.7 Petition for repeal of the Contagious Diseases Acts, 1878. Source: *The Shield*.

extension may well have shared a certain worldly tolerance of promiscuity and the inevitability of prostitution; this might best be described as a variation of the 'classic moralism' identified by Michael Mason.[74] Something else again might be found in the views of vice-chancellors and public school headmasters for whom a certain degree of worldliness was tempered by sincere desires to protect the morals as well as the health of the young men under their charge: their support

---

[74] M. Mason, *The making of Victorian sexual attitudes* (Oxford, 1994), pp. 43–62.

for regulation has more of the emerging 'anti-sensual' moralism than that of the 'classic' variety. And even more strongly can this be found in the ranks of the divines who supported the CD Acts – typically the Anglican Establishment at the heart of the British *ancien régime*, many of whom continued to support the Acts at least up to 1881, but also including some Catholic priests sharing their concern for public decency.[75] To their ranks we may also add policemen, magistrates and other authorities for whom public order was a principal motivation. There was therefore in the extensionist movement a *mixture* of military, medical and moralist rationales for regulation, a structure of support that was far from homogeneous, varying as it did from place to place, and which was as a result rather more vulnerable than its Establishment make-up may make it seem.

Despite their ambitions to introduce the CD Acts across the country, it also soon became clear that any extension was likely to be as piecemeal as the introduction of the original legislation. Responding in 1868 to a question in Parliament about the possibility of extending the Acts, for instance, the Duke of Somerset replied that, 'if the Act were made to apply to the whole country at once a feeling might be raised which would not be favourable to the gradual extension of the Act, and he would therefore suggest that it should, in the first instance, be extended to some large towns, such as Liverpool, for instance, and other places with which the army and navy were connected, and he did not see why Dublin should be excepted'.[76] It was appreciated that the move to extend the Acts was likely to generate opposition, and a gradual strategy was thought to be preferable. Even *The Lancet*, always an aggressive proponent of a universal rather than a piecemeal policy, had to accept that extension of the Acts would have to proceed borough by borough, making the case too that London, with its exceptional character, required exceptional legislation.[77] Early on, however, the capital was considered far too large a leap, on grounds of cost and practicability, as well as visibility and vulnerability to criticism, despite being, in the words of the Marquess Townshend, 'the very hotbed of the disease' and the place, if anywhere, where the provisions of the Acts were most necessary.[78] In cities like Liverpool, with established lock hospital provision and sympathetic professional support, there were better grounds for optimism; there, in any case, regulation of a sort was already practised 'by knitting together and strenuously applying Acts already on the Statute Book'.[79] We shall see in the next chapter the nature of this *informal* system of regulation in Liverpool and why the city suggested itself so strongly to extensionists as a beachhead for a civilian version of the Acts. By 1875, in fact, the scaling down of

---

[75] For Anglican support of the Acts, see 'The alleged increase of immorality', *The chronicle of Convocation. Being a record of the proceedings of the Convocation of Canterbury the tenth Victoria Regnante, sessions, Feb. 8, 9, 10, 11, 1881* (London, 1881), 20 July 1881.
[76] *The Times*, 16 May 1868, p. 6.   [77] *The Lancet*, 24 April 1869, p. 573.
[78] *Hansard*, 203:98, 12 July 1870.
[79] McHugh, *Prostitution and Victorian social reform*, pp. 76, 78.

the extensionist argument was tacitly admitted, but with cities like Liverpool very much in the van as testing grounds for civilian regulation:

> Under present circumstances we do not aim at so wide and immediate extension of the Acts as before, but the case of certain seaport towns not subject to the Acts, which are known to be hotbeds of disease introduced by sailors of the merchant service of our own and of foreign countries, is so glaring, and is attended by such disastrous consequences, that we feel it our duty to call for the special interference of Parliament to repress the evil.[80]

The ambitions of these extensionists, however, even in their immediate and specific targets, would never be fulfilled. For the major effect of their campaign was to stimulate an unprecedented, countrywide opposition, in the shape of various groups formed to resist the extension of the CD Acts and arguing for their ultimate repeal. The resistance to British regulationism – the movement for 'repeal' or 'abolition' – first took shape at a meeting in Nottingham at the Social Science Congress, which led to the founding of the National Anti-Contagious Diseases Acts Association (later, the National Association for the Repeal of the Contagious Diseases Acts) in 1869. The National Association, local branches having been amalgamated in 1870, initially excluded women, but it was to be complemented by a Ladies' National Association (LNA) the following year. This was the organisation led by the redoubtable Josephine Butler, spearhead of the feminist activism against the Acts that was lampooned by opponents as the 'revolt of the women' and the 'shrieking sisterhood'.[81] To some extent, the National Association has been neglected by historians, overshadowed as it has been by the LNA and by the high public profile of Butler and the other female repealers. The Radical MP James Stansfeld's organisational skills and political nous have been widely noticed, all the same, and the eventual repeal of the Acts greatly credited to him. The work of the London solicitor William Shaen, a veteran of reform causes, should also be recorded, along with the relocated Nottingham publisher F. C. Banks and the academic lawyer Sheldon Amos. These London men directed the patient, even plodding, work that became necessary after the hopes for early repeal of the Acts were dashed in the early 1870s. The activities of the Sheffield industrialist Henry Wilson in the provinces and the country at large to some degree complemented the metropolitan work of the London-based and London-dominated National Association (NA).

The geographical tensions within the movement remained difficult to bridge, however, with Wilson notably lambasting both the NA's inactivity and incompetence at organising a national agitation, and its metropolitan bias into the bargain. Throughout the movement for repeal suspicions were repeatedly cast on the metropolis, along with dark hints that the leaders of the NA were subject

---

[80] Association for Promoting the Extension of the Contagious Diseases Acts, *6th Report* (London, 1875).
[81] See Walkowitz, *Prostitution and Victorian society*, pp. 121, 94.

to the corrupting influence of the capital. It is probably unfair to deride these men's efforts in contrast to the more prominent platform agitation that was taking place in the provinces; McHugh has ably defended these metropolitan reformers against the imputation of sloth and co-option.[82] Nevertheless, the more cosmopolitan, intellectual, secular and freethinking, or at least less religiously fervent, leaders of the NA were geographically, socially and politically distanced from the provincial centres of support for the repeal movement. As Walkowitz notes, 'Male leaders were generally wealthy industrialists and merchants residing in northern cities, although a core of important repeal supporters lived in Bristol and London. Politically important in their own locales, they nonetheless saw themselves as provincial "outsiders" from the London social and political establishment that upheld the CD Acts.'[83] The women of the LNA were also disproportionately provincial, its numerical and financial strength in the 1880s, for instance, being found in York, Liverpool, Bristol, Leeds and Newcastle, in addition to London.[84] Bertrand Taithe has further observed that the LNA was strongest in the north, its membership shifting from the west and the south of England to the north and the east in the early 1870s, and then to centres in Yorkshire and in the southwest; Ireland, on the other hand, appears to have had more homogeneous support for repeal, being neglected as a field for canvassing by the regulationist party.[85] The importance of Liverpool, hometown of Butler since the year of the first CD Act, and a stronghold of the movement, should again be emphasised. As one of the principal targets for the extension of the Acts, and a city with a tradition of informal regulation of prostitution, Liverpool was always likely to be the key battleground.

Overwhelmingly nonconformist, in contrast to the preponderance of Church of England support for the regulationist cause, the repealers were also drawing on an established tradition of northern radicalism, tracing the circuits of electoral reform activity as well as evangelical and dissenting religion. As Ogborn observes, 'The presentation of this political identity through the moral force of the language of northern radical dissenting religion formed a powerful platform, perhaps the only one able to challenge the hegemony of the southern medical and military establishment.'[86] Vital Christianity was particularly well represented in the campaign against the Acts, and in particular the missionary zeal brought by their female and feminist opponents. In some ways the LNA was more in tune with the national agitation, at least in its early proactive years, being more moralistic and passionate, better placed to articulate a denunciation of regulationism that resonated with the respectable working class. It was effective in extending the agitation out from the confines of Parliament and committee, and into

---

[82] McHugh, *Prostitution and Victorian social reform*.
[83] Walkowitz, *Prostitution and Victorian society*, p. 99.
[84] *Ibid.*, p. 134.   [85] Taithe, 'From danger to scandal', pp. 101–3.
[86] Ogborn, 'Law and discipline', p. 48.

the country and the expanded political public sphere. In this respect, the use of sensationalist stories to whip up indignation, the indictment of a debauched aristocracy, the denunciations of instrumental rape and the brutalisation of women were particularly important: all these were used to appeal to the heart and to the conscience. This was a political use of scandal and outrage, a melodramatic fix, or 'melo-propaganda' as Bertrand Taithe puts it, inappropriate and ineffective in the commissions of enquiry but well suited to the extramural electoral campaigning that produced some of the movement's notable successes.[87] This early form of the politics of social purity was not a later graft onto a principled feminist agitation; it was there from the beginning, part of the political agitation against the Acts.

Although several political contests were marked by this kind of platform politics, the Colchester election of 1870 is the most famous.[88] Josephine Butler was a great supporter of organised electoral pressure, and took to the streets of Colchester personally to direct the agitation there against the attempt to bring Sir Henry Storks into Parliament as a Liberal MP. Storks, it should be noted, was targeted not just because of his military background and his strong support for the CD Acts. As High Commissioner of the Ionian Islands and then Governor of Malta, Storks had presided over the operation and elaboration of stringent systems of police regulation of prostitution, regimes that were repeatedly cited as proof that contagious diseases legislation was successful in halting the progress of venereal disease. To come from a colonial regulationist background like this to one of the principal domestic towns subjected to CD legislation, was too much of a temptation for repealers pursuing the strategy of electoral pressure. One of the handbills published against Storks' candidacy for the borough singled out this colonial experience in one of its stanzas:

> You succeeded at Malta, King Stork, King Stork,
> In expelling disease with a fork, with a fork:
> Yet the evil recurs,
> For nature demurs
> To be crushed by enactments, O Stork, King Stork.[89]

The repealers' own candidate, J. Baxter Langley, appealed to the electors of Colchester by portraying Storks as 'one of the principal supporters of the most immoral and unjust legislation which has disgraced the civilization of Europe'.[90] This campaigning pressure split the Liberal vote and, following Langley's

---

[87] Taithe, 'From danger to scandal', p. 279.
[88] Others were Bath in 1873, Oxford in 1874, Pontefract in 1875, East Cornwall in 1879. Careful attention was given to selecting boroughs where pressure would be most felt: McHugh, *Prostitution and Victorian social reform*, p. 94.
[89] See Walkowitz, *Prostitution and Victorian society*, p. 107.
[90] *The Times*, 25 October 1870, p. 13.

withdrawal, prompted many to abstain, allowing the Tory candidate to romp home by over 500 votes. The violence visited upon Josephine Butler and the other repeal agitators was acknowledged as a major factor in detaching Liberal votes from the government's candidate; the embarrassment to the government was only temporary, but the public profile of repeal was enormously enhanced by this demonstration of their ability to mobilise local opposition.

This was an early but isolated highpoint of the electoral strategy, and the fortunes of the repeal movement subsequently waned. After the early successes and high hopes, the mid-1870s found supporters at a low ebb, demoralised by the Liberal defeat of 1874 and the persistently inconclusive debates on the Acts. At both local and national levels, it seems as if the active, public and popular phases of the agitation had run their course.[91] Repeal activity went on – the routine of lectures, meetings, petitions, finding converts and bolstering supporters – and there was an important offshoot as we shall see into opposing continental and colonial regulationism; but there were few victories and little of substance to show for all this effort. As has already been noted, the subjected districts were mostly fallow ground for repeal activity. Though local scandals could be seized upon and publicised, this was largely reactive and opportunistic; more significant seemed to be the danger that sympathetic social purity advocates might be co-opted by the regulationist approach of policemen and doctors. All in all, the end of the decade seemed to mark a movement at best at a standstill.

In three years, however, the CD Acts would be suspended, and by 1886 swept off the statute books altogether. For all their inability to forward the agitation, particularly in the heartlands of regulation, the repealers had made enough of a nuisance of themselves in the provincial towns that were critical for Liberal electoral success. Having grafted their demands onto the Liberal programme, once the Liberals were back in government, in 1880, it required only a modest Parliamentary push, carefully timed to take advantage of the Home Rule crises, to extirpate the Acts. Their opponents were not, by then, strong, if they ever had been. Opinion in the country, influenced by the lurid exposés of white slavery, child prostitution and homosexuality in high and low places, made any concerted defence of the double standard unlikely, whilst the practical benefits of contagious diseases legislation were more and more subject to doubt. The repeal movement may have ground to a halt, but extension was also a lost cause early on in the 1870s; and the failure of this project must in retrospect be seen as a principal cause for the failure of the CD Acts themselves. In 1872, Home Secretary Bruce conceded the long-term unsustainability of the Acts, in accepting the conclusions of the commissioners who had reported the previous year, on the undesirability of partial and exclusive legislation: 'After giving the subject the most attentive consideration the Government had arrived at the same conclusion. They thought it impossible to maintain in certain limited districts and with a large civil population, a system of

[91] Walkowitz, *Prostitution and Victorian society*, p. 170.

law that was incapable of extension to other parts of the country. The Government were of opinion that the system of compulsory and periodical examination could not be made the basis of general legislation.'[92] Though secure in their respective domains, the two movements were also entrenched, and neither could have any expectations of a decisive victory in the field. The final battle would thus be waged in Parliament, where the political power of the regulationist lobby was extremely weak; the persistent efforts of the repeal lobby had exhausted the patience of their opponents, and embarrassed the undecided. The repeal party, after sixteen years, had achieved their aim; 'Their efforts resulted in the dismantling of a threatening system of police control over the individual, the abandonment of a medically ineffective attempt to regulate public health by compulsion, and the recognition that the law should not be used to underpin a double standard of sexual morality.'[93] The national experiment in 'partial legislation', bringing in regulationist policing in 'privileged places', before attempting to extend the statutes place by place, had comprehensively failed. With the demise of the CD Acts, the most explicit form of regulationism in Britain came to an end.

Outcomes

What were the legacies of the Contagious Diseases Acts? What difference did they really make? In some respects, we might be tempted to consider them relatively insignificant, considering that the Acts were so geographically restricted, and in full operation for at best a decade and a half. They may indeed look like a 'flirtation with regulation', a brief interruption to the progress of a country congenitally suspicious of central state intervention, whose culture and common law traditions enshrined the liberty of the subject.[94] The Acts would be, in this quite widespread view, an anomaly or aberration, quickly discarded in a return to more conventional and time-honoured methods of policing public order and the public health.[95] Such a reading contrasts markedly with the equally widely held but contradictory notion that the Acts were a social, cultural and political watershed.

In truth, there was no *single* legacy, and some of the confusion about the historical significance of the Acts surely comes down to the fact that several outcomes were involved, in different registers and relating to different constituencies. What may have been of relatively minor importance in terms of the numbers of people directly affected, as a quickly abandoned experiment in social medicine, may have been in the sphere of politics and government of much more profound and

---

[92] *Hansard*, 209:334, 13 February 1872.
[93] McHugh, *Prostitution and Victorian social reform*, p. 273.
[94] *Ibid.*, p. 16.
[95] In Smith's view, 'the popular distrust of "centralisation" and "medical despotism" did save Britain from the bureaucracy of "medical police" that afflicted Prussia and France': Smith, *The people's health*, p. 418.

lasting significance. It is essential to bear in mind therefore both the local policing of prostitution and the wider policing of sexuality. In the first place, for the women involved in the sex trade and the working-class communities from which they were overwhelmingly sourced, it has been emphatically argued that the Acts, brief as their reign was, had large and lasting effects in *professionalising* prostitution. As is well appreciated, systems of regulation tend to create, rather than just codify, a distinct class of recognised prostitutes. It was one of the main complaints of repealers that once identified and inscribed on a register it was difficult for women to shake off this shameful ascription. The likes of Acton had emphasised the fluidity of sex workers' lives – their ability to move back into the ranks of the respectable working class after relatively short prostitute careers – and other defenders of the Acts argued that women were encouraged and enabled to move out of the profession. Despite these claims, however, the Acts appear to have operated in the main to professionalise the cohort of women who were caught up in its administrative net, to turn prostitution from an opportunity into something more like a career, albeit a stigmatised and increasingly marginalised one. Judith Walkowitz has most influentially suggested that the Acts helped to create an 'outcast' group, detached and socially segregated from their peers in the casual proletariat.[96] Most women who worked as prostitutes within and beyond the subjected districts were undoubtedly little different from other migrants who fuelled the nineteenth-century expansion of British cities. They were typically young, single women who moved from the local countryside in search of work. That theirs was not respectable 'work', or even recognised as 'work' at all, was more of a problem for bourgeois observers than for the women themselves, or perhaps for many other workers for whom social and geographical mobility was an accepted condition of existence. Women working as prostitutes may have been somewhat more mobile, uprooted perhaps by family strife or breakdown, by romantic disillusionment or the dissolution of relationships, but they were in no sense the class apart as some social investigators attempted to portray them. The CD Acts, however, imposed their logic and interests upon this situation. As Walkowitz summarises:

The Contagious Diseases Acts were part of institutional and legal efforts to contain this occupational and geographical mobility. At the local level, they were used to clarify the relationship between the unrespectable and respectable poor, and specifically to force prostitutes to accept their status as public women by destroying their private associations with the poor working-class community.[97]

There is inevitably only indirect evidence for such a process. Demographic analysis of registered women gives some indication of the nature of the class of public women that the Acts are argued to have created. The age of women

---

[96] See Walkowitz, *Prostitution and Victorian society*, and the earlier statement by Walkowitz and Walkowitz, '"We are not beasts of the field"'.
[97] Walkowitz, *Prostitution and Victorian society*, p. 192.

registered under the Acts, for instance, was a few years older than typical in areas beyond the subjected districts, and this age profile tended to increase over time. If a study of Victorian York is considered as a control, we note that from 1837 to 1887 half of the prostitute women there were under the age of twenty even at the point of their last reporting and recording by Frances Finnegan.[98] In most systems of regulation, by contrast, women tended to be disproportionately in their early and mid-twenties. The subjected CD districts fit this pattern pretty well. Whilst in the early years of the Acts the numbers of younger women were relatively high – in 1865 70% of registered women in Plymouth and Devonport for instance, and 35% of those in Chatham, were under twenty-one – this proportion fell quickly – by 1871 to 17% and 29% respectively. At the other end of the age range, there were disproportionately more women in the older cohort – in 1870, 10% of women in Plymouth were over thirty-one years of age, rising to 26% by 1881, and the figures for Chatham were 5% in 1865 rising to 21% in 1881.[99] The absence of young prostitute women is questionable – younger women may have been deterred or redirected by the Acts, though it was also in the interests of the authorities to downplay the existence of juvenile prostitution – but there still appears to be no doubt that registered women stayed longer in their prostitute careers. The falling numbers of brothels and prostitutes in the subjected districts also suggests a move to a more 'professional' cohort of women. This might be called a kind of modernisation of prostitution, even a move towards contemporary conditions of 'sex work' as we would now recognise it.

The local landscape of prostitution in the subjected districts may be used to reinforce this characterisation. As Walkowitz also suggests, prostitute women's social isolation was typically accompanied by a certain geographical segregation of the areas where they lived and worked. The advantages to the police of having prostitute women clustered in relatively well-defined neighbourhoods needs little emphasis. Speaking of London, for instance, the regulationist Berkeley Hill pointed out that 'The great majority of women to whom prostitution is the business of life live together in localities that are perfectly well known to the police. This peculiarity very much facilitates the supervision necessary for the purposes of examination and control.'[100] All the more so was this rationale applicable in the subjected districts. In Plymouth, for instance, registered women were clustered in courts and alleys surrounding the Octagon on Union Street, the principal thoroughfare; in Southampton, the equivalent was the neighbourhood of Simnell

---

[98] F. Finnegan, *Poverty and prostitution: a study of Victorian prostitutes in York* (Cambridge, 1979), p. 76.

[99] Joyce, *The Chatham scandal*, p. 129.

[100] B. Hill, 'Illustrations of the working of the Contagious Diseases Act. IV – The venereal disease among prostitutes in London', *British Medical Journal*, 23 May 1867, pp. 505–6, p. 505.

Street, in this case distanced from the commercial heart of the city.[101] It can be argued that this *localisation* of prostitution is a clear sign of the role of police management in professionalising the commercial sexual economy, and prominent examples are given in subsequent chapters of this book.

Whilst this is a compelling thesis, we do need to introduce another note of caution, specific in the first instance but ultimately of wider significance. As far as micro-geographies of prostitution go, clusters of residences of sex workers in particular streets and neighbourhoods was not necessarily the direct product of CD Act regulation, nor did it always work in their favour. Many of these 'vice areas' were very well established in the moral geography of nineteenth-century towns, and long survived the short career of the Acts.[102] The Brook, in Chatham, North-lane in Aldershot, Barracks Street in Cork, and many other moral locations were synonymous with prostitution in the subjected districts; but these were not necessarily distinctive of managed sexuality. Nor were these places quite as regular and regularised as defenders of the Acts suggested. Encomiums to the good order and respectability of the registered women in the subjected districts were always likely to be wildly optimistic; in truth there was little sign of the disciplined sexual economy that regulationists envisaged and advertised, and that was castigated by Josephine Butler as 'pretty, proper vice'.[103] To return to Cork for but one example: though the improved condition of the city's streets was much remarked upon, the existence of a localised brothel district remained a matter of scandal to the respectable inhabitants. In Cork, the brothels in St Finbarr's parish, in the streets and lanes around Barracks Street south of the Lee, were locally notorious, and the Acts seem to have little effect in disciplining the neighbourhood's criminal fraternity and sorority. Complaints about disorderly prostitution abounded, and this was, for the local newspaper, simply 'a nest of the foulest infamy'.[104] Whilst the authorities were said to be powerless to do anything about the district, in 1876 a small band of Catholic priests, possibly acting with the aid of the constabulary, succeeded in 'disestablishing' the brothels of Barracks Street. This destruction of a recognisable brothel quarter, accompanied by a liberal sprinkling of prophylactic holy water, produced these hosannas from the *Cork Examiner*:

This Catholic land has known in recent years many a wondrous outpouring of God's grace; but we doubt if it has known any so wondrous as that which a few days since descended upon the southern part of this city of ours, sweeping away a foul plague spot,

---

[101] Walkowitz, *Prostitution and Victorian society*, p. 197.
[102] See for instance M. Ogborn and C. Philo, 'Soldiers, sailors and moral locations in nineteenth-century Portsmouth', *Area*, 26 (1994), 221–31.
[103] Josephine Butler, quoted in McHugh, *Prostitution and Victorian social reform*, p. 143.
[104] 'A crusade against immorality', *Cork Examiner*, 27 June 1876, p. 2.

and changing almost in an instant, a street of sinners, the vilest and most hardened, into a street of penitents.[105]

Later apologists for the work of the Acts would claim these results for themselves, and we must remember that repression and regulation typically went hand in hand; yet it is an indication all the same that the restriction of prostitutes to particular districts did not *in itself* discipline them and improve the standards of public morality. Indeed, regulationists alternately championed and challenged this localisation of brothel businesses.

It is wrong to use the existence of brothel districts in themselves as evidence that the Acts changed the fundamental geographical pattern of prostitution. As we shall see in the next two chapters, other towns not under the Acts had their own prostitution areas, some the result of social and economic processes encouraging clustering, but others the products of formal and informal policing that bears comparison with the regimes introduced by the Acts. Berkeley Hill's comment on London quoted above indicates that 'containment' of the brothel economy was a principle of nineteenth-century policing of much more general application. Districts of brothels and houses of accommodation are simply not exclusive signs of the transformations effected by contagious diseases legislation. In any case, not all the CD districts were organised in this fashion: though keen to emphasise the notorious neighbourhood of the Brook in Chatham, Brian Joyce categorically states that there was no distinct red light district in the town.[106]

The wider point is that it is hard to provide a real control group for the districts under the Acts, given the heterogeneity within and beyond their jurisdiction. Again, it is ultimately misleading to think that a policing regime existed under the legal authority of the Acts in the subjected districts that was wholly distinct from that existing outside it. Even the more convincing statistics as to the age range of prostitute women, and the implications for their careers as public women, is not quite definitive. We simply do not know enough about the demography and changing social status of women in the rest of the country. The forms in which prostitution occurred and managed may well have produced cohorts of women of different ages and backgrounds, so that streetwalking women in one city, say, may not be straightforwardly compared with those working in 'brothels' or other such houses in another. Moreover, we must particularly remember that the landscape and nature of commercial sexuality was changing across the country. Whilst the number of brothels and registered prostitute women fell markedly in the subjected districts, for instance, in many other parts of Britain the same pattern was found.

How much more difficult is it to assess the suggestion that prostitute women accepted and internalised the identity fostered by the operation of the Acts? In some cities, the implied recognition offered by the Acts seems to have been seized

---

[105] 'Extraordinary social reform in the city', *Cork Examiner*, 3 July 1876, p. 2.
[106] Joyce, *The Chatham scandal*, p. 205.

upon by women used to being despised and abused. Cork was the place where prostitutes referred to themselves as 'Queen's women', 'in the employment of Her Majesty', much to the repealers' disgust.[107] But it is difficult to discern the specific inflections here; harder still to see this as passive acquiescence to the demands of a regulationist regime.[108] There are very few statements from prostitutes themselves, none unmediated. Regulationists were quick to argue that prostitute women were compliant, even enthusiastic, but their logic is sometimes hard to follow. Supporters of the Acts stated for instance that young and inexperienced women were frightened off the life by the horror of genital examinations, but that, once hardened, women paid little attention to it and complied without protest; statements like these depended upon the pre-existence of a distinction between the relatively innocent and the relatively incorrigible. On the other hand, opponents collected testimonies of women's revulsion and resistance to incorporation under the Acts. It is surely better to exercise caution in commenting on the Acts' contribution to the social construction of wholly novel sexual identities.

Whilst the suggestion of professionalisation is alluring, it remains difficult to single out the Acts as *directly* responsible for a thoroughgoing transformation in the conditions and the nature of prostitution. Walkowitz's very influential and widely cited arguments – not only that prostitution became the preserve of a smaller and more readily identifiable number of women, but also increasingly stigmatised even amongst the working classes, and moving from a female- to a male-dominated trade – were, we should note, never confined to the operation of the Acts. Indeed she accepted that the changes she charts may simply be an acceleration of processes occurring elsewhere, albeit less quickly and intensively.[109] Just as importantly, these were changes that can be seen as much the result of the repeal agitation than of the operations of formal regulation. This is because repeal promoted the rise of a purity politics that had the potential to bear down even more repressively on women's citizenship rights.

This brings us neatly enough to the place of the Acts in the context of the longer-term changes in the philosophies of state intervention into sexuality. As Anne Scott notes, 'Sanitary discourse became a battleground in a wider struggle, which used debates about hygiene and "purity" to define the limits of state power'; troublingly, sanitarian ideas about moral and physical pollution were central to both medical interventionists and female purity campaigners.[110] Others have also noticed that repealers and regulationists shared certain presumptions and prejudices, not least a willing blindness to some of the social and economic reasons for prostitution. Bertrand Taithe remarks that '[i]t is one of the paradoxical issues of the repeal discourse that it eventually worked out

---

[107] McHugh, *Prostitution and Victorian social reform*, p. 144.
[108] Walkowitz, *Prostitution and Victorian society*, p. 233.   [109] *Ibid.*, p. 210.
[110] A. L. Scott, 'Physical purity feminism and state medicine in late nineteenth-century England', *Women's History Review*, 8 (1999), 625–53, p. 632.

similar conclusions and took on board some of the rhetoric of regulationism', as in the language of pollution.[111] This was not simply a matter of shared discourse though; the possibilities of practical collaboration between regulationists and fellow travellers of the repeal movement had been demonstrated by the willingness of the likes of the social purity campaigner Ellice Hopkins to co-operate with municipal police forces in repressing the most flagrant public manifestations of prostitution. One effect of the repeal movement's success was thus to open up a discursive and political space in which purity campaigners could make common cause with their erstwhile opponents, allying moral with medical prophylaxis and inviting greater state intervention into the realm of sexual behaviour and relations.

The alliance between social purity reformers, appalled by moral decay, and 'neoregulationists', concerned with the spread of social disease, ushered in new repressive practices of moral surveillance that would be targeted not so much at the common prostitute but at all forms of deviant sexuality.[112] Promiscuity rather than prostitution – 'wayward' rather than working girls – would come to be the targets of this new regime, along with male homosexuals, white slavers, child abusers and so on.[113] For these reasons, Richard Price has portrayed the 1880s – which saw not only the demise of the CD Acts but also the rise of the influential Criminal Law Amendment Act of 1885 – as a crucial turning point, the older, truly 'Victorian' traditions of campaigning through voluntary associations of moralistic but still civil libertarian stripe giving way to an endorsement of state supervision and an intrusive regulation of morality: 'The contagious diseases campaign had exposed the contradictions and instabilities of the ideology that underlay the public and private spheres of civil society and had ended up contributing to a shift in the very ordering of those spheres.'[114] To a large extent, Walkowitz's subsequent work on the changing social geography of late-Victorian London reinforces this suggestion that the 1880s saw a decisive reorientation of British society, in which the repeal of the CD Acts marked no return to core 'Victorian values' but only a stage in the transition to a more repressive scripting of vice and virtue that transgressed the conventional boundaries between state and citizen.[115]

[111] Taithe, 'From danger to scandal', p. 210.
[112] See for instance L. Bland, *Banishing the beast: English feminism and sexual morality 1885–1914* (Harmondsworth, 1995), F. Mort, 'Purity, feminism and the state: sexuality and moral politics, 1880–1914', in M. Langan and B. Schwarz (eds.), *Crises in the British state 1880–1930* (London, 1985).
[113] B. Littlewood and L. Mahood, 'Prostitutes, magdalenes, and wayward girls: dangerous sexualities of working class women in Victorian Scotland', *Gender and History*, 3 (1991), 168–75, L. Mahood, *Policing gender, class and family: Britain, 1850–1940* (London, 1995).
[114] R. Price, *British society 1680–1880* (Cambridge, 1999), p. 226.
[115] J. R. Walkowitz, *City of dreadful delight: narratives of sexual danger in late-Victorian London* (London, 1992), J. R. Walkowitz, 'Going public: shopping, street harassment,

Even here we may still be going too far. Walkowitz herself argued that, whilst there were the beginnings of a new disciplinary regime for working-class women, there were also new possibilities for middle-class women – and others – to explore their sexual subjectivity.[116] Looking for absolute discontinuities, between repeal and social purity in the history of feminism for instance, or between *laissez-faire* and interventionism in the history of public health, is bound to be as misleading as an insistence on essential continuity. This was a period of flux, not simply the abandonment of one distinct regime for another. Medically speaking, even if we restrict our purview to the career of the venereological campaigns, it is fair to say that the demise of the CD Acts was rather *less* significant than has sometimes been claimed. Whilst some very prominent medical historians have suggested that Britain returned to a 'voluntary' system of treatment that was only interrupted by the 'atypical' CD Acts, Pamela Cox has recently and rightly pointed out the survival and extension of medical coercion – particularly for prostitutes and other suspected women and girls, but even for infected soldiers – for many decades; so repeal only appears to mark a watershed in British public health and tactics of sexual governance, whereas 'compulsory strategies remained a crucial part of British VD management up until at least the 1940s'.[117] The British state and medical establishment, far from rejecting regulation, as Peter Baldwin and others have claimed, found other ways to enforce the treatment of specific groups. Formal regulation, in any case, may be thought of as dormant rather than dead, reappearing in the crisis of the world wars in the form of regulation 40D of the Defence of the Realm Act (DORA) in 1918, and again in a 1942 addition, regulation 33B, to the Emergency Powers (Defence) Act of 1939. These wartime powers take the career of British regulation into the late 1940s, and end, interestingly enough, more or less contemporaneously with the dismantling of the French system of regulated brothels. And, although there is little comparison between the discontinuous domestic British policies and the consistent regulationism and neo-regulationism of France, it will not in the end do to argue that the British experience of regulationism began in 1864 and ended in 1886. To put it shortly, the history of British regulationism is not the history of the CD Acts alone.

Orientation

This conclusion is important for the wider history and geography of the British regulation of prostitution, not only on the mainland but also abroad. I have

and streetwalking in late Victorian London', *Representations*, 62 (1998), 1–30.
[116] Walkowitz, *City of dreadful delight*. See also F. Mort and L. Nead, 'Sexuality, modernity and the Victorians', *Journal of Victorian Culture*, 1 (1996), 118–30.
[117] P. Cox, 'Compulsion, voluntarism, and venereal disease: governing sexual health in England after the Contagious Diseases Acts', *Journal of British Studies*, 46 (2007), 91–115, p. 92.

addressed in this chapter the central role that the Contagious Diseases Acts have been assigned in the historiography of British regulationism. For better or worse, the Acts have dominated discussion, perhaps no more so than in synoptic cultural studies that have portrayed the Acts as representative of a systematic and pervasive 'regulationist discourse', a wider project of containment aimed at combating the 'frightening alternative geography' of contagion associated with prostitute women, and indeed perhaps of women themselves.[118] Such arguments inevitably tend to overstate the coherence, comprehensiveness and efficacy of the Acts, and they also tend to conform to the portrayal of the Acts as a turning point for social policy and the state, not to mention for Victorian culture and society as a whole. It is the stuttering introduction of these various local regulationist regimes that must be emphasised, however, together with their unsystematic and uneven qualities, and their essential messiness. They did not and could not introduce in Britain a wholly new, wholly distinct regime of sexuality, nor one that we can clearly say decisively transformed British society. We should clearly recognise the Acts' limits and limitations, and be circumspect about their ultimate significance; we cannot assume, as Philippa Levine rightly again reminds us, that the Acts represent a significant historical watershed.[119]

Often without awareness of any contradiction, other studies have suggested that the Acts were merely a short-lived flirtation with regulation, an erratic turn to continental-style medical policing, quickly contested and consigned to history.[120] These narratives have just as misleadingly portrayed the rise and fall of the Acts as the rise and fall of British regulationism itself. What such portrayals miss, first of all, is the fact that the Acts were interventions into a British map of prostitution policy that was itself deeply heterogeneous and equally unsystematic. What went on beyond the remit of the subjected districts was not a landscape of *laissez-faire* in terms of the policing of prostitution; as the next two chapters in this book show, there were other, local regimes of regulation in Britain that predated and preempted the CD Acts. Furthermore, although they were caught up in the same political struggles, these regimes outlasted the Acts, indicative in itself that British authorities' commitment to regulationism could and did survive their legislative repeal. If the Acts do not represent a decisive turning point for British policy on prostitution, social hygiene and public order, neither should their repeal be taken as decisive for the fortunes of regulationism.

---

[118] L. Nead, *Myths of sexuality: representations of women in Victorian Britain* (Oxford, 1988), p. 129. See also S. Bell, *Reading, writing and rewriting the prostitute body* (Bloomington, 1994), pp. 55–64.

[119] P. Levine, 'Rough usage: prostitution, law and the social historian', in Adrian Wilson (ed.), *Rethinking social history: English society 1570–1920 and its interpretation* (Manchester, 1993), pp. 266–92, p. 284.

[120] McHugh, *Prostitution and Victorian social reform*, p. 16.

This point may be made even more strongly when the career of contagious diseases legislation in the colonies is considered. Beyond Britain, regulationism survived and, even in the face of determined opposition, prospered for decades after the demise of the CD Acts. The later chapters in this study show how important these colonial regimes were, and how their fortunes were caught up in the empire-wide political history of British regulationism. This was not, as I have previously insisted, simply a case of prostitution regulation being exported from Britain to the colonies. Even if we lay aside the argument that the Irish stations under the CD Acts already demonstrate that these were, in part, colonial statutes, it is clear that the British experiment with regulation in the British (and Irish) subjected districts was part of a much greater gathering of experience and expertise at regulating prostitute women in the colonies. Not just the colonial legislation, but the CD Acts themselves, need to be placed in the context of British imperialism.

This recontextualisation and reorientation of the CD Acts provides a frame for the following chapters. Attention to the messy geographies of the Acts reminds us that they were clumsy and circumscribed interventions into the landscape of commercial sex, limited in their impact and perhaps most important for the intense opposition that they generated, both nationally and empire-wide. Their fortunes must be coupled but not identified with those of British regulationism, which took the form of local geographies of regulation in both the domestic and colonial arenas. The political geography and geopolitics of British regulationism was more complex than much of the historiography of the CD Acts has hitherto suggested.

3

Liverpool, localisation and the municipal regulation of prostitution in Britain

According to official measures, Liverpool was the city with the greatest prostitution problem in England. Proportionate to its population, it had the greatest number of brothels and 'known prostitutes', and topped the Victorian league table for prosecutions for prostitution offences throughout the second half of the nineteenth century. In the comparative moral geography constructed by national criminal statistics, Liverpool stood out in this regard as one of the true shock cities of the age: if prostitution was the 'great sin of great cities', Liverpool was clearly one of the country's greatest sinners. The *Morning Chronicle* survey of the labouring poor called it 'perhaps the most depraved sea-port, not only in Great Britain, but in the world'.[1] The Navy Report of 1867 likewise claimed that 'Liverpool is the *hotbed of syphilis*, where disease flourishes and is *sown broadcast over the world*'.[2]

As this chapter demonstrates, this characterisation was a source of concern and controversy both at the local and national scales, particularly given the contentious history of regulationist policies in Victorian Britain. Although Liverpool was never regulated under the Contagious Diseases Acts, it was deeply implicated in the politics of prostitution that they generated. Both the scale and the scandal of the borough's prostitution problem made it an obvious target for advocates of nationwide regulationism, and it was repeatedly canvassed in the 1870s as one of the principal candidates for the extension of the Acts to civilian towns. Just as inevitably, it was early on recognised as a crucial political battleground by repealers and moral reformers determined to resist the march of what they saw as tolerated vice. They recognised in Liverpool not just a city vulnerable to regulationist

---

[1] *Morning Chronicle and London Advertiser*, 27 May 1850, p. 6.
[2] From the Navy Report of 1867, p. 34, quoted by J. Birkbeck Nevins, *The health of the Navy: an analysis of the official report for 1876, and of the special return relating to five ports under and five ports not under the Contagious Diseases Acts, which was ordered to be laid before the House of Commons, on the 4th July, 1877* (London, 1878), p. 3, emphasis in original.

experiments in 'partial legislation', however; they also considered that Liverpool *already* had an *informal* system of regulation, in the form of the discreet strategy of supervision and 'containment' of brothel prostitution long operated by the borough police in conjunction with the city's magistrates. Although the extensionist campaign was unsuccessful, the controversies it engendered trained a political spotlight on these local and specific practices. The informal management of prostitution came under particularly close scrutiny in the 1880s, when the national ascendancy of social purity was confirmed with the passage of the Criminal Law Amendment Act, and when the demise of the CD Acts signalled the intolerance of any 'tolerated' prostitution. By that time Liverpool's distinctive approach to policing prostitution had become a political issue of national importance. The borough police, together with its magistracy and political class, was to become notorious for prostitution policy that could be taken as regulationist in spirit if not in name.

The systematic management of prostitution by the police and the magistracy in Liverpool certainly approximates formal regulationist policies, and most particularly in its techniques of enclosure and spatial surveillance, the policy that in the borough was termed 'containment' or 'localisation' and that we might today call segregation or zoning. The point here is not to add Liverpool to the list of regulationist regimes, however; as the next chapter demonstrates, other towns in Britain have an even better claim to that status. The intention is rather to place Liverpool on the map of prostitution policy in Britain, as the exemplar of a *more* managed and thus *more* 'regulated' approach, in contrast with other municipalities that rejected such 'toleration' of vice. It is necessary to note once more that the business of commercial sexuality outside the subjected districts under the CD Acts was not homogeneously *unregulated*, a landscape of *laissez-faire*, or alternatively of *repression* of prostitution; we have instead a range of different approaches to managing prostitution, policies that became identified with particular cities under particular political regimes. If the identification of Liverpool as an example of regulated prostitution remains contentious, in the Victorian policy spectrum Liverpool was clearly aligned with the principles of regulationism rather than with the aggressive attempts to repress prostitution attempted by some other towns. This association of Liverpool with managed and regulated prostitution was well recognised by contemporaries, supporters and opponents alike. This chapter examines how Liverpool became a precedent and a model for other municipalities to follow – or, from the perspective of moral crusaders convinced of the borough authorities' complicity with the brothel economy, a byword to be avoided at all costs.

Whether Liverpool deserved its notoriety compared to other towns is much more problematic. Liverpool *did* have a very significant commercial sexual economy – hardly surprising given its nature – but police and criminal statistics did not straightforwardly reveal its problem with prostitution; instead, they constructed it, in discourse and political practice. Police statistics fed moral reformers' denunciations of the city's police and political leaders, but their veracity was called into question by those who supported the idea of managing prostitution, both in Liverpool and beyond. Confronting the statistics of prostitution head on, and rejecting as a farce the supposed success of other towns in repressing prostitution, the proponents of the system in Liverpool sought to redraw the municipal map of morality, and to align it more accurately with what they saw as the realities of prostitution in Victorian Britain. This chapter also concerns, then, the political geographical imagination of prostitution in Victorian Britain, examining the ways in which the phenomenon of prostitution and the geographically differentiated policies for its management were constructed as forms of *knowledge*. I am interested here in one of the key ways in which Victorian Britain was 'mapped' as a moral phenomenon, shaped as a form of social reality, for spatialisation was central to both the regulation and the *representation* of prostitution. There was also no consensus on the nature of prostitution, no policy formula of universal application, no homogeneity in its treatment. Instead, prostitution remained ambiguous and policy remained variegated, at least until the final years of the nineteenth century. No account of Victorian prostitution, nor of Victorian sexuality in its supposed 'home base', should ignore this plurality of practice, both discursive and material. It is a fundamental part of my argument in this book that the British 'metropole' was distinctively differentiated, such that there was no single model of metropolitan practice and policy that could ever be exported to the rest of the British world.

In emphasising the heterogeneity of prostitution policy in nineteenth-century Britain, geographical differentiation is identified as central to the national-scale integration of knowledge and practice. On the one hand, it was at the *municipal* level that prostitution policy was most energetically pursued; but, on the other, these municipal policies were understood through comparison with each other, contributing to the *national* policy debate. Though grounded in the practices of the locality, both local and national governmentalities are invoked in this chapter. With the geographically differentiated framework for governance in mind, I begin by considering first the political geography of prostitution that was revealed by the compilation of Victorian criminal statistics.[3]

Political geographies of prostitution

Knowledge about prostitution was not confined to self-appointed scientific experts and moral reformers, to the likes of Acton and Parent-Duchâtelet. There was another set of knowledges about prostitution, one that derived from the administration of

[3] For a useful discussion of geography and governmentality, see R. S. Rose-Redwood, 'Governmentality, geography, and the geo-coded world', *Progress in Human Geography*, 30 (2006), 469–86.

law and justice and the bureaucratic machinery of the modern state. This was encoded in the administrative data gathered by the agents of what Edward Higgs has felicitously called the 'information state'.[4] The criminal statistics compiled by the Home Office from data provided by local police forces are significant for being a state-sponsored representation of prostitution. This form of knowledge enabled certain characteristics of prosecutions for prostitution offences to be presented for analysis, commentary, and action, all within the context of the statistical analysis of nineteenth-century criminal activity as a whole. The difficulties of using such statistics are very great, as all commentators have noted, but it is possible to sidestep objections by concentrating on the statistics and their mapping as a political phenomenon in itself, as a practice of knowledge rather than as a direct representation of reality. We can look at these figures not as a guide to the *truth* of Victorian sex work and its geography, but rather to examine what kinds of work, cultural and political, this spatial representation of prostitution accomplished.

It should be noted immediately that the *history* of nineteenth-century crime has been rather more commented on than its geography. Historians who have worked on criminal statistics have typically done so in order to comment on the phenomenon of the fall in recorded criminal activity in the second half of the nineteenth century, a period that Vic Gattrell characterised as an era of unequivocal success for the British 'policeman-state'.[5] There are many qualifications to the use of these statistics that do not need to be rehearsed here, but Gattrell insists that, whatever the relation of these statistics is to the actual incidence of criminal activity, it is legitimate to accept that there *was* a fall in real as well as recorded crime, given that we would expect other developments in the system of criminal prosecution to have increased these figures, not lowered them. Although some sexual offences are exceptional to this general trend, those associated with prostitution do decline in real terms, as Gattrell's overview suggests. We may be allowed some confidence in the fact that the statistics for many of the offences concerning prostitution fell steadily throughout the second half of the nineteenth century. Summary prosecutions in England and Wales dropped for instance from 22,586 in 1858 to 17,216 in 1897, and indictments from over 2,050 in 1858 to under 453 in 1886. In Ireland, the equivalent figures are 13,208 in 1865, falling to 3,021 in 1898,

---

[4] E. Higgs, *The information state in England: the central collection of information on citizens since 1500* (London, 2003).
[5] V. A. C. Gattrell, 'Crime, authority and the policeman-state', in F. M. L. Thompson (ed.), *The Cambridge social history of Britain, 1750–1950* (Cambridge, 1990), p. 292. See also V. A. C. Gattrell, 'The decline of theft and violence in Victorian and Edwardian England and Wales', in V. A. C. Gattrell, B. Lenman and G. Parker (eds.), *Crime and the law: the social history of crime in western Europe since 1500* (London, 1980), pp. 238–370, and V. A. C. Gattrell and T. B. Haddon, 'Nineteenth-century criminal statistics and their interpretation', in E. A. Wrigley (ed.), *Nineteenth-century society: essays in the use of quantitative methods for the study of social data* (Cambridge, 1972), pp. 336–96.

and 509 in 1865, falling to 187 in 1884.[6] These figures suggest – for whatever reason – that prostitution was lessening as a phenomenon for the criminal justice system. These of course also need to be taken relative to the increase in population, revealing an even more precipitous decline. It is true that the statistics for prostitutes prosecuted under the vagrancy laws suggest that prostitution may have been simply being tackled using different statutory means; prosecutions under this heading rose from the 1860s through to the mid-1880s, and, though they fell considerably to the end of the century, the figures were much the same as they had been forty or fifty years earlier.[7] Even bearing in mind the rise in population, these figures suggest less of an unqualified triumph for purity or policing. Paula Bartley also reminds us that these figures may suggest changes in the police response to prostitution rather than the extent of prostitution itself.[8] Nevertheless, most commentators agree that the second half of the nineteenth century saw a fall in the numbers of women who resorted to prostitution as well as those who were recorded by the justice system: 'on scarcely anyone's showing do prostitution levels rise in nineteenth-century England; in real terms, indeed, there is almost unanimity that they fall.'[9] Contemporary commentators took notice of this apparent fall in prostitution activity, even if they continued to believe that prostitution was as much a problem as ever.

The debate over numbers in the abstract and the substantive argument over the relative success of the Victorian 'policeman-state' have tended to obscure the *geography* of recorded crime that these figures represent, however. This is, too often, either ignored or taken as read, assimilated uncritically to general analysis of urbanisation, industrialisation and modernity. At this level of discussion, few would disagree with the general conclusions of the Liverpool venereologist Frederick Lowndes:

> The history of all countries, in all ages, has shown that prostitution has always prevailed to a greater or lesser extent, being most prevalent in large towns and cities; less prevalent, but by no means absent in smaller towns, in villages, or even in the most rural districts.

[6] The source for this information is the returns of judicial statistics for England and Wales, and for Ireland, contained in the British Parliamentary Papers.
[7] This is particularly important for Liverpool, where increasing recourse to the vagrancy laws appears to have been policy after 1872. Home Secretary Henry Bruce (*Hansard* 209:335–6, 13 February 1872) noted that the Vagrant Act had lately been applied for the first time with any vigour, and with eminently satisfactory results; Bruce noted that if a woman was thought by police and magistrates to be living a disorderly life, and if found to be suffering from contagious disease, she would be detained in the prison infirmary or in some certified hospital until she was cured, or for a maximum period of nine months. He added, somewhat disingenuously, that '[n]o compulsory examination would in that case be necessary'.
[8] P. Bartley, *Prostitution: prevention and reform in England, 1860–1914* (London, 2000), pp. 167–8.
[9] M. Mason, *The making of Victorian sexuality* (Oxford, 1994), p. 78.

Political geographies of prostitution 81

The extent of prostitution is greatly determined by the number of inhabitants in any town or city, and also by other circumstances, such as the presence of soldiers, naval seamen, marines, or merchant seamen. Hence garrison towns and seaports have always had an unenviable notoriety for the large number of prostitutes which they always attract to them; and for the horrible condition in which these poor creatures are too often found to be living by the few persons to whom this is known.[10]

Others, though rather less convincingly, might concur with William Acton's general commentary on the geography of prostitution:

prostitution abounds not only in places where large numbers of unmarried men are collected together, but also where in the course of their daily work the sexes are brought into close and intimate relations. Factory towns, therefore, must be included in the list of places peculiarly liable to the presence of prostitution, though perhaps in this case the prevailing mischief may be more accurately termed general immorality, or depravity, than prostitution proper; the difference, however, is not very great, and, for the purposes of this work, immaterial ... We may, however, expect to find large cities contribute in a greater degree than other places to the manufacture and employment of prostitutes. Here always abound idle and wealthy men, with vicious tastes, which they spare neither pains nor expense to gratify. Here also are the needy, the improvident, and readily recruited. The close proximity of luxury and indigence cannot fail to produce a demoralizing effect upon the latter. Garrison, seaport, and factory towns, and large cities, are all places peculiarly liable to the presence of prostitution, containing as they do, within themselves in an eminent degree the seeds and causes of vice. Some places, such as London, combine within themselves all these qualities, and are therefore notable and exceptionally exposed to this evil. It is impossible to suppose that in such localities prostitution can ever become extinct.[11]

The criminal statistics portrayed a much more nuanced picture, however, and one that went beyond and sometimes conflicted with these commentaries. The Victorian statistician James Hammick offered a particularly careful and considered analysis of the 1867 figures, and, though rightly suspicious of particular returns from particular police divisions, he was willing to draw the conclusion that prostitution was a product of certain *types* of town, particularly the great commercial ports, but excluding London.[12] His tabulation of crime and prostitution, idiosyncratic as it is, followed the usual Victorian practice of aggregation into categories of places, and his conclusions have been endorsed in passing by Judith Walkowitz.[13]

[10] F. W. Lowndes, *Prostitution and venereal diseases in Liverpool* (London, 1886), p. 1.
[11] W. Acton, *Prostitution, considered in its moral, social, and sanitary aspects, in London and other large cities and garrison towns. With proposals for the control and prevention of its attendant evils*, reprint of 2nd edition, 1870 (London, 1972), p. 177.
[12] J. T. Hammick, 'On the judicial statistics of England and Wales, with special reference to the recent returns relating to crime', *Journal of the Statistical Society*, 30 (1867), 375–426.
[13] *Ibid.*, p. 391; J. R. Walkowitz, *Prostitution and Victorian society: women, class, and the state* (Cambridge, 1980), pp. 21–2.

	Criminal class, one in	Total prostitutes separately, one in
Metropolitan district	216.8	475.7
Seats of the small textile manufactures	146.3	443.1
cotton and linen manufactures	141.0	524.7
woollen and worsted manufactures …	139.1	623.2
Commercial ports	108.1	198.9
Agricultural towns	99.0	263.4
Hardware towns	89.7	564.0
Pleasure towns	89.7	239.4

Here, then, in support of Lowndes but in contrast to Acton, the commercial ports preponderate, but the industrial towns are greatly underrepresented. We may point too to the relative insignificance of London as a centre of recorded prostitution. Though inevitably prominent in the general discourse of Victorian criminality – London is described in Mayhew's *London labour and the London poor* as 'the grand central focus of operations, at once the emporium of crime and the Palladium of Christianity' – in terms of these offences London is remarkably insignificant.[14]

For prostitution crime, the contrast between London and Liverpool is particularly marked. It is *Liverpool*, not London, that stands out from the criminal returns. London had roughly one in six of the recorded brothels of England and Wales in 1870, but so too did Liverpool, a city many times smaller. By the early 1870s, Liverpool had surpassed London in terms of prostitutes prosecuted as vagrants and also in terms of summary prosecutions for prostitution offences. For these summary prosecutions Liverpool had lagged behind the capital in the mid-nineteenth century, with 2,600 offences in 1858 compared to nearly 10,000 in London, but in the later decades the numbers were very similar, in the range of 5–6,000 in the 1870s and 1880s, and 3–4,000 in the 1890s. In other words, whilst summary prosecutions for prostitution offences in London more than halved in the later decades of the nineteenth century, in Liverpool they rose dramatically and fell less sharply as the century wore on, ending the century still some way above the mid-century figure. It was Liverpool, therefore, not London, which dominates the criminal statistics, at least for England

---

[14] W. Tuckniss, 'The agencies at present in operation within the metropolis, for the suppression of vice and crime', in H. Mayhew, *London labour and the London poor*, volume IV, reprint of 1861 original (New York, 1968), pp. xi–xl, p. xv.

and Wales.[15] On almost any measure, Liverpool was the capital of prostitution in Victorian England.

An even clearer picture of the statistical prominence of Liverpool can be gained when one corrects these absolute figures for the enormous difference in overall population, by mapping the figures for summary prosecutions relative to the female population in the age range fifteen to forty for the counties and police districts of England and Wales. Victorian analysts tended to focus on the locality of crime, noting that 'the economic condition of the different counties in England and Wales differs considerably from the peculiarity of race of their inhabitants, and from the special character of their principal industries.'[16] The resulting mapping of crime was a feature of their portrayal of the social body. Drinking for instance was exceptionally well recorded, and the cartographic portrayal of a more drunken *North*, a more drunken *Lancashire*, and a more drunken *Liverpool* was widely disseminated. Not only were northern towns three and a half times more drunken than southern towns, but Liverpool was revealed as the most drunken of the lot with a rate of drunkenness of 420 per 100,000, the nearest competitor being Newcastle with 372 per 100,000 (Figure 3.1).[17] For prostitution, no exact equivalents exist to these maps. Mayhew's *London labour and the London poor* did, however, map out the mid-nineteenth century prosecutions for keeping disorderly houses, or brothels, and also female criminality, dominated as this category was by prostitution offences.[18] Mayhew's maps are curiously misaligned with contemporary prejudices, however. Female criminality is predictably high in London and Lancashire, but also prevalent in the agricultural counties of Hereford and Gloucester. Brothels are prominent in Middlesex and the industrial northwest, but Hereford and Worcester are not far behind. It is a picture from which no firm conclusions are drawn. By the later nineteenth century, however, a more straightforward geography of prostitution was forthcoming. If a Victorian functionary had been asked to do for these prostitution offences what was done for drunkenness and many other offences, Figure 3.2 shows what might have been produced, taking 1871 merely as an example. Here, it is the preponderance of Lancashire that is striking, followed by Tyneside, Glamorgan and – in a very much weaker sense – the Metropolitan Police District. There is far

---

[15] Note that the well-informed Josephine Butler wrote in 1868 that her home city had 9,000 women making their way by prostitution: I. Sharp (ed.), *Josephine Butler and the prostitution campaigns: diseases of the body politic, volume I: the moral reclaimability of prostitutes* (London, 2003), pp. 7, 18.

[16] L. Levi, 'A survey of indictable and summary jurisdiction offences in England and Wales, from 1857 to 1876, in quinquennial periods, and in 1877 and 1878', *Journal of the Statistical Society*, 43 (1880), 423–56, p. 434.

[17] See P.P. 1895 [300] CVIII.271, *Extract from introduction to judicial statistics, 1893*, p. 39.

[18] Mayhew, *London labour and the London poor*, pp. 485–7, 503–4.

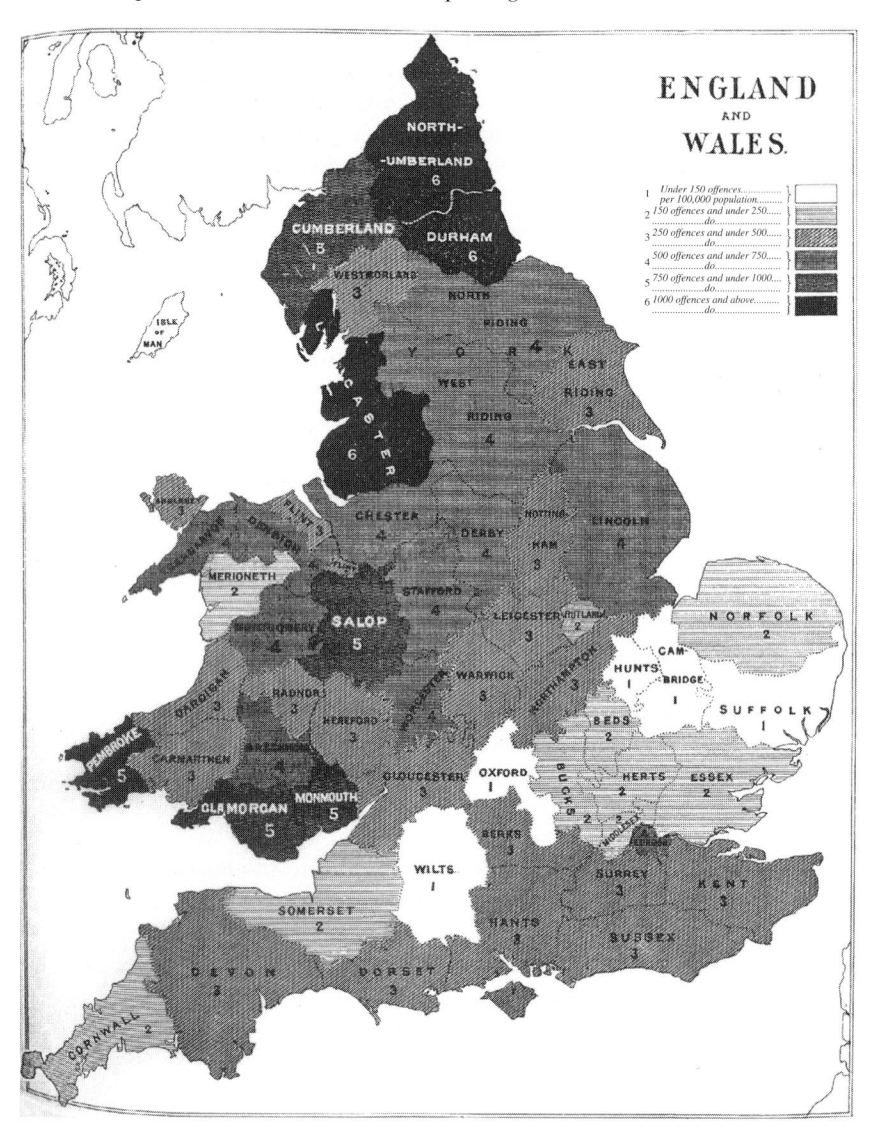

Figure 3.1 Offences for drunkenness in England and Wales per 100,000 population, 1892. From the Introduction to Judicial Statistics 1893, P.P. 1895 CVIII.

less of a north–south divide here than is to be found with other criminal statistics, and there is no need to reproduce the singling out of the industrial districts that are found in the Victorian reports. In fact, it would be more accurate, if we were truly to imagine a Victorian analysis, to play down the role of industrialisation; prostitution was dissociated, in Victorian discussions, from the industrial districts

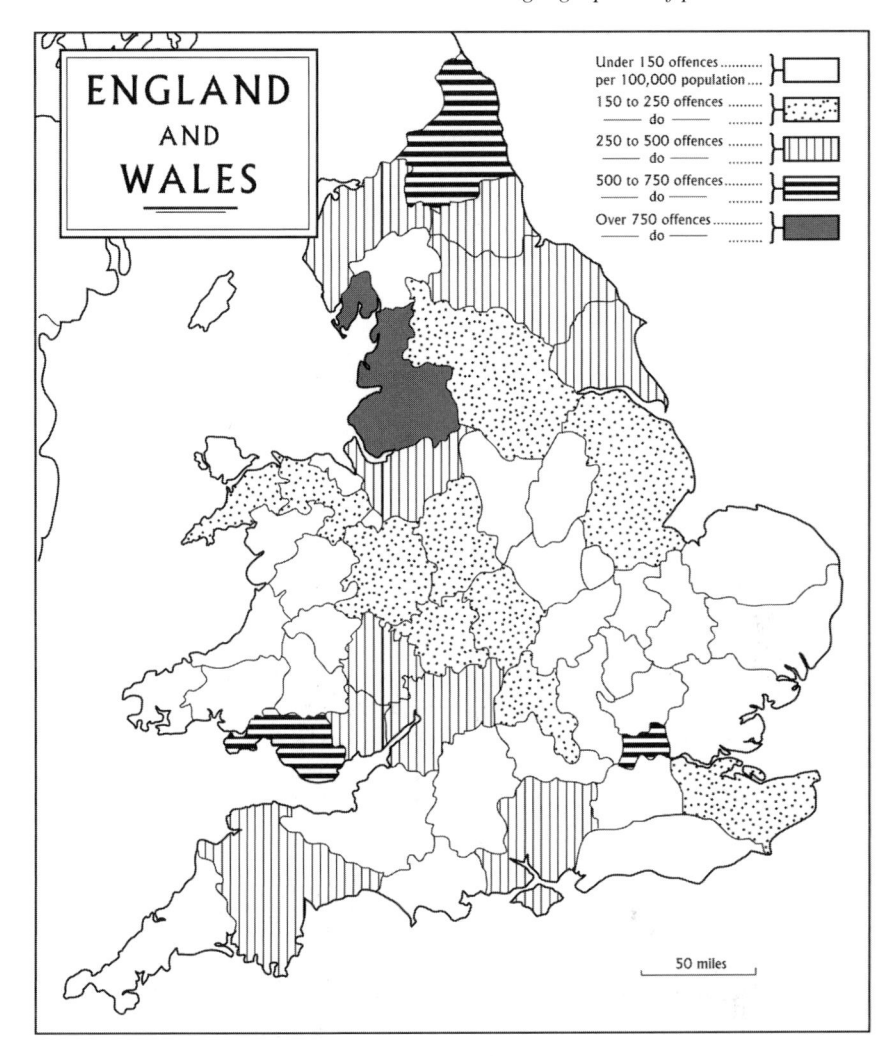

Figure 3.2 Prostitution offences in England and Wales in proportion to the female population aged 15–40, 1871. Source: judicial statistics.

and the industrial towns. It is important to stress that the statistical prominence of Lancashire is owing to the massive pre-eminence of Liverpool; the industrial towns of southern Lancashire – Manchester and its satellites – make only a very limited contribution to the overall figures. It is Liverpool, not industrial Lancashire, which stood out in the map of Victorian immorality. This would have been perfectly clear to Victorian criminal statisticians, and not surprising given the constancy in which the northern counties are singled out for opprobrium, particularly for summary offences. As the statistician Leone Levi had it, adding a characteristic aside to the criminal contribution of Irish immigrants: 'In offences Durham and Lancaster carry the palm. If race be considered an element in the frequency of crime, it may be noticed that the Irish element is most prominent in the north-western and northern counties.'[19]

Whether it is wise to push these statistics as far as this is thus a matter of debate. The historian of Victorian sexuality Michael Mason is certainly too sanguine, making a particular virtue of the police statistics for 'known prostitutes': 'Since they reflect police wisdom rather than the judgements of a court, they are to some extent exempt from the arbitrariness that makes most crime statistics uninformative.'[20] On the other hand, in one of the most pessimistic views, Hera Cook notes that both the fundamental instability of nineteenth-century definitions of the prostitute and the fact that policemen categorised women according to different criteria render the figures virtually useless.[21] The statistician Hammick himself argued that 'it is impossible to accept as entirely trustworthy the police returns of reported offences', particularly given the lack of precise rules for the guidance of the police; and he singled out the discrepancies between the neighbouring towns of Liverpool and Manchester, with high and low figures respectively.[22] Another of his contemporaries similarly insisted that 'the reported numbers of the criminal classes in all the large towns are mere approximations to the actual numbers, and are nearly, if not quite, valueless for the purposes of comparison'.[23] We too must be careful not to claim that this is an accurate representation of the geography of Victorian sex work. There are numerous caveats, perhaps the least important of which is the difficulty in using and mapping Victorian statistics. The fragility of such information, the conversion of acts and behaviours and attitudes into digits and tables, is rather more pertinent, but again this is not the most crucial difficulty. Much more problematic is the problem of police statistics identified by Howard Taylor: that these are the products of heterogeneous police forces, whose budgets, priorities and political programmes effectively determined their pattern of prosecutions.[24] It is hard, as a result, and perhaps impossible, to place any confidence in the police statistics, particularly in their aggregate and comparative form, as reflections of the actual state and nature of sex work in the boroughs of the kingdom.

---

[19] Levi, 'A survey of indictable and summary jurisdiction offences', p. 435.
[20] Mason, *The making of Victorian sexuality*, p. 78.
[21] H. Cook, *The long sexual revolution: English women, sex, and contraception 1800–1975* (Oxford, 2004), p. 79.
[22] Hammick, 'On the judicial statistics of England and Wales', pp. 392–3.
[23] J. T. Bunce, 'On the statistics of crime in Birmingham, as compared with other large towns', *Journal of the Statistical Society*, 28 (1865), 518–26, p. 520.
[24] H. Taylor, 'Rationing crime: the political economy of criminal statistics since the 1850s', *Economic History Review*, 51 (1998), 569–90.

The fact that these statistics are the product of police forces with very different interests and strategies is, however, *precisely* what makes them useful when considering the problem of prostitution and the policies directed towards it. Neither Hera Cook's objections nor Michael Mason's confidence in the ability of policemen to identify prostitutes properly attends to the *political* geography of policing in Victorian Britain. Discrepancies between municipal standards of reporting are indicative of different policing regimes, not merely a lack of epistemological uniformity. As noted, James Hammick singled out differences between Liverpool and Manchester, and so did the Parliamentary report recommending the omission of the 'so-called Police Tables of Character' from future judicial statistics:

> The recent inquiry into the Manchester Police Force shows in a striking manner how little reliance can be placed on returns of a similar character. The annual report of the Chief Constable for Manchester contained a table which purported to include all suspected brothels, but it transpired that it included only houses in respect of which the police possessed such evidence of their being brothels as would enable them to take proceedings against the occupiers. It was even stated in the evidence that this was done in accordance with Home Office instructions. As a matter of fact no such instructions had ever been given by the Home Office, and the tables giving the number of brothels had been discontinued in the Judicial Statistics so long ago as 1872.[25]

The key issue in this regard was the deliberate *underreporting* of brothels by the Manchester police, a charge that had been levelled for many years by the likes of Liverpool's chief constable William Nott-Bower, who objected to the fact that Liverpool was repeatedly portrayed as consistently more immoral than its neighbouring borough as a result. Of such figures, which purported to prove that cities such as Manchester had only a handful of brothels, Nott-Bower simply had this to say: 'the figures condemn themselves, and prove conclusively how utterly *worthless* such statistics are'.[26]

We will come to this dispute between Liverpool and Manchester subsequently, but the point here is that these figures for prostitution crime were a form of political geography, a knowledge constructed by local and national agencies and deployed in the struggle at the municipal level between competing moral regimes. Liverpool, with its commitment to managing prostitution, stood repeatedly condemned in its *knowledge* of brothels and prostitution, whilst Manchester's repressive strategy purported to be successful in cleaning up the borough. These statistics are a portrait of the social body, then, not an anatomy. They are a new form of knowledge composed of but separate from the innumerable discretionary identifications and local criminal proceedings. These maps of prostitution must be taken as an indication of the moral and political construction of the reality of

---

[25] P.P. 1900 [Cd.123] CIII.1, *Report on criminal statistics for England and Wales, 1898*, pp. 191–2.

[26] J. W. Nott-Bower, *Houses of ill-fame, &c. Report of the Head Constable* (Liverpool, 1890), p. 7.

prostitution in the late Victorian period, the establishing of a 'spatial discourse of the social body', as Pamela Gilbert puts it, for 'The social body was a concept increasingly associated with spatial forms of knowledge, especially geographical distributions.'[27]

Liverpool's immoral geographies

At one level, however, the criminal statistics simply confirmed Liverpool's reputation as a city with a perhaps unmatched problem with prostitution. If we consider the history of prostitution in the borough, we must first acknowledge its intransigence and infamy. As a commercial port, one of the great imperial entrepôts, a flourishing prostitution economy was inevitable: as the venereologist Frederick Lowndes put it, unexceptionally, 'Liverpool, being a very large seaport, with a large floating population (a number of seamen estimated at from forty to fifty thousand being present at any given time) … possesses all the conditions which tend to create and foster prostitution.'[28] The city was distinguished, and for critics disfigured, by the ranks of prostitutes living and loitering in the dockside streets and courts. Foreign visitors disembarking in Liverpool took the opportunity to comment on this startling introduction to English life. Herman Melville, for instance, drawing on his first visit to the city, took stock of 'the denizens of notorious Corinthian haunts in the vicinity of the docks, which in depravity are not to be matched by anything this side of the pit that is bottomless'.[29] Beyond the docks, too, in the slums and rookeries of the city, prostitution flourished as an all too characteristic component of the black economy of the female poor.[30]

Many agreed that, bad as it was, there had been *some* improvement in Liverpool over the years, at least in terms of combating the most flagrant public immorality. Reflecting in the 1850s on conditions half a century earlier, Richard Brooke noted that 'The streets of Liverpool frequently exhibited sad scenes of profligacy; abandoned women paraded them in considerable numbers, indulging in disgusting language, noises, and riotous conduct, without any effectual interference from the police'; he went on to say that 'It may, perhaps, be very true that vice is quite as prevalent now as it was at that period, but certainly it is not so openly displayed or so disgustingly prominent.'[31] Michael Mason has noted that some accounts of Liverpool stress the good order and even the elegance of the prostitutes of

[27] P. K. Gilbert, *Mapping the Victorian social body* (Albany, 2004), pp. 21, 4.
[28] Lowndes, *Prostitution and venereal diseases*, p. 2.
[29] H. Melville, *Redburn* (1849), cited in P. Aughton, *Liverpool: a people's history* (Preston, 1990), p. 143.
[30] See W. Bevan, *Prostitution in the borough of Liverpool. A lecture, delivered in the Music Hall, June, 3, 1843* (Liverpool, 1843).
[31] R. Brooke, *Liverpool as it was: 1775 to 1800* (Liverpool, 2003), pp. 299–300.

the borough, whilst others simultaneously condemned these women's 'unbridled lewdness'.[32] The *Morning Chronicle* correspondent, for instance, classed the abandoned women of the town amongst the 'land-sharks', 'parasites and plunderers' who preyed upon the sailors, in the courts of the likes of Denison Street, 'one of the most turbulent, dissipated, and in every way disreputable in the town'.[33] The inconsistency of these accounts, notes Mason, makes it hard to form a clear idea of the nature of prostitution in Liverpool.[34]

For those concerned with prostitution in the later nineteenth century, however, three aspects of Liverpool's moral geography stood out, inoculating them in various ways to the more mollifying accounts of improvement. The first was the continuing high levels of venereal infections, and a more insistent consciousness of their threat to the health of society and to the life of the nation. Earlier moral reformers had not ignored venereal disease, of course, but they had not singled it out in this way as the most deadly consequence of the social evil. In 1843, William Bevan's condemnation of prostitution in Liverpool, for instance, had numbered disease as only one of a series of social costs of prostitution, including such vaguely defined categories as the engendering of 'unnatural spirit' amongst those who practised the profession.[35] In the context of debates over the Contagious Diseases Acts, the moral dimensions of 'social plague' had given way in many quarters to an emphasis on *physical* infections. Lowndes, for example, in recommending that the provisions of the CD Acts be extended to Liverpool and to other 'hot-beds of disease', opined that the disease rate amongst the 2,000 or more prostitutes in the city was between 35 and 38 per cent – a potential source of infection that was uncatered for by the city's provision of lock accommodation.[36] He contrasted this to what he considered to be the very effective state of affairs in Plymouth and the other towns under the supervision of the Acts, where there were improvements not only in social hygiene but also in public morality: 'There were none of those crowds of drunken seamen and low prostitutes which one sees in most sea-ports; and even in those streets where brothels now exist, the most perfect quiet and order prevailed, and no noise nor disorder was to be heard from any of the houses.'[37] Such reflections drew upon regulationist thinking and were bound up with the attempt to extend the schedules of the Contagious Diseases Acts to Liverpool.

A second cause of concern was the significance of Irish immigrants for the economy of prostitution in Liverpool, a theme that was developed alongside these calls for regulationist legislation. Inevitably, given the demographic history of

[32] Quoted in Mason, *The making of Victorian sexuality*, p. 75.
[33] *Morning Chronicle*, 26 August 1850, p. 5.
[34] Mason, *The making of Victorian sexuality*, pp. 74–5.
[35] Bevan, *Prostitution in the borough of Liverpool*.
[36] F. W. Lowndes, *Prostitution and syphilis in Liverpool, and the working of the Contagious Diseases Acts, at Aldershot, Chatham, Plymouth, and Devonport* (London, 1876).
[37] *Ibid.*, p. 25.

Liverpool, and the history of sectarianism and anti-Irish racism in the borough, the contribution of Irish women and girls to the ranks of prostitutes was constantly affirmed. In 1858, for instance, J. T. Danson flatly opined that Liverpool's prostitutes were 'nearly all Irish'.[38] In the same regulationist pamphlet quoted above, Lowndes observed merely that the Irish were overrepresented in prostitution, citing the 1850s statistics that put the Irish-born as making up 44 per cent of the city's prostitutes, and adding that they were disproportionately represented in the lowest classes of prostitutes, serving in the 'black men's brothels' of the city's northern districts.[39] A dozen years later, after the repeal of the CD Acts, Lowndes returned to this theme:

> It is well known that Irish women in their own country are, even amidst very unfavourable surroundings, a most virtuous class, and yet they furnished the largest proportion of prostitutes in this city thirty years ago. I am sorry to add that they have generally belonged to the lowest and most degraded class of prostitutes, living in brothels situated in the very worst streets of the borough, and resorted to by the numerous negroes always present in Liverpool as ships' cooks, stewards, seamen, and labourers. The condition of these women, both physical and moral, is deplorable, and their reclamation is a prospect of which the most hopeful might despair.[40]

Prostitution in Liverpool was racialised, therefore, the immigrant Irish being, for the respectable population of the second city of the Empire, a pre-eminent source of moral and physical contagion. The Irish were 'a permanent residuum of misery' that contributed an enormous financial, sanitary and criminal burden to the respectable classes of the borough.[41] Their reputation as one of the mainstays of Liverpool's criminal classes was long established, and the continuing contribution of Irish women to prostitution was regarded by most as incontrovertible.

It is important to note further that these representations of the city's prostitution economy were very clearly spatialised. Liverpool's brothels were typically appraised in terms not just of character, but also of location and environment. The brothels and accommodation houses of north Liverpool, which contained some of the poorest districts and some of the areas of most dense Irish settlement, were said to be the resorts of the lowest class of prostitutes. These women were reported as living 'in the lowest class of brothels in streets well known to the police as the worst in town, being the abodes of thieves and other bad characters, as well as of prostitutes'.[42] Prostitution here merged into the general degraded environment of the criminal poor, again disproportionately populated by the Irish. In the south,

---

[38] Cited in J. Belchem, *Merseypride: essays in Liverpool exceptionalism* (Liverpool, 2000), p. 114, note 53.
[39] Lowndes, *Prostitution and syphilis*, p. 8.
[40] Lowndes, *Prostitution and venereal diseases*, pp. 3–4.
[41] *Morning Chronicle and London Advertiser*, 20 May 1850, p. 6.
[42] Lowndes, *Prostitution and venereal diseases*, p. 19.

but more particularly in the centre of the city, by contrast, were to be found a wholly distinct class of prostitutes:

> Well-dressed, residing in brothels which are well built houses in streets apparently quiet and respectable, and near to streets of undoubted respectability. These brothels are mostly to be found in the centre of the city, and they have a great tendency to congregate, several streets, all situated together, and of considerable length, being mostly composed of brothels.[43]

This socially and geographically differentiated prostitutional economy may in itself explain why observers sometimes commented on the good order of Liverpool's prostitutes, sometimes on their shamelessness and degradation. For pro-regulationists, although the concentration of prostitution in particular districts did not in itself prevent what they saw as the rampant propagation of venereal disease, the separation of brothels from the criminal neighbourhoods and their relative good order were more promising than the chaotic, unstructured conditions of the city's northern margins.

A third area of concern was the association of prostitution and drink, which took on significance in the later nineteenth century as temperance campaigns were stepped up. This association was of equally long standing, but in Liverpool the development of prostitution and exceptional levels of drunkenness, on the one hand, and prostitution and the drink industry in the borough, on the other, were remarked upon with special force in the second half of the nineteenth century. 'Drunkenness and prostitution are twin abominations', the reformer William Logan, no stranger to Liverpool, had announced.[44] Peter Burne's ironically intemperate attack on intemperance also saw drink as behind the social phenomenon of prostitution, and singled out Liverpool for its moral failures, claiming that prostitutes formed an outrageous one in fifty-nine of the population.[45] In the vital statistics Liverpool stood revealed as the most drunken borough in England, with a rate of drunkenness of 420 per 100,000, the nearest competitor being Newcastle with 372 per 100,000; together with the equally dismal figures for prostitution, these painted a quite desperate portrait of the city's inhabitants. Lowndes unsurprisingly condemned both phenomena, commenting that 'Intemperance is a most inseparable companion of vice, and both lust and drink have, as is well known, a tendency to beget each itself and each other.'[46] Inevitably, too, he singled out the low and degraded, disproportionately Irish, prostitutes of north Liverpool: 'these women are exceptionally low and degraded; constantly appearing in the Police Courts as confirmed drunkards, as well as for soliciting and disorderly

---

[43] *Ibid.*, p. 12.
[44] W. Logan, *The great social evil: its causes, extent, results, and remedies* (London, 1871), p. 60.
[45] P. Burne, *The teetotaler's companion; or, a plea for temperance* (London, 1847), pp. 53–4.
[46] Lowndes, *Prostitution and venereal diseases*, p. 17.

conduct; and being themselves especially liable to assaults from their drunken and degraded male associates.'[47] Drink in this sense was only one more sign of the moral failings of the Liverpool poor.

There were others, however, who took the association between drink and prostitution in quite another direction, one that directly challenged the political establishment in the city. The connections between drink and prostitution were the focus of late nineteenth-century moral and political social purity campaigns in Liverpool, with the links of the city's political leaders to the brewing and drinks trades the central issue, together with alleged complicity in an economy of prostitution that accompanied the culture of drinking. The most powerful refrain had it that the city's Tory masters had no interest in taking action against brothels and prostitutes, since doing so would cut the custom of the public houses and cut into their profits.[48] The Reverend Richard Armstrong's extraordinary 1890 pamphlet, *The deadly shame of Liverpool*, laid out the charges with a finely calculated calumny. The principal evil, he affirmed, was 'the knitting together of the wholesale liquor trade, of drunkenness, and of prostitution on an enormous scale, in one vast, compact interest, and the power which that interest has obtained within the governing bodies of Liverpool'.[49] The systematic and cynical diversion of monies from the poor to the rich, via both the brewhouses and the brothels, was the foundation of the brewers' fortunes and their political power in the city. The magistrates' bench, upon which sat Alderman John Hughes, legal adviser to the two great Liverpool brewers Walker and Cain, was charged with refusing to enact the repressive provisions of the Criminal Law Amendment Act; the Watch Committee and the police, under Sir William Nott-Bower, were equally unwilling, it seemed, to challenge the economic and political hegemony of the Tory brewers. In this indictment of Liverpool's entire political establishment, Armstrong put the case for the energetic suppression of known brothels, and the extirpation of this lingering source of municipal shame.

The details of this campaign are considered below, but the divergent views of Lowndes and Armstrong will serve to indicate the contours of the debate about prostitution in late nineteenth-century Liverpool. For pro-regulationists such as Lowndes, the problem of venereal disease in Liverpool authorised the extension of the Contagious Diseases Acts to the city, the attempt to regulate and better manage a prostitutional economy that could not be wished away. In the face of the failure of this campaign, the management of the brothel economy by the municipality, with its degree of supervision and control over brothel districts long established and well known to the police, was preferable to futile attempts to suppress

---

[47] *Ibid.*, p. 19.
[48] P. J. Waller, *Democracy and sectarianism: a political and social history of Liverpool 1868–1939* (Liverpool, 1981), pp. 106–7.
[49] R. A. Armstrong, *The deadly shame of Liverpool. An appeal to the municipal voters* (London, 1890), p. 5.

prostitution entirely.[50] Lowndes, who became police surgeon in 1877, was closely linked to a coterie that included the Chief Constable of police, Nott-Bower, and the city's Watch Committee, all of whom believed that their responsibility was the regulation rather than the repression of prostitution. On the other hand, for social purists like Armstrong, the inaction of the police against flagrant and visible brothel districts in the heart of the city pointed to police and municipal complicity with prostitution, and, worse, a corrupt synergy of interests between the brothel keepers and the borough's political class. For these critics the policies developed in Liverpool were straightforwardly regulationist and clearly immoral. They aligned themselves with the currents of social purity politics that flowed from the successful campaign against the Contagious Diseases Acts, and which aimed at what Lucy Bland has called the purification of the public world.[51] This was the political context for the development of prostitution policy in Liverpool, a development that would put the borough at odds with national legislation and the cultural and political ascendancy of the purity parties by the last decade of the nineteenth century.

Prostitution and municipal policy

We need also to consider Victorian Liverpool in the context of the various municipal experiments in prostitution policy that characterise the period as a whole. As has been noted, discussion of Victorian prostitution has been dominated by the short but contentious career of the Contagious Diseases Acts. Far less attention has been given to the management of prostitution in areas outside their very restricted remit. They did not extend to London, let alone to the second city and seemingly unchallenged capital of prostitution, Liverpool. For most of the nineteenth century, the vast landscape of British prostitution was barely touched by central state intervention, with the attempt to extend the Acts in the 1870s nationwide a resounding failure. Prostitution policy in Victorian Britain was largely directed and inspired by municipal experiment and discretion, resulting in a distinctively variegated policy map.

We still know far too little about the policing of prostitution in the municipalities. Linda Mahood's major work on Glasgow remains the most significant contribution, insofar as she describes the city's policy as both example and exemplar.[52] In Glasgow, aggressive suppression of brothel prostitution and street solicitation,

---

[50] Lowndes, *Prostitution and venereal diseases*, p. 40: 'it appears to me unwise to set the law in motion against brothels which have existed in the same locality for many years, except for very grave reasons, or with the certainty that they will be respectably tenanted in future.'
[51] L. Bland, *Banishing the beast: English feminism and sexual morality 1885–1914* (Harmondsworth, 1995), ch. 3.
[52] L. Mahood, *The magdalenes: prostitution in the nineteenth century* (London, 1990).

more or less formally combined with the agency of lock hospital and magdalen, constituted a system of police repression that contrasted sharply with the regulationist approach encoded in the CD Acts and practised in the towns under their schedule. For some critics, this did not quite go far enough, and the charge of 'veiled regulation' was laid, but in the national context Glasgow clearly represented the *repressive* extreme of municipal prostitution policy. Significantly, this model was copied not just in Scotland, but also in a number of English cities including Manchester, Birmingham, Sheffield and Leeds. In Birmingham, for instance, Paula Bartley has demonstrated how powerful was an alliance of class ideologies, a feminine civic gospel, and a range of private philanthropic ventures driven by common philosophies of moral education, reform and protection. For Bartley, the 'complex mixture of repression, protection, and liberation' that may be found in the work of the local branch of the National Vigilance Association from 1885 can be traced in earlier theories and practices of moral politics in Birmingham.[53] She rightly points out that a local and regional perspective is a necessary counterpoint to national surveys with overly assertive and generalised accounts of moral politics, and to suggest that similar local enterprises, taken together, constituted an 'archipelago of reform'.[54] In cities like Birmingham, the agencies of social rescue and the activities of social purists certainly take centre stage.

In our context, though, it is *Manchester* that most concerns us, the neighbouring Lancashire city offering an example of proactive policing that contrasted with the apparently lax and *laissez-faire* Liverpool. Edward Mynott, in an important unpublished thesis, has shown how Manchester's approach to policing prostitution developed in direct emulation of Glasgow's repressive strategy, with seemingly very close co-operation between the police and purity reformers, and with apparent success in ridding the city of both brothels and prostitutes.[55] Like Birmingham, Manchester could claim to have taken the lead in tackling prostitution through a combination of repression and rescue work. Manchester's claim to be, as one incoming Chief Constable put it, 'the most moral town in England' was ultimately destroyed by scandalous revelations in the 1890s of police collusion and corruption, and evidence of a manipulation of the crime statistics bordering on fraud. The success of its 'zero tolerance' approach, if we may be allowed an anachronism, was exposed by the end of the nineteenth century as a straightforward sham. Nevertheless, the very public, political contrast for much of the late nineteenth century between the *repressive* strategy of Manchester and the '*tacit regulation*' of Liverpool is compelling.[56]

---

[53] P. A. Bartley, 'Seeking and saving: the reform of prostitutes and the prevention of prostitution in Birmingham 1860–1914' (PhD, Wolverhampton University, 1995), p. 195.
[54] *Ibid.*, p. 119.
[55] E. Mynott, 'Purity, prostitution and politics: social purity in Manchester 1880–1900' (PhD, University of Manchester, 1995).
[56] *Ibid.*, p. 443, emphasis added.

The Liverpool system, in the period 1872 to 1890, was one of pragmatic policing or management, for which the tag of *laissez-faire* was never really appropriate. The origins of this policy are difficult to trace, in their informality and their studied pragmatism, but there is no reason to doubt that this approach to prostitution, preferring to maintain brothels in places where they might more readily be supervised, was a long-standing practice in Liverpool, and possibly the most typical approach of municipal police forces generally. In Dublin, for instance, the existence of a central brothel district – the famous 'Monto' – was widely recognised; although again not evidence of a formal commitment to regulationism, it followed the axioms of the policy, and was considered by commentators and critics to be an iconic example of the police and municipal toleration of prostitution. It may well be that Liverpool and Dublin and other cities are typical, and Manchester, Birmingham and Glasgow the exceptional cases. Be that as it may, it was Liverpool that became identified with the implicitly regulationist approach to policing prostitution.

Chief Constable William Nott-Bower, one of the most prominent policemen in the realm, and arguably the major architect of prostitution policy in the city, offered in this regard a perfectly clear and concise statement of regulationist philosophy:

Brothels and prostitution have existed in all ages of the world, and the evils in connection therewith may be checked and moderated, but cannot be suppressed by human effort, and the attempt to effect suppression by men of the highest character, and with the best possible intentions, has frequently served only to aggravate the evils they desired to subdue.[57]

Though sometimes charged by its critics as a *'laissez-faire'* or 'let-alone' system, this was in fact a *proactive* policy. In Nott-Bower's mind, this was an 'even and systematic' policy of controlled intervention. The police would take action against brothels and houses of assignation only if one of the following conditions was met: if young girls were found to be living in the house; if robberies were suspected to have taken place there, even if no convictions had been achieved; if they were of 'a notoriously bad character'; if they had been opened in a street hitherto free of such houses; or if two or more inhabitants complained and were willing to provide evidence to substantiate that complaint. This pointedly pragmatic policy, Nott-Bower averred, recognised the limitations of both the existing statutes and of the moral law. For the Chief Constable, this was the only humane, sensible and, above all, realistic policy towards prostitution. The alternatives, particularly the attempts to suppress prostitution altogether, were not only futile but would also make the problems associated with the trade worse. The only effect of such policing, Nott-Bower pointed out in a common refrain, was to 'broadcast' prostitution throughout the city, introducing it into hitherto 'respectable'

---

[57] *Head Constable's special report book 1886–1890*, Liverpool Record Office, 352 POL 2/11, 23 December 1889.

neighbourhoods, and driving it underground and out of any possibility of effective police supervision.

It is for exactly this reason that Nott-Bower poured scorn on the criminal statistics that claimed to demonstrate the failings of Liverpool's people and their leaders. Though these appeared to show that the city's standards of morality lagged behind the likes of Manchester and most of the other towns in the kingdom, these statistics were – he noted – based on entirely false premises. The possibility for instance that Manchester had only five brothels in 1890, or Glasgow fifteen, or Sheffield none at all, was for him simply ludicrous: 'The Head Constable would only say that the figures condemn themselves, and prove conclusively how utterly *worthless* such statistics are.'[58] For Nott-Bower, this entire comparative project, this attempt to portray the social body by way of moral cartography, was a waste of time. This echoes the complaints of the *Morning Chronicle*'s Liverpool correspondent in 1850, that 'the science of statistics is one which does not flourish in this town' – except of course that in this case *only* Liverpool's returns were worthy of being believed.[59]

The central issue for supporters of regulating prostitution was the purported underreporting of brothels by the Manchester police, a charge that had been levelled for many years by Nott-Bower. In the first place, there was ample evidence for statistical undercounting, an evident massaging of the figures for political purposes; furthermore, though, the fact that these few were only those brothels categorised 'known to the police' indicated that prostitution had simply been driven into discretion and invisibility by the repressive policy. As Nott-Bower pointedly argued:

> It is at least open to question whether, by procuring for Liverpool such powers as are already possessed by Manchester, any really substantial good would be effected, though doubtless the number of prosecutions would be increased and the statistical returns probably improved.

Nott-Bower went on to add, striking an ingenuous and ingenious note: 'This however is of course a matter entirely for the Public, and not for the Police.'[60] He would leave it up to others whether they really wanted to know about prostitution in the city, or pretend to themselves and others not to know.

Indeed, in this view, the statistical portrayal of prostitution in Liverpool could be adduced not as a mark of shame but as the sign of a *successful* prostitution policy: 'That the police of Liverpool know of 443 brothels in this town, whilst the police of Sheffield know of none within that borough, may possibly be proof of the superior local knowledge of the Liverpool police and of the advantages of the system under which they work.'[61] This may also be used to explain the seeming

---

[58] Nott-Bower, *Houses of ill-fame*, p. 7.   [59] *Morning Chronicle*, 24 June 1850, p. 5.
[60] *Head Constable's special report book 1883–86*, Liverpool Record Office 352/POL/2/10, 15 June 1885.
[61] Nott-Bower, *Houses of ill-fame*, p. 6.

contradiction in the figures between a system of toleration in Liverpool generating high levels of prosecutions for prostitution offences, and a system of repression in Manchester producing many fewer prosecutions. Quite apart from the real differences in prostitution levels between the boroughs, we can point to the fact that Liverpool aggressively policed prostitutes and brothel-owners working outside the areas in which it was more or less tolerated, whilst Manchester was institutionally interested in playing down the problem of prostitution, paradoxically prosecuting less often. Both suggestions follow from the fact that the statistics were no real guide to the actual levels of prostitution in the boroughs; they had everything to do with the different policies adopted in the neighbouring towns.

The debate over statistics aside, this was the example that Liverpool set for the nation: a policy of managing prostitution, rather than repressing it. It was a policy that closely followed the formulae of regulationist thinking, which certainly survived, albeit informally, and albeit at a municipal level, the demise of the CD Acts at home. This was a system of regulation, for its proponents, of which Liverpool could be proud rather than embarrassed. As Nott-Bower went on to say in his report to the Watch Committee, with a sideways glance at the graphic revelations of homosexual activity in other cities, and with an assumption of heterosexual purity as hopelessly heroic as that of Manchester's virtual eradication of prostitution:

The Head Constable will only say in conclusion that whilst the character of Liverpool, in regard to the social evil, has been unduly blackened by some who might be supposed to desire her fair fame, it is at least a source of satisfaction to know, beyond doubt, that no town is so free as Liverpool from the grosser outrages of female virtue, whilst the hideous and unspeakable crimes which have lately disgraced so many other large towns in the Kingdom have not been heard of in this City.[62]

This system of policing could be portrayed as both modern and progressive, attentive to the eternal weaknesses of human nature and also in the best interests of both the women who degraded themselves and the clients who degraded them. In the context of British society, this was one of the closest equivalents to the policy of regulationism espoused across the Channel and across Europe. If it was expressed in a distinctively British idiom, it nevertheless shared in those systems' commitment to social hygiene and discipline.

Localisation, containment and social geography

Late-nineteenth-century Liverpool was, therefore, an important political exemplar for regulation – not the regulationism of the CD Acts and their continental cousins, but with a similar commitment to managing rather than attempting to suppress the sex trade. The area where the similarities between formal regulationist regimes and those, like Liverpool, on the spectrum of regulationism are most glaringly

[62] *Ibid.*, p. 10.

obvious is the stance taken towards the social geography of prostitution. As we have seen, the formal regulationist regimes attempted to confine prostitution in brothel houses, and often (though not necessarily) in certain well-designated brothel districts. The attempt to enclose prostitution was the basis for the disciplining of the prostitute. In Liverpool, this approach was referred to as a policy of containment, or 'localisation'. This was based around the restriction of brothels, as far as possible, to certain carefully managed districts of the city. Nott-Bower's reminiscences make this clear, and also serve to establish the link between knowledge and power emphasised by Corbin as the ambition of regulation: 'to enclose in order to observe, to observe in order to know, to know in order to supervise and control.'[63] As we have seen, the question of knowledge was central to the issue of policy; we may add, following Corbin, that the ability to place the prostitute, to enclose her in brothels and in known neighbourhoods, was an essential element of this administrative practice of knowledge. In Nott-Bower's words:

> There were, necessarily, in a town like Liverpool, many such houses in existence, but they were generally located in special streets. They were *'known* to the Police,' who did not as a rule take action against them, for it was felt that any action taken would not result in decreasing the number of such houses, but only driving them into neighbourhoods unaffected by the evil, and where (so far as any chance of prosecution was concerned) they would be *'unknown'* to the Police.[64]

It was consistently argued that containing houses of prostitution within their current locales, by vigorously repressing houses that appeared in areas hitherto free of the taint of commercial sexuality, was conducive to proper supervision and management: 'The Head Constable', the Watch Committee was informed in 1881, 'has always felt it necessary to lay down clear principles of action in the consistent carrying out of law; and with relation to this branch, he is only too well aware, that to remove houses of the kind named from any neighbourhood is only to distribute them into streets where they did not formerly exist, and so greatly aggravate the evil intended to be removed.'[65] These principles, even after the national demise of regulationism, and even after the passing of the Criminal Law Amendment Act in 1885, continued to be the cornerstone of Liverpool's prostitution policy. The venereologist Frederick Lowndes, for instance, the great enthusiast for regulation, insisted that, whilst the provisions of the Criminal Law Amendment Act were welcome, they should not be implemented in such a way as to disturb the geography of tolerated prostitution in the city: 'It appears to me to

---

[63] A. Corbin, *Women for hire: prostitution and sexuality in France after 1850* (Cambridge, MA, 1990), p. 16.
[64] W. Nott-Bower, *Fifty-two years a policeman* (London, 1926), pp. 140–1, emphasis in original.
[65] *Head Constable's special report book 1880–1883*, Liverpool Record Office 352/POL/2/9, 23 May 1881.

be unwise to set the law in motion against brothels which have existed in the same locality for many years, except for very grave reasons, or with the certainty that they will be respectably tenanted in future.'[66]

Commitment to principle, and consistency of purpose, meant, moreover, that the Liverpool police had an exceptionally precise knowledge of the geography of commercial sexuality. Abraham Hume's mid-century identification of streets of crime and immorality, apparently produced with help from the municipality, suggests that police surveillance was already established with some precision.[67] In 1882, too, the Chief Surgeon of the Liverpool Lock Hospital provided the commissioners investigating the Contagious Diseases Acts with a map of the principal streets containing brothel houses, a map compiled with the help of the borough police. This has not survived, but in 1890 the police themselves provided a report to the Watch Committee detailing eight 'brothel districts' in Liverpool containing 421 brothels, and 994 prostitute women (Figure 3.3).[68] This figure may be compared to the roughly 1,200 prostitutes who were noted as being 'known to the police' in the later decades of the nineteenth century: we might surmise that somewhere in the region of 80 per cent of sex workers on the police's unofficial registers were placed in this zone of implicit if not formal surveillance. The figures are summarised in the appendix to this chapter but it should be emphasised that the Chief Constable's report proceeds street by street and court by court, providing a quite extraordinary mapping of commercial sexuality in late Victorian Liverpool. Drawn up in such a detailed and regimented form, it is hard to avoid the comparisons with much more explicitly regulationist regimes.

The epicentre of this system of containment was, undoubtedly, Blandford Street (Figure 3.4). When Armstrong noted of the city's brothel district that '[s]ome of the streets are almost entirely composed of houses of ill-fame, some of the courts contain no other dwelling of any kind', he could be thinking of no other thoroughfare.[69] Blandford Street was locally notorious, and amounted to a shorthand or synecdoche for the entire landscape of prostitution in the city. The *Liverpool Citizen*, for instance, ran a story entitled 'The Results of a Visit to Blandford Street!' in which it was reported that one unlucky drinker was enticed into a house of ill repute in the street, and has been ever since in one of these 'traps for Hell'.[70] We do not have to rely upon anecdote and sensation journalism, however, for the statistical details of the police report may be utilised further. The precision of the Liverpool police's regulation and registration of brothel

---

[66] Lowndes, *Prostitution and venereal diseases*, p. 40.
[67] Rev. A. Hume, *Condition of Liverpool, religious and social; including notices of the state of education, morals, pauperism, and crime*, 2nd edition (Liverpool, 1858).
[68] See the appendix to this chapter.
[69] Nott-Bower, *Houses of ill-fame*, p. 11.
[70] *Liverpool Citizen*, 18 September 1889, p. 4.

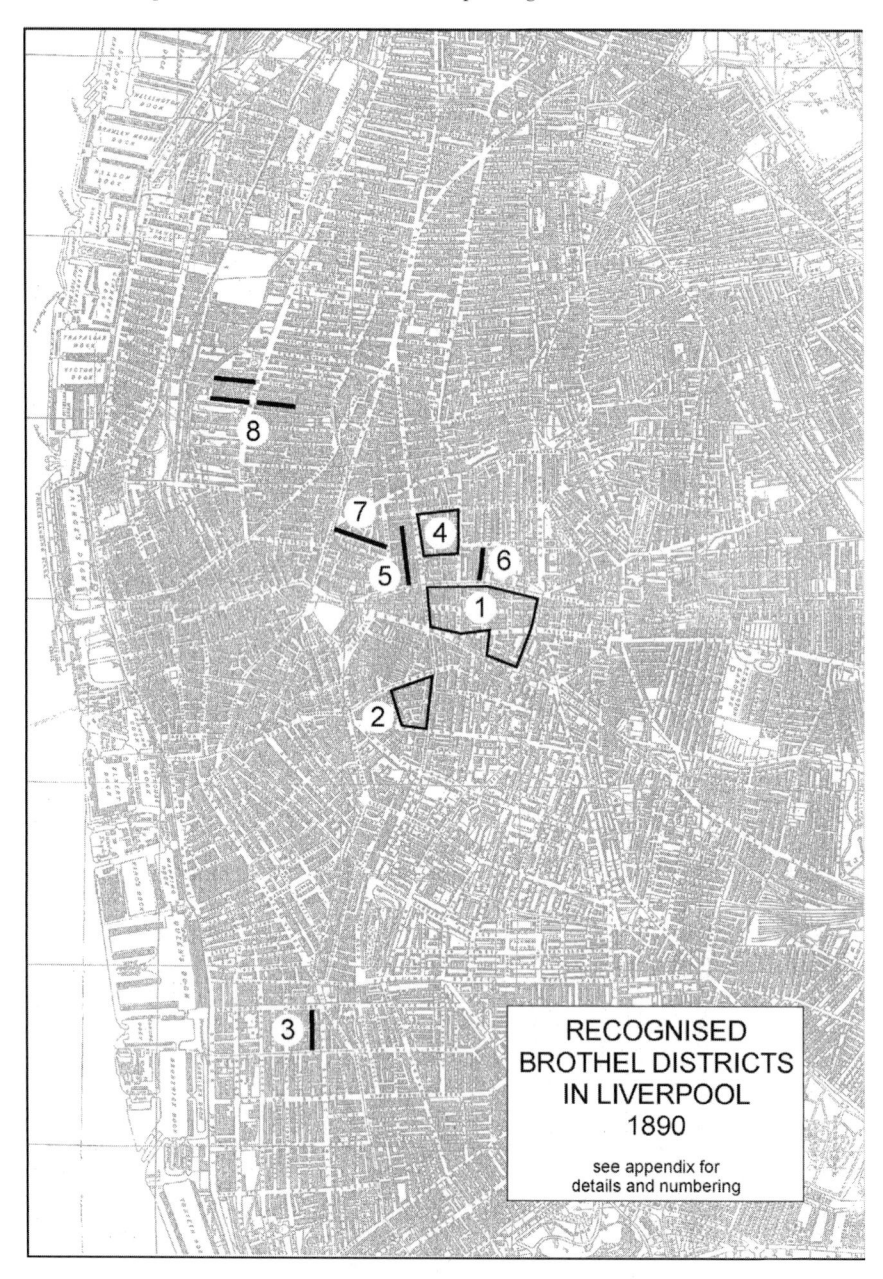

Figure 3.3 Brothel districts in Liverpool, c.1890. Source: Liverpool Record Office, 352/POL/2/12, *Head Constable's Special Report Book 1890–2*, 2 September 1890.

Figure 3.4 Blandford Street, Liverpool, c.1890. Courtesy of Liverpool Central Library.

prostitution, unofficial and discreet as it is, might well be unique. It offers us the opportunity to try to reconstruct something of the nature of these houses and the women who worked in them. Working backwards from 1890 to the census of 1881, we can move beyond location and locale to the social structure of these brothel houses and their residents. Using the 1881 census, it is easy if not quite straightforward to produce a list of putative brothels, given that we know that these districts – and particularly that of Blandford Street – had an association with commercial sexuality over many decades. Proceeding on the assumption that such houses typically (if not exclusively) contain an older, female head of household, with one or more, younger female residents, unrelated to each other and to the householder, it is possible to provisionally identify these brothel and accommodation houses. Sometimes their residents are listed as dressmakers, milliners, seamstresses or tailoresses, and so on, but the majority are without legitimate employment, and a few are straightforwardly enumerated as 'unfortunates'. I have still tended to be cautious, and to give houses the benefit of any doubt, usually passing over single householders, and also usually excluding those listed as servants within the household. The presence of male visitors and the location of the household within the environs of many suspected houses

	1881 (putative)	1890 (recognised)
Brothels with 6 resident prostitutes	1 (6 women)	2 (12 women)
Brothels with 5 prostitutes	0 (0 women)	2 (10 women)
Brothels with 4 resident prostitutes	10 (40 women)	6 (24 women)
Brothels with 3 resident prostitutes	30 (90 women)	33 (99 women)
Brothels with 2 resident prostitutes	40 (80 women)	123 (246 women)
Houses of accommodation	70 (70 women)	69 (69 women)
Total	151 (286 women)	235 (460 women)

have influenced my judgement, certainly, but this exercise is still likely to under- rather than over-represent the numbers of brothels. Even with this exercise of caution, over 150 suspected brothels and nearly 300 suspected prostitute women can be identified in the Blandford Street district in 1881, 65 per cent and 62 per cent of the respective 1890 figures.

These 'brothels', if they truly can be taken as such, are to be found in tightly clustered courts and sections of streets: a microgeography of commercial sexuality in which, we may surmise, a combination of business imperatives and police supervision forced prostitute women and their houses to associate and bind themselves together. Certain streets are particularly good examples of this process. The half of Oakes Street that falls within the police-recognised district contains thirty-one brothels, whilst the half that falls outside it contains not a single one. Norman Street, which runs into Oakes Street, contains thirty brothel households out of only forty-eight for the entire street. In this area, then, the visibility and density of prostitution businesses is striking, confirming the reality of localisation in Liverpool. Broken down into household structure, we can also essay the comparison shown in the table above between suspected houses in 1881 and the police statistics for known brothels and houses of accommodation in the district in 1890.

There is a reasonably close comparability between these figures that indicates a remarkable stability in the structure of the enclosed prostitution business in Liverpool. There does seem to be variation *within* this district – in 1880, for instance, there are many more brothel houses in Norman Street than in Lambert Street, the reverse of the 1890 figures – but the similarity in numbers and structure for the Blandford Street area as a whole is notable. This suggests, if not precisely confirms, the municipal management, in fact the authorisation, of Liverpool's prostitution trade.

From the census statistics we may also essay a portrayal of these suggested brothel residents themselves, again to forward this characterisation. First, the average age of this suspected prostitute cohort is nearly twenty-five, a relatively advanced age. 50 per cent of these women are in the age bracket twenty-one to twenty-five, which may again be compared to the 50 per cent of prostitutes in Victorian York recorded by Finnegan as under the age of twenty.[71] Of course, here we are considering brothel residents, rather than the presumably much younger streetwalkers and other members of the casual and independent sexual proletariat. In Blandford Street and its environs we have by contrast what looks like a more 'professional' cadre of women, more firmly ensconced in a world of enclosed prostitution. We may indeed better compare these women with the registered sex workers of the continental systems of regulation. In France for instance, most *filles soumises* were registered between the ages of twenty-one and twenty-five, even if the typical age of *filles de maison* seems to have been considerably older.[72] In Russia, in 1889, 42 per cent of brothel prostitutes were aged twenty to twenty-five, and in late nineteenth-century Italy registered prostitutes were typically in their early twenties.[73]

Secondly, the geographical origins of these putative prostitutes suggests that over 40 per cent were born in the city of Liverpool itself, and this figure rises to around 60 per cent if we include the rest of Lancashire and Cheshire. Yet again, we may compare this geographical breakdown to the prostitutional topography of continental regulationism. This is a marked contrast to the figures from the mid-nineteenth century cited by Lowndes, in which a majority of prostitutes taken into custody by the police came not just from outside the city and its neighbouring counties, but from outside of England itself – including the 44 per cent from Ireland.[74] Lowndes, without considering the effects of the Irish Famine, or the intervening years, dwells in 1886 on the large proportion of the prostitutes who come from Ireland. Some modern commentators have followed this lead in disparaging the Irish poor.[75] It is certainly possible to use the Chief Constable's crime reports to get a fuller picture of the origins of prostitutes, and to support this characterisation. The age, degree of education, and countries of persons apprehended for a variety of offences determined summarily was tabulated annually, no doubt helping those interested to identify the sources of moral deviance and deterioration. The proportion of Irish women apprehended for prostitution offences under the Vagrancy Act remains relatively constant, being 26.33% in the police year 1874–5, 20.65% in the year 1884–5, and 21.87% in 1889–90. This visible Irish group would have made an easy target for those

---

[71] F. Finnegan, *Poverty and prostitution: a study of Victorian prostitutes in York* (Cambridge, 1979), p. 76.
[72] Corbin, *Women for hire*, pp. 42–3.
[73] See L. Bernstein, *Sonia's daughters: prostitutes and their regulation in imperial Russia* (Berkeley, 1995), p. 99, M. Gibson, *Prostitution and the state in Italy, 1860–1915* (New Brunswick, 1986), pp. 107–9.
[74] Lowndes, *Prostitution and venereal diseases*, p. 3.
[75] See for instance W. R. Cockcroft, 'The Liverpool police force, 1836–1902', in S. P. Bell (ed.), *Victorian Lancashire* (Newton Abbot, 1974), p. 160.

who were convinced that Liverpool's problems were only exacerbated by the children of Erin. But, of the putative prostitutes derived from the 1881 census, a mere 15% were Irish – and this is a figure almost exactly proportionate with Liverpool's Irish-born population as a whole. Now this does not necessarily mean that the ranks of Liverpool's sex workers were not disproportionately Irish; and there may well be reasons why brothel prostitutes were less likely to be immigrants. It could well be, with the suggestion of a bifurcated prostitution trade in mind, that the Irish were indeed overwhelmingly to be found in the city's margins, in the more or less unsupervised sexual economy rated by critics as the lowest end of the profession. But they would have to be there in remarkable numbers to justify Lowndes' and others' figures; there is no evidence, here at least, to suggest that this characterisation of the trade is anything but caricature.

All this is evidence of course for the relative success of the Watch Committee and the Liverpool police in managing the sex trade in the later nineteenth century. If we can take these women to be representatives of Victorian Liverpool's largest red light district, once again we are directed to a portrait of a *managed* system of prostitution, an informal regulationist regime with perhaps closer comparisons to the continent than to the situation of avowedly repressionist neighbours like Manchester.

Abolitionism, social purity and the end of tolerance

This 1890 police report was a portrait of a world that was soon to vanish, however, for the strength of purity reformers and vigilance activists was increasing, and the room for manoeuvre for municipalities was shrinking. For the moral reform party, in all its variety, the 1880s saw significant victories – the Contagious Diseases Acts were suspended, and repealed, and a new piece of legislation, the Criminal Law Amendment Act of 1885, had specifically outlawed the keeping of brothels. More than that, it had encouraged concerned citizens, drawn of course from the ranks of respectability, to complain of suspected houses and to initiate prosecutions. It has been suggested that the formation and activity of vigilance groups led to a dramatic rise in prosecutions of brothel-keepers, with police forces and vigilance groups acting in close co-operation to suppress brothels. Certainly, in places like Birmingham and Manchester, whose police chiefs signed up to the National Vigilance Association, there is evidence for a concerted campaign to banish brothels, using the tools provided by the 1885 legislation. The diversion of the energies and activities of feminists into social purity campaigns that were every bit as marked by the class and gender double standards as the regulationist policies, has been rehearsed by many historians. Some are willing to argue for the achievements of purity activists, but most have seen their results as oppressive and unjust, their efforts at protection paradoxically exposing working-class women to greater surveillance and coercion. Although these moral reformers came in many guises – the White Cross Army, the Social Purity Alliance and the National Vigilance Association being only the most well known – Paula Bartley has called this 'a more or less consistent policy of repression'.[76] From the perspective of the state rather than private philanthropy, Frank Mort has characterised this period as 'a new, more coercive system of state intervention into the domain of sexuality'.[77]

The ascendancy of this 'repressive system' may be exaggerated in its speed, spread and eventual success, however.[78] Bartley has pointed out that co-operation between police and purity activists was far from universal, with the Criminal Law Amendment Act a dead letter in many areas, and Mort has summed up the resistance of politicians and administrators to cede power to busybody moralists in the localities as the response of the 'reluctant state'.[79] In fact, in many cities the police and local authorities were far from convinced of the merits of private moral reformers and the workability of the Criminal Law Amendment Act. In Liverpool, to take perhaps the most important site of resistance to municipal puritanism, the provisions of the Act were resisted from the start, with no change to the policy of localisation that had continued for several decades. The immediate rearguard action was to investigate the workings of legislation – both national and local – in a number of towns, prominent amongst which were Glasgow, Birmingham, Manchester and Sheffield, where a repressive system was in force. The greatest effort, though, as ever, was to compare the contrasting operations of the police in Liverpool and Manchester. It was emphasised that Manchester, empowered by the provisions of its 1875 Improvement Act, could take summary action against brothels in a manner that was impossible in Liverpool; but there was no conviction that changing the local statutes would achieve anything but an improvement in the borough's statistical returns.[80] Instead, Nott-Bower stuck to the wisdom of the policy of tolerance, that is, 'to diminish the number of these houses, but also to localize, and bring under the closer supervision of the Police, those which remain'.[81]

It is precisely this concentration of known brothels that laid the police open to attack, though, to the charge that it was 'soft' on prostitution, effectively conniving at its existence and indeed even encouraging it. Purity groups, having succeeded at the national, legislative level, increasingly turned their attention towards pressurising local police and politicians to enact the law and banish known brothels

---

[76] Bartley, *Prostitution*, p. 155.
[77] Mort, *Dangerous sexualities*, p. 105.
[78] Bland, *Banishing the beast*, p. 109.
[79] Bartley, *Prostitution*, pp. 161–8, Mort, *Dangerous sexualities*, pp. 126, 126–30.
[80] Liverpool Record Office, *Head Constable's special report book, 1883–1886*, 15 June 1885.
[81] Nott-Bower, *Houses of ill-fame*, pp. 4–5; Nott-Bower, *Fifty-two years a policeman*, p. 141.

from their boroughs. In Liverpool, the activities of these reformers were trained on police and politicians alike, confronting them with evidence of brothels and streetwalking women in the city, and enjoining them to use the new statutory powers to eliminate these evils. Liverpool's record of seeming equivocation and footdragging was compared by them, unfavourably, with that of Manchester and other municipalities who appeared to be much more proactive and successful in dealing with prostitution offences. To these critics, the city's policy towards prostitution disgraced the very name of Liverpool.

The efforts of the Liverpool Vigilance Committee were particularly important in portraying the actions of the police force and watch committee as out of step with both local and national opinion. As they described it in their retrospective complaint of the city fathers:

Four hundred houses were so tolerated and protected, and this policy of protection and toleration, inaugurated by the Chief Constable, had the support of the Watch Committee, and the majority of the members of the City Council. By the Watch Committee, a manifesto, in favour of a stricter administration of the law, was treated with contempt, though it was signed by the Bishop, the Archdeacon, and many leading citizens.[82]

This was a knowledge that could not be confined to either expert or administrative circles; instead, it was an open secret, common knowledge, which only served to point out Liverpool's moral equivocation with vice. Once again, we see here an emphasis on the entanglement of prostitution policy with the politics of knowledge itself. In the context of the Criminal Law Amendment Act, and the new powers for ratepayers and vigilance groups to pressure the police to repress all known brothels, this geographical knowledge was politically charged and an incitement to protest and political activism.[83] This is how a special committee of magistrates in the borough, seeking to align Liverpool with the letter and spirit of national legislation, put it in 1889:

Whether the large number of brothels then known to the police, to exist has increased or diminished we have no means of ascertaining, but that a very large number of such houses do exist is within the common knowledge of all persons even superficially acquainted with the City.[84]

Efforts on this occasion failed in the face of stonewalling by Nott-Bower and the Watch Committee. But the pressure of purity campaigners outside the magistracy, and political opponents within it, was beginning to be felt. The old Tory establishment in Liverpool was for the first time in fifty years on the defensive, attacked on a number of fronts, and beginning to lose political control of the

---

[82] *Vigilance Record*, October 1892, p. 72, cited in Bartley, *Prostitution*, p. 167.
[83] Bland, *Banishing the beast*, pp. 101–5.
[84] *City of Liverpool. Report of the special committee of magistrates on the state of the laws affecting houses of ill-fame within the city, and to consider the best mode of putting the laws in force* (Liverpool, 1889), p. 4.

borough. The two areas where it was revealed to be extremely vulnerable were the problems of drink and of prostitution. Drink, as noted above, was an issue that had dogged the city's leaders for many years, not only for the extraordinarily high levels of drunkenness recorded in Liverpool but also for the apparent lack of political will to use the licensing system to combat the evil. For instance, the temperance campaigner Dr Lundie accused the Chief Constable of 'preferential application of the licensing laws and allowing the moral condition of the town to degenerate to an appalling degree', with only a single publican brought before the court on licensing charges.[85] Other critics argued that the Tories' connections with the drinks and brewing industry were to blame, and that the political establishment actively encouraged intemperance. These were the same charges as were laid against the toleration of prostitution, of course, albeit in a different register. The fiercest antagonists of the Tory establishment had no hesitation in linking the two, and, as we have seen, the Reverend Richard Armstrong drew particular attention to the concentration of brothels in the centre of the city, which he saw not as toleration but as a concession to the interests of brothel-owners. Nothing else, for these outraged moral reformers, so proved collusion and complicity than this geography of managed prostitution. The presence of such 'hot-beds of vice' in the heart of the city was in itself a condemnation of the municipality's morals.

This was an extraordinary attack on the vested interests of the borough, and, by placing the problem of prostitution at the heart of the city's political system, very publicly pronounced the city's shame. The Tory establishment responded in kind, attacking Armstrong for maligning Liverpool's reputation: one Conservative councillor attacked his Radical and Liberal opponents for 'calling Liverpool an immoral town'.[86] This accusation of civic treachery was a particularly stinging rebuke. The moral reputation of Liverpool was at stake, in these late-nineteenth-century politics of prostitution. Liverpool was held up to the light of bad publicity, compared to its municipal rivals and found wanting. The importance of the local municipal comparison, which I have emphasised throughout this chapter, also took substance from the international moral politics of prostitution, however. For their part, social purity reformers could point to the moral unacceptability of 'French' and 'continental' systems of regulated prostitution. The *Liverpool Daily Post* was, for instance, appalled by the prospect of Liverpool adopting what it called a 'burlesque' version of the continental approach to prostitution regulation:

As a matter of fact ... neither the Continental system nor the Liverpool burlesque of it is of the slightest efficacy in checking the progress of the epidemic of immorality. The only

---

[85] On the purity crusade launched by Armstrong in 1889, see N. Collins, *Politics and elections in nineteenth-century Liverpool* (Aldershot, 1994), p. 210.
[86] Waller, *Democracy and sectarianism*, p. 106.

difference between the two is that in this locality all the consequences are infinitely more deplorable. The fact that a certain district in a Continental city is assigned to residents of a particular class by no means prevents persons of that class from occupying houses in other and more reputable districts of the same city; and this is just as true of Liverpool as it is of Paris, Berlin, or Vienna. You may assign fixed limits to a certain class of people, but by no exercise of human power or ingenuity can you keep them within those limits or prevent the spreading beyond them of their pernicious influence. What, then, becomes of the value of the known as distinguished from the unknown?[87]

It was one thing to be seen as the poor relation of Glasgow and Manchester. It was quite another to be classified in the same breath as depraved continental regimes, even as a burlesque bastardisation of their practices.

In 1890, when these campaigns came to a head, the Conservatives were in full retreat, and the Liberals continued to press the moral issues of temperance and vice. The result was a surprise victory for the Liberals in the municipal elections and a shift in the balance of power on the Watch Committee. Accordingly, the old policy of segregation and toleration began to give way to repression. The Bishop of Liverpool and the entire Anglican establishment were recruited to the cause – a far cry, note, from the hierarchy's characteristic support for the Contagious Diseases Acts. The Watch Committee and the Chief Constable were shortly instructed to use the powers of the Criminal Law Amendment Act to close down the city's recognised brothels. Duly galvanised, most of the brothel houses were cleared, much to the satisfaction of the purity party. The *Liverpool Review* turned its attention to portraying Nott-Bower as the scourge of the streets, in the new guise forced upon him by the political transformation of the borough (Figure 3.5).[88] The Reverend Armstrong complacently surveyed the difference that a couple of years could make, and welcomed the demise of the 'to all intents and purposes police-protected' districts of the city.[89] The vigilance and licensing campaigner Shilton Collin reported in the same year that the fifty-year 'recognition of houses of ill repute by the municipality' that had given Liverpool a deservedly bad name was finally over.[90] Almost overnight, twenty or more years of police management of recognised brothels had come to an end.

Conclusions

In this chapter, I have outlined the context in which municipal models of prostitution policy were developed in the later nineteenth century. I have referred

---

[87] *Liverpool Daily Post*, 8 January 1890, pp. 4–5.
[88] *Liverpool Review*, 28 February 1891.
[89] R. A. Armstrong, *Two years ago and now. An appeal to the municipal electors* (London, 1892), p. 6.
[90] Quoted in Mynott, 'Purity, prostitution and politics', p. 444.

DRABS AND DUCHESSES.

SENSIBLE CITIZEN.—" Say, Captain, can't you give some attention to the Duchesses in the Carriage? The Drabs in the gutter have had enough of it."
CAPTAIN NOTT BOWER.—" I take my orders from the Watch Committee."
SENSIBLE CITIZEN.—" Ah ! "
CAPTAIN NOTT BOWER.—" Yes."

Figure 3.5 'Drabs and duchesses': Liverpool Chief Constable Nott-Bower attacked for picking on working-class women. Source: *Liverpool Review*, 28 February 1891.

both to discursive and political practice, in terms of the political epistemology of prostitution represented by the mapping and comparative analysis of the criminal statistics, and to the varieties of prostitution policy that were adopted. Liverpool, in this context, was the exemplar of a managed policy of tolerance that contrasts markedly with other forms of administration and policing to be found in cities like Glasgow, Birmingham and Manchester. If Liverpool does not reproduce the features of formal regulationist systems, it was nevertheless a close cousin to regulationism, derivative of the same philosophy and politics, and nowhere more obviously is this the case than in its reliance on a spatial policy of containment, concentration, segregation or 'localisation'. This reliance on a geographically organised and structured brothel system made it a highly visible and politically vulnerable target for moral reformers who aligned such 'toleration' with the pernicious aspects of regulationism. Their campaigns, local and national, eventually promoted a political about-face, the scouring of the brothel districts in Liverpool, and the hounding of their inhabitants. This was clearly never likely to be a victory for prostitute women: 'classed alongside pornographers and child abusers, the working prostitute's freedom was – whatever the reason – to be curbed.'[91] Social purity activists usually rejoiced at the expulsion of brothels and the forced discretion of prostitutes, without worrying too much at what happened to the women themselves. But it was a defeat – even a small, partial and temporary one – for those who promoted the regulation of prostitution in Britain. The campaign to extend to Liverpool the benefits and privileges of the Contagious Diseases Acts had been abandoned in the early 1870s; a generation later, even the discreet, modest and informal supervision of prostitution was deemed politically unacceptable, backward-looking and incompatible with British values.

[91] Bartley, 'Seeking and saving', p. 213.

Appendix: recognised brothel districts in Liverpool, 1890

No. 1 district: *Blandford Street and Oakes Street district ('the area bounded by Islington, Moss Street, Daulby Street, Pembroke Place, Anson Street, London Road and Norton Street')*

    2 brothels with 6 prostitutes living in each
    2 brothels with 5 prostitutes living in each
    6 brothels with 4 prostitutes living in each
    33 brothels with 3 prostitutes living in each
    123 brothels with 2 prostitutes living in each
    69 houses of accommodation
    235 in total

No. 2 district: *Segrave Street and Pellew Street district ('the area bounded by Copperas Hill, Russell Street, Blake Street, Brownlow Hill')*

    2 brothels with 5 prostitutes living in each
    14 brothels with 4 prostitutes living in each
    19 brothels with 3 prostitutes living in each
    17 brothels with 2 prostitutes living in each
    3 houses of accommodation
    55 in total

No. 3 district: *The South End ('Prince William Street, Gore Street')*

    4 brothels with 6 prostitutes living in each
    2 brothels with 5 prostitutes living in each
    9 brothels with 4 prostitutes living in each
    14 brothels with 3 prostitutes living in each
    11 brothels with 2 prostitutes living in each
    3 houses of accommodation
    43 houses in total

No. 4 district: *Queen Anne Street district ('Soho Street, Springfield Street, St Anne Street, Mansfield Street')*

    4 brothels with 4 prostitutes living in each
    17 brothels with 3 prostitutes living in each
    15 brothels with 2 prostitutes living in each
    36 houses in total

No. 5 district: *Clare Street*

    2 brothels with 3 prostitutes living in each
    11 brothels with 2 prostitutes living in each
    2 houses of accommodation
    15 in total

No. 6 district: *Bidder Street*

    4 brothels with 3 prostitutes living in each
    9 brothels with 2 prostitutes living in each
    1 house of accommodation
    14 houses in total

No. 7 district: *Circus Street*

    2 brothels with 4 prostitutes living in each
    3 brothels with 3 prostitutes living in each
    7 brothels with 2 prostitutes living in each
    1 house of accommodation
    13 houses in total

No. 8 district: *Vauxhall Road ('Clement Street, Charters Street, Maguire Street, Ford Street')*

    1 brothel with 4 prostitutes living in each
    3 brothels with 3 prostitutes living in each
    6 brothels with 2 prostitutes living in each
    10 houses in total

Source: Liverpool Record Office, 352/POL/2/12, *Head Constable's special report book 1890–2*, 2 September 1890.

4

A private Contagious Diseases Act: prostitution and the proctorial system in Victorian Cambridge

The late-nineteenth-century operation of police and magistrates in Liverpool was 'regulationist' in nature, even if it lacked the formal qualities of stricter regimes. At a municipal level, it is evident that some local authorities could discreetly corral, and thereby to better manage, the sex workers that it could not or would not attempt to prosecute out of existence. There was another form of prostitution regulation in Britain, however, one that had quite different origins but which produced a very similar landscape, and which more surely deserves the name. This was the policing of prostitution in the University towns of Oxford and Cambridge, the 'proctorial' system, as it was known in both places, which authorised the inspection and detention of suspected prostitutes. These were anomalous regimes, anachronistic even, given that their existence depended upon medieval statutes that were increasingly out of step with the legal framework of modern Britain. As corporate privileges, these were also *private* forms of regulationism, far removed from the aegis of the state: one critic even referred to the Cambridge system as a 'private Contagious Diseases Act'.[1] Specific and exclusive, these were *lex loci*, peculiar to the University towns, and together one more addition to the complex patchwork of laws and regulations concerning the policing of prostitution in nineteenth-century Britain that has already been emphasised. They might easily be treated, and dismissed, as no more than oddities with little significance beyond the boundaries of these towns and the small world of university life. Directly affecting few people, they marked no great change in sanitary science or philosophies of state. Yet they were notable beyond their jurisdiction because they offered an important precedent for those who believed that regulationist regimes could and should be introduced for both military and civilian populations, and because they became caught up in the late Victorian politics of prostitution. In the era of the CD Acts, the issue of the policing of prostitution in the University towns took on an importance quite disproportionate to its scale.

[1] R. C. B., 'The proctorial system', *Cambridge Review*, 4 (1883), p. 392.

This chapter examines the nature of the proctorial systems, and reconstructs the landscape of regulated prostitution in Cambridge in particular detail. It provides a further discussion of the role of repression and regulation in the policing of commercial sexuality, and confirms the importance of 'localisation' or containment in the overall strategy of toleration. It not only provides a closer commentary on the experience of those women caught up in the workings of regulationist practices than is offered elsewhere; some consideration can also be given here to the role of their undergraduate clients. This is instructive because the existence of regulationist practices in Oxford and Cambridge drew special attention to the *class* as well as gender privileges that they institutionalised. Unlike the garrison towns, where the immediate beneficiaries of regulationist systems were overwhelmingly common soldiers and sailors, in Oxford and Cambridge the proctorial systems could be presented as systematically privileging the rights of worldly middle- and upper-class undergraduate men over those of vulnerable and innocent working-class women. The reputation of undergraduates as sexually indisciplined was thus introduced into the debates over the regulation of prostitution in Britain. Bearing this in mind, this chapter considers the sexual experiences of the undergraduate and the culture that formed him, and the active promotion in the later nineteenth century of a more moral model of masculinity.

The universities and the proctorial system

Prostitution was, as enemies and defenders of the universities admitted, a constant attendant of university life. In his classic treatise on prostitution, William Acton noted the exceptional circumstances of the university towns, and the stimulus to vice provided by their 'floating population of unmarried males'.[2] William Tait had earlier offered the observation that, 'as is exemplified in various classes of students, particularly those of law and medicine, the most learned are often the most prone to give free vent to their sexual passions'.[3] In Oxford, it was said that the 'perpetual and unceasing flow of youth into the city, at an age when the passions are warm, when perhaps, for the first time they are released from the guardianship of friends, possessing wealth often profusely granted by indulgent parents, must naturally tend, unless restrained, to the production of a large amount of vice'.[4] And, in Cambridge, in exactly the same way, it was said that it could hardly

---

[2] W. Acton, *Prostitution, considered in its moral, social, and sanitary aspects, in London and other large cities and garrison towns. With proposals for the control and prevention of its attendant evils*, reprint of 2nd edition, 1870 (London, 1972), p. 55.

[3] W. Tait, *Magdalenism. An inquiry into the extent, causes, and consequences, of prostitution in Edinburgh* (Edinburgh, 1842), p. 20.

[4] 'Public morals: prostitution in Oxford', *Oxford Protestant Magazine*, 1 (1847), quoted by A. J. Engel, '"Immoral intentions": the University of Oxford and the problem of prostitution, 1827–1914', *Victorian Studies*, 23 (1979), 79–107, p. 80.

be expected that a university could exist 'without some special developments of the Kingdom of evil'.[5]

Without doubt, prostitution flourished in both Oxford and Cambridge. Classification is imprecise and invidious, but it may be estimated that, at any one time, something like one or two hundred more or less professional sex workers existed in each of the university towns. These figures are not exceptionally high, even if they do not take into account the larger set of women for whom casual assignations might have been a temporary expedient or a more or less innocent adventure, but they are comparable with some of the garrison towns. They indicate that, for the determined undergraduate, sexual opportunities with women of the town were not difficult to find. William Acton had added, however, that, if the extent of local prostitution in the university towns was not much in excess of 'the usual average of towns of similar dimensions', this was the result of policies enacted there for the regulation of prostitution.[6] Oxford and Cambridge had long developed special policing systems for protecting undergraduates from the dangers associated with public women, by registering suspected prostitutes, examining them for communicable venereal diseases, and confining them for reasons of both punishment and prophylaxis. The antiquity of these practices is worth remarking, as it demonstrates better than anywhere else the continuities between medieval, early modern and modern regulationist regimes. Regulations for protecting the scholars can be traced in fact to a series of medieval awards, which were periodically restated in the early modern era, and reinvigorated in the first decades of the nineteenth century. In Cambridge, the responsibility of the Vice-Chancellor to subject prostitutes and other 'idle and disorderly' persons to banishment or a prison term had developed as part of a broad remit of civil and criminal jurisdictions granted by the Crown in the Middle Ages out of solicitude for its academic subjects.[7] The initial emphasis on the repression of prostitution had long given way, however, to consistent attempts at regulation, these statutes coming to be invoked only to remove prostitutes from the public streets and to control disorderly houses. By the early nineteenth century, it was the duty of the Vice-Chancellor's court in Cambridge to examine suspected prostitutes, to hear their accounts, to register their names, and to order a medical inspection if warranted. The early Victorian Vice-Chancellor thus assumed his medieval predecessor's responsibility for safeguarding the health, reputation and prospects of the young

---

[5] H. C. G. Moule, quoted in *Cambridge Chronicle*, 11 December 1880, p. 7. See also *Cambridge Chronicle*, 7 February 1852, p. 7, 5 February 1859, p. 6, 4 November 1865, p. 5.

[6] Acton, *Prostitution*, p. 55.

[7] A. B. Cobban, *The medieval English universities: Oxford and Cambridge to c.1500* (Aldershot, 1988), P. Kibre, *Scholarly privileges in the Middle Ages: the rights, privileges, and immunities of scholars and universities at Bologna, Padua, Paris, and Oxford* (London, 1961).

men nominally in his charge, but this responsibility was more precisely defined and effected by the removal or regulation of infectious, solicitous and disorderly women from the public streets, rather than their banishment from the town.

In Oxford, there is a similar emphasis on the continuity of ancient custom and the transformation of modern practice. Whilst the powers there were equally old, a multifarious amalgam of ecclesiastical and secular jurisdictions that had come in time to assume the status of a single authority, these powers were increasingly subject to challenge and clarified accordingly. In the early years of the nineteenth century, John Walker's barbed correspondence with the *Oxford Herald* continually drew attention to what he considered the wholesale illegality of the Vice-Chancellor's powers in respect to the taking of prostitutes from the streets and the searching of disorderly houses: 'By what statute of the University, or law of the land, the conviction, and consequent commitment to prison, by the Vice-Chancellor, is justified, the writer (though he has taken the greatest pains in examining the statutes) is not able to discover.'[8] The University responded to these questions by setting its powers on a new legal footing, under the clauses of the 1822 University Police Act, and its powers to imprison prostitutes in the town gaol were renegotiated in 1824 in a process that reconstituted the traditional privileges in a new bureaucratic and political framework.[9] After that date, what was described as 'the old practice of indiscriminate custody' was replaced by a rather more careful attention to the circumstances in which women were arrested and detained.[10] The University and the city also agreed to share the costs and responsibility for policing prostitution, the University supporting a night police and paying, to begin with, 10d per day for every 'common prostitute' imprisoned in the city gaol.[11] In Oxford, therefore, the University and the borough closely collaborated in the regulation of prostitution.

If the Vice-Chancellors of the Universities had ultimate responsibility, it was their agents, the proctors, who carried out the surveillance and coercion. These men – clergymen-fellows nominated by the colleges by rota – and their servants – or 'bulldogs' – were in effect the Vice-Chancellor's private *police des moeurs*, patrolling the city's streets after dark on the lookout for disorderly women, whom they apprehended and registered and if necessary delivered to the University court for interrogation and possible incarceration. Acton summarised this system by stating that, '[f]or the purposes of discipline at the Universities, large powers are

---

[8] [John Walker], *Curia oxoniensis: or, observations on the statutes which relate to the University Court; on the illegality of searching houses; on the procuratorial office; and on the University Police Act* (Oxford, 1825), pp. 111–12.

[9] See Engel, 'Immoral intentions', pp. 80–3.

[10] Letter from Mayor T. H. Taunton to the Vice-Chancellor, 7 November 1826, in 'Papers relative to a payment made to the city for the support of prostitutes confined in the city gaol by the authorities of the University', Oxford University Archives (hereinafter, OUA) NEP/A/7.

[11] Engel, 'Immoral intentions', p. 81. This practice seems to have ceased in 1869.

entrusted to certain officers called proctors, part of whose duty is to prevent any intercourse between undergraduates and women of the town, the latter being liable to arrest and imprisonment if caught *flagrante delicto*'.[12] This was delicate work, of course, involving discretion as well as discipline: the Oxford proctors recommended for the benefit of future incumbents that the 'utmost tact and judgement' was required in their 'varied, distracting and laborious' duties.[13] It was particularly emphasised that a good proctor is one who knows 'the character of every one of these unfortunate but in many instances most depraved creatures, and who extends to them every kindness & leniency which can be made consistent with a proper sense of his duty to the University'.[14] On the other hand, this benign view of the proctors' work should not mislead us to the essentially disciplinary nature of their duties; perhaps more representative is the self-portrait provided by the great geologist Adam Sedgwick, when he was newly attired in his proctor's robes, as an 'accomplished moral scavenger'.[15] Archdeacon William Emery, in reference to his time as a proctor at Cambridge, spoke too of the objective of 'continually harassing vice, by forcing the purveyors of the evil to be on the move, and by keeping temptation out of the way'.[16] Diligent proctors like these could certainly find plenty of work in the streets of Cambridge: in a single day in 1828, Sedgwick committed seven women to the University's private Bridewell, the Spinning House.[17] Inevitably, the proctors were feared and resented, and not only by the practising prostitutes subject to their authority; they were also targets for the complaints of 'town' against 'gown'. The role of the proctors was the greatest point of contention for critics of the system to which they lent their name, given that they were given 'the liberty of deciding on the characters of all the female inhabitants of the place, and of condemning them, from partial representations, or individual caprice'.[18]

There was one further institution, however, which came to symbolise the regulation of prostitution in the Universities, and to focus the attention of antagonists. This was the Spinning House in Cambridge, located on St Andrew's Street (Figure 4.1a,b, Figure 4.2), which was the place of examination and confinement

---

[12] Acton, *Prostitution*, p. 155.
[13] 'Henry Pritchard, Procuratorial experiences and observations 1852–1853', OUA WP.γ.8. (21), pp. 35, 1. See also: Junior proctor's manual, 1830–, WP.γ.8. (19); Senior proctor's manual, 1837, WP.γ.8. (2); Senior proctor's manual, 1897, WP.γ.87/5; Senior proctor's book 1902–3, WP.γ.7. (6); and University Police: general instructions, 1850, OXFU.24.
[14] OUA WP.γ.8. (19), Junior proctor's manual, 1830–, pp. 66–7.
[15] A. Desmond and J. Moore, *Darwin* (London, 1991), p. 54.
[16] 'The alleged increase of immorality', *The chronicle of Convocation. Being a record of the proceedings of the Convocation of Canterbury the tenth Victoria Regnante, sessions, Feb. 8, 9, 10, 11, 1881* (London, 1881), 20 July 1881, p. 395.
[17] Desmond and Moore, *Darwin*, p. 54; see too P. Searby, *A history of the University of Cambridge, volume III: 1750–1870* (Cambridge, 1997), pp. 459–60.
[18] Walker, *Curia oxoniensis*, p. 11.

Figure 4.1 Two views of the Spinning House, St Andrew's Street, Cambridge, c.1890. Courtesy of the Cambridgeshire Collection, Cambridgeshire Libraries Service.

Figure 4.2 'A curious group of buildings in Cambridge': the Spinning House in the local landscape of morality. Courtesy of the Cambridgeshire Collection, Cambridgeshire Libraries Service.

for women taken on and from the streets. In Cambridge – unlike Oxford – the proctors and the University had their own private Bridewell: women suspected of being prostitutes could be held in the Spinning House for terms of up to three months, if after medical inspection they were found to be suffering from venereal disease. The antiquity of the Spinning House as a place of confinement for women is attested to in its name, a variant on the Amsterdam *Spinhuis*, the influential female reformatory built in 1597; but, whereas that institution confined women for 'private' crimes such as adultery, the Spinning House came in time exclusively to detain 'public women'.[19] It became a cornerstone in the landscape of morality instituted in Cambridge by the proctorial system, widely disliked in the town but also repeatedly censured in the national media as an icon of the University's exploitation of townswomen and of the town in general. After the death of a woman detained in the Spinning House in 1846, for instance, it was described by the national press as a 'den of abomination', 'a wretched, dirty, and ill-managed place', and a place whose disgraceful condition was the responsibility of 'an arbitrary, tyrannical and irresponsible corporation'.[20] The Spinning House would become the icon of the regulationist policing practised by both Universities.

The Times, which was prompted to join in with some of the criticism of the Spinning House and its operations, nevertheless repeatedly approved of the *principle* of protecting students in the University towns:

---

[19] See M. Ogborn, *Spaces of modernity: London's geographies 1680–1780* (London, 1998), pp. 43–4.

[20] 'Proctorial authority', *The Times*, 8 December 1846, p. 7; 'The Spinning House abomination', *Morning Chronicle*, 2 January 1851, p. 15; *The Times*, 11 December 1846, p. 4. See *The Spinning House abomination, from the special commissioner of the Morning Chronicle* (Cambridge, 1851).

The object with which these powers were originally granted being, of course, the preservation of the morality of the students – an object quite as important in the present day as it was three hundred years ago – it is hardly proper to denounce them generally, or indeed on any other ground save that of their interfering unnecessarily with the liberty of the subject.[21]

Whatever reservations it had on the subject, in the era of the Contagious Diseases Acts, *The Times* was even more willing to invoke the impress of necessity. The agitation for the Acts had picked up upon the existence of the powers of the Universities, and pro-regulationists were keen to use them as a significant precedent. Sir John Liddell, in the 1862 report on venereal disease in the armed forces, took note of the special legislation that existed at Oxford and Cambridge, 'where public women can be imprisoned as rogues and vagabonds'.[22] *The Lancet* pointedly asked, two years later, why the military and naval authorities should be refused powers no greater than those exercised by the proctors of Oxford and Cambridge.[23] And the author of the prominent military pamphlet, *Soldiers and the social evil*, argued most forcefully that 'in our Universities the cause of *morality* alone, in the special case of the great gathering together of youth there, effected of old a Law against prostitution, which still enables recognised Officers to interfere and apprehend public women'.[24] A rhetorical question inevitably followed from the author:

Why may not a MEDICAL 'OFFICER OF HEALTH', (without endangering the liberty of the subject, or invading the privacy of our homes) be charged with the oversight and control of public women, with power to inform of and cause to be apprehended for inspection all such (well enough known alas!) who, being found contagious, should be detained in Hospital, and after cure, be *confined penally*, for a period, in a SPINNING HOUSE? Suppose for this end no general Law can be applied, yet are not Garrison Towns, and especially Camps, as really exceptional cases as the University Towns? Why then may not Spinning Houses or HOUSES OF CORRECTION be instituted (with LOCK HOSPITALS connected) as well as in our Camps of Instruction as in our places of Education?[25]

Those minded to regulationism could therefore insist that, where circumstances called for special measures, it was entirely appropriate that local regimes of surveillance and inspection be instituted, even if this went against the temper of society or of the times. As the solidly pro-regulation *Times* again noted,

---

[21] *The Times*, 11 December 1846, p. 4.
[22] *Report of the committee upon venereal disease in the Army and Navy* [1863], NA WO 33/12/188.
[23] 'Venereal disease in the Army and Navy', *The Lancet*, 19 March 1864, p. 329.
[24] *Soldiers and the social evil. A letter addressed by permission to the Right Hon. Sidney Herbert, MD, Secretary of State for War, by a chaplain to the forces* (London, 1860), p. 4.
[25] *Ibid.*, p. 9.

As it is not long ago that attention was drawn to the jurisdiction exercised by certain officers in the University of Cambridge, our readers will be able to appreciate another question which has now arisen on the same subject. It must be quite unnecessary for us to explain that in a place where 1,200 or 1,500 young men are congregated some especial authority is required for the preservation of public morality. This authority is lodged in the hands of the Proctors, who are appointed annually for the discharge of such duty, and who are expected to keep the students from consorting with women of loose character and to impede as far as possible the traffic which such women pursue ... If the jurisdiction available for such purposes at Cambridge is extraordinary in its nature, we do not see that it can be for the disadvantage of the place ... All peculiar courts and jurisdictions are naturally objectionable to Englishmen, but where the conditions of life are so exceptional as in University towns, they must be met by exceptional regulations.[26]

The same argument could be made, as the editorialist intended it should, for the garrison towns proposed for the 'partial legislation' that the CD Acts would come to represent. The fact that Oxford and Cambridge were *civilian* towns meant moreover that regulation might, once established, legitimately be extended from the military garrisons to the population at large. In the mid-nineteenth century, the existence and operation of the proctorial system in the University towns could be considered as a key argument for the extension of regulationist policing in Britain.

Regulated prostitution in Victorian Cambridge

If we focus on Cambridge, the nature of the regime at a local level and its landscape of managed sexuality can better be apprehended. The fact that proctorial records in Cambridge contain a list of brothels and of the residences of suspected women of ill-fame amply confirms that regulation rather than repression was the aim of the University authorities.[27] Further, as we have seen in the previous chapter, one characteristic of such policies of 'tolerance' was the concentration of prostitution in a segregated sex district or vice zone, thereby making registration and surveillance that much easier. Like Liverpool, there was no licensed sex district authorised by overt legislation, but Cambridge was no exception to the general rule that regulation implied the geographical 'containment' of prostitution. In Victorian Cambridge, this prostitutional space by and large had a single name: that of 'Barnwell', the working-class district that lay to the east of the wealthier, respectable town of Cambridge proper. Its position on the road to Newmarket and to Stourbridge Fair had earned it an early reputation for both licit and illicit leisure, one eighteenth-century diarist noting that 'bawdy'

---

[26] *The Times*, 3 December 1860, p. 6.
[27] Cambridge University Archives (hereafter CUA) Min.VI.6, Proctorial syndicate (1849–1900), flyleaf.

Barnwell consisted of 'good-natured girls for the use of the colleges'.[28] The racy student guides of the early nineteenth century also archly referred to Barnwell's 'Cyprian tribes', and made 'French pox' and 'Barnwell ague' synonyms.[29] But, when the area was engulfed by the working-class housing that had worked its way towards it in the early nineteenth century after the enclosure of the common fields in 1807, Barnwell assumed a more threatening association with crime and moral decay. By then, many would have agreed with the *Cambridge Chronicle* that Barnwell was 'the rendezvous for hundreds of men and women who roll onwards, and upwards to the deepest atrocities'.[30] The 'long degraded and misled populace' of the neighbourhood made it in the bourgeois imagination the 'focus of villainy' in Cambridge.[31] But, for all the opprobrium, it was convenient from the viewpoint of social hygiene and prostitution regulation for brothels and commercial sexuality to be kept by the University authorities to this district as far as possible; in this way, the University – like the borough police in Liverpool – might be said to have connived with prostitution.

Reconstructing the geography of brothels and suspected houses from town and University records confirms the extent to which Barnwell came to dominate the trade in commercial sexuality in Cambridge. By the 1860s and 1870s, the houses of ill-fame in the other poor areas of the town – Castle End, the New Town and the rest of eastern Cambridge – had given way to a marked concentration in Barnwell, and moreover to a small number of streets, of which Wellington Street was by this time by some way the most notorious, remaining for many years the primary centre for brothels and prostitutes' residences (Figure 4.3).[32] The lodgings of women arrested by the University proctors also attests to its primacy: by the 1850s, the town of Cambridge, and its satellite neighbourhoods, were ceding place to Barnwell in terms of prostitutes' residences, many of which must have operated as receiving houses

---

[28] N. Mansfield, 'Grads and snobs: John Brown, town and gown in early nineteenth-century Cambridge', *History Workshop Journal*, 35 (1993), 184–98, p. 191.

[29] *Gradus ad Cantabrigiam: or, new university guide to the academical customs, and colloquial or cant terms, peculiar to the University of Cambridge* (Cambridge, 1824), p. 122; *Gradus ad Cantabrigiam: or, a dictionary of terms, academical and colloquial, or cant, which are used at the University of Cambridge* (Cambridge, 1803), p. 16. See also the reference to 'Barnwell wh——s' in 'Socius', *The Cambridge tart: epigrammatic and satiric-poetical effusions; &c. &c. Dainty morsels served up by Cantabs, on various occasions* (London, 1823), p. 21.

[30] *Cambridge Chronicle*, 15 January 1853, p. 8.

[31] 'The dens and traditions of Barnwell', *Cambridge Chronicle*, 8 January 1853, p. 8.

[32] Information on brothels and receiving houses comes from a number of sources: Proctorial syndicate records (CUA Min.VI.6), Spinning House committals books (CUA T.VIII.1–3), the inmate books of the Cambridge Female Refuge (Cambridgeshire Record Office, hereafter CRO, R.60.27.1–2), and the police court reports in the *Cambridge Chronicle*.

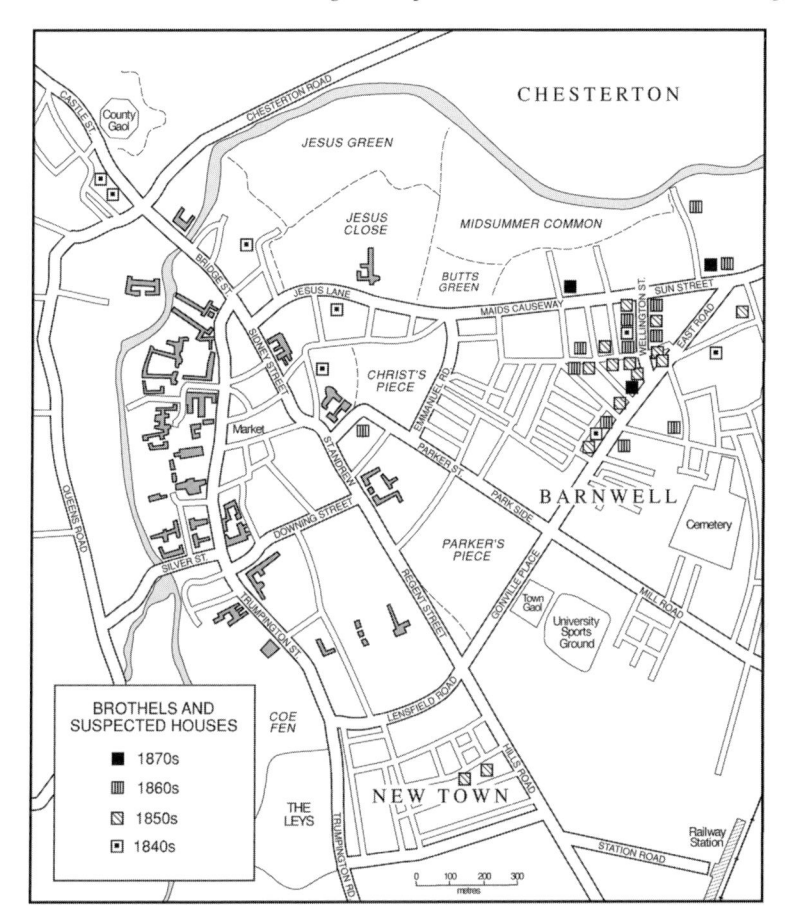

Figure 4.3 Brothels and suspected houses in Victorian Cambridge. Source: Spinning House commitals books, CUA T.VIII.1–3, and police court reports, *Cambridge Chronicle*.

of some sort (Figure 4.4).[33] Domesticated prostitutional activity from mid-century onwards thus became concentrated in a small number of streets, well known to police and proctors alike. The proctors were empowered to enter such suspected houses, but they were understandably reluctant to do so; instead, they kept them under surveillance, and watched for the ingress and egress of undergraduates. Only in aggravated cases was action taken against these houses.

The privacy of the receiving house and the brothel made a rather notable contrast to the actions taken against suspected women in polite public space. In

[33] Spinning House committals books, CUA T.VIII. 1–3.

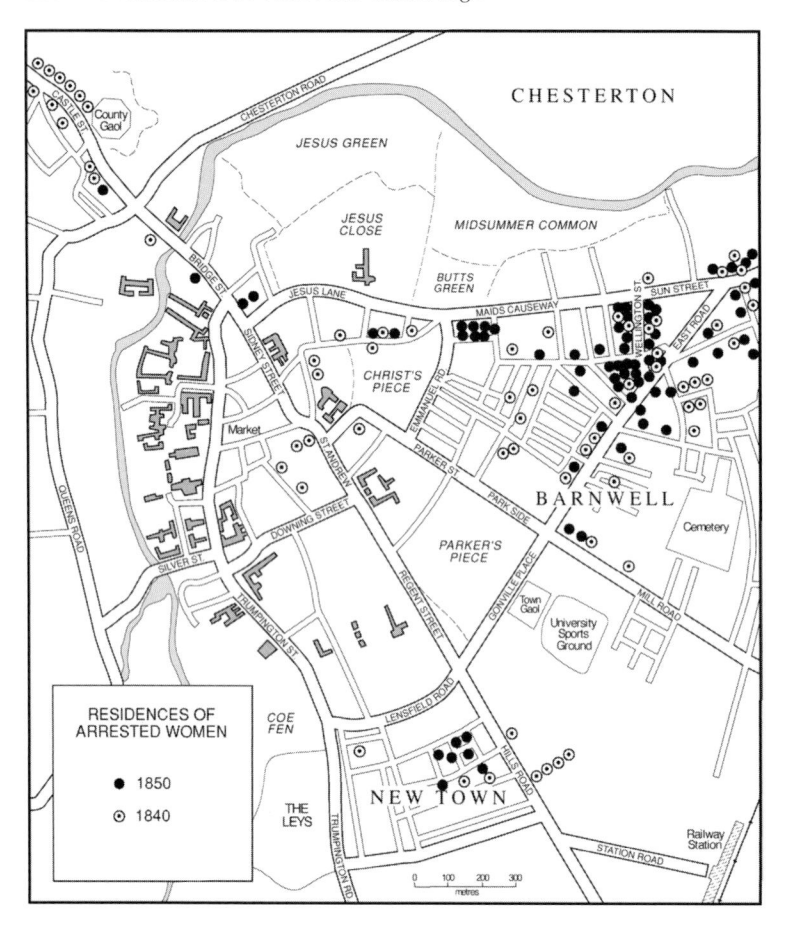

Figure 4.4 Residences of women arrested in Cambridge by the proctors, 1840 and 1850. Source: Spinning House commitals books, CUA T.VIII.1–3.

contrast to the ostensibly 'private' world of the brothels and receiving houses, the streets and 'public' spaces of the respectable town of Cambridge served as the focus of repressive policing. The emphasis on the 'public' evils of prostitution, the attack on the overt sexualisation of public space that soliciting entailed, is clearly evident in the equation of prostitution with 'streetwalking'. Though occasionally dignified by the mocking title of 'nymphs of the *pavé*', streetwalkers were written into Victorian narratives as the epitome of prostitution and its dangers. In Victorian Cambridge, with its 1,500 or so undergraduates (or 'gownsmen') protected behind high walls in the private world of the colleges but subject to public temptation in the streets of the town, this concentration on the public nature of the prostitution problem was powerfully resonant. The prostitute was portrayed here

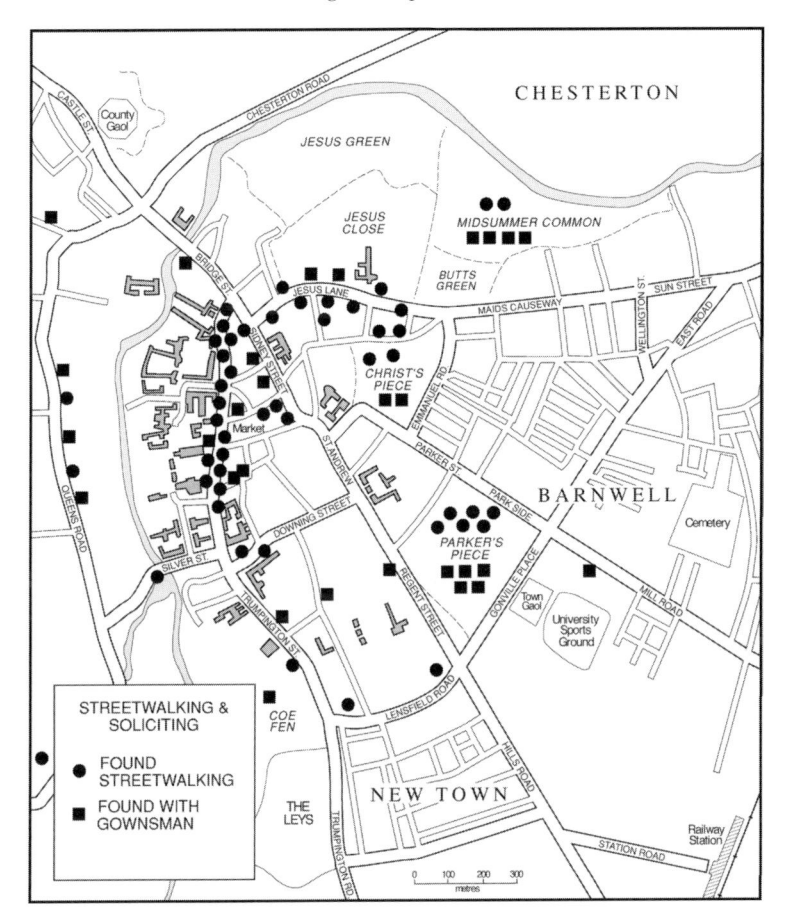

Figure 4.5 Locations of streetwalking and soliciting offences in Cambridge, 1823–94.
Source: Spinning House commitals books, CUA T.VIII.1–3.

as the aggressor, the temptress, the instigator; and it was her public presence that was thus felt to be the real problem of prostitution. The geography of soliciting, as it was constructed by the operations of the proctors, was a mirror image of that of brothels and residences: this was the 'public' side of prostitutional space to be repressed rather than managed. The problem for the University was that prostitutes advertised themselves on the promenades of King's Parade, Trinity Street and Trumpington Street, or in the shadily marginal zones such as Jesus Lane and King Street, or else again in the open public spaces like Parker's Piece, Christ's Pieces and Midsummer Common (Figure 4.5).[34] In the respectable streets, these

[34] *Ibid.*

women became nuisances, following or pawing undergraduates, pulling their gowns, interrupting their strolls and damming the free flow of the streets' respectable 'passengers'. There were those who simply made an exhibition of themselves in the streets, drunk or brawling with their bullies or with each other. On the one hand, such women introduced an unwanted 'public' element into the promenades of 'private' men and their wives and families; on the other, they were dangerous 'privateers' who made a mockery and a danger of public space. One offended undergraduate, pushed at by a prostitute, took her to the police court for the sake of public decency, and expressed his opinion that 'the improprieties allowed in the streets of London and other large towns of England were inconceivable to foreigners'.[35] More heinous still was the plain fact that open, public spaces like Parker's Piece and Midsummer Common were places for sexual transactions. The proctors not uncommonly found undergraduates coupling with women in alleyways, parks and fields.

The unacceptability of such 'public' prostitution was written into the operation of the proctorial system. The latter worked out the spatial logic of regulation by registering prostitutes and suspected women found soliciting in Cambridge, and through the threat of incarceration, driving them from the public spaces of the town into the domesticated *milieux* of the brothel and the working-class districts, principally Barnwell. That way, so the University authorities reasoned, the respectable inhabitants of Cambridge would be protected from public exhibitions of immorality, and the vulnerable and the easily led might be prevented from falling into temptation. 'The plan', as Professor Sedgwick frankly put it, was simply 'to keep young men out of the way of temptation, and to extinguish every aggravated case.'[36] Those determined to procure sex – and Sedgwick was hardly alone in insisting that human nature, by which he meant male nature, was invariably liable to temptation – would always do so, but they could be channelled to Barnwell and to the privacy of the brothel, whilst the University did all it could to make sure that the undergraduates' partners would be free from disease, by taking them out of the circuits of sexual exchange whenever they were found to be infectious.

This way of proceeding was subject to the same objections registered by all antagonists of regulationism. These practices effectively underwrote the double standard, by treating the male undergraduate leniently, seeking to protect his health at the expense of the townswomen who were his sexual partners. *The Times* remarked in this regard that 'The surplus penalty paid by a street-walker in Cambridge is paid to protect an undergraduate from temptation. His frailty is corrected by her liability.'[37] At the same time, *all* women in public spaces were potentially suspect, running the risk of apprehension, medical inspection and incarceration purely on the suspicion of a private morals police, and the verdict of

[35] *Cambridge Chronicle*, 7 November 1857, p. 8.
[36] *Cambridge Chronicle*, 29 January 1859, p. 7.
[37] *The Times*, 17 December 1846, p. 4.

a private hearing under the sole authority of the Vice-Chancellor. The University would increasingly find it difficult to refute the charge that it condoned male licence whilst visiting its worst punishments upon prostitutes, townswomen and the female working poor of Cambridge in general.

Even the presence of a network of institutions designed to keep young women out of the prostitution business, or to release them from its grip, could not shake the charge that the University connived at prostitution. Symbolically, the presence of a magdalen or refuge for fallen women might have gone some way to countering the charge: and a Female Refuge in Cambridge, founded and run by evangelical churchmen in the University, had existed from 1838, eventually located right in the heart of Barnwell's slums, behind the newly built Christchurch on Newmarket Road.[38] The Refuge, however, was not conceived as an alternative to the proctorial system but as an adjunct to it; its secretary summed up its relationship to the Spinning House in these words: 'we have always found the Spinning House a kind of *feeder* to the Refuge.'[39] The Female Refuge was typically quick to add its support to the proctors, another member of its committee insisting that 'special powers are necessary, not only here but elsewhere, for dealing with the solicitation of boys and young men'.[40] There was always some confusion therefore about whether the Refuge protected women from the dangers posed by undergraduates, or *vice versa*, or whether indeed it performed both these services at once.[41]

Many remained unconvinced of the altruism of the University, however. Even within its own ranks there was sporadic dissent. None was fiercer than the pamphlet war that erupted in the 1830s, in which the relationship between the town of Cambridge and the district of Barnwell came to be considered of central importance. In a wholesale condemnation of his alma mater, which he pointedly described as a 'prostitute mother', one particularly disaffected son, Robert Mackenzie Beverley, lambasted the sexual morals of a city that he described as 'wholly given to fornication'. The University, Beverley insisted,

has a religion of rituals joined to a debased standard of morals, which legitimates impurity to preserve wealth, and oppresses with ceremonies those whom it deprives of consolation. Learning here is an accumulation of refined trifles … Mental exertion is rewarded with

---

[38] For the records of the Refuge, see CRO R.60.27.
[39] Letter from John Scott on the beneficial effects of the proctorial jurisdiction, in Guard Book 1548–1900, CUA CUR 41.1.116, emphasis in original. For magdalens as adjuncts to regulationist systems, see L. Mahood, *The magdalenes: prostitution in the nineteenth century* (London, 1990).
[40] *Cambridge Chronicle*, 8 January 1892, p. 8. Many committee members were proctors or ex-proctors themselves.
[41] 'It is, surely, rather an accident developed by circumstances than a property belonging to the nature of the System, that the Proctor should be the most successful of all Town missionaries, and the Spinning-house be the easiest transition to the Home of Mercy!', 'The proctorial system at Cambridge', *The Magdalen's Friend*, 2 (1862).

sloth, and gifts to the belly oppress the ardour of talent. Young men who come for instruction are too often infected with the general depravity, and go away with a load of debt and the empty honour of a degree. Men of prayer are in eminent peril of backsliding, and repentant debauchees lapse into heresy. Fellowships are a temptation to a sinful celibacy, and religious tests encourage deceit and foster dissimulations. In one word, the University seems to be a slaughterhouse of conscience and a kingdom of evil.[42]

Not content with this extraordinary attack, Beverley singled out the relationship between Cambridge and Barnwell as proof of the University's corruption: 'who has not heard of Barnwell?' he asked: it was a town 'set apart and dedicated to sin' – 'prostitutes swarm there, and Cambridge and Barnwell are to all intents and purposes now one town'.[43] Defenders of the University barely demurred at this characterisation of Barnwell, but contented themselves with trotting out familiar justifications for regulation. Adam Sedgwick, for one, argued that the University 'protects her modest sons, as far as she is able, from every exhibition which might tempt them to sensuality'; and that, if students were licentious, 'they have, by their own deliberate acts, to look for the secret haunts of misery and sin; – if they go wrong, it is because they are prone, by their own nature, to the ways of evil.'[44] In a further comment, addressed directly to Beverley, this classic regulationist formulation was mapped out in the very geography of Barnwell and Cambridge:

You say 'that Barnwell and Cambridge are to all intents and purposes the same town.' If you mean mere contiguity or situation you are right, but if you mean to convey the imputation that the former is therefore a common place of resort, the charge is as false as a charge can possibly be. It is scarcely possible for two other places to be so near, and yet so thoroughly distinct. The line of demarcation is widely drawn, and if you wish to know by what, I answer 'Public Opinion,' and in the greater part of the society here the name of the former is interdicted.[45]

Or, as yet another put it, the University and colleges and their rules are 'a breakwater against the tide of temptation which sets in from Barnwell and the town, and the low tide which sets in from the previous bad habits, and the full purses, or the good prospects of some of the young men'.[46] But that even the University's most stalwart defenders could only protest that Barnwell was a necessary evil points to

---

[42] R. M. Beverley, *A letter to His Royal Highness the Duke of Gloucester, Chancellor, on the present corrupt state of the University of Cambridge* (London, 1833), pp. 11, 45.

[43] *Ibid.*, p. 17.

[44] A. Sedgwick, *Four letters to the editors of the Leeds Mercury in reply to R. M. Beverley, Esq.* (Cambridge, 1836).

[45] 'An undergraduate of the University of Cambridge' [William Forsyth], *A Letter to R. M. Beverley, Esq.*, Cambridge, T. Stevenson, 1833, p.10.

[46] F. R. Hall, *A letter to R. M. Beverley, Esq., containing strictures on his letter to His Royal Highness the Duke of Gloucester, Chancellor of the University of Cambridge, on the present corrupt state of the university* (Cambridge, 1834), p. 19.

the fact that this was an argument informed by and amounting to regulation. The landscape of Cambridge was the product of a culture with an established ideology of sexuality, one that condoned male sexual error as natural and that made the women of the town the focus of its systems of moral and medical discipline.

The promiscuous paradigm in Oxbridge culture

This brings us to the sexual culture of the Universities in the nineteenth century. As Beverley's correspondence shows, together with his equivalent, John Walker, in Oxford, for those who did not share the Universities' priorities, the phenomenon of prostitution and the system of proctorial regulation represented nothing less than wholesale corruption. Shorn of the dictates of pedagogy and the naturalisation of male sexuality, managed prostitution pointed simply to the licentiousness of the undergraduate body. Proctorial connivance in the exploitation of townswomen indicated not merely profligacy, however, but also political corruption. Radical critics of the Universities identified the exploitation of women by men, town by gown, the poor by the rich, as a flagrant example of the abuse of entrenched privilege: politically, prostitution had become for early and later nineteenth-century critics a potent symbol of the rottenness of the old regime. In a missive aimed at parents considering sending their children to Cambridge, for instance, another wholly alienated early nineteenth-century alumnus argued that:

> it is but too notorious that the university is an extensive school of vice and profligacy under all their forms. It is absolutely fearful to reflect on what even I have witnessed; and I do not indeed well see how it is possible for any youth to stem the universal torrent of corruption; while it is most certain that there is an extremely small proportion of young men who ever think seriously of any study or learning while they are at the university, or consider it as any other than a place on which they may amuse themselves with every species of fashionable vice.[47]

In Oxford, John Walker had spoken in the same terms, condemning as an engine of oppression a proctorial system which 'by vainly endeavouring to suppress one immorality, encourages another more atrocious, of which the cruel effects are perceptible in the frequent seduction and consequent ruin of females in the city and neighbourhood of Oxford'; the system 'first compels women to become prostitutes [by encouraging seduction], and then punishes them for being so.'[48] In the wake of the Spinning House scandal of 1846, 'Oxoniensis' advised *The Times* that police power in Oxford was even more arbitrary than it was at Cambridge, flippantly requesting the editor to pass this information on to the Russians, for 'it may give the Emperor a useful hint, or at least teach him

---

[47] 'Cantabrigiensis' [or 'A.H.'], 'The regrets of a Cantab', *London Magazine and Review*, 4 (1825), 437–46, p. 446.
[48] Walker, *Curia oxoniensis*, p. vi.

that in the midst of our civilization and advancement our noblest institutions still cherish a system as unmanly, as oppressive and as brutal as any his own dominions can boast'.[49]

Whilst these intemperate views rhetorically indulged their authors' outrage and resentment, it is important to register the close correspondence between the proctorial system and the sexual culture of the Universities. There was, certainly, a more or less sympathetic regard to what was deemed inevitable, natural and excusable. Adam Sedgwick, as we have seen, had forcefully denounced any form of draconianism with regard to punishing University men, declaring that he had recommended himself for the position of proctor 'because it was known that he was a friend of the Undergraduates, and loved young men, and could make allowance for them and their sins, if they committed any'.[50] Equally characteristic may be the attitude related in the memoirs of the Bishop of Bristol, G. F. Browne. As a proctor at Cambridge later on in the century, he claimed to understand the undergraduate temper, and, being assured of 'the manliness and the straightness of the general run of undergraduates', advocated a sympathetic discipline that avoided all signs of high- and heavy-handedness:

Proctorial discipline differs from any other discipline with which I have been concerned. You are dealing with high-spirited young men, at an age when you yourself used to test your safety-valves by a little harmless turbulence now and again. In dealing with such men, it is very easy for an unsympathetic or an inexperienced official to treat some wholesome ebullition as a grave offence. How often one has to let a culprit see that his scrape was as natural to him as the infliction of the penalty is to the disciplinary officer.[51]

It is important to note therefore that the Universities did not only attempt to regulate prostitution, but also the masculinity and sexuality of their charges. Sexual offences were not to be treated lightly, but they were to be understood with an eye to the nature of youth and the mentoring of men. Recourse to prostitutes, in this view, could never entirely be prevented; the duty of the University was rather to protect the undergraduate from dissipation and disease without retarding his progress to maturity and manhood.

These assumptions about youth and masculinity were a hallmark of the regulationist systems in Oxford and Cambridge. Human nature – that is to say, once again, *male* nature – made the young man only too liable to temptation from 'syrens and harpies'.[52] If undergraduates fell into sin, their errors were correctable, even self-correctable. What the Universities could do was to ensure, as far as they were able, that they were protected from moral and physical contamination. Such thinking was hardly unusual, of course: the focus on a practical

---

[49] 'Police power in the Universities', *The Times*, 10 December 1846, p. 7.
[50] A. Sedgwick, *Four letters*. See also *Cambridge Chronicle*, 30 May 1834, p. 4, and 5 February 1859, p. 7.
[51] G. F. Browne, *The recollections of a bishop* (London, 1915), pp. 139, 141.
[52] J. F. R., *Cambridge Chronicle*, 15 November 1833, p. 4.

morality is perfectly representative with the double standards of the 'classic moralism' that Michael Mason has identified as a central current in Victorian sexual attitudes.[53] But it is salutary to see these arguments marshalled in the context of an adolescent masculinity whose implicit vulnerability mandated not a monastic isolation but rather a watchful and active *tolerance*. Nor can this toleration be separated from the important pedagogic theme of the independent student who must be treated no longer as a schoolboy but as a young man with his own estate, and for whom too much regulation would hinder the development of his judgement and maturity. The blunt question was whether it was *natural* – at that stage of life – to game, brawl and whore. For many observers in the nineteenth century, sexual irregularity could be excused as both impossible and inexpedient to restrain, and in any case as a self-correcting stage on the road to manhood. The undergraduate's journey to manly maturity was the great object of the system, with the welfare of women a strictly secondary concern: masculinity, not femininity, was the issue of moment. The collegiate system itself was designed to counter the destabilising and dangerous effects of this liberation from the bosom of the family, at 'a very critical time of life, with strong passions and little self-control'.[54] The ambiguous ethos of the Oxbridge college as a surrogate family and household bolstered the notion that students were to be cosseted within its confines and protected in particular from the world of women outside the college gates. Cardinal Newman, with regard to Oxford, was quite clear on the responsibilities of alma mater:

> It is impossible for masses of young men to be congregated for the purposes of study, without danger of a lower standard of morality becoming current among them than could be endured in the bosom of families. Young men are prone to wink at young men's peculiar excesses. When the mild and sweet influence of mothers and sisters is removed, male natures become uproarious. After close study will follow violent exercises; after exhausting labour, intemperate eating and drinking; and if drunkenness can be tolerated, we have no security whatever against worse debasements.[55]

But the inevitable result of the collegiate ethos was the emphasis placed on the inferiority of women, and on the danger of that class of 'wayward' girls and common women who facilitated such 'worse debasements'. Sexual difference, being conscripted 'as a primary explanatory concept for signifying differentiation generally', firmly embedded the view of women as sinful, sexual temptresses in the 'Oxbridge' cultural system.[56]

---

[53] M. Mason, *The making of Victorian sexual attitudes* (Oxford, 1994), pp. 43–62.
[54] CUA T.XI.1, Award of Sir J. Patteson, 1855, p. 179.
[55] J. H. Newman, 'National universities', *Cambridge Chronicle*, 18 September 1875, p. 6. Compare E. H. Perowne, 'Religion in the Universities', *Cambridge Chronicle*, 8 May 1875, p. 7.
[56] P. R. Deslandes, 'Masculinity, identity and culture: male undergraduate life at Oxford and Cambridge' (PhD, University of Toronto, 1996), p. 46; this is published as

In matters sexual, moreover, young men turned above all to their peers for their codes and systems. What we might think of as 'underworld' constructions of masculinity, celebrating sexual adventure within a promiscuous paradigm, can be easily exampled within the Universities. At the 'unrespectable' end of the student spectrum, the 'fast' man remained a viable model of undergraduate masculinity throughout the century. The 1824 edition of a Cambridge student guide, for instance, came with a handy supplement on the two ways of proceeding to the BA degree, the orthodox 'reading' method being contrasted with an alternative 'varmint' version:

Now the *varmint* way to proceed to BA degree is this – Cut Lectures, go to Chapel as little as possible, dine in hall seldom more than once a week, give *Gaudies* and *Spreads*, keep a horse or two, go to NEWMARKET, attend the six-mile bottom, drive a drag, wear *varmint* clothes and well-built coats, be up to smoke, a rum one at Barnwell*, a regular go at New Zealand*, a staunch admirer of the bottle, and care a damn for no man.[57]

For the uninitiated into the geography of prostitution in nineteenth-century Cambridge, the asterisks explained that Barnwell and 'New Zealand' were celebrated as the residences 'of the Cyprian tribes'. These casual references to sexual opportunities suggest that profligacy was more than simply an accepted part of the lives of one cohort of students: it was offered rather as a model of masculine behaviour. Carried over into the nineteenth century with evident ease, he offered generations of students a model of masculinity that endorsed and celebrated sexual licence.

How far can we say that the undergraduate body deserved the reputation for debauchery it had inherited and attracted? This is a question that must necessarily remain frustratingly obscure, and the nature of the disciplinary apparatus in the Universities means that we can only catch glimpses of student sexual experiences. Records of students apprehended with women deemed to be prostitutes are sporadic and only modestly enlightening. There is only one source that allows a more detailed, and for want of a better, a systematic picture of student sex lives. This is the *Liber niger* maintained by the Oxford University proctors since the seventeenth century.[58] Both Cambridge and Oxford devoted a considerable bureaucracy to the registration and surveillance of those it deemed to be 'prostitutes', but the 'Black Book' represents the sole surviving continuous record of students engaged in sexual misdemeanours. Although it is not exclusively devoted to sexual infractions, this

P. R. Deslandes, *Oxbridge men: British masculinity and the undergraduate experience, 1850–1920* (Bloomington, 2005).

[57] *Gradus ad Cantabrigiam: or, new university guide to the academical customs, and colloquial or cant terms, peculiar to the University of Cambridge* (Cambridge, 1824), p. 122. Note that 'New Zealand' was the mocking name for the New Town, home to several brothels in early nineteenth-century Cambridge.

[58] *Liber niger sine registrum nebulosum* ('Black Book'), OUA P.R. 1/23/3; the records that I have been allowed to consult run from 1840 through to 1899.

record of the most prominent undergraduate offenders is notable for their pre-eminence. Registered in the proctors' formulaic dog-Latin, undergraduates are portrayed in the Black Book in variously compromising situations and activities, ranging from the more or less innocent to the definitively dissolute, such as:

cum duabus famae haud dubiae mulieribus, quibus herbam nicotinam dedit, e fenestra cubiculi sui collocutus est [having a conversation from his dorm window with two women of ill repute, to whom he gave cigarettes]

... *in loco vulgo dicto 'Dog Kennel Lane', cum meretrici colloquens* [conversing with prostitutes in 'Dog Kennel Lane']

... *inter alios nebulones, convivio intempestivo cum meretricibus, habitu quodam barbaro (dicto Bloomer) vestitis, in domo famosa apud villam de Abingdon* [among other ne'er-do-wells at a well-known house outside Abingdon, revelling with prostitutes dressed in what are popularly called 'Bloomers']

... *post mediam noctem turbulentus et ebrius per plateas vagans a custodibus pacis percontabatur ubi mulierculas invenire posset, postremo ad domum malae famae perveniens pulsando et clamando ingressum postulabat* [wandering riotous and drunk after midnight through the main streets, and demanding of the police where he might be able to find low-class women, finally arriving at a house of ill repute, where he was found shouting and knocking at the door demanding entry]

... *in infamem domum, ibidem cum meretrice concumbens deprehensus est* [he was found in a house of ill-repute found reclining with a prostitute][59]

These evocative little scenes can be roughly classified into the following tally of undergraduates found in compromising situations, all taken from the period from 1840 to 1899:

Found with, near, or talking to 'prostitutes'	85
Walking in the streets with 'prostitutes'	56
Found in a receiving house or 'prostitute's' rooms	53
Walking in the streets with servant girls or other townswomen	46
Found with, near, or talking to servant girls or other townswomen	28
Found in a brothel or house of ill-fame	28
Found in a tavern with 'prostitutes'	20
Found with women in alleyways or fields, and engaged in sexual activity	14
Travelling in a vehicle (boat, carriage, train) with prostitutes	8
Offences involving the corruption of boys or youths	7
Harassment of respectable women in the streets	6
Paying suit to a servant or townswoman	3
Attempted abduction of a young girl	2
Cohabitation	1

---

[59] 'Black Book', entries from 1851, 1862, 1870, 1886 and 1892.

What is notable in the first instance is that Oxford University's disciplinary net caught up young men involved not only in commercial sexual transactions but also those apprehended in the company of maidservants and working women. Whilst the proctorial systems at Oxford and Cambridge were intended primarily to police sex workers, the duty to protect undergraduates inevitably involved a more general and indiscriminate moral surveillance. The fact that the proctors resorted to terms as various as *'meretrices'*, *'oppida'*, *'mulieres'*, *'villana'* and *'puella'* indicated the problems involved. Identification of townswomen as 'prostitutes' was always contentious and a potential source of great embarrassment to the Universities.

The sources that survive therefore hardly indicate a general dissipation, but they do indicate the range of sexual relationships that could exist between undergraduate and townswoman, and the inability of University discipline to accommodate this diversity. One further question to which the survival of University records does offer some greater guidance, however, concerns the social background of these offenders. Is there any truth to the suggestion that students from more privileged upbringings were more prominent in promiscuity? Looking again at the Oxford cohort from the *Liber Niger* in the period 1840 to 1899, we may identify 112 students belonging to *Alumnae Oxoniensis's* 'armiger' class, 79 to that of 'gentlemen', 84 the sons of 'clerks', 9 the sons of medical men, and a single student of 'plebeian' origin. Added to these is a motley selection including the sons of an archdeacon, a baronet, several military officers and a Wesleyan minister. We can present these in tabular form:

Social origin	n	%
Peers	1	0
Knights and baronets	5	2
Esquires	112	36
Gentlemen	102	33
Clerks in holy orders	90	29
Plebeians	1	0
Pauperes pueri	0	0

This may be compared with earlier analyses which found that the ranks of esquires and above comprised some 30% of the total undergraduate population, that of gentlemen 28%, clergymen and medical men 30% and plebeians 11%.[60] It may be significant that virtually none from the very poorest backgrounds are represented, but, with the drastic underrepresentation of the plebeians excepted, the Black Book's social constituency is close to the composition of the University as a whole. There is a slight suggestion that gentlemen commoners are overrepresented,

---

[60] Compare J. C. Mitchell, 'The political demography of Cambridge 1832–1868', *Albion*, 9 (1977), 242–71, and Stone, 'Oxford student body', pp. 13–14.

but overall there is little here to back up that especial target of the moralists, the aristocratic debauchee.

There still remain immense, and probably unbridgeable, gaps in our knowledge about student sexual liaisons. Fragmentary bureaucratic records offer only limited glimpses into the world of sexual activity, and of course they say nothing about the emotional nature of this experience. We can perhaps only infer from the bluster and bravado of student peer culture, and suggest that the clubbable masculinity of the common room might easily translate into a treatment of women as little more than outlets for sexual energies. It is certainly not too difficult to find evidence of the coarsest misogyny, such as the likes of Francis Bradley Paget, of Trinity, who appeared before the Cambridge police court charged with throwing water from his lodgings over two local women, Catherine Mowlam and Ann Rumbelow. To the remonstrance of the policeman sent to investigate, Paget replied: 'Oh, they're only —— —— , and that will wash the —— off them.' When the policeman declared that he had made a mistake in calling them 'dirty whores', or whatever words he had used, Paget replied: 'All the women in Cambridge are —— .'[61]

Women and the trade in prostitution in Victorian Cambridge

What, then, of the women who were caught up in the workings of the proctorial system? Again, as with the undergraduates, the records are unusually revealing, if equally inevitably to be treated with a great deal of caution. Women suspected of prostitution and apprehended by the proctors in both towns were all duly registered and interrogated. If we return to our principal focus on Cambridge, we see that, in absolute numbers, the proctors arrested some 1,500 women in the period 1823–94, mostly in the 1830s, 1840s and 1850s, after which time a series of controversies forced the University's proctors into relative quiescence; the corresponding figure for Oxford, from 1822–62 is 1,298 arrested women (Figure 4.6).[62] Contemporary estimates of up to 200 prostitute women at any one time cannot have been too far from the mark: J. H. Titcomb, of the Cambridge Female Refuge, denied the charge that 1–200 prostitutes existed in Barnwell alone, but then promptly gave the true figure as a curiously precise 107.[63] The highest number of arrests in a single year was as many as 363, and the decennial averages in the 1840s climbed past 200.[64] These figures hide multiple arrests but they indicate nevertheless the scale of the prostitution business in Cambridge. The difficulty with assessments

---

[61] *Cambridge Chronicle*, 26 February 1870, p. 7. See also Mansfield, 'Grads and snobs'.
[62] The source for these figures and the following is the Spinning House committals books, CUA T.VIII. 1–3.
[63] 'A vindication of Barnwell', *Cambridge Chronicle*, 15 January 1853, p. 8.
[64] By comparison, Engel, 'Immoral intentions', pp. 84–5, hazards a figure of 3–500 'common prostitutes' in Oxford, of which 100 or so were habitual streetwalkers.

a. Cambridge

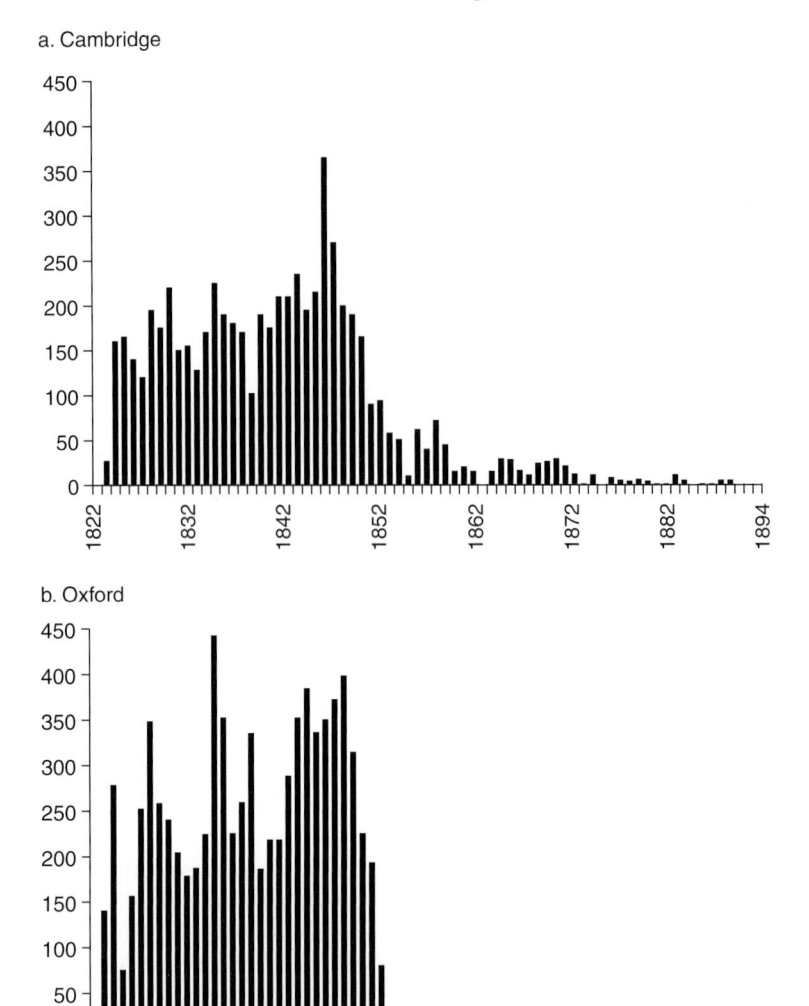

b. Oxford

Figure 4.6 Arrests of suspected prostitutes in Cambridge, 1823–94, and Oxford, 1822–53 (a. Cambridge; b. Oxford). From CUA T.VIII.1–3, Spinning House committals books and OUA MS.Top.Oxon.e.242–7, University Police reports.

like these remains though the fact that the Victorian definition of 'prostitute' was necessarily imprecise and highly elastic in its use; regulationist attempts at registration as a result both imposed on women the label and role of professional prostitute, as well as calling into being the spectre of an accompanying cohort of casual, unregistered prostitutes who had eluded detection. With these problems in mind, it is difficult to take the University's records as anything more than a confirmation of the objectifying power of the discourse and procedure of regulation itself. Arrested women were in effect forced to conform to stereotypes of female criminal sexuality, and to a homogeneity, that they could never have possessed in reality.

All the same, it is possible to say something about the background of the women arrested over the seventy or so years of operation of the modern proctorial system in Cambridge. The average age of women apprehended on suspicion of prostitution was nineteen, with a median of eighteen years, a figure that, as with other characteristics of prostitutes' lives, remained more or less constant throughout the nineteenth century. The fact that most women were to be found in their late teens and early twenties is roughly comparable to the findings of other studies of prostitution in Britain, but considerably younger than suggested for Liverpool and in regulationist regimes elsewhere. The fact that the women arrested were not younger still may reflect the Victorians' unwillingness to countenance the sexual agency and vulnerability of very young girls. On the other hand, older women were not unknown in Cambridge, with a sizeable number of women arrested for streetwalking in their thirties and forties.

These women typically originated in the small villages and the country parishes surrounding Cambridge, though many came from much further afield (Figure 4.7). It is true that women might base themselves in the country districts to evade the powers of the proctors, and entertain their clients from the University there. William Acton commented in this regard on the role of the country districts, with women moving to towns and districts beyond the jurisdiction of the proctors; others simply referred to the fact that 'the district immorality was poured into [Cambridge] every market-day'.[65] But the emphasis on the population of the rural districts is hardly surprising, given that Cambridge was a magnet for workers of all kinds, especially female workers. There is little to suggest that these women were anything but typical of the generation of immigrants to working-class Cambridge. Barnwell was certainly characterised by a considerable amount of migration and a high turnover of people, with half of all heads of households born outside of the borough, and half of these people outside the county. This was, generally, a society of the young, the poor and the migrant, attracted by the jobs either directly or indirectly provided by the University. Women arrested for prostitution offences were certainly drawn fairly and squarely from the labouring and artisan classes. Parents' occupations make clear that mothers were active as charwomen, laundresses, servants and dressmakers, whilst fathers were drawn either from the ranks of the unskilled – labourers, gardeners and the like – or those of the artisanate (Table 4.1). In both cases, a substantial number of college servants (bedmakers, cooks, groundsmen and gardeners) are to be found. In addition, only 40 per cent indicated that both parents were living, suggesting that a

---

[65] Acton, *Prostitution*, pp. 154–5; 'The late pro-proctors: important meeting in the Arts' School', *Cambridge Chronicle*, 5 February 1859, p. 7.

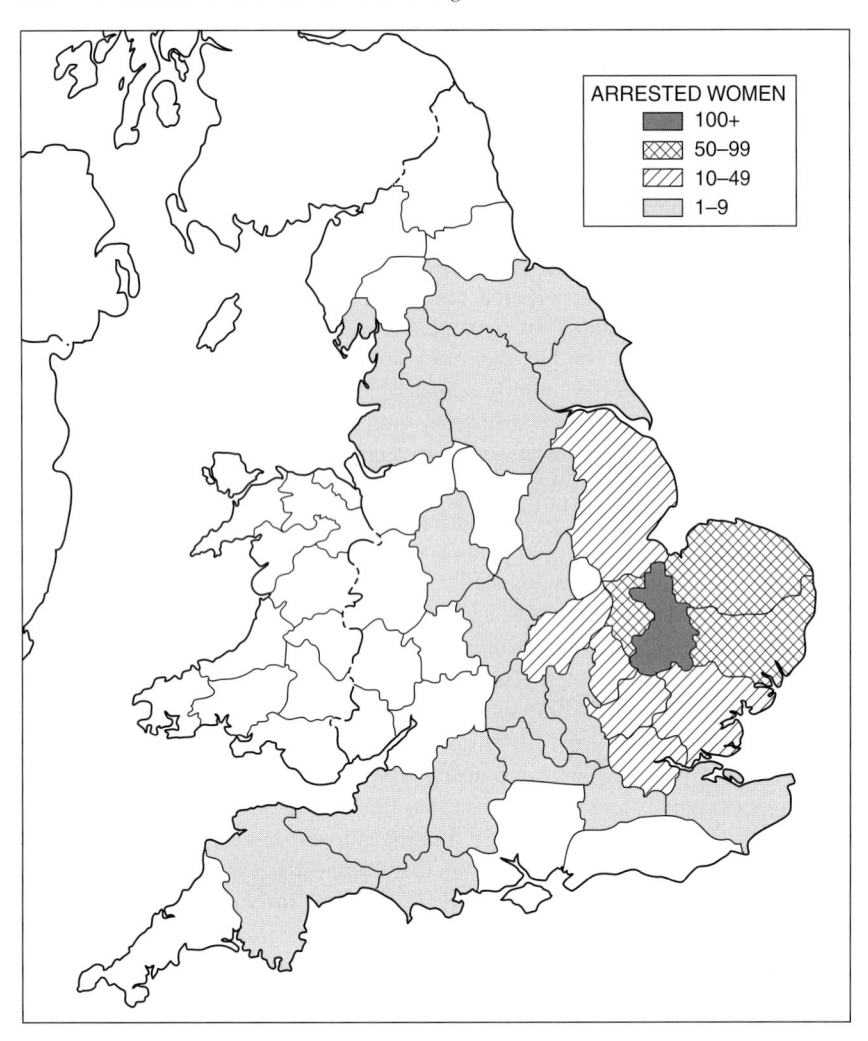

Figure 4.7 Geographical origin of arrested women in Cambridge, 1823–94. Source: Spinning House commitals books, CUA T.VIII.1–3.

disrupted family background was a part of many prostitutes' experiences. But, as with the geographical background of these women, it is hard to find distinctive qualities about this cohort of working-class women. It may in any case be a mistake to ask why these women took up prostitution, or lifestyles that might have laid them under suspicion, rather than other forms of work.

The 'professionalism' of this cohort of arrested women is also of necessity very difficult to determine. There is no sharp line of division between country girls and

Table 4.1 *Occupations of parents of women arrested by Cambridge proctors as suspected prostitutes, 1823–94, by employment classification*[a]

Agriculture, forestry and fishing (farmers, turfseller)	3
Food, drink and tobacco (baker, brewers, butcher, corn merchant)	5
Coal and petroleum products (coalporter)	1
Metal manufacture (blacksmiths)	2
Vehicles (coachmaker, coachtrimmer, wheelwright)	3
Metal goods not otherwise specified (hardware dealer)	1
Textiles (draper, lacemaker)	2
Leather, leather goods and fur (furrier)	1
Clothing and footwear (dressmakers, bootmakers, shoemakers, tailors)	13
Bricks, pottery, glass, cement, etc. (brickmaker)	1
Timber, furniture, etc. (basketmaker, cabinetmakers, carver and gilder, cooper)	5
Paper, printing and publishing (printers)	2
Construction (bricklayers, carpenters, painters, plasterer, stonemason)	17
Gas, electricity and water (gas worker)	1
Transport and communication (boatman, carrier, engine driver, flyman, horsekeeper, porter, waterman)	7
Insurance, banking, finance and business services (auctioneer)	1
Professional and scientific services (clerks, nurses, surgeon)	6
Miscellaneous services (bedmaker, charwomen, college servants, cricket ground custodian, cricketer, gamekeeper, gardeners, housekeepers, laundresses, publicans, saddlekeeper/innkeeper, servants, travelling fiddler, washerwomen)	60
Public administration and defence (relieving officer, sailors, soldiers)	5
Not classified (foreman, labourers)	33
Not occupied (brothelkeeper, prostitute)	2

[a] Source: Spinning House committals books, CUA T.VIII. 1–3.

domestics erroneously or feloniously found on the streets or talking with undergraduates, and the hardened professional prostitute inured to her lot. However, it is impossible to disregard completely the indications of professionalism that do exist in the records of arrests. Whilst nearly half of arrested women were apprehended by the proctors and their servants once only, and recidivism, at least by this measure, was not very high, there was a cadre of women who spent years on the city's streets, and in and out of the carceral institutions of Cambridge. These women's experiences closely correspond to those of other Victorian female criminals, with a high number of arrests and punitive detentions, for relatively short sentences, eventually arriving at a point at which authority became reluctant to prosecute the clearly 'incorrigible'. Records indicate an average period on the streets of only a year and a half, but if only repeat offenders are considered this figure rises to nearly three. Of those who were repeat offenders, half were reapprehended in the first three months, 70% in the first six months, and 86% within the first year. The interval between arrests could be many months, certainly, but there was a considerable number rearrested quickly, regularly and often. If only a tiny percentage (2.9%) were active ten years after their first arrest, those arrested more than once could find themselves arrested several times over the next few months or years. In addition, half the cohort made at least one appearance before the police courts, for offences such as drunkenness and disorderly behaviour, pickpocketing and threats. Such appearances before the magistrates compounded women's criminality, and added to the longevity and adhesiveness of their status as 'public women'. It was, moreover, not unusual for recalcitrant women to shuffle regularly between the Spinning House and the town gaol. The length of a prostituted woman's 'career', therefore, might extend over a considerably greater period than the University's records suggest. Something like 10 per cent were arrested ten or more times. At the very extreme were women like Rhoda Grant, who spent over two decades in the town working in the business of prostitution. Grant was born in the Cambridgeshire village of Bourn in 1817 or 1818, the daughter of a mat-maker, and was first arrested at the age of 18 in 1835, at which time she was living in the deprived and despised thoroughfare of Gas Lane. By her own testimony never in extreme poverty, though in the habit of drinking, Grant continually walked the streets after – she claimed – her seduction in Cambridge by a gownsman, except for a brief period in which she spent the best part of a year in the Female Refuge, before leaving in 1849 after a disagreement. She was living on her own in the notorious Union Row in 1851, and in Maria Stevens' Wellington Street brothel in 1856. She was last apprehended by the proctors in 1857, by which time she had made sixty-nine appearances before the proctors, together with seven Police Court appearances for brothel disturbances and for stealing from clients; she was also an inmate of the County Gaol at least four times. There is every indication that the proctors had given her up by this time as an 'incorrigible' for whom the terrors of the Spinning House offered little deterrent.[66]

The overall impression, therefore, is a mixed one: of a relatively small number of confirmed and 'professional' prostitutes mixed in with a larger number of women apprehended for casual assignations or even more or less innocent flirtations. Such records say little about the lives and careers of townswomen involved in prostitutional activity, of course. More detail is only possible through glancing at other records, particularly those of the Cambridge Female Refuge, and through indications of their agency in resisting the powers of authority. The two hundred

[66] Information from Spinning House records and police court reports, and from the Cambridge Female Refuge Minute Book, CRO R.60.27.2, 22 March 1848.

or so women who passed through the doors of the Refuge in fifteen years' worth of minutes are not a representative sample, by any means. Reformatories tended invariably to select the young, the new to the streets and the most tractable; nor can we assume that all these women were involved in commercial sexuality as we would understand it. Nevertheless, these women do provide much greater detail of their lives than can be ascertained from other records, and, even if this information was elicited in the scripted manner of the interrogation or confession, it has the advantage of being virtually in transcript form.

These Refuge inmates' narratives focus heavily on dislocation and translocation, telling as they do of broken homes and estranged families, sexual harassment, peripatetic working lives, quarrels with employers, seductions and rapes, failed courtships and cohabitations, and attempted suicides. Hannah Stittle's journey to the magdalen, for instance, was succinctly recorded in shorthand form: '21 years of age – born at Dry Drayton – illegitimate – her Mother died 16 years ago – was brought up by an aunt – went to service in a Public House at Broughton when 13 years old – fell into sin between 3 & 4 years since.'[67] Susanna Bowler found herself with only a stepfather who used her and her sister very cruelly and turned them out of doors.[68] And Amelia Sparrow summed up her fortunes in the following words: 'I have neither father nor mother, have been in the Cambridge Union 3 months, brought up at Ipswich by a Stranger, have no known settlement, have had two places in London, been on the town since August last, my last place was at Mr Miller's a Baker in Tooley Street, left there in May & went to Colchester, there I first commenced bad ways.'[69] Many traced their fall to a craving for excitement, bad company and influence. Elizabeth Fuller was persuaded to attend a country feast at the village of Barton, stayed out late, and was 'introduced by a female friend of light character to a young collegian from Cambridge to whom she surrendered herself'.[70] Martha Stevens was matter-of-factly invited by another girl to come to Cambridge and live in sin.[71] Public spaces like fairs were commonly written into these narratives of seduction and fall: Lavinia Robinson 'met a man in a booth who gave me beer & had his way of me'; Jane Aves 'went to the Fair without my Mistress' permission & fell into sin'; Mary Ann Beadsworth was found to be 'living in a sinful way since last Midsummer Fair; was led wrong by a Gentleman whom she met in a Booth.'[72] Others, like Mary Russell, claimed to have drifted into prostitution only after a series of relationships: 'I was never, strictly, *upon the Town* more than one week. I left him (Mr ——) or rather he left me, last week. I do not know with certainty where he now is. he is not the person

---

[67] Cambridge Female Refuge Minute Book, CRO R.60.27.1, 3 December 1839.
[68] *Ibid.*, 7 February 1842.   [69] *Ibid.*, 5 March 1838.   [70] *Ibid.*, 9 July 1839.
[71] Cambridge Female Refuge Minute Book, CRO R.60.27.2, 25 January 1848.
[72] *Ibid.*, 11 July 1843, 21 April 1846; Cambridge Female Refuge Minute Book, CRO R.60.27.1, 20 August 1839.

who first took me from home. *he* was also a gownsman. the latter is a fellow of a College. it was after the first person left me that I went upon the Town.'[73]

Such narratives cannot be taken at face value. As 'profound aporias of agency', these are generic narratives of 'attenuated autonomy and fractured identity', in which these women 'fail to present or maintain an authentic, private, or self-regulating identity'; their engagement both with others and with the world around them is constructed as a testament to the dangers that existed to all women who dared to leave their domestic confines.[74] The language of these accounts – 'led into sin', 'went into sin', 'fell into sin', 'threw myself into sin', 'suffered into sin' – all helped construct the prostitute as a fallen woman whose loss of agency was catastrophic and only with great difficulty reclaimable. To some extent this reflected the exigencies of a world in which women might easily find themselves friendless and alone, in debt, in distress or in thrall; the fact that women were prepared to suffer the rigours of a reformatory is evidence in itself of their vulnerability. This was brought home most tragically in 1876, with the murder of a young prostitute, Emma Rolfe, fifteen years old, who had gone with a client, a Robert Browning, onto Midsummer Common for the purpose of sex. He had intended to kill a girl from whom he believed he had contracted gonorrhoea, but slit Rolfe's throat instead. Before he was executed in the town gaol, Browning ruefully observed: 'I didn't give the poor girl much time to repent or reflect, I can't say which.' A crowd of townspeople attended her burial in Mill Road cemetery, exhibiting a wordless solidarity expressive of the state of feeling in the town towards the prostitute's lot.[75]

If Emma Rolfe represents the extreme vulnerability and victimisation of women engaged in prostitution, we must not let her stand for all such women. Although discussions of prostitutes' agency or lack of it have become somewhat circular and inconclusive, it is still worthwhile emphasising the active roles of female sex workers, and in particular their resistance to the power of authorities such as the police and the University. Quite apart from the complex trajectories of these women's lives, of which official records offer only a glimpse, and which indicate the insufficiency of narratives of a failure of agency, it is clear that women in this situation often refused the ascriptive and disciplinary dictates of regulationist thinking and practice. That apprehended women had constant recourse to false names and accounts, or learned to tailor their responses to elicit the greatest sympathy and leniency, is one facet of such resistance. The violent responses of women confined in the Spinning House or

---

[73] Cambridge Female Refuge Minute Book, CRO R.60.27.2, 17 September 1844, emphasis in original.

[74] A. Anderson, *Tainted souls and painted faces: the rhetoric of fallenness in Victorian culture* (Ithaca, 1993), pp. 47, 63, 2.

[75] *Cambridge Chronicle*, 25 November 1876, pp. 4, 8, and 16 December 1876, p. 8. See also the depositions in the case of Robert Browning, Norfolk Assizes, National Archives ASSI 36/21.

Female Refuge amount to another. At the Female Refuge, many, like Sarah Fordham, who 'fell into sin for the sake of making a living', were very matter-of-fact about the circumstances that drew them into prostitution. Elizabeth Christian likewise noted that she was 'first led to such sin by not having work to do'; Clara Duncan was simply 'advised to come up to Cambridge for the purpose of prostituting myself'.[76] Episodes of resistance are as much in evidence here as in other refuges and reformatories. Asked why she wanted to leave the magdalen, Charlotte Dorrington confessed that 'I have never been comfortable since I have been in the House. I have a shocking bad temper and others have also – I have been uncomfortable and do not intend to stay till next week ... I intend to go *now*.'[77] Similarly, Eliza Battel stated that she had nothing to complain of in the Refuge, but that 'she thought it was quite time for her to do something for herself'.[78] Sarah Letteridge more succinctly insisted: 'I can't stay – I *must* go – I *will* go.'[79]

Women's resistance was, moreover, bound up with popular resentment of authority. On 26 February, for instance, Sarah Crowe, after having been warned off the streets, refused to accompany a proctor's man, and resisted violently, at which time a mob of several hundred on Downing Street had collected to help her. 'They cried out "Shame, shame. Don't let him take her". Some one called out, Punch their heads.'[80] Rescues of suspected prostitutes were regularly attempted and effected, the fifth of November being a particular flashpoint: Elizabeth Ison, apprehended by the police in 1859, noted that on that traditional evening of town-gown standoffs she was 'following the mob, who were endeavouring to get up a row, and being recommended to 'move on' by a gentleman in blue, she refused to do anything of the sort for such a —— cad, and told him she would see him (further) first'.[81] So the 'gown' did not have it all its own way. Women found themselves subject to an extraordinary disciplinary surveillance in the University towns, but even the humblest might find ways to evade or to resist the proctors and their allies. In time, moreover, the agitation against the Contagious Diseases Acts and against all forms of regulation would turn the tide of public opinion against the practices of the Universities, allowing such women to place the proctors in the dock, both metaphorically and literally.

Reform and repeal

In both Oxford and Cambridge, the inequities of the proctorial system became a recurrent feature of town versus gown rivalries in which the exploitation of

---

[76] Cambridge Female Refuge Minute Book, CRO R.60.27.2, 16 March 1847, 17 November 1847, 6 April 1852.
[77] *Ibid.*, 19 April 1842.   [78] *Ibid.*, 19 July 1842.   [79] *Ibid.*, 19 November 1844.
[80] Deposition of PC William Maltby, Guard Book, 1548–1900, CUA CUR 41.1.150.
[81] *Cambridge Chronicle*, 12 January 1859, p. 8.

townswomen by the Universities and their students could stand in for a whole raft of grievances felt by the townspeople as a whole. Indeed, the system became the most intractable question to be resolved between the two. In Oxford, the night watch was given up in the early 1860s, their powers transferred to the borough, at the University's request; the University, under attack for the abuse of its unconstitutional and unnecessary powers, effectively ceded its responsibilities to the municipal authorities. In Cambridge, however, though the University also gradually ceded the bulk of its special privileges to the borough during the nineteenth century, the right to apprehend suspected prostitutes was jealously guarded in the face of much agitation against it and many reviews of its operations. This was true throughout the 1850s and the great age of University reform. Relations between the borough and the University were amongst the issues settled by the arbitration of Sir John Patteson in 1855. Although the award largely came down in favour of the retention of University privileges, the process generated considerable debate over the proctorial system. The University and its defenders continued to argue the evenhandedness of its justice, stressing the benefits accruing to the town by insisting that the system protected townswomen from the attentions of young men, and this was a position that Patteson came wholeheartedly to accept:

Where a considerable part of the population consists of young Men at a very critical time of life, with strong passions and little self-control, greater powers must necessarily be given to some authorities, as well as to restrain the young Men themselves, as to guard them from the solicitation of Prostitutes, and also to protect the respectable Inhabitants of the Borough from molestation and annoyance.[82]

But this was not the end of the matter, with resentments simmering through the ensuing decades. The University was always able to count on the support of many amongst the respectable and the ratepaying classes, but by the later nineteenth century the question had become a firmly political one, with not only local but also national opponents seizing on the issue as symbolic of the chains in which the borough was kept by the University. For them, the proctorial system was 'opposed to the spirit of the English constitution, subversive of the liberty of the subject, repugnant to the feelings of the inhabitants of this town, and wholly inoperative as affecting the objects which they profess to accomplish'.[83]

Even before the passing of the Contagious Diseases Acts, the climate of opinion in the Universities was changing. Particularly significant in this regard were the Cambridge controversies of 1859 and 1860. In 1859, following successive discoveries of undergraduates in town brothels, two proctors with strong evangelical sympathies had attempted to come down hard on one of the students involved, assuming that the recently reformed University statutes empowered

[82] CUA T.XI.1, Award of Sir J. Patteson, 1855, p. 179.
[83] 'Memorial of a meeting at the Hoop Hotel', *Cambridge Chronicle*, 18 February 1860, p. 5.

them to treat the male client as strictly as the female prostitute had been in the past. The result was a damaging standoff between the proctors, George Williams and F. J. Jameson, the college tutors, and the Vice-Chancellor. The latter censured the proctors, arguing that discretion should have been exercised as it was a first offence. Williams and Jameson promptly resigned, and an acrimonious meeting was held in the Arts school to discuss their interpretation of the new statutes.[84] At this meeting, Jameson noted that the offence involved was a frightful, if common, evil, and protested 'as a member of a Christian University, and as a working clergyman in Cambridge', against the ruinous laxity affirmed by the Vice-Chancellor's Court. Speaking to the gallery, Jameson argued that the time was ripe for a thoroughgoing moral reformation:

If, Mr Vice Chancellor, the University announces in a Court from which there is no appeal, that fornication is a light offence, and one which demands no punishment, what must be the effect on the character of the hundreds of our students, who at an age when they need every defence against the temptations of Academic life, look to her as their moral as well as intellectual guide? ... Is she commending herself to the confidence of the country, as a place where a large number of our future religious teachers may safely be trained, when such is the model of moral instruction which she sets before them? And is *this* the moment for re-asserting the principles of laxity on which we too long have acted, when we are entering on a new era in the University, and when the eyes of the public are upon us?[85]

At 'the opening of a new academical era', as Jameson put it, 'The present controversy is really between the antiquated views of discipline still to be found in our body and the growing opinion that if our University is to stand well in the face of the country she must foster a higher moral tone than hitherto.'[86] Adam Sedgwick, now in his seventies, and an ex-proctor of the old – temporising – regime, spoke up in support of the Vice-Chancellor's censuring of the proctors' actions. Confessing his ignorance of the case, Sedgwick was nevertheless stringent in his condemnation of the proctors' judgement:

Suppose they went with Draconic fury to attack a man who had the great misfortune to be caught, he hesitated not to say that the academic prospects of that man would be blotted out. Consider what human nature is: how liable it was to fall! How impossible it was to construct laws or to execute them with such severity as to prevent impurity! ... And with regard to morality, good gracious, was a man to have his prospects blighted for ever, because he fell before temptation? It was certain – he knew it to be true – that men on the bench of BISHOPS – and good men too – would have been in a state of degradation, that men sitting upon the official bench of the sovereign would have been degraded, if

---

[84] See CUA VCCt/I/21, Acta Curiae 1846–61, 2 November 1858, 12 December 1858, CUR 40, Vice-Chancellor's Court, case of Alexander Henry Green.
[85] 'The late pro-proctors and the Vice-Chancellor', *Cambridge Chronicle*, 22 January 1859, p. 4.
[86] *Cambridge Chronicle*, 29 January 1859, p. 8.

this miserable system of allowing no pliancy were adhered to, if no feeling were allowed whereby you might win a man back who had gone astray.[87]

This salvo proved to be, however, in its blunt recapitulation of the tenets of classic moralism, entirely embarrassing in the context of political reform. Even his defenders asked that the Woodwardian Professor be excused on account of his great age, for belonging to a former generation ill at ease with contemporary realities, and as 'one who has breathed the atmosphere of laxity which was characteristic of the Georgian period of our history': 'I think this principle will explain the otherwise strange phenomenon, that in these days men of advanced age, though themselves moral and virtuous, are frequently found, I will not say defending, but palliating and attenuating immorality.'[88] Sedgwick's indulgence towards the vices of students could be made to seem, in the reforming era, as anachronistic as his geology. The *Record* deemed it instead a fitting occasion for 'a bold testimony against a sin which, like a dreadful ulcer, is eating into the very heart of our universities and carrying swiftly to perdition some of the choicest sons of the nation'. Despite the current campaigns for a higher morality, it went on to condemn the University for 'that timid, temporizing spirit which is afraid to do good lest it should do evil, and which retreats to the shelter of a blind antiquity ... They will have the thanks of old debauchers whose career of shame they have thus accredited, and of youthful profligates to whose excesses they have been so indulgent.'[89] For its part, the radical *Guardian* lamented 'that the old traditions of the venial nature of immorality and incontinence still haunt the lodges and common rooms of Cambridge, diffusing an atmosphere very prejudicial to the purity of Christian youth'.[90]

Worse than this internal dissension, which had the effect of accentuating divisions between the University and the evangelical clergy in its ranks, and which pitted the University against the march of morals, was the controversy over the apprehension of five women the following year. These women had been participants in an undergraduate expedition to a 'Bachelors' Ball' in the village of Great Shelford, but were seized from the omnibus chartered to take them there.[91] The women involved claimed entire innocence, and with help from borough agitators set in motion actions against the Vice-Chancellor for false imprisonment. Their counsel pointedly asked why students at Cambridge needed such protection when students at London, Edinburgh and elsewhere did not: 'Cambridge was the only

---

[87] *Cambridge Chronicle*, 5 February 1859, p. 7.
[88] *Cambridge Chronicle*, 12 Feburary 1859, pp. 4–5.
[89] *Record*, quoted in *Cambridge Chronicle*, 29 January 1859, p. 8.
[90] *Guardian*, 2 February 1859, p. 89.
[91] See R. Parker, *Town and gown: the 700 years' war in Cambridge* (Cambridge, 1983), p. 151.

place in which this relic of monastic institution was allowed to subsist.'[92] The law did not recognise private gaols, another lawyer noted, and the Vice-Chancellor might as well have committed her to his own private wine-cellar. Edwin James QC went on:

> If the same so-called justice was meted out to the men at Cambridge, men who were wandering through the streets of Cambridge habitually and soliciting the poor girls, the University authorities would have a great deal more to do, and would have to employ a much larger number of 'bull-dogs'.[93]

The effect of these twin controversies – and the verdicts generally went with the plaintiffs – was to usher the University authorities into an era of prudence bordering on complete inaction. Save for a flurry of activity in the late 1860s and 1870s, interestingly coincident with the heyday of the Contagious Diseases Acts, apprehensions by the proctors in Cambridge were virtually brought to a halt. And, although some feared that the habitués of the Haymarket would descend upon the town *en masse*, no effective proposals for returning the system to its former levels of vigilance were attempted.

The important point here remains that the charges brought against the University were almost exactly the same as those that were levelled at the Contagious Diseases Acts. A correspondent to the repeal journal, *The Shield,* observed that 'one can easily understand how the members of a University which has long accustomed itself to over-ride the personal liberty of women, and to act extra-legally with regard to persons not in any way within its jurisdiction, should be found ready in so large a number to support a system like the Contagious Diseases Acts, which proposes to subordinate all the most sacred personal rights of women to the fancied immunity of vicious men'.[94] Moreover, since 'streetwalker' and prostitute were essentially interchangeable terms, critics argued, any woman in a public space was suspect. The several cases of supposed mistaken identity turned on the proctors' rights to apprehend women in public, and Liberals and radicals protested this un-English interference with ancient rights; as *The Telegraph*, grinding the sharpest axe, put it:

> Cambridge is ... no fit place for a decent and respectable woman to live in. Many and many have been the outrages perpetrated in the Town by the Proctors and their bulldogs, for it is seldom that the poor, however grievous their wrongs, can obtain such assistance as will enable them to prosecute a cause, whose defenders are backed by the funds of a wealthy University. Young girls, of stainless character and modest manners, have been seized in the streets, their garments half torn off by their brutal assailants, scoffed at as

---

[92] See Proctorial Suit, Kemp v. Neville: CUA CUR 41.2 and CUR 41.3. and *Cambridge Chronicle*, 23 June 1860, p. 9.
[93] *Cambridge Chronicle*, 1 December 1860, supplement.
[94] W. C. E., 'The Cambridge "Spinning-House" – proctorial "protection" of students', *Shield*, 24 February 1872, 839–40, p. 839.

prostitutes, subject to humiliating examinations by medical men and foully insulted by the cross-questioning of their secret judge, and, after suffering this most abominable and lawless treatment, have been released, with or without punishment, utterly unable to vindicate themselves. The Proctors and their bulldogs are the terror and the opprobrium of Cambridge.[95]

Opponents of the system constantly pressed this point: wasn't this system of prostitutional and public space really a matter of procuring clean women of the town for the use of undergraduates? And wasn't 'privacy' – the University's secrecy, its private privileges, the jealous protection of its members – claimed at the expense of the young women made irredeemably public in the exchange? Despite one supporter's claim that 'the nature of their offence makes them court privacy, and public morals require it', it was hard to avoid the impression that whatever advantages of the separation of public from private accrued only to the undergraduates and to the University.[96] Public space, and the right to inhabit it, became the key point at issue. Whilst the proctors were the guardians of good order to some, they had become to others 'bloated erotic pedants', 'busy and *impertinent prigs*' who abused their uniquely extensive powers to take up any woman in the streets on suspicion of prostitution; and in a neat inversion *The Telegraph* went on to accuse the proctors of 'not confining their operations to the night time, but parading the streets in broad day'.[97] By the time that proctors rather than the prostitutes could be accused of intruding outrageously into public space, the system's day had gone. Even the Cambridge Union passed censure on the proctorial system in 1883 – the year of the suspension of the CD Acts – one debater damning it as 'a permanent Coercion Act which the Irish do not suffer, and a relic of the days when women were burnt for witchcraft'.[98]

Conclusions

In the era of the Contagious Diseases Acts, the Universities had proved to be not only a useful precedent for regulationists but also a stick with which to beat them. For the repeal-minded, the Universities were well worth watching: the sanitationist B. W. Richardson used his medical report on Cambridge, for instance, to criticise the nature of regulationist legislation and the prospects of their general application to the civil population:

Prostitution is theoretically under great control in Cambridge, the University law in reference to the suppression of open prostitution being all that the most rigid law makers

---

[95] See 'Barnwell Gorger', quoted in *Cambridge Chronicle*, 8 December 1860, p. 7.
[96] *Cambridge Chronicle*, 24 November 1860, p. 8.
[97] *Cambridge Chronicle*, 10 March 1860; *Telegraph*, quoted in *Cambridge Chronicle*, 24 March 1860, p. 5.
[98] *Cambridge Review*, 4 (1883), p. 312.

could desire. It is notorious, however, that prostitution is very rife, and I learned that not less than 200 women of loose character, and who *sub rosâ* pursue their peculiar calling, were known to the authorities. The prevalence of venereal disease is very great, and I received as an authority I cannot doubt that very few of the young men who go through University life escape one or other forms of the disease. This is one of the sad reflections that casts itself over the University life, and it is a point of the greatest difficulty to know how to meet the evil. The present system at Cambridge, in which the presence of vice is concealed by the suppression of its appearance, certainly does not give much evidence of success, nor offer inducements to our legislators to extend that particular plan to the country at large.[99]

The Universities' actions were to be condemned not only from a medical but also from a moral point of view. It is significant that the great feminist repealers took a special interest in the undergraduate bodies, given that they were of the same class and that they would become the leaders of tomorrow. Josephine Butler, for instance, knew both Universities well, and her campaigns for the education of women had prepared her for both the general prejudice against women and the double standard of sexuality. It is reported that Butler was early on exposed to the atmosphere of Oxford in the 1850s, and offended by the levity and hypocrisy of the common room. Responding to rumours that a don had seduced a young girl who had borne his child, Butler apparently expressed the hope that the don would be brought to a 'sense of his crime', only to be advised that a 'pure woman ... should be absolutely ignorant of a certain class of evils in the world'.[100] In 1879, supported by her great ally and friend, the Cambridge professor James Stuart, she would commend social purity to the undergraduates; two years later, she made a tour of the Oxford colleges, determined to 'speak on this subject if only 20 words to *everyone* I meet at Oxford even casually'.[101] Stuart himself argued that the preventative measure of addressing the 'low tone so often existing among men' was as important as the curative work of women's rescue agencies.[102] Another purity advocate advised Cambridge undergraduates that 'you can do much in your University here to carry out that end by not tolerating loose talk, not tolerating light ways of treating impurity in any form; representing it always as a serious matter, a serious wrong doing, and by never permitting yourself or others to jest upon it or to

---

[99] B. W. Richardson, 'The medical history of Cambridge', excerpted from *The Medical History of England, The Medical Times and Gazette: A Journal of Medical Science, Literature, Criticism, and News*, volume II (1864), pp. 559–601, 628–32, 657–61, p. 660.

[100] H. Cook, *The long sexual revolution: English women, sex, and contraception 1800–1975* (Oxford, 2004), p. 92, quoting from Josephine Butler, *Recollections of George Butler* (1892).

[101] J. Jordan, 'Introduction', in J. Jordan (ed.), *Josephine Butler and the prostitution campaigns: diseases of the body politic, volume III: the constitution violated: the parliamentary campaign* (London, 2003), pp. 10, 173.

[102] J. Stuart, 'Social purity', *Cambridge Review,* I (1879), 84–5.

treat it lightly'.[103] Ellice Hopkins, too, appealed directly, and in the most emotional terms, to the manliness and patriotism of the undergraduates of Oxford:

Bearing on my woman's heart the shame and sin and anguish of my own sisters, my hands always full of children degraded by the fearfully debased manhood in our midst – never for one moment have I lost faith in the men of England. It isn't English![104]

In the 'Oxbridge' of the later nineteenth century, with the rise of social purity organisations within the student ranks, the promotion of sport as an outlet for undergraduate energies, and with the influx of female undergraduates, it was increasingly difficult to defend the proctorial system and the temporising, worldly culture on which it depended. The energy expended against finding and securing suspected prostitutes in the first half of the nineteenth century was increasingly directed in the second half at the undergraduate offender: promiscuous *men*, as opposed to promiscuous women, were now posed as the pre-eminent problem. One indication of this is that the stock literary figures of the debauched Oxonian and the vicious Cantab were being replaced by a more rigid fictional morality, in which sexual incontinence was deplored and chastity prized. The improving mid-Victorian university novel continued the theme of student profligacy and promiscuity, but only as a foil to a new model masculinity, one that dispensed with the older genre's tolerance and worldliness. At Oxford, Tom Brown is the epitome of the new university hero, whilst, at Cambridge, Frederic Farrar's Julian Home similarly counselled the unwary against 'the foul haunts of squalid dissipation and living death'.[105] That these new university fictions coincided with the era of political reform at Oxford and Cambridge suggests that the universities would be judged in part by the standards of undergraduate morality, institutional reform by the prospects for the reformation of men. The most heartfelt critique of indulgence is Farrar's Julian Home, who advises his erring friend to reject the doctrine of wild oats and worldly experience – 'loathly experience!' – by bearing in mind the women he has ruined:

Remember the wretched victims of your infamous passions, and tremble while you desecrate and deface for ever God's image stamped on a fair human soul. Think of those whom your vileness dooms to a life of loathliness, a death of shame and anguish, perhaps an eternity of horrible despair. Learn something of the days they are forced to spend

---

[103] J. M. Wilson, *An address to the Cambridge University Association for the Promotion of Purity of Life* (Cambridge, 1883), p. 6.

[104] See R. M. Barrett, *Ellice Hopkins: a memoir* (London, 1907), p. 170, cited in E. Mynott, 'Purity, prostitution and politics: social purity in Manchester 1880–1900' (PhD, University of Manchester, 1995), p. 146; see also S. Morgan, '"Wild oats or acorns?" Social purity, sexual politics and the response of the late-Victorian Church', *Journal of Religious History*, 31 (2007), 151–68.

[105] T. Hughes, *Tom Brown at Oxford* (London, 1861), F. W. Farrar, *Julian Home: a tale of college life* (London, 1859), p. 333.

that they may pander to the worst instincts of your degraded nature; days of squalor and drunkenness, disease and dirt; gin at morning, noon, and night; eating infection, horrible madness, and sudden death at the end. Can you ever hope for salvation and the light of God's presence while the cry of the souls of which have been *the murderer* – yes, do not disguise it, the *murderer*, the cruel, willing, pitiless murderer – is ringing upwards from the depths of hell?[106]

Debates over the reformation of the Universities thoroughly examined the ethos and the purpose of university education, and were increasingly coloured by the advance of social purity and the legislative attacks on the double standard. As the nature of 'Oxbridge' and its role in the national culture was placed on the political agenda, the undergraduate's sexual life was perhaps at no time under such careful scrutiny: Paul Deslandes has recently emphasised the importance of Oxbridge to the construction of British and imperial masculinity in the Victorian and Edwardian era, an identity inseparable from the homosocial and heterosocial parameters of the undergraduate experience, and thus inseparable from questions of both gender and sexuality.[107] In these conditions, sexual licence could no longer be winked at, and the transformation in attitudes is palpable. Concerns for youth, masculinity and sexuality, powerful in themselves let alone in combination, had never entirely escaped critical surveillance, but these took on a particularly charged political significance in the 1850s and 1860s and beyond, to the repeal of the Contagious Diseases Acts and the retreat of the old moral order on a broad front.

The end of these regimes came quickly, and like the Contagious Diseases Acts after some years of abeyance. In the early 1890s, in response to the imprisonment of yet more apparently innocent women in both Oxford and Cambridge, one final assault on the institutional double standard was mounted. *The Modern Review* asked why the ordinary law was not good enough for the undergraduates at the Universities, adding that 'Only one of two conclusions can be arrived at in the matter – either that their moral virtue is of an exceedingly frail character and needs extraordinary care and attention in order to grow to a healthy maturity; or else that these young men are the salt of the earth, and everyone besides may be sacrificed lest haply one of them should fall.'[108] In Cambridge, the authorities quickly threw in the towel, and the proctorial system, statutorily alive for several hundred years, came to an ignominious end with the tearing down of that icon of regulation, the long abominated Spinning House.

[106] Farrar, *Julian Home*, pp. 264–5, 266.
[107] See Deslandes, *Oxbridge men*.
[108] 'The sins of our cities', *The Modern Review*, 4 January 1893, p. 330.

5

Sexuality, sovereignty and space: colonial law and the making of prostitute subjects in Gibraltar and the British Mediterranean

Whilst the two previous substantive chapters have considered the policing and management of prostitution in Britain, this chapter and the next present examples of colonial regulationist regimes. This chapter needs some preliminary justification, however, since it may seem perverse to begin a consideration of the colonial regulation of prostitution with the distinctly minor colonies of the British Mediterranean. Gibraltar and the other mid-nineteenth-century British possessions of Malta and the Ionian Islands are insignificant compared, say, to the immensity and the importance of British India. As accidents of conquest, legacies from the rounds of struggle between the great powers, they belong more to the old empire than to the new. They were retained largely so that they might be denied to other states, and valued for their military and strategic situation rather than for any grander designs of colonial settlement or exploitation. It is thus hard to see them as exemplars of British colonial dominion in the high imperial era. What is more, only Malta fits our conventional timeline of decolonisation, having gained its independence in 1964. The Ionian Islands were united with Greece exactly a hundred years earlier, a signally early instance of British concession in the face of implacable nationalist resistance, and Gibraltar maintains its connection with the United Kingdom, embarrassment about its apparently anomalous attachment to imperial and colonial status only serving to emphasise our difficulties in placing it within the established narratives of empire.[1]

Accordingly, the British Mediterranean remains marginal to the analysis of colonial rule that has come to dominate the historiography. Some of the predominant themes of colonial and post-colonial studies – the putative rule of racial difference, the dispossession by othering of indigenous peoples, the cultural chasm between the colonisers and the colonised – are all rather less readily applicable to Britain's European colonies than they are to those in which 'white' colonisers

---

[1] See the excellent critical commentary of D. Lambert, '"As solid as the Rock": place, belonging and the local appropriation of imperial discourse in Gibraltar', *Transactions of the Institute of British Geographers*, 30 (2005), 206–20.

confronted 'non-white' natives.[2] Since comparisons between the nearer and the further forms of British colonial rule remain controversial, raising as many questions as they answer, we may simply follow Terry Eagleton's observation that '[i]t is possible to rank different forms of colonialism according to their degrees of visibility', and assert that these specks of British imperial power in the Mediterranean remain all too easy for the historian of British colonialism to overlook.[3]

The British Mediterranean deserves greater notice from those interested in the nature and mechanics of colonial rule, however. From our particular perspective, Malta, Gibraltar and the Ionian Islands certainly take on greater importance than they have previously been accorded. Though peripheral to most accounts of colonial regulationism, these places were long prominent in the justification of contagious diseases legislation in Britain. As has already been noted in passing, Malta under the governorship of Sir Henry Storks was held up as a particularly successful example of how such legislation might be used to combat venereal disease, which was supposed by supporters of the system to be virtually eradicated on the island by the mid-1860s. Indeed, the only disappointment Storks seems to have expressed was the fact that he had not the power to inspect the wives of soldiers as well as the common prostitutes of the island. In his previous administration of the Ionian Islands, moreover, Storks had also attempted to address the problem of prostitution, and again claimed more or less total success in eliminating disease from Zante, Cephalonia and Corfu, where it is clear that women were inspected at least twice a month for disease, by use of the speculum, and that prostitutes paid a small fee to the police surgeon for their examination.[4] Malta and the Ionian Islands were straightforwardly regulationist regimes, stringently policed in the service of social hygiene.

For advocates of the Contagious Diseases Acts and their extension throughout Britain, these central Mediterranean stations were indeed more important than other ostensibly more significant colonies where medical measures were in place, because their success in tackling disease was regarded as wholly indisputable.

---

[2] Irish studies provide an exception: see L. P. Curtis, *Apes and angels: Irishmen in Victorian caricature*, 2nd edition (Washington, 1997), for the best-known study of the Victorian racialisation of the Irish. Drawing on some of this analysis, in an exceptional study of the Ionian Islands, Thomas Gallant suggests that the use of related stereotypes amounts to the construction of a subordinate colonial identity of the islanders as 'the Irish of the Mediterranean'; however, he also sharply criticises the dominant Saidian model of cultural opposition: T. W. Gallant, *Experiencing dominion: culture, identity, and power in the British Mediterranean* (Notre Dame, 2002).

[3] T. Eagleton, 'Afterword: Ireland and colonialism', in T. McDonough (ed.), *Was Ireland a colony? Economics, politics and culture in nineteenth-century Ireland* (Dublin, 2005), p. 326.

[4] In this chapter, note that I use the prevailing nineteenth-century British and Italian names for the Ionian Islands and their communities, rather than the current Greek equivalents: thus Corfu rather than Kerkyra, and Zante rather than Zakinthos, and so on.

These colonies – however small, however now neglected – became the pattern stations for the kind of medical surveillance and supervision envisaged by promoters of the CD Acts both at home and elsewhere in the Empire. Most important early on was the persuasion of the influential Skey committee on venereal diseases which first recommended the introduction of periodic medical examination. Admiral Sir William Fanshawe Martin, one of the most prestigious witnesses to the commission, used the experiments in Malta strongly to urge the extension of the CD Acts from the garrison towns to the whole country:

> There should be no trifling in this matter – the disease is ruining multitudes of innocent as well as of guilty, it embarrasses the service, squanders the public money, and saps the stamina of the population ...
>
> Your experience of the results of the surveillance at Malta, and elsewhere, leads you to be decidedly in its favour? – Most decidedly, and I think we shall neglect an important national duty if we do not enforce it in Engand.[5]

Subsequent supporters of the CD Acts, such as the pioneer female doctor, Elizabeth Garrett, and the ideologue of regulation, C. W. Shirley Deakin, similarly took the view that Malta under Storks' government conclusively proved the wisdom of the sanitary policing of prostitution.[6] In 1868, John Brendon Curgenven, secretary of the movement for extension of the CD Acts to the civilian population of the British Isles, also argued that the sanitary regimes not just of Malta but also of Gibraltar and the Ionian Islands demonstrated the efficacy of medical surveillance. Curgenven even claimed that regulation in these three stations had led there to the near disappearance of prostitution as well as venereal disease. The moral, for him, was straightforward: 'while the Government and the local authorities are instituting measures of prevention in our possessions in all parts of the world, does it become us to look quietly on the ravages of this disease amongst ourselves, and take no steps to check its fatal progress?'[7] From the opposing perspective, these near-at-hand colonies were just as salutary. Josephine Butler lamented the fact that the arbitrary operation of the Maltese regulations was virtually unrestricted by countervailing authority; and, for her, Malta was an ominous warning of the kinds of regulation that could be installed in all of the British colonial possessions: 'The iron police rule which it establishes over women, and the unbounded discretion which it places in the hands of constables are typical of the lengths to which Englishmen will go in tyranny when dealing with a dependent race,

---

[5] *Report of the committee*, P.P. 1867–8 (4031) XXXVII.425, p. 1072.

[6] E. Garrett, *An enquiry into the character of the Contagious Diseases Acts of 1866–1869* (London, 1870), p. 12; C. W. S. Deakin, *The Contagious Diseases Acts: the Contagious Acts '64, '66, '68 (Ireland), '69. From a sanitary and economic point of view* (London, 1872).

[7] J. B. Curgenven, *The Contagious Diseases Act of 1866, and its extension to the civil population of the United Kingdom* (London, 1868), p. 12.

Colonial law and prostitute subjects in Gibraltar   155

and acting in collusion with Government experts at home, sheltered from public criticism by the strong doors of the Departmental Offices.'[8]

Precisely because these regimes were considered so important at the time to the progress of British regulationism, this chapter considers their contribution to British colonial rule in the Mediterranean in some detail. After glancing at Malta, briefly, and at Corfu in a little more depth, the central substantive example we come to focus on is that of the garrison colony of Gibraltar. Gibraltar, it should be noted, because it lacked formal regulationist statutes, has suffered even greater neglect in terms of its contribution to the British regulation of prostitution than the Mediterranean colonies in general, and is only inconsistently noted even in survey. In Malta and Corfu, as this chapter points out, where regulationism was more readily apparent, the British also had the advantage of inheriting systems of supervision of prostitutes: to an important extent, contagious diseases legislation relied on the precedent and experience of these earlier regimes. Because of their scale and insularity, furthermore, Malta and the Ionian Islands offered the most workable model of medical prophylaxis, an example that other places could only look upon with envy. Recall that, because of the partial legislation in the British Isles, the possibility that prostitute women might slip in and out of administrative surveillance always counted against the successful operations of the CD Acts. Small islands like Malta and Corfu, by contrast, where legislation could be brought into universal operation, were the ideal form for prophylactic campaigns against contagion, venereal disease in particular. Their site and situation made the colonial campaign against contagious disease there at once exemplary and at the same time impossible exactly to reproduce. Gibraltar was different, however, in ways that makes its system of regulation of prostitution more interesting and significant than the other two colonial possessions. It was the most important of the British possessions from a military perspective, the most vulnerable from the point of view of public health as well as imperial security, and it was also the home to what was regarded as 'the lowest and most dissolute garrison of the British army'.[9] Moreover, since Gibraltar is not of course an island, many of the complaints about the free movement of diseased women resurfaced there with particular force, particularly given the ease of travel to and from the Spanish mainland. These were concerns that were all the more pressing where vital questions of health and security were considered. We will see in Gibraltar, as a result, more of the opportunities that existed in a colonial context for the regulation of prostitution and more of the insistent difficulties that medical surveillance typically faced. Lastly, like Liverpool or Cambridge, it is arguably the *absence* of

---

[8] J. E. Butler, *The revival and extension of the abolitionist cause: a letter to the members of the Ladies' National Association* (London, 1887), reprinted in I. Sharp (ed.), *Josephine Butler and the prostitution campaigns: diseases of the body politic, volume V: the Queen's daughters in India* (London, 2003), p. 30.

[9] P. Dietz, *The British in the Mediterranean* (London, 1994), p. 68.

specifically regulationist legislation that makes Gibraltar's experiment in policing prostitution so instructive.

Prostitution regulation in the British Mediterranean

It is important, first, to emphasise the fact that in the British Mediterranean the legal powers pertaining to prostitution regulation were no absolute novelty. Regulationist measures go back much further than is typically appreciated, and, in the case of Malta and the Ionian Islands, in addition to not being *modern*, it can be argued that these were not even *British* in origin. In Malta, the practice of inspecting prostitutes for disease was traced as far back as 1530 and the arrival of the Knights of the Order of St John. As the pro-regulationist doctor Lyon Playfair summarised to the House of Commons, 'At Malta traders in vice have been inspected since the time of the Knights, though by custom merely.'[10] The presence of the Knights, who were monks in name only, contributed to a flourishing market for prostitutes, and the demands of public decency led to various attempts to control their movements and appearance, including proposals to confine them to particular districts of the capital, Valletta. The medical historian Paul Cassar observes that efforts to restrict prostitutes became in time limited to the 1631 statutes that excluded public women from certain specified streets in the centre of the city, a provision that survived well into the twentieth century, whilst other laws regulated the entrance to their houses, and prohibited them from frequenting taverns.[11] These early modern ordinances serve to demonstrate the wider concern for social and sexual order found in other European cities at this time, where 'the importance of maintaining the distinction between the "public" women and the rest of the (presumably "private") female populace became a recurring legal theme'.[12] As Mary Elizabeth Perry notes for Seville, such 'protective rules for prostitutes established boundaries for the deviance that could be tolerated in this city'.[13] It was not just public order that was the aim of early modern legislation on prostitution, however. Awareness of the terrible scourge of venereal disease, the great pox, also prompted the medical supervision of prostitutes. Specifically,

---

[10] *Hansard*, 201:1329, 24 May 1870.

[11] P. Cassar, *Medical history of Malta* (London, 1965), pp. 225–6; these were St John's, St James's and St George's streets.

[12] D. Shemek, *Ladies errant: wayward women and social order in early modern Italy* (Durham, NC, 1998), pp. 28–9.

[13] M. E. Perry, *Gender and disorder in early modern Seville* (Princeton, 1990), p. 140. For more detail on Seville, see M. E. Perry, 'Deviant insiders: legalized prostitutes and a consciousness of women in early modern Seville', *Comparative Studies in Society and History*, 27, 1 (1985), 138–58. See also D. Y. Ghirardo, 'The topography of prostitution in Renaissance Ferrara', *Journal of the Society of Architectural Historians*, 60 (2001), 402–31.

Cassar has noted that the periodical examination of prostitutes was introduced after the Order took possession of Malta, and that it was maintained during the first half of the nineteenth century, with public women being directed, after 1832, to the venereal ward of the Women's Hospital in Valletta.[14]

There is some strong continuity, therefore, between these early modern regulations and the techniques of the British colonial era. Intriguingly, too, it was only after the system was challenged in 1859, prostitute women apparently having found that personal examinations were not sanctioned by law but only by *tradition*, that moves were made to put this regime on a clear legal footing. It took this revolt of public women – perhaps prompted by the efforts of reformers – to force the British authorities to introduce *explicit* contagious diseases legislation in Malta. Under the British Ordinance IV of 1861, prostitutes were liable to examination three times in each month by a police physician, and if diseased could be confined until cured, in the Lock pavilion of the Central Hospital. So, whilst it is easy to mistake this as the *beginning* of the British regulation of prostitution in Malta, some kind of regime of medical inspection was likely to have been in place from the very start of the British colonial occupation of the island, and this an inheritance from much earlier times. Furthermore, the governors of Malta were able to hold on to a system that they considered eminently successful in combating venereal disease well into the twentieth century. Responding in 1888 to calls for the repeal of colonial contagious diseases legislation, for example, the Maltese journal *Public Opinion* objected that there is 'no reason why this Island should be converted into a pest house for the propagation of the foulest and most insidious diseases which undermine the health and the life, not only of the immediate sufferers but of innocent generations yet unborn'.[15]

Far from being immediate novelties of colonial rule, then, prostitution regulation in Malta simply continued an established system of surveillance, long accepted and jealously retained. Elsewhere in the British Mediterranean, the longevity of regulationist laws relating to prostitution can also be demonstrated. In Zante, the historian and anthropologist Thomas Gallant has noted the statute of 1835 that prohibited public women from loitering in the streets and restricted them to working from brothel houses in areas not frequented by respectable people.[16] Public women there were to register with the police and be examined in their houses once a month by a doctor appointed by the Chief of Police, at their own expense. If this doctor found upon examination that a public woman was suffering from venereal disease, then he was to take her to the police station where she would be detained in the public gaol, again at her own expense, until such time as she was considered cured. The efficacy of the statutes relating to the behaviour of prostitute women is always open to question, as they were not all energetically enforced, and Gallant follows the likes of Nicholas Thomas and Timothy Mitchell in arguing that sanitary

---

[14] Cassar, *Medical history of Malta*, p. 228.   [15] Cited in *ibid.*, p. 230.
[16] Gallant, *Experiencing dominion*, pp. 65–6.

laws including the regulation of prostitution were symbolic as much as they were utilitarian, meant to draw exemplary distinctions between the civilisation of colonial society and the disorder of native communities.[17] But he observes still that the laws were enforced with vigour where British troops were involved, and particularly those that related to the spatial segregation of prostitutes. As Gallant states in conclusion: 'The aim of the prostitution law is clear: segregation of the women away from polite society, regulation of the type of women who could ply the trade, and protection from venereal disease for male clients … [T]he police aggressively patrolled the spatial boundaries of prostitution.'[18]

Gallant suggests, all too loosely, however, that, in Zante, 'the Greeks turned to the system employed in France', borrowing from the French system of tolerating prostitution in order to bring in better discipline and public order.[19] It is far more likely that in the Ionian Islands the French *themselves* introduced a regulationist regime at some point during their two periods of occupation between 1797 and 1814. In Corfu, for instance, there survives an 1814 register of *pubbliche meretrici*, numbering the individual prostitute women in the French and Greek quarters of the town of Corfu, and recording the houses where they were permitted to work.[20] This date comes scant months after the surrender of the French forces, and over a full year before the islands were officially established as a protectorate at the Congress of Vienna. Given the elaboration of French regulationism in the Napoleonic era, and its Napoleonic introduction to French colonies and conquered territories, it is almost certain that the important military base of Corfu was protected in this way from the ravages of venereal disease. It is also entirely possible that some form of regulation of prostitution was a feature of the Venetian imperial administration of Corfu and the other islands, taking the history of regulation there even further back, and aligning it with the equivalent practices in early modern Malta.[21] In any event, regulating prostitution in the Ionian Islands was likely *not* a British colonial innovation; its origins lie in other imperial administrations and other experiences of colonial domination.

Nevertheless, the medical supervision of prostitution perfectly suited the nature of British rule in the islands, right from the beginning of the protectorate and the quasi-dictatorial governorship of Sir Thomas Maitland all the way through to the equally autocratic Sir Henry Storks at its end. Certainly the British exercised their protection of the islands' inhabitants without much encouragement of

---

[17] N. Thomas, *Colonialism's culture: anthropology, travel and government* (Oxford, 1994); T. Mitchell, *Colonising Egypt* (Berkeley, 1991).
[18] Gallant, *Experiencing dominion*, p. 66.   [19] *Ibid.*, p. 65.
[20] Corfu Archives (TIAK), E.A. 22³ 1814.
[21] For prostitution and its policing in Venice, see R. Sennett, *Flesh and stone: the body and city in Western civilization* (London, 1994); and, on the general policing of sexuality, G. Ruggiero, *The boundaries of eros: sex, crime and sexuality in Renaissance Venice* (Oxford, 1985).

self-government. The Ionian Islands were described in 1838 as '[a] sort of middle state between a colony and a perfectly independent country, without in some respects possessing the advantages of either', and the struggle of the islanders for representative government, against an entrenched administration that offered only sporadic and inadequate liberalising initiatives, is well narrated.[22] It has been argued that the British and Greek communities led increasingly separate lives, the latter increasingly disillusioned and Anglophobic, whilst the three thousand or so British soldiers in the islands, aided by a High Police with arbitrary powers, smothered outbreaks of radical and revolutionary sentiment. The nature of this kind of colonial rule in the Ionian Islands may be starkly illustrated by the comments of the then self-important minor official George Ferguson Bowen, who saw little chance of the Ionians ever being able to be brought into a system of representative government: 'Above all, let not the Government at home fall into the fatal error of imagining that a Protected State, situated as the Ionian Islands now are, can be governed on the same principles as a British Colony, or other integral part of the Empire.'[23] Using tropes familiar from colonial rule elsewhere, Bowen advised the childlike and 'inflammable Oriental population' of the islands that they could only hope to be governed for the foreseeable future by the benevolent despotism of the British Protectorate.[24]

It is significant that the state of morality of the islanders was also described as thoroughly depraved, and moreover tainted with 'the vices and lax manners' of their former Venetian overlords.[25] In these circumstances, it is hardly surprising that the British continued throughout the early nineteenth century with a regulationist regime designed to protect the health of the soldiery from the contamination of venal native women. The archives in Corfu amply confirm this. In addition to the 1814 register, there are surviving examples from the period 1824–51 which suggest that there were around sixty or seventy public prostitutes regularly inspected by doctors and sent to the hospital if found to be diseased.[26] In the second half of the 1840s, there is a more or less constant number of around sixty registered women. These numbers are surprisingly small, but there is every

---

[22] Lord High Commissioner Sir Howard Douglas, describing the Ionian Constitution in 1838, cited in M. Pratt, *Britain's Greek empire: reflections on the history of the Ionian Islands from the fall of Byzantium* (London, 1978), p. 127.

[23] [G. F. Bowen], *The Ionian Islands under British protection* (London, 1851), p. 139; for Bowen's career, see B. Knox, 'British policy and the Ionian Islands, 1847–1864: nationalism and imperial administration', *English Historical Review*, 49 (1984), 503–29.

[24] *Ibid.*, pp. 52, 122. See Gallant, *Experiencing dominion*, on the stock tropes of English condescension. For a nationalist reply to this attack, see 'An Ionian', *The Ionian Islands; what they have lost and suffered under the thirty-five years' administration of the Lord High Commissioners sent to govern them. In reply to a pamphlet entitled 'The Ionian Islands under British protection'* (London, 1851).

[25] Bowen, *The Ionian Islands*, p. 5.   [26] TIAK, E.A. 22[8] [1824]; 23/793, 1169 [1834–41].

indication that they were well organised and marshalled by the colonial authorities, part of an extremely close management of commercial sexuality in the island. Analysis of the surviving register for the period 1846–51 provides further information about the nature of prostitution in Corfu. Only just over half these women (53 per cent) are listed as of Corfiot extraction, and only a handful more came from the near mainland of Greece or Albania. The other Ionian Islands, particularly Zante, provide a further 16 per cent of the registered prostitutes, but Malta provides 10 per cent of these women on its own, and Sicily, Naples, Venice and Tripoli, taken together, nearly match this contribution. There is in addition a significant number of women of British or Irish extraction, and a lone American, who in total make up another 8 per cent. To the latter cohort of women might be added the three women who are listed as having resided at some point in time in England. This is a set of women therefore that is drawn not just from Corfu town and its suburbs, the local countryside and the rest of the island, but also from a mobile population moving within the Mediterranean and closely connected too to the British Isles. The impression that this cohort of women suggests, reinforced by the fact that Malta and the other Ionian Islands had regulated systems of prostitution, is of a migrant sexual proletariat, some of whom followed the British garrisons from one regulated station to the next.

We might also expect to find some evidence of clustering of the houses where prostitutes lived and worked. Most of the locations in Corfu mentioned in the registers belong to the old town, the Venetian buildings of Campiello, a district reputed to have taken its name from the prostitutes who lived there, and well known for prostitution. Its extramural location, and its association with the similarly marginalised Jewish quarter, is also suggestive.[27] But regulated prostitution in Corfu does not seem to have resulted in any strong clustering in particular streets, and the picture is one more of dispersal and isolation. Reference to houses is in any case not at all specific, with neighbourhoods in the vicinity of the churches or other public landmarks indicated rather than any more precise description. This is in contrast to the recording in the short register of public women from 1814. By the 1840s at least, there seems to be no need for any greater specificity, perhaps owing to the medical and social discipline that the British colonial authorities seem to have been able to bring to bear on the registered women. These women presumably lived in and amongst the rest of the civilian population, in the Venetian courts and alleys of Campiello but also in or around the town's more prestigious streets and promenades. Not only does a brothel quarter appear to be absent, then: it seems unlikely that brothels of a stereotypical stamp existed either. We are probably better to consider a far less hierarchical structure, with individual women pursuing fairly independent prostitute careers.

Everything else in the registers of women reinforces this conclusion. About 20 per cent of these women were inscribed in every single month of the six years

[27] See Sennett, *Flesh and stone*, pp. 237–41.

covered by the register, and nearly one-third were recorded in sixty or more of these seventy-two months. The average length of presence of women on this register is over three years, and there is nothing to suggest that many of these women were not registered long before the beginning of 1846 and remained long after the end of 1851. Conversely, only one-quarter was listed on the register for less than twelve months in total, and a mere six were only inscribed once within this period. This is quite distinctive: there is hardly any sign in Corfu of the large number noted elsewhere, up to a half of all those arrested, of women who only come into contact with the system of regulation a single time. There does not, in other words, appear to be any significant class of those women labelled elsewhere as 'wayward' or 'amateur', women who are almost immediately warned off, or weaned off, a life of prostitution. The ages of women registered also suggests this conclusion. Recording is inconsistent, sometimes wildly so, and perhaps amounting to no more than guesses on behalf of the police officials, but, if they are accepted as approximately correct, the mean age of a little over twenty-five is a notably high figure, and yet another indication of a mature cohort pretty much confirmed in a prostitute profession. Moreover, before being entered onto the register for 1846–51, 25 per cent of these women are noted as having first been inscribed between one and five years previously, 13 per cent from five to ten years previously, and 15 per cent as having spent over ten years as a registered prostitute in Corfu; to this tally can be added the average of three years on the register noted above. At the upper end of the scale there were two women recorded as in their sixties whose careers appear already to have spanned nearly four decades.

In Corfu and Malta, in short, we have the most apparently successful examples of the British colonial regulation of sexuality. In these places – small islands with limited and manageable populations, where the British could exercise a dominant authority under near autocratic powers – prostitutes and other women could most easily be policed. As a result, at least if the example of Corfu is taken to be representative, a small but stable cohort of more or less professional prostitutes could be kept firmly under moral and medical surveillance. Indeed, if the records are to be believed, fewer than half of the Corfu women are recorded as having been sent to the hospital for a syphilitic infection even a single time during their period of inscription, evidence perhaps for the success of such a regime of inspection and such a regimented cohort of women in combating the spread of venereal disease in Corfu. Although the medical treatments for syphilis and the other diseases were basic, to say the least, and almost wholly ineffective, with a small number of women like this, easily supervised and regularly inspected for communicable infection, it may well be the case that medical detention could drive down levels of disease. Places like Corfu – and Malta – could in all probability be justified as models of medical discipline, as the British supporters of regulationism claimed.

In the rest of this chapter, however, I turn to a detailed study of Gibraltar, the third British Mediterranean possession, which is important precisely because of the inability of the British there to control the civilian population in this exemplary manner. In Gibraltar are revealed the insistent difficulties of colonial regulation, and it is in the struggles over the control of prostitute women that the nature of colonial regulationist policing may be brought most easily to light.

Prostitution regulation in Gibraltar

Gibraltar was and is one of the smallest British colonial possessions, barely a couple of square miles of real estate connected by a narrow isthmus to the Spanish mainland (Figure 5.1). Environmentally ill-favoured, it would hardly be a prize of any distinction were it not for the strategic considerations that led to its seizure from the Spanish in 1704, and the highly charged political legacy that has dogged British–Spanish relations ever since. This history and geography have made Gibraltar a 'rock of contention' throughout the three centuries of British control.[28] War and the threat of war is one of the constant themes in Gibraltar's British history, and this takes us back to the military justification of prostitution regulation. Gibraltar was a garrison town, home to a few thousand troops and their commanding officers under the control of a military governor, but, like other garrisons, drunkenness and ill discipline, encouraged by the beer shops provided by the civilian population, were a constant concern for the military authorities.[29] Prostitution was a similarly pressing phenomenon, and it is hardly surprising then that there should have developed in Gibraltar the same kinds of measures for the regulation of prostitution that the CD Acts sanctioned in the English and Irish garrisons. Although the CD Acts were specifically limited to the domestic stations, confronted with the same problems Gibraltar was eager to institute its own localised practices; as in the British stations, special, particular and partial measures were called for, and instituted.

Gibraltar was not just another 'domestic' garrison, however. It was also a colonial possession where questions of sovereignty over 'alien' territory and peoples were raised most insistently. Civilians were quickly attracted to Gibraltar by the labour needs offered by the naval base and the garrison, to speak only of legitimate employment. Immigration to the colony proceeded apace in the nineteenth century, with the civilian population – the great majority Spanish – coming to outnumber the military personnel by some ten to one. Women who came to prostitute themselves in Gibraltar in the nineteenth century were little different from the rest of the civilian population. These women were sex workers whose primary reason for being in the colony was an economic one. But prostitute work in nineteenth-century Gibraltar cannot be considered simply as an economic enterprise.

---

[28] G. Hills, *Rock of contention: a history of Gibraltar* (London, 1974).
[29] P. Dietz, 'Gibraltar', in P. Dietz (ed.), *Garrison: ten British military towns* (London, 1986), pp. 177–200, K. Hendrickson, 'A kinder, gentler British Army: mid-Victorian experiments in the management of army vice at Gibraltar and Aldershot', *War and Society*, 14 (1996), 21–33.

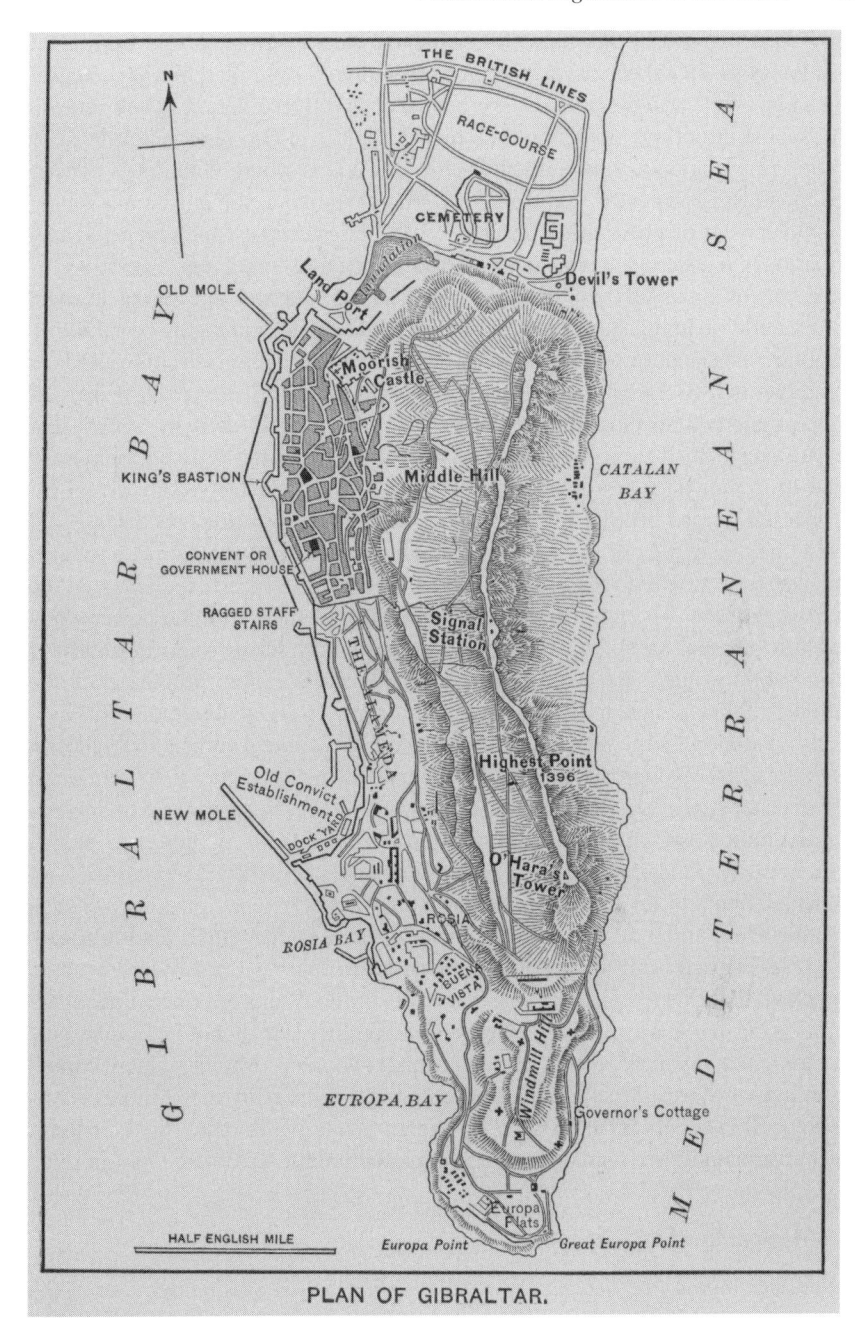

Figure 5.1. Plan of Gibraltar in the late nineteenth century. Source: H. M. Field, *Gibraltar* (London, 1889).

It was also marked by military, political, medical, imperial and governmental considerations. In particular, questions of *sovereignty* were from the very beginning a key element in the politics of prostitution and its regulation in Gibraltar.

The most important element of colonial discipline in Gibraltar as it related to prostitute regulation was the colonial law, and this is where Gibraltar's experience most decisively parts company with that of the domestic garrisons. Whilst its management of prostitution had clear affinities with the operation of British regulationist legislation at home and abroad, no specific contagious diseases ordinance was ever passed in Gibraltar. Nor, unlike Malta and the Ionian Islands, could it build on long-established customs and statutes for managing prostitution. Gibraltar instead developed unique sanitary measures. Its governors relied on legislative and disciplinary machinery inherited from the very earliest days of conquest and colonisation, on laws relating to the status of civilian 'aliens' that allowed non-British subjects to reside and work in Gibraltar only on temporary permits rescindable at any time by the Governor. This exclusively colonial legislation was not framed in order specifically to control either prostitutes or disease, but it could be made to work for regulationist purposes because women who refused or neglected to submit to regular medical examination could be expelled from the city and garrison. The government and police had in theory all the powers they needed to compel prostitutes to comply with sanitary supervision: in Gibraltar these 'public women' were enrolled as 'public visitors' whose permits could be rescinded if they proved to be uncooperative or otherwise troublesome. This system provided for a large measure of control over prostituted women, the majority of whom were Spaniards temporarily resident in the brothels of the city's red light district. It provided for the registration of prostitutes, their periodic inspection and their hospitalisation if found to be diseased, with the power to banish them from the territory being the lever to ensure obedience. The workings of this legislation and its effects on the economy and geography of prostitution in Gibraltar are examined in detail subsequently, but its effects can be readily stated. What these statutes did was to professionalise the cohort of prostituted women, to enclose them in recognised houses of prostitution, and to concentrate them in a more easily surveyed and disciplined urban space. It should be emphasised once more that it was the *legal* restrictions under which prostitute women worked that effectively shaped the landscape of commercial sexuality in Gibraltar. It was the colonial law, with its exercise of sovereign power within a political territory, which made possible a regulationist regime in Gibraltar.

Prostitution, law and discipline

Before we come to the nature of this regime in practice, this recognition of the importance of colonial law enjoins us to consider at a more abstract level the relationship between the disciplining of prostitution and the law. As I have earlier noted, following the work of Foucault, Corbin and others, it has become convenient to think of the regulation of prostitution as a modern, disciplinary project.

But the place of the law in these developments remains obscure and ambiguous. The association of regulationism with disciplinary power encourages us to assume that the legal basis for the regulation of prostitution is actually something of an irrelevance, a view that historians of the French system have encouraged. The legal status of Parisian regulationism was at best inconclusive, its proponents appealing to a motley collection of statutes whose shaky authority was defended only on the grounds that prostitutes had already put themselves beyond the law, so that they were liable to be policed 'by measures whose relation to the statutory code was itself deviant': 'If the prostitute is an outlaw, so in a sense is the police administration that maintains her legal alienation.'[30] Jill Harsin has also observed that 'the very familiarity of the regulatory system obscured the fact that it was, within the legal environment of the nineteenth century, a complete anachronism'.[31] Disciplinary surveillance of prostitute women would seem in the paradigmatic French case to have *no* recourse or substantive relation to law at all – the latter is something of an arbitrary contrivance irregularly and inconsistently invoked. A realm of practices developed in France, as Andrew Aisenberg argues, 'without reference to claims about sovereignty'.[32] In our earlier cases, too, of Liverpool and Cambridge, we have seen that disciplinary regulation of prostitution largely sidestepped questions of legal sovereignty and the modern right to liberty of the subject. These were characteristically informal regimes, using the authority of statute and sanction where possible, but just as characteristically relying upon tradition, discretion and improvisation. As we have also seen, this left these regimes open to characterisation as legal anachronisms incompatible with English modernity.

This view of regulationism as founded on discipline rather than dependent upon the modern legal framework of rights and sovereignty has clear affinities with Foucault's view of law as essentially *pre-modern*, merely an adjunct of sovereignty and centralised coercion and destined to be supplanted if not replaced by disciplinary power, and occasionally relegated to the role of concealing the pervasiveness of disciplinary technologies. The recent publication of Foucault's 1975–6 *Collège de France* lectures intriguingly raises the relation of war to discipline, but the antithesis of law and discipline is made there as insistently as ever: 'The discourse of discipline is alien to that of the law; it is alien to the discourse that makes rules a product of the will of the sovereign.'[33] In Foucault's analysis,

---

[30] C. Bernheimer, *Figures of ill repute: representing prostitution in nineteenth-century France* (Cambridge, MA, 1989), pp. 28–30.

[31] J. Harsin, *Policing prostitution in nineteenth-century Paris* (Princeton, 1985), p. 95.

[32] A. Aisenberg, 'Syphilis and prostitution: a regulatory couplet in nineteenth-century France', in R. Davidson and L. A. Hall (eds.), *Sex, sin and suffering: venereal disease and European society since 1870* (London, 2001), p. 16.

[33] M. Foucault, *'Society must be defended': lectures at the Collège de France 1975–1976* (New York, 2003), p. 38. However, see A. W. Neal, 'Cutting off the king's head: Foucault's *Society must be defended* and the problem of sovereignty', *Alternatives*, 29 (2004),

discipline finds itself in direct conflict with the juridical order of sovereignty. But 'to conceive of sex without the law, and power without the king', as Foucault once advised in *The history of sexuality*, is, in the context of the regulation of prostitution, completely mistaken.[34] Foucault was eager to divest us of our anachronistically sovereign understanding of power, but to rule out the power of law would be just as obviously absurd. Alan Hunt and Gary Wickham have very effectively criticised the thesis of law's expulsion or displacement from the disciplinary society, arguing for a view of discipline and law as supplementary, forging 'distinctive and pervasive forms of regulation at the very heart of modern government'. In their theorisation of the policing functions of state and society as legal governance, they insist that disciplinary power is not opposed to law, but rather that law has been 'a primary agent in the advance of new modalities of power'.[35]

The modernity of regulationism cannot consist, therefore, in its rejection of law *for* discipline. It is straightforwardly a mistake to identify 'law' with a 'sovereign' power derived from absolutist authority, as a relict of the early modern era, or to conceive in a corresponding way of law as purely 'negative' in its effects. Miles Ogborn has argued in his specific treatment of the Contagious Diseases Acts that British regulationism used law not simply to bulwark but to *produce* the 'positive' effects associated with disciplinary power: 'The legal apparatus provided an acceptable basis for state intervention in the sphere of morality. More than just legitimation, it provided the central mechanisms and institutions which enabled the apparatus to be constructed.'[36] It is better then to regard at least the *British* regulationist project characteristically as *combining* law and discipline in its construction and socio-spatial operation. Law was, then, and indeed still is, an essential element of the disciplinary regulation of prostituted women.

Sovereign power and colonial law in Gibraltar

In the case of Gibraltar, we have a particularly detailed case study of this process at work. There, the disciplinary regulation of prostituted women depended perhaps to a unique extent on law and the legal struggles over jurisdiction, residence and nationality that resulted. Sovereignty, far from being an abstraction, an anachronism or an irrelevance, was, in these particular colonial conditions, always the issue at hand. Gibraltar was claimed by right of military conquest, and held in the name of the British sovereign. The military governor's authoritarian powers over its inhabitants were not even to be complemented by civilian

---

373–98, for the argument that Foucault was advancing a much more complex analysis of sovereignty that emerged alongside the rise of the modern nation-state.

[34] M. Foucault, *The history of sexuality, volume I: an introduction* (New York, 1980), p. 91.

[35] A. Hunt and G. Wickham, *Foucault and law: towards a sociology of law as governance* (London, 1994), pp. 22, 65.

[36] Ogborn, *Discipline, government and law*, p. 221.

authority until well into the twentieth century. Gibraltar was a colony, from 1830 onwards, but its status as a garrison and a fortress took clear precedence over civilian interests throughout the nineteenth century. Gibraltar had a substantial civilian population – the garrison of three or four thousand men was early in the century overwhelmed by immigrants – but it had few who could claim to be 'citizens'. Without a British settler community of any size, there was a stark divide between the British military and the 'alien' resident population. These 'alien' workers and their families – the majority were Spanish, but there were notable Genoese, Portuguese, Maltese and Jewish components – had no automatic rights of residence, none of the conventional trappings of citizenship. They were allowed into the colony only on temporary permits; and by the late nineteenth century it was not unusual for daily workers amounting to the entire strength of the British garrison to cross the barrier from Spain every day. Thousands of other 'aliens' were suffered to reside on the Rock, but even the most privileged were supposed to leave the colony at least one day in the year, demonstrating that they were not permanent residents. These 'aliens' could be removed from the colony at any time, at the Governor's discretion and behest.

Given the tiny size of Gibraltar, what the authorities feared most was overpopulation and overcrowding, two pressing concerns exacerbated by the periodic deadly epidemics which swept the colony. Uncontrolled immigration and population growth threatened Gibraltar's fragile demographic, sanitary and political regime. The permit system was designed to limit the numbers working and residing on the Rock, although it had the added advantage of allowing for the administrative registration and magisterial surveillance of the non-British population in Gibraltar. There was one intractable problem, however, and a legal one at that. Under British law, automatic right of residence had to be granted to those born in Gibraltar itself. Men and women who were born in the colony were deemed to be inalienable, and irremovable: 'natives' in the sense of being naturalised and invested with rights, rather than in the sense of colonial othering and condescension. Their presence constituted a kind of demographic time bomb with the potential to subvert the authority of the colonial power. As the numbers of 'natives' inevitably rose, so correspondingly diminished the Governor's autocratic power over the civilian population. To counter this problem, the Governor retained the right to approve all marriages in Gibraltar, and sporadically enforced the rule that 'alien' men could only marry providing that they left the colony long before any legitimate child might be produced. A further refinement required all women married to 'aliens' to quit Gibraltar for their accouchements. These measures were all designed to reduce the growing numbers of resident foreigners in the colony, and specifically 'to prevent the increase of the fixed population of an alien character'.[37] These were the basis, as Stacie Burke and Lawrence Sawchuk

---

[37] F. S. Flood, 'History of the permit system in Gibraltar' (Gibraltar Government Archives [GGA] Box: *History of the permit system 1704–1871*), p. 65.

have argued, of a distinctive 'reproductive politics' in Gibraltar, admitting that these attempts were only partially effective even when they were fully enforced.[38] Successive steps only seemed to provide further loopholes: for instance, whilst the 1844 doctrine of naturalisation helpfully required a woman married to an alien to relinquish her British nationality for her husband's, it raised the vexing possibility that 'alien' women might contract marriage with British subjects solely in order to stay on in the garrison. The British Naturalization Act of 1844 was ruled inapplicable, but one woman, a Spanish prostitute named Carmen Hernandez, did mount a challenge to the legal interpretation of the law, forcing the Gibraltarian authorities to insist on the Governor's overriding power to expel any foreigner from the Rock.[39]

That Carmen Hernandez worked as a prostitute in Gibraltar was no irrelevance, for control over the flourishing prostitutional economy had also come to depend on the laws restricting the movements and civil relations of 'foreigners'. The issue here was not overcrowding or overpopulation *per se*, but the retention of the right to expel women, as aliens, from the colony. Like all other alien workers, prostituted women were allowed into the colony only on sufferance, on temporary day permits or on residence permits which required them to leave the colony for at least one day in the year. It is a significant *technicality* rather than just a euphemism that these women were understood as 'public visitors'. They were supervised by the same police force dedicated to controlling the alien population through the permit system. They were controllable not because they were prostitutes *per se* but because they were legally aliens. The power of expulsion was critical to the management of prostitution because disorderly women could be banished outright and venereally diseased women compelled to seek treatment. Effectively, legislation controlling an alien civil population provided for the regulation of a subset of prostituted women considered as inevitable and even necessary but also potentially dangerous. In the regulationist system which emerged in Gibraltar, the authorities could comfortably accept the presence of numerous prostitutes but, retaining the power to banish them if non-compliant, could register them as sex workers, compel them to submit to weekly physical examination by medical officers, and to attend the civilian hospital if they were found to be exhibiting signs of venereal disease. Anything that threatened these powers, such as the purchase of nationality leading to automatic right of residence, opened up the possibility of unrestrained commercial sexuality and epidemic propagation of disease. The 'reproductive politics' of nineteenth-century Gibraltar identified by

---

[38] S. D. A. Burke and L. A. Sawchuk, 'Alien encounters: the *jus soli* and reproductive politics in the 19th-century fortress and colony of Gibraltar', *History of the Family*, 6 (2001), 531–61.

[39] *Ibid.*, p. 540. For the readiness of prostituted women to use the law in their own defence, see M. W. Hill, *Their sisters' keepers: prostitution in New York City, 1830–1870* (Berkeley, 1993).

Burke and Sawchuk were thus at the same time a *regulationist politics* designed to manage prostitution in the city, garrison and colony.

The Gibraltarian authorities had long and consistently stressed the *local* necessity for this kind of regulation of prostitution. In 1887, when local powers were seriously imperilled by the domestic repeal of the CD Acts, Chief of Police William Seed noted that:

> Gibraltar is a place apart and special rules are necessary. The bulk of prostitutes are Spaniards, who very well know that to be allowed to live in Gibraltar it is necessary that they should submit to examination. They come to ply their calling here with the knowledge that they are to submit to the examination and as they do so voluntarily I cannot see any hardship in it. It is simply a contract they enter into. If they do not wish to enter into the contract they need not come. Besides this, in Spain if they wish to reside in a public brothel they must submit to examination so that they enter Gibraltar brothels on the same understanding that they enter Spanish houses of the same sort.[40]

The nature of these special measures had been, however, an open question for a generation, and reliance on the permit system was a matter of expedience rather than preference. The stirrings of contagious diseases legislation in Britain and Ireland had been a significant boost to the regulationist project in Gibraltar. A lock ward for the treatment of diseased women had been in existence in 1856 – together, no doubt, with some form of registration and compulsion of prostitutes. But in 1864 the War Office (later to be joined by the Admiralty) provided for the subvention of funds in its support of the inspection of prostitutes.[41] Whilst CD legislation authorised regulation in the domestic (including Irish) garrisons there was, however, no equivalent *legal* basis for colonial practices. There was, instead, a rather mixed bag of colonial orders and ordinances. What should be noted about British colonial regulationism in general is the fact that the imperial government accepted the doctrine of *local* necessity and special powers whilst resisting the opportunity to extend domestic CD legislation to the colonies. Desiring to put the control of prostitution on a clear legal footing, Governor of Gibraltar Sir Richard Airey had initially requested that the colony be included in the British CD legislation, but was firmly reminded in 1868 that the Act could not in *any* circumstances be extended to a colony:

> the Act is expressly limited by clause 4 to certain stations at home, and that there is no intention of discussing a further act so as to include any Garrison abroad or Colony in the first schedule, but that whatever steps are taken should be effected by local laws or ordinances; and I am to add that all other Colonies which have been invited to take steps have been requested to do so on this plan.[42]

---

[40] Memorandum, William Seed, Chief of Police, to Colonial Secretary, 13 April 1887 (GGA, Box: Venereal Disease & other contagious diseases (hereafter 'Box A').

[41] See 'Lock hospital and Contagious Diseases Act – all the papers, correspondence &c. belonging to this question with a precis' (GGA, Box A).

[42] War Office memorandum to Under Secretary of State, Colonial Office, 14 February 1868, in 'Lock hospital and Contagious Diseases Act' (GGA, Box A).

Airey was advised instead to frame a local ordinance, based on what was recognised as the remarkably successful legislation operating for some time in Malta. A CD ordinance for Gibraltar was accordingly drafted by the energetic, authoritarian and abrasive Police Chief Frederick Solly Flood, only for this to be abruptly halted upon the appointment of a Royal Commission to investigate its workings.[43] It is clear that, in part at least, domestic controversy dissuaded the Colonial Office from ratifying a specific regulationist ordinance. In 1870, Malta's former Governor, Sir Henry Storks, was attacked at home precisely because of his presiding over what was seen as the licensing of prostitution there. In these circumstances, it was deemed politically inexpedient to proceed with such explicit legislation.

This meant, in Gibraltar, falling back on 'Local Law or Regulations', which effectively meant the permit system by which civilians could be registered as 'aliens' and expelled from the colony if necessary. The laws in force regarding the alien population gave the police the power to implement a regulationist system in Gibraltar, although they had previously been enforced with discretion if not outright inconsistency. Upon his appointment in 1865 as police magistrate, Frederick Solly Flood had proceeded methodically to enquire into the permit system, and argued strongly for its strict enforcement, together with all the regulations designed to control the future growth of the 'native' population, particularly where the problem of prostitution was concerned. His efforts were concentrated on confirming and strengthening the powers of removal contained in the permit system and its philosophy. Their operation would take on greater importance in subsequent years, once the impossibility of specific contagious diseases ordinances was confirmed. What Flood found initially was not very encouraging, however. The inadequacy of the statutes, together with their lax enforcement, and the abundant legal loopholes, all appeared to conspire against him. Most importantly, though, the ever-present possibility of the naturalisation of prostitutes threatened the entire system of regulated sexuality. Flood's comments demonstrate how closely the problem of the alien population and the right of residence was bound up with concerns over sex work in Gibraltar:

The principal mischief was the purchase of the British nationality which the statute attached to the alien wife of a British subject. During the three years which a similar enactment was in force a regular tariff was established according to which alien women of bad character purchased from transitory and British subjects by means of the ceremony of marriage British nationality and the consequent privilege conceded to them to lead an abandoned life in Gibraltar without fear of removal and to add to the population of

---

[43] For the draft 'Ordinance for the Prevention of Contagious Diseases in Gibraltar', see GGA, Box: Ordinances. Ordinances, Draft Ordinances & Orders in Council, 1832, 1867, 1869 & 1894–1895.

Gibraltar by giving birth to illigitimate [sic] children who as native British subjects would grow up a permanent burden to the Fortress.[44]

As Flood wrote to the Governor in 1866, even more pithily, this situation simply confirmed for him 'the right of infamous alien women (if married to British subjects) to lead an abandoned life and set the Police Regulations at Defiance and fill Gibraltar with their bastards.'[45] This was not all, however, for Flood perceived that the hostility of the civilian population threatened not only the moral, medical and military functioning of the colony but also the entire rule of law and British sovereign authority in Gibraltar:

> For some few years past there has gradually been growing up a determination on the part of extraneous authorities, practically to take the Government of Gibraltar out of the hand of Her Majesty Queen Victoria, and to dictate to Her Government, the mode how the Civil Affairs of this Fortress may be administered, as if it was a dependency of a Foreign Government, and for the benefit of any interest except that of England.[46]

Flood faced numerous legal difficulties in Gibraltar, which continued after he had become the colony's Attorney General, and personal attacks were seen by him as part of a conspiracy 'to secure the disregard of English law by English officers through the hands of the British Government itself'.[47] His initial attempts to put the practices of registration and removal on a secure footing were stymied by the confusions and ambiguities of the colonial legal system.[48] The question of whether laws passed in the British Parliament had force in Gibraltar, after the grant in 1830 of colonial status, was a matter of some complexity, leading to an acrimonious dispute with the Chief Justice, Sir James Cochrane.[49] The latter suggested that Gibraltar should be deemed, as far as possible as its military character allowed, as a town of England, and 'considered with respect to its Laws, to be an integral part of the United Kingdom'.[50] Flood, however, considered that proposal to be 'subversive of the Sovereignty of the Crown, the power and authority of the Governor, & all the rights and privileges of the people'.[51] It would certainly not authorise the kinds of registration that he considered fundamental to the colony's social and sexual order. Flood remained absolutely single-minded

---

[44] Flood, 'History of the permit system', pp. 79–80.
[45] NA CO 91/285, Flood to Governor Airey, 9 November 1866.
[46] NA CO 91/285, Flood to Freeling, 17 September 1866. [47] *Ibid.*
[48] See P. Howell, 'Colonial law and legal historical geography: an argument from Gibraltar', in A. R. H. Baker and I. S. Black (eds.), *Home and colonial: essays on landscape, Ireland, environment and empire in celebration of Robin Butlin's contribution to historical geography* (London, 2004).
[49] The two were completely at deadlock, eventually refusing even to speak to each other: see NA CO 91/289, Airey to the Duke of Buckingham and Chandos, 8 July 1867.
[50] NA CO 91/285, Sir James Cochrane to Governor Airey, 24 December 1866.
[51] NA CO 91/285, Flood to Acting Colonial Secretary, 25 December 1866.

172   *Colonial law and prostitute subjects in Gibraltar*

about the need to control what he called 'the evils of a crowded alien and semi-alien population'.[52] Prostitutes remained the very symbol of this civilian, 'alien' threat to British authority and even to the survival of Gibraltar itself: 'an infamous native population, which is daily increasing, and which is eating up the very vitals of Gibraltar, adding to its frightfully over-crowded condition and endangering the very existence of the Garrison.'[53]

Flood's attempt to replace 'Anarchy' with 'Law' rested ultimately on the possibilities of legal ordinances.[54] He consistently maintained that British sovereignty, gained by right of conquest, made British military and imperial interests paramount. Legislation could not be based on civil considerations, nor could the population be treated as British citizens. The rights of the civilian population – 'of whom not one tenth is capable of comprehending the nature of the English Constitution of laws or even understanding a word of the English language' – made the application of English statute law for him entirely inadmissible.[55] In the end a solution would have to be found that translated the peculiar situation of the colonial garrison into a workable system of local statutes. This would mean, as in Oxford and Cambridge, a *lex loci* explicitly recognising *local* necessities. This law of place was gained by the passing in 1873 of the Aliens Order in Council that set forth the military necessity of controlling the civil population and gave clear authority for it to be strictly enforced. More specifically, it provided the legal framework under which a regulationist practice could flourish in Gibraltar, here described in straightforward summary:

No ordinance based on the English Contagious Diseases Acts, lately repealed, has ever been enacted in Gibraltar, but there exists an indirect control over prostitutes, exercised through the law of Gibraltar relating to aliens, with the result that certain prostitutes, generally the majority, agree to submit to periodical examination. By the law of Gibraltar, no alien can enter or remain in the place without a day ticket, or permit of residence granted by the authorities. Even a labourer coming in from Spain for his day's work, has to obtain a day ticket from the Inspector of Police at the Barrier. An alien desiring to live in Gibraltar can only do so on a permit of residence issued to him or her by the Police magistrate under the Aliens Order in Council, on the application of a resident, who must be a person of some responsibility. A prostitute's permit would be, in the first instance, either for 30 days, or for a quarter of a year, and would be renewed afterwards for periods not exceeding 30 days, but must not exceed 364 days in the whole year, one day being spent out of the garrison. The granting or withholding of permits is in the discretion of the Police Magistrate, and an alien prostitute's permit of residence is not granted unless she is certified to be free from venereal disease, and is not renewed, unless she submits to weekly examination at the Civil Hospital. If she refuses or neglects to present herself for examination her permit is not renewed, and she has to leave the garrison like any other

[52] NA CO 91/285, Flood to Freeling, 30 August 1866.
[53] NA CO 91/285, Flood to Freeling, 5 August 1866.
[54] NA CO 91/285, Flood to Freeling, 15 April 1867.
[55] NA CO 91/285, Flood to Freeling, 12 August 1867.

alien ... Permits are not granted for such alien women unless the inmates, who are British subjects, submit regularly to the weekly examination.[56]

In subsequent years, sanitary ordinances covering the notification and treatment of infectious diseases were grafted onto this legislative trunk, with the explicit intention of strengthening the police's control over prostitutes and the transmission of venereal disease. Whilst it fell short of the legal clarity that only a dedicated CD ordinance could provide, the law in Gibraltar in this form was able to provide the basis for the systematic regulation of prostitution in the colony.

Prostitutional space in Gibraltar

What was the effect of this legislation on the civil population, specifically the prostituted women who were its subjects? Like sex workers in similar systems, these women were conscripted into the machinery ensuring social and sexual order. Along with their names, addresses, backgrounds and status, their careers were recorded in great detail, enabling them to be carefully monitored and if necessary disciplined. Though few records now survive, during the operation of the system these women would have been systematically inscribed in the registers of permits of work and residence, in the population censuses, and in the tabulated results of their weekly medical examinations. As one memorandum noted, 'Matters relating to prostitutes and their examination are under the charge of the chief of police, who keeps a book in which their names, residence, and the results of their periodical inspection are entered, the book being examined and signed weekly by the surgeon in charge'; it is significant that the author went on to concede that 'this book is of no legal authority, and is merely kept for information'.[57] Whilst the permit law generated its own records, the existence of a register of prostitutes, though a simple elaboration, was regarded as a discreet and informal measure. As I have indicated above, it was not a legal substitute for a contagious diseases ordinance. Nevertheless, police magistrates and military medical officers worked closely to ensure that these women did comply with medical requirements and with standards of decorum: those who offended against these precepts were liable to be banished from the garrison, either temporarily or permanently. Right up until the end of the system, after the First World War, the authorities continued to keep up this close surveillance of Gibraltar's prostitute population.

The problems encountered in defining prostitution were kept to a minimum in a colony where the status of 'public visitor' was straightforwardly authorised by law. To an extent unknown in Britain, but common in the colonies, women were recognised and licensed as prostitutes. Commentators in Gibraltar could

---

[56] Memorandum, n.d., 'Regulations affecting prostitutes in Gibraltar' (GGA, Box A).
[57] Memorandum, 'Regulations affecting prostitutes in Gibraltar', (GGA, Box A).

speak authoritatively and precisely about the numbers of public women, and their places of work and residence. In numerical terms, the ranks of prostituted women ranged from 100 to 150 and more – quite a significant number in proportion to a civil population that did not exceed 20,000 even at the century's end. In 1887, the chief of police reported that there were 153 'recognised' prostitutes, consisting of 70 natives and 83 aliens. In 1901, 108 alien and 30 native prostitutes were recognised, and in 1903 the number was 110 in total, 'all willing to submit to examination'.[58] The figures for various dates are provided in Table 5.1.

These numbers and their relative stability – for all that individual women came and went – strongly suggest a well-organised and authorised prostitutional economy. This is an impression bolstered by the very stable number of brothel houses, which were well known and regularly inspected by medical officers. In every census since 1871 we can identify fourteen to sixteen brothels (defined here as houses with more than three women present at the time of the census). These were often very well established and professionally run, their ownership or control remaining in the hands of individual brothel-keepers for many years. The 'first-class' brothel for officers that existed on the road to the Devil's Gap, for instance, was proudly described by its mistress, Enriqueta Thomas, as having existed from a time 'exceeding the memory of any living inhabitant of Gibraltar'.[59] Thomas, who was first recorded as a brothel-keeper at 35 Arengo's Lane in 1871, headed the brothel in its last years, having taken over from a Cristina Gonzalez who appears to have had its running for over twenty years. A building like this was firmly embedded in the social as well as material landscape, testimony to the longevity and seeming permanence of the business of prostitution in Gibraltar.

A few other examples will indicate the opportunities for women to work themselves up through the ranks of prostitution to head their own households and institutions. Dolores Fernandez, a twenty-one-year-old from Malaga, was working at 23 Serruya's Lane in 1891 as a public visitor. Though still at No. 23 in 1901, she was by 1921 running her own brothel on the same street, having completed at least thirty years in the business. Another woman, an immigrant from Mogador in Morocco, also saw out three decades in Serruya's Lane, the most prominent street in terms of Gibraltar's prostitutional economy, having progressed in that time from public visitor and boarder to full-time brothel-keeper. To give one last example:

---

[58] William Seed, Chief of Police, to Colonial Secretary, 13 April 1887 (GGA, Box A); 'Prostitutes in disorderly houses', 24 May 1901 (GGA, Box: Venereal Disease (1) (hereafter 'Box B')); 'Venereal disease, reports as to increased number of venereal cases in military hospital', 26 June 1903 (GGA, Box: Venereal Disease (2) (hereafter 'Box C')).

[59] File, 'Withdrawal by police of permits of residence of alien women residing in C.P. 841 (a brothel)', 24 April 1919 (GGA, Box B).

Table 5.1 *Residence and status of sex workers in Gibraltar, 1868–1921*[a]

	Number (percentage in italics)												
	1868	%	1871	%	1881	%	1891	%	1901	%	1913	%	1921	%
Identified women	113		131		122		97		138		127		92	
Residing in brothels	67	*59*	93	*71*	79	*65*	91	*94*	100	*72*	118	*93*	83	*100*
Living in own lodgings	46	*41*	38	*29*	43	*35*	6	*6*	38	*28*	9	*7*	0	*0*
Brothel residents:														
Native	17	*25*	36	*39*	31	*39*	17	*19*	24	*24*	5	*4*	2	*2*
Alien	50	*75*	57	*61*	48	*61*	74	*81*	76	*76*	113	*96*	81	*98*
Independent women:														
Native	12	*26*	16	*42*	18	*42*	4	*67*	8	*21*	6	*67*	0	*0*
Aliens	34	*74*	22	*58*	25	*58*	2	*33*	30	*79*	3	*33*	0	*0*
Total native	29	*26*	52	*40*	49	*40*	21	*22*	32	*23*	11	*9*	2	*2*
Total aliens	84	*74*	79	*60*	73	*60*	76	*78*	106	*77*	116	*91*	81	*98*
Number of brothels	12		16		16		14		15		16		14	
Average number of brothel residents (including brothel-keepers)	4.4		4.1		4.4		6.5		6.7		7.4		6.1	

[a] Source: Gibraltar censuses. The category 'native' includes a small number of British-born women and other British subjects. Note that identification of non-brothel prostitutes in the 1891 census is difficult, leading to an underestimation of their numbers: results for this year should therefore be treated with caution.

Benedeta Montero was recorded as a prostitute working independently in Abacasis Lane in 1868, and in 1871 residing with another woman at 33 Serruya's Lane; as Benedeta Montero Glynn, she was working in 1881 in a household of three at 20 Serruya's Lane; but she was heading her own brothel with seven resident women in 1891 and 1901 a few doors down the lane. Cases like theirs were unusual – most women recorded by the system of registration were Spanish 'aliens' on temporary permits, glimpsed once or twice by the administrative machinery before vanishing into obscurity. But a lifetime's career in Gibraltar's brothel economy was clearly viable, and it was a path traced by many women in the second half of the nineteenth century. This underlines the fact that prostitutes were able – in some situations – to establish in their profession 'a significant degree of autonomy and control in their professional lives, both as individual workers and in managerial roles'.[60]

Looking at the ages of sex workers in Gibraltar (Table 5.2) we can note that, in comparison to other places, the average age of prostituted women is also relatively advanced, as we might expect. In comparison, brothel residents tend to be younger than women working independently and from their own lodgings, and their status as either natives or aliens makes no difference to this. Nor do natives and aliens differ significantly, and though there is a suggestion that, over time, native prostitutes residing in their own lodgings are increasingly older than their alien counterparts the small numbers of identifiable independents makes this a hesitant one. Most importantly, however, these figures and those relating to residence indicate that the nature of the prostitution business in Gibraltar changed significantly as these decades wore on: from a younger to an older cohort of women. These figures point, in other words, to a more organised and structured sexual market; if it had long been a 'profession', then we may see it becoming more 'professionalised' as the nineteenth century ended and the twentieth century began.

We can take this point a little further, though. The records which survive suggest that, if the business of prostitution in Gibraltar was increasingly structured, this was owing above all to the law and its policing. The careers of individual women point to their entrepreneurial role in creating and maintaining the landscape of prostitution in Gibraltar, but the other indicators demonstrate that it was authority from the top down, rather than agency from the bottom up, which structured the profession. What is striking from an analysis of the census and other records is, first, the monopolisation of the prostitutional economy by brothel houses together with the apparent growth in their size, and, secondly, their increasing concentration in urban space. Brothels – in my analysis, recall, houses with an identified brothel keeper, and with at least two prostitute women resident in the house at the time of the census – come to outweigh the contribution of women working out of their own lodgings. The proportion of women residing in such houses rises more or less steadily from 59 per cent in 1868 to 100 per cent in 1921 (see Table 5.1). Their average size, excluding the brothel-keeper herself, increases from 4.4 to 6.4 residents (this not counting women who may have been non-resident at the time of the census), whilst the ages of brothel-keepers also shows a marked increase (see Table 5.2). All this points to a movement from a rather more independently organised to an almost completely brothel-dominated system run by older female brothel-keepers who had grown up in the profession. None of the above means that *no* independent women prostituted themselves as time wore on – the continuing existence of clandestine forms of prostitution must be suspected – but it does indicate that for the *regulated* business of prostitution, brothel-houses were increasingly common and in all probability encouraged by the colonial state.

[60] Hill, *Their sisters' keepers*, p. 324.

Table 5.2 *Ages of sex workers in Gibraltar by residence and status, 1868–1921*[a]

	1868	1871	1881	1891	1901	1921
Average age of brothel-keepers/ heads of houses	36.2	37.9	39.6	42.5	41.9	48.9
Average age of brothel inmate	22.0	22.8	22.3	23.5	25.2	26.6
Average age of non-brothel inmate	25.4	26.1	29.5	28.9	29.4	–
Average age of native prostitute	23.9	24.4	25.6	26.8	28.0	–
Average age of native prostitute in brothel	22.0	22.5	22.8	28.6	25.6	–
Average age of native prostitute in lodgings	24.2	25.1	28.4	24.4	34.1	–
Average age of alien prostitute	23.8	24.7	25.6	23.4	26.3	26.6
Average age of alien prostitute in brothel	22.0	23.0	22.2	23.0	25.1	26.6
Average age of alien prostitute in lodgings	26.1	26.3	29.4	40.0	28.5	–
Average age of prostitute	24.1	24.6	25.6	23.9	26.6	26.6

[a] Source: Gibraltar censuses. See caveat to Table 5.1 above.

There are two reasons why this should be so. In the first place, regular brothels were more amenable to inspection and control than independent accommodation houses, and were at a greater distance from the clandestine and 'amateur' prostitution that regulationists most feared. Secondly, more specifically and critically, Gibraltar-born women or other British subjects working out of brothel-houses could be compelled to submit to medical examination when their counterparts in independent lodgings could not: as one surgeon attested, 'pressure is brought to bear on British suspects who are prostitutes and who reside in brothels where there are alien women, in order to induce them to submit to the same kind of examination'.[61] The persistent difficulty with the legislative machinery in force, and I will return to this point, is the fact that its provisions could only be legally extended to *alien* prostitutes. 'Native' women were, in formal terms, beyond the scope of the law. When a British subject was a brothel resident alongside alien women, however, the law could lean on the brothel-keeper to ensure that she attended the hospital and accepted the authority of police and medical officers. For both these reasons it would be no real surprise if the police magistrates put as much pressure as they could to domesticate prostitution in the regular brothel economy.

This may be confirmed if we take into account the accompanying concentration of brothels in the immediate vicinity of Serruya's Lane. Long famous for

[61] Memorandum from Port Surgeon to Colonial Secretary, received 22 April 1887 (GGA, Box A).

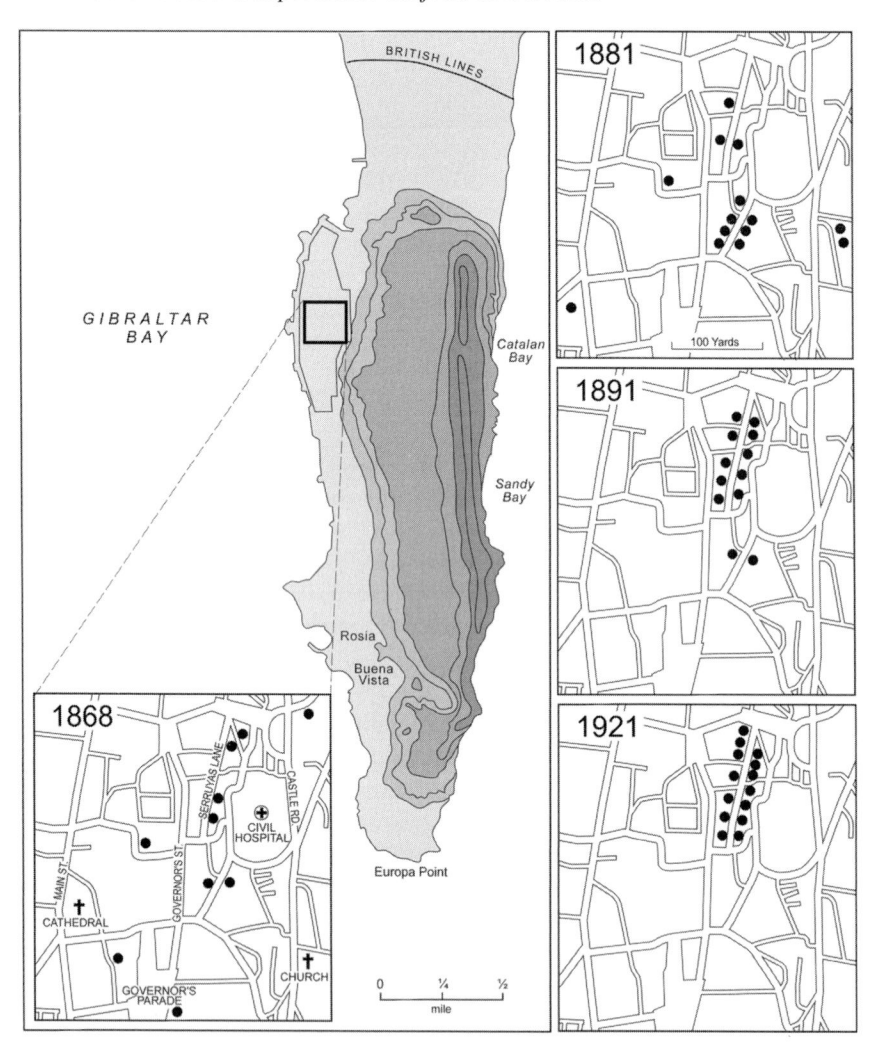

Figure 5.2. Location of brothels in Gibraltar, 1868–1921

its brothels and accommodation houses, Serruya's Lane was at the heart of the 'Ramps' district that was the effective red-light district of Gibraltar. Prostitution was always localised and concentrated. Yet the censuses indicate that it was, under the impress of the law and police practice, ever more so. Its outliers, in the form of both individual lodgings and regular brothels, seem to have disappeared over the half-century under consideration here (Figure 5.2). What was left was the central brothel street of Serruya's Lane – and by 1921 every single acknowledgeable brothel was located there. There is no direct evidence of which I am aware to confirm this as government policy, and there would be no legal authority to authorise the residence of 'native' prostitute women in any case, but their power to resist the police was limited. In 1901, the Acting Attorney General noted that even native women 'would not, I think, disregard an intimation from the chief of Police not to occupy any premises which it may be desired to keep closed, and if they did, they could be expelled and re-admitted only on conditions'.[62] The comments of the Chief of Police a year later similarly suggest the importance of indirect pressure and police pragmatism:

> before 1893, alien women were made to live in houses under the control of a mistress who looked carefully after the health of the girls living in her house. This system was objected to in 1892 and the Chief of Police was instructed not to put any pressure on these women but to allow them to live where they liked. Since then they have lived where they please and many of them now live in single rooms by themselves and are under no control whatever. Since my appointment in 1895 I have discouraged their living in single rooms by themselves as much as I can without using actual pressure, and the result has been good.[63]

Alternatively, as happened later, with the closure of the brothel at Devil's Gap, the permit of residence of alien residents could simply be rescinded. Despite the memorial of its madam, Enriqueta Thomas, who cited the ill consequences of officers and men mixing in the houses and in the single street of Serruya's Lane, this Gibraltar institution finally came to its end in 1919.[64]

Whatever the exact chronology, these remarks point to the overall philosophy of regulationist policing that encouraged concentration and brothel residence over dispersal and independence. Space was both target and opportunity of medical police. By the beginning of the twentieth century the situation was almost all that the authorities could desire. Whilst drunkenness, disease and disorder were ever-present features, the perceived necessity of catering to the sexual requirements of service personnel led the authorities in Gibraltar to play a central role in seeking to mitigate its problems. As an exercise in law and order the regulation of prostitution is distinctive for its thoroughness and apparently systematic control. Though lacking a specific legal backing, the authoritarian powers over the entire civilian population lent medical policing effective powers to shape and structure Gibraltar's prostitution economy.

Tackling the 'native' problem

For all its apparent success in ordering the business of prostitution, however, the practice of regulation in Gibraltar was still forced to confront the intractable

---

[62] File, 'Prostitutes in disorderly houses', 24 May 1901 (GGA, Box B).
[63] Chief of Police to Colonial Secretary, 29 January 1902 (GGA, Box C).
[64] "Withdrawal by police of permits of residence of alien women residing in C.P. 841 (a brothel)', 24 April 1919 (GGA, Box B).

problem of the naturalised or 'native' prostitute. It was noted with something like despair that native prostitute women were 'under no inducement, as far as the police are concerned, direct or indirect, to submit to examination', and even if they did so they were reported as being irregular in attendance.[65] This had always been the principal reason for considering specific contagious diseases legislation in Gibraltar. In 1867, one military surgeon pointed to the inadequacy of the laws at present 'which, altho' they confer ample powers for the removal of aliens known to be diseased ... those enjoying the rights of British subjects, cannot be dealt with in the same manner'.[66] Flood's abortive attempt at framing a Contagious Diseases Ordinance was animated by the inability of the legislation to authorise compulsion against Gibraltar-born women, but in 1887 the Port Surgeon lamented that 'it is a great pity that all well known prostitutes in this Colony are not placed on the same footing as the Alien Women'.[67] By that time, proponents of extending regulationism to native women were handicapped by the repeal of domestic CD legislation and by the fact that the Colonial and War Offices had made it clear that no form of compulsion could be exercised on prostituted women in the future. Although the case for regulation continued to be made, there could be no question of specific legislation. So, whilst the imperial government could not transfer CD laws to the colonies in the 1860s, the defeat of domestic regulation nonetheless meant that all such ordinances abroad must promptly be extinguished. Gibraltar's Governor fought a rearguard action against this decision, but was eventually overruled.[68]

For those convinced of the necessity of retaining regulationist measures, there were, in Gibraltar, two legislative ways round this problem. The first was to add on an apparently neutral medical legislation to the aliens ordinances. Tinkering with sanitary legislation allowed venereal diseases to be classified under the general heading of infectious diseases, and made subject to the ordinary machinery of notification and treatment. In this way regulationism for all might be smuggled in by the back door. The Sanitary Order Further Amendment Ordinance of 1901 accordingly allowed the Chief of Police to require women to attend the Colonial Hospital or elsewhere if there had been notification of their diseased condition. This was drawn up, with the full consent of the War Office, Colonial Office and Admiralty, along the lines of Indian cantonment regulations and, for all that it was intended to circumvent association with venereal disease ordinances was blatantly a regulationist enterprise.[69] It was so recognised by its opponents, who understood it as a further step by which the imperial government was surreptitiously bringing

[65] Memorandum, n.d., 'Regulations affecting prostitutes in Gibraltar' (GGA, Box A).
[66] Surgeon Major R. Dominshetti [?] to Assistant Adjutant General [?], 28 September 1867, 'Lock hospital and Contagious Diseases Act' (GGA, Box A).
[67] Memorandum from Port Surgeon to Colonial Secretary, 14 April 1887 (GGA, Box A).
[68] See 'Precis of correspondence relative to contagious diseases systems' (GGA, Box A).
[69] J. Chamberlain to Governor Sir R. Biddulph, 8 December 1899 (GGA, Box B).

regulationism home from the colonies: 'This Gibraltar Ordinance clearly shows that the present Government has *reversed the whole policy* so far as Crown Colonies (of which Gibraltar is one) are concerned.'[70]

The second step, and it was allied with the first, was quite arbitrarily to remove – as far as venereal disease and prostitution were concerned – the exemption that Gibraltar-born or naturalised women had enjoyed. The Sanitary Order Amendment Ordinance was conceived with its legislative twin, a 1900 amendment to the 1885 Aliens Order in Council referred to informally as the 'Strangers Order in Council'. Under this amendment the Governor would simply be given the same powers over 'certain British subjects' – prostitutes – that he exercised over aliens: 'Draft Ordinance empowers the Governor to declare persons not complying with Sec. 3 of Ordinance to be strangers, and a *Native* prostitute can then be dealt with in the same way as an alien. The combined operation of the Ordinance and O. in C. will enable the Governor to terminate the residence in Gibraltar of any prostitute, native or alien, who would only thereafter receive a permit of residence and get it renewed on furnishing a certificate of health.'[71] The British government had long made it clear that no system of compulsion of prostitutes could be authorised, but the sweeping powers that this so-called 'Strangers' ordinance authorised were, in conjunction with the sanitary ordinance, simply regulationism by another name. As the anti-regulationist critic Joseph Edmondson put it:

Under the combined operation of the two ordinances of 29th June, 1900 (re 'Aliens'), and of 29th March 1901 ('Sanitary amendment'), the whole system has been, or may be restored and applied to aliens and natives alike; *and that without the mention of Regulation, licensing or medical examination in either of these measures.* Thus do these Ordinances come up to the Regulationist's Ideal of establishing the system by enactments which 'understand Regulation without expressing it.'[72]

The care with which this legislation was drawn up and introduced, the paths that the memoranda traced within the British government and the imperial network, the elaborate evasion of explicit forms of compulsion, all betray the preoccupation with legalism characteristic of British attempts to regulate prostitution. Regulation was too vulnerable at home and abroad to the social purists' charges that the state was complicit with vice. In direct legal terms, the repeal of the CD Acts had made regulation a dead letter. The argument for local necessity that had sustained colonial measures was no longer defensible on these grounds. Instead, proconsuls and their agents, convinced of the necessity to combat venereal disease, were forced to improvise, though still with recourse to the law. The ordinance on 'aliens' in Gibraltar remained the central legal framework to encourage

---

[70] J. Edmondson, *By stealthy steps: regulation in Gibraltar* (London, 190[?]), GGA, Box C, p. 1, emphasis in original.
[71] Printed Memorandum 'Venereal' (GGA, Box B).
[72] Edmondson, *By stealthy steps*, p. 5, emphasis in original.

or compel compliance, but it could only be made fully effective by recourse to a legal fiat that gave the Governor the power to alienate *any* undesirable person. This change of status, from 'native' to 'stranger', made them instantly coercible, bringing them for the first time under the full control of Gibraltar's colonial authorities. The results may be seen in the landscape of prostitution I outlined in the previous section, and it is perhaps the central mechanism by which a potentially disorderly and clandestine business could be structured and constrained. Complete regulation was impossible without full legislative authority; discipline impossible without law.

The demise of regulation

By the start of the twentieth century, the prostitution question had thus been brought firmly within a strengthened administrative machinery, and the reach of the law extended to the entire civilian population. The prostitution business was seemingly ever more professionalised and disciplined. Brothel prostitution was all but hegemonic, and the brothel quarter had acquired an ever-greater presence and permanence. Medical inspections of Serruya's Lane testified to its general salubrity: finding no case of venereal disease in the hundred women examined there, two army medics opined that 'most of these women are well nourished, cleanly in habits and enjoy good health. We were surprised to find such healthy young women following such calling.'[73] Indeed, police magistrates and medical officers tended to be increasingly sceptical of servicemen's claims to have been infected by residents of Serruya's Lane.[74] Though there were those who regarded them with suspicion, many medical officers refused to believe that the district's well-regulated brothels formed a centre of infection.

Rates of venereal disease nevertheless began to increase again, a phenomenon that would cause greater and greater alarm in the years leading up to the First World War. In 1911, the admission ratio per 1,000 strength was 123, and, in 1912, 128. In the words of Governor Archibald Hunter: 'These figures are ghastly reading.'[75] Some blame was put on the servicemen themselves, their indiscipline leading them to engage with women beyond the reach of medical order, but of course more was heaped on the women themselves. Indeed, a new landscape

---

[73] Report of Major J. Tobin, RAMC and Major C.E.P. Fowler, RAMC, 9 January 1912 (GGA, Box C).

[74] See for instance John Bennet, Chief of Police, to Colonial Secretary, 13 July 1905: 'All the girls living in the houses indicated have been examined by a doctor during the past week and have been certified to be free from disease. I attach a certificate signed by Dr Lyons showing that "Gloria" was examined only yesterday and found free from disease. This shows that the information given by the soldiers is quite useless' (GGA, Box C).

[75] File, 'Venereal disease among the troops in the garrison', 10 February 1913 (GGA, Box C).

of indisciplined sex was mapped out: a territory of clandestine 'amateurs', of women who prowled in the shadows of the Almeda gardens, and of the brothels of La Linea just across the border with Spain. Here is one commanding officer, responding to eight cases of venereal disease among his troops admitted on successive days:

Thanks for letting me see enclosed report from Chief of Police. Really don't know what we can do!!! There must be some free lancers abroad who indulge in al fresco performances in the Almeda or elsewhere. I cannot believe that all this increased venereal is the result of picnics, fairs, & Linea. There is some woman or women who are poisoning the unsuspecting soldier. One can take some steps with the professional lady, but it is very difficult to deal with the amateur.[76]

Measures to patrol the city and to prevent soldiers' excursions to Spain failed to stem the tide of anxiety, and for the first time more drastic measures seemed called for, including, for all their earlier sanitary testimonials, placing the city's brothels out of bounds or suppressing them entirely. The War itself made the entire question of prostitution a matter of urgency, with regulationism back on the agenda, together with propaganda, prophylaxis and straightforward repression. Under the impress of military necessity any complacency over the regulated brothel was rapidly extinguished. In 1916, the Deputy Surgeon General dismissed the health certification of Gibraltar's brothel inmates as worthless and argued that 'the presence of these women under present conditions as the chief focus of venereal infection constitutes a danger to the general health and an increasing loss to the Navy of the services of men at a time when these services are most required'. Calling for the exclusion of all 'alien' prostitutes during the period of the War, he went on to denounce the entire enterprise of regulation:

In this matter it is my opinion that supply creates a demand to a greater extent than demand creates a supply, especially in a place such as Gibraltar. Men arriving in ships find here not only no difficulty in the way of their desires, but every facility offered, together with a guarantee that the women are free from disease.
  If alien prostitutes be abolished the demand, in my opinion will decline. No doubt a certain number of irregular prostitutes will exist: but in so small a place as Gibraltar there should be no difficulty in locating them and bringing them under police supervision.

A certain proportion of Fleet men when on leave gravitate or follow the line of least resistance. They go from grog-shop to brothel with the tide, since, not only is there little if any functional resistance to such a course but every facility offered. Were real difficulties placed in their way many having no very definite purpose would be deflected from the common course.[77]

---

[76] Memorandum from Colonel Murray, 13 August 1910 (GGA, Box C).

[77] See memorandum from Rear Admiral B. Currey, Senior Naval Officer, to H.E. Lt Gen. Sir Herbert S. G. Miles, Governor and Commander-in-Chief, 28 April 1916 (GGA, Box C).

There were others who cautioned against drastic action, insisting by contrast that it was demand – men's sexual urges, imperious and insistent – that created supply. Approved by nature it was simply impossible to hope that the young soldier could avoid its directives:

> To discuss an impulse so approved by nature that for its direct encouragement the flowers put on their gorgeous blooms, and the birds their brilliant plumage, as if it were a cultivated growth like a taste for beer or Botticelli, is absurd.
>
> The real question to be faced, from the point of view of what ever person concerned you [sic] may be discussing the question, is which is best? to permit opportunity to be given for this demand to be satisfied with free and willing agents in certain specified localities, or to leave this desire in some cases to turn men to unnatural forms of vice, and in others to treble the pursuit by them of the servant girl class, or increase the custom of unsupervised professional masquerading as an amateur.[78]

Although the advice not to expel the prostitute class does not seem to have been followed, the brothels were to be put out of bounds. The days of the tolerated Serruya's Lane brothels were numbered. In 1916, one concerned Admiral accepted that, whether or not it reduced the extent of venereal disease infection, the exclusion of such women 'would certainly free the Authorities from the stigma of knowingly permitting women to reside here for immoral purposes, a stigma no British Government can openly admit'.[79] After the crisis of the war years, the tide had turned once more against regulationism. The National Council for Combating Venereal Diseases recommended in 1921 that toleration of prostitution in Gibraltar, should be brought to an end. Recommending the 'absolution [sic] of a prostitution area', the commissioners particularly regretted its central situation within the town and the vicinity of public houses. During their stay in Gibraltar, it is significant that the commissioners were offered enthusiastic help and hospitality by the Governor General Sir Horace Smith-Dorrien, and by his wife.[80] His aid was not long forthcoming: an advocate of barrack reform and an enthusiast of wholesome sports and games, in 1922 Smith-Dorrien promptly closed down the entire brothel quarter, bringing to a close the era of regulated prostitution in Gibraltar.[81]

Prostitution itself did not disappear, of course. Serruya's Lane's sex workers simply decamped across the Spanish border to La Linea, installing themselves in a single street appropriately called Calle de Gibraltar.[82] From 1922 onwards, however, prostitution would be literally beyond the pale. The sex workers who had catered

---

[78] War Office memorandum, 13 December 1916 (GGA, Box B).
[79] Currey to Miles, 28 April 1916 (GGA, Box C).
[80] *General report and recommendations submitted to the Colonial Office for transmission to the colony by the National Council for Combating Venereal Diseases Commission*, May 1921.
[81] H. Smith-Dorrien, *Memories of forty-eight years' service* (London, 1925), p. 495.
[82] Stewart, *Gibraltar the keystone*, pp. 212–13.

to the demands of the soldiers and sailors of Gibraltar for generations were now marginalised in space as much as they were marginalised in society. They were fully outside of the law in the sense that they were outside colonial jurisdiction.

Conclusions

We have seen in this chapter that the regulation of prostitution in the British Mediterranean was both consistent in philosophy and divergent in form. The regimes in place at Malta, in Corfu and the other Ionian Islands, and in Gibraltar, were characteristically colonial institutions in their attempts to discipline the lives of the prostitute women who served the sexual needs of the British troops stationed there. Each demonstrates the prioritisation of the health and the security of the British garrison state over the civil rights of the women who worked as prostitutes. In these colonies such women were conscripted into a notably professionalised and well-managed business of prostitution; in this way prostitution regulation reshaped civil society according to the needs of the British colonial power. We can say, with Philippa Levine, that 'colonial authorities … defined, judged, and ordered local societies in an imperial image'; this was as true for the Mediterranean colonies as it was for the overseas empire and the contact zones between white and non-white peoples.[83] On the other hand, it is the diversity of the origins and nature of the machinery by which women were regulated that is notable. In Malta and the Ionian Islands, the British had significant precedents upon which to draw, both customary and formal. The colonial regulation of prostitution could be elaborated in part from these earlier regimes, or at the very least take strength from their historical sanctioning of regulated sexuality. In Gibraltar, however, though regulationism was also of very long standing, rooted as it was in the early history of the colony, it was fashioned from the initial powers of conquest; Gibraltar's status as an imperial fortress counted for as much here as its later manifestation as a colony. In Gibraltar, regulationism never needed the formal sanction of contagious diseases legislation, as it was made possible by the authoritarian powers over the civil population, by the fact of British sovereignty itself. In Gibraltar, the considerations not only of war but also of *law*, as it related to sovereignty and civilian rights, were of central importance; and they were complemented by the need for a military-medical discipline recognised early on by Gibraltar's colonial authorities. Prostitute women were required to be regulated on grounds of hygiene and order, as in the towns under the Contagious Diseases Acts and in other domestic regimes; but they needed to be made imperial subjects as well as moral and medical ones. It was, above all, the colonial law that allowed this to happen.

Something of the *ad hoc* quality of the British experience of regulating prostitution is also brought out by these examples, however. The one institution that

[83] Levine, *Prostitution, race, and politics*, p. 179.

might have harmonised these regulationist regimes was the law; but the British authorities had long denied themselves the possibility of laws of universal imperial application, insisting instead that British dependencies should frame local ordinances suited to local necessities. British colonial regulationism was always therefore partial and particular, so that even to speak of a characteristic 'colonial' regime of sexuality, however tempting, should be questioned. But the question of imperial Britain's sovereign power over its colonial subjects, the question, that is, of *law as sovereignty*, is everywhere insistently raised, and, in such settings, the *legal* status of prostitute subjects was of paramount importance. The British project of regulating prostitution was inevitably imperial and international, crossing political boundaries and raising pressing questions of the racial and sexual subjection of women who were *never* characterised as the juridical subjects of metropolitan legal discourse. It helped, in short, to draw up the legal-moral boundary between the metropolitan world, in which the liberty of the subject was supposedly sacrosanct, and colonial settings, in which such liberties could be suspended where necessary.

As I have argued for Gibraltar, it was the prostitute's legal status that was the primary issue in the regulation of prostitution there. The prostituted woman found herself 'othered' by a law drawing distinctions between 'natives' and 'aliens', residents and 'visitors', subjects and 'strangers'. It was the law that governed her relationship to space and territory and the rights that were bundled with them. It was the law that ensured the inseparability of sexuality and sovereignty. In Gibraltar, jurisdiction over territory and population, and the authorisation of legal distinctions of citizenship and nationality serves to demonstrate the ways in which rights of residence could be intertwined with sexual rights – making sovereign law and sovereign power a crucial determinant of the nineteenth-century 'governmentalisation of the sexual field'.[84] The disciplinary regulation of prostituted women depended to a unique extent on legal authority and on legal struggles over jurisdiction, residence and nationality. The regulation of prostitution depended in Gibraltar on lines of jurisdiction that were drawn both on the ground and within the territory itself, legal boundaries which, again *contra* Foucault, were 'productive' in their effects, producing identities and ensuring their compliance with disciplinary technologies. It is not the juridical subject – the exemplary rights-bearing citizen – who is central to this story. Regulation in Britain may have policed the boundaries of citizenship by placing prostituted women outside its protection – but in Gibraltar most such women never possessed these liberties in the first place. In their case, under Gibraltar's colonial law, the key juridical relation was not that which existed between state and citizen, but that between colonial authority and 'alien' residents. It is the legal authority of sovereign power, not the discourse of constitutional rights, which is bound up here with the operation of disciplinary power. This has certain affinities with the emphasis in Giorgio Agamben's work,

[84] A. Hunt, *Governing morals: a social history of moral regulation* (Cambridge, 1999).

contra Foucault, on the importance of sovereign power, and on the possibility of the sovereign suspension of rights in particular – that is, the use of the law to revoke the citizenship of certain individuals, belonging to certain groups, to produce persons outside the protection of the law.[85] In the case of Gibraltar, it was the right of residence that continued to be withheld from the majority of civilians who lived and worked on the Rock. Their place in the territory was conditional, even arbitrary, a legal fact that acted as a bulwark, not a hindrance, to colonial order. The troubling and dangerous mobility of prostituted women could be countered by legislative and policing technologies that attempted to keep civilians from becoming citizens. The discipline, comformity and compliance of prostituted women was produced by constructing their legal identity as 'aliens'.

Whilst colonial law in Gibraltar offered unique possibilities for disciplining commercial sexuality in the colony, it was not, however, watertight; it also offered possibilities for women to challenge and evade the administration of prostitution. As the historical anthropologist Thomas Gallant notes in his study of colonial rule in Zante, law should not be seen as the handmaid of imperial social control: 'Law was not merely the blunt instrument of imperial rule, it also created new opportunities and spaces for the subject population both to resist the hegemonic designs of their rulers and to contest power, status, and reputation among themselves.'[86] The law can be 'a shield for the powerless as well as a weapon for the privileged'.[87] The ability of prostitute women to challenge the authorities in Gibraltar, formally or informally, in the courts in the case of individuals like Carmen Hernandez or Enriqueta Thomas, or simply by naturalising themselves or their children by marrying British men or giving birth in the colony: these strategies testify to the resourcefulness of women who otherwise appear to be placed beyond the protection of the law. Even if this battle in Gibraltar was ultimately lost, by a legal sleight of hand that rendered at a stroke all civilians strangers, and even if prostitute women were in the end forced to remove themselves over the border to Spain and beyond British jurisdiction, their willingness to use the law to challenge the colonial authorities remains salutary.

---

[85] See especially G. Agamben, *Homo sacer: sovereign power and bare life* (Stanford, 1998), and *State of exception* (Chicago, 2005).
[86] Gallant, *Experiencing dominion*, p. 150.
[87] T. Eagleton, *Holy terror* (Oxford, 2005), p. 53.

6

Race and the regulation of prostitution in Hong Kong and the overseas empire

The previous chapters in this book have considered the elaboration of British regulationist regimes either at home or close to home. This chapter moves rather further away from the metropolis by considering the regulation of prostitution in one important part of the British overseas empire, taking Hong Kong – once termed the 'Gibraltar of the East' – as an example of the distinctive regimes of regulated sexuality that were installed in the wider colonial world.[1] I say example, rather than exemplar, as the differences between colonies were always great, sometimes extremely so, and the British authorities in any case made it a point of administrative principle and imperial propaganda to tailor colonial policies to local circumstance. The scholarship on the regulation of prostitution and of sexuality in the overseas colonies is large and growing, and may be taken now to point up the differences as much as the similarities between them. We must be cautious about portraying these overseas regimes, in all their variety, as collectively representative of the 'colonial', particularly insofar as a fundamental contrast with practices to be found in the British 'metropolis' is imputed. For reasons that I have elaborated on earlier, this distinction between colonial and metropolitan practices has to be critically analysed rather than assumed or asserted. The previous chapter in itself advises caution in equating the colonial world with some or all of Britain's overseas possessions.

The example of Hong Kong given here may still be used to indicate something of the general nature of British attitudes and policies towards the regulation of its imperial subjects in farther flung colonies, distant as they were from British, European and 'white' institutions and seemingly sharing nothing of their values. The specifics of Hong Kong's history should not preclude attention to broader questions of imperial governance, not least because the activities of repealers

---

[1] The phrase comes from Governor Sir George Bowen who wrote in 1883 of Hong Kong as a garrison town rather than a colony: see F. Madden and D. Fieldhouse (eds.), *The dependent empire and Ireland, 1840–1900: advance and retreat in representative self-government* (New York, 1991), p. 495.

raised the stakes in this regard, the latter being particularly vigorous in drawing connections between colonial regimes that they refused politically to see as *sui generis* and impelled only by local necessities. Historians of the management of sexuality in the British Empire have followed their lead by suggesting shared characteristics of colonial regulationist regimes, but most particularly in conditions of racial subordination 'where sexual contact between people of different races threatened to destabilize the dichotomies upon which the imperial system was built'.[2] It has been fairly said in this regard that contagious diseases legislation enacted in such colonies were more ambitious, more thoroughgoing and more extreme than to be found in the domestic CD Acts.[3] So brothels were typically recognised and legalised, and prostitutes formally conscripted by card and register, measures that could never be countenanced in Britain. There was little attempt either to reform prostitute women, little by way of a sop to those who considered regulated prostitution simply a matter of attempting to provide safer sexual opportunities for venal men. The ultimate priorities of the military-medical management of sexuality were made quite explicit. There was, moreover, no restriction of regulationist legislation to military rather than civilian communities: in the colonies, regulation of prostitution meant the management of women and the indigenous civilian population generally. Colonial regulationism was never therefore justified in the territories in which it operated as a matter of 'partial legislation' or 'privileged sites' in the sense of the CD Acts in Britain. This was a matter instead of intrusive, authoritarian government founded on the subject status of the native population.

The nature of one such regime is examined in this chapter in detail, and the importance of race to the landscape of regulated prostitution is indeed the predominant theme. The measures enacted in Hong Kong involved the licensing of brothels and the registration of prostitutes, the medical inspection only of women whose clients were Europeans, and their incarceration if found to be in a contagious state. In strictly separating brothels intended for non-Chinese clients from those for the Chinese, these ordinances confirmed the central importance of race in the attempt to promote or impose sexual discipline. The exigencies of colonial policy may thus be easily stated: regulation of brothels was a matter of imperial policy designed to protect Europeans from disease by policing the contact zones where they came into direct sexual engagement with women predominantly of the migrant Chinese community. The spatially organised system of licensed

---

[2] M. Harrison, review of Levine, *Prostitution, race, and politics*, in *American Historical Review*, 109 (2004), 483–4, p. 483.

[3] See S. Banerjee, *Under the Raj: prostitution in colonial Bengal* (New York, 1998), p. 66, P. Howell, 'Prostitution and racialised sexuality: the regulation of prostitution in Britain and the British Empire before the Contagious Diseases Acts', *Environment and Planning D: Society and Space*, 18 (2000), 321–39, pp. 328–9, P. Levine, *Prostitution, race, and politics: policing venereal disease in the British Empire* (New York, 2003), p. 52.

prostitution in Hong Kong was part of a series of measures that together formed 'a powerful network of overlapping schemes of control and surveillance'.[4]

It was rather more than this, however, and this chapter's conclusions depart from those of previous studies by emphasising the role of race in limiting and shaping, rather than extending, the disciplinary modernity represented by colonial sexual regulation. At the same time, the geography of segregation of brothel clients points to the articulation of a political project that *conceded* rather than merely imposed the rule of racial difference. Acceptance of segregated prostitution limited colonial medical intervention through its acknowledgement of Chinese sensitivities, which British condescension persisted in calling native 'prejudices'. Without disputing the bluntly authoritarian nature of British colonial rule, regulationism in Hong Kong can be seen as inscribing distinctive 'boundaries of rule', with an emphasis on pragmatic calculation rather than disciplinary domination.[5] In Foucauldian terms, this chapter argues, race was the product as much as the producer of a geopolitical technology, part of a locally constituted colonial governmentality, rather than merely the imposition of some universal form of colonial power. This specific articulation of race and space, at once characteristically authoritarian and carefully circumscribed, was central to the government of sexuality in colonial Hong Kong.

Regulating prostitution in the overseas empire

Regulationism in Hong Kong needs first to be considered in the context of policies in Britain's other overseas colonies, however. Any survey of British practices can demonstrate that regulationist regimes were established in these colonies at a notably early stage. Linda Bryder's otherwise useful review of the historiography of sex, race and colonialism has it quite wrong when she writes that after the passing of the British Contagious Diseases Acts 'similar measures were soon enforced in the colonies'.[6] It was rather the other way round, with both formal and informal practices being pioneered in several overseas colonies some time before 1864, and in some cases long before that date. Whilst it is true that in some of the colonies with regulationist ordinances formal legislation did postdate the British Acts, this does not invalidate the important point that contagious diseases acts were

---

[4] C. Munn, *Anglo-China: Chinese people and British rule in Hong Kong, 1841–1880* (Richmond, 2001), p. 344.

[5] For 'boundaries of rule' see the discussion of colonial categories in A. L. Stoler, *Carnal knowledge and imperial power: race and the intimate in colonial rule* (Berkeley, 2002), pp. 22–40; the spatial implications of the phrase are developed in the context of imperial medicine in A. Bashford, *Imperial hygiene: a critical history of colonialism, nationalism and public health* (Basingstoke, 2004).

[6] L. Bryder, 'Sex, race and colonialism: an historiographical review', *International History Review*, 20 (1998), 791–822, p. 815.

'pre-eminently imperial legislation, designed to ensure the security of the British Empire' and that they appeared first, and arguably first achieved their *characteristic* form, in the colonial margins rather than in the imperial metropolis.[7]

Even if we exclude from our purview the Mediterranean possessions and the antiquity of their measures for the control of prostitution and disease, the overseas colonies provide the *earliest* precursors of domestic regulationism. The case of British India is by far the most studied and the best known, for better or for worse.[8] The origins of the system there – and I mean this in the genealogical rather than the teleological sense – can be found in the archipelago of lock hospitals that emerged in the late eighteenth century and proliferated in the early years of the nineteenth. These emerged at more or less the same time as the spread of lock hospitals in Britain, but they clearly operated in a very different, much more blatantly coercive fashion; from the very beginning, even when soldiers were subject to medical inspection, it was the prostituted woman who was the real focus of the discipline they imposed. In fact, there was a long-standing military effort in India dedicated to seeking out and treating diseased women, one that probably dates back well into the eighteenth century; but older, irregular and customary practices were increasingly replaced in the early nineteenth century with a more systematic campaign involving the compulsory registration and coercive treatment of women in the cantonments and their surroundings.[9] The lock hospitals constructed from 1805 onwards in Madras, the most enthusiastic of the presidencies, and advertised as providing the 'wholesome restraint' needed to counter 'the bitter scourge of unlawful embraces', seem to have been the pioneer institutions.[10] Seventeen hospitals were in place in Madras by 1808, though most of these institutions were short-lived. In 1807, Bengal had adopted similar measures at its principal stations, and the building of hospitals was authorised by the East India

[7] E. B. van Heyningen, 'The social evil in the Cape Colony 1868–1902: prostitution and the Contagious Diseases Acts', *Journal of Southern African Studies*, 10 (1984) 170–97, p. 173.
[8] Among many important commentaries: K. Ballhatchet, *Race, sex and class under the Raj: imperial attitudes and policies and their critics, 1793–1905* (London, 1980); Levine, *Prostitution, race, and politics*; D. M. Peers, 'Soldiers, surgeons and the campaigns to combat sexually transmitted diseases in colonial India, 1805–1860', *Medical History*, 42 (1998), 137–60; J. Whitehead, 'Bodies clean and unclean: prostitution, sanitary legislation, and respectable femininity in colonial North India', *Gender and History*, 7 (1995), 41–63.
[9] Peers, 'Soldiers, surgeons', p. 150; M. S. Kumar, '"Oriental sore" or "public nuisance": the regulation of prostitution in colonial India, 1805–1889', in L. J. Proudfoot and M. M. Roche (eds.), *(Dis)placing empire: renegotiating British colonial geographies* (Aldershot, 2005), p. 162.
[10] British Library, Oriental and India Office Collections (OIOC), F/4/200, 'Establishment of lock hospitals' [Madras] 1805–7, F/4/277, 'Statement of the expenses of lock hospitals' [Madras].

Company's Board of Directors in all three of the Indian presidencies in 1810. The limitations of this early attempt to regulate the sex trade should be emphasised, however. It was never politically or administratively secure, and Bombay was distinctly less committed than the other presidencies, its medical officers critical of the efficacy and expense of lock hospitals. Cumulative concerns of this sort – together with vociferous moral objections – brought these piecemeal experiments to an abrupt end, first in Bengal in 1830, and then in India as a whole by 1835. Nevertheless, the principles of medical police had been laid out, and a definite precedent established.[11] In any event, even after formal proscription, concerned commanders and surgeons simply fell back on the unofficial, *ad hoc* measures of controlling disease by controlling prostitutes. Douglas Peers has pointed not only to the reintroduction of lock hospitals in all but name but also to the surreptitious rebuilding of a system of regulated prostitution: thus, he notes, 'even before the Contagious Diseases Acts were passed, and perhaps in the knowledge that such legislation was in the offing, the government of India had quietly gone to work reinventing the lock hospital'.[12] Opponents of regulationism were quick to register the precedence and priority of these Indian military experiments, whether officially sanctioned or surreptitious. The Dean of Carlisle, Francis Close, reported that '[t]he spirit of the Acts in question has, we are assured, been in operation there for many years, and not a few of their direct enactments have been enforced', and the great repeal campaigner James Stansfeld spoke significantly of 'a separate, earlier, and more important system of regulation'.[13]

When, therefore, regulationist measures were reintroduced in the era of direct rule after the so-called 'Mutiny', British colonial authorities in India could build upon both existing institutions and more than half a century of official or unofficial regulationist experience. The British sanitary commissioners of 1863 straightforwardly recommended 'the re-organization of the measures formerly adopted in the three Presidencies, with any improvements which subsequent experience and consideration may point out as being required to meet the necessities of each locality'.[14] Imperial security was the question of utmost importance, venereal disease having assumed an even greater significance as the threat of other diseases

[11] See the evidence of Grierson, Appendix 2, to the *Royal Commission on the sanitary state of the army in India*, P.P. 1863 (3184) XIX, Part I. As early as 1805, military surgeon Whitelaw Ainstie called for the institution of a 'Military Police of Health' in India: OIOC F/4/226, 'Mr Surgeon Ainstie's plan for preserving the health of the European soldiers', 1806.

[12] Peers, 'Soldiers, surgeons', p. 159.

[13] F. Close, *An examination of the witnesses, and their evidence, given before a Royal Commission upon the administration and operation of the 'Contagious Diseases Acts, 1871'* (London, 1872), p. 5; J. Stansfeld, *Substance of the speeches of the Rt. Hon. James Stansfeld, MP, on the Contagious Diseases Acts* (London, 1875), p. 260.

[14] P.P. 1863 [3184] XIX. Part I, *Royal Commission on the sanitary state of the army in India, volume I: Report of the commissioners*, p. lxii.

temporarily receded and the reliance upon British servicemen increased. This was also the period at which Victorian colonial sanitary science was at its peak of influence and authority. It is essential, as I have already argued, to emphasise the importance of the expert authority of the Indian soldier-surgeons to the development of contagious diseases legislation both in India and in Britain. We might then say that British regulationism in the late 1850s and 1860s developed upon both a colonial *and* a domestic front, with many of the same personnel active in both theatres. In India, the political work of such advocates resulted in the Cantonment Act of 1864 – the same year as the first of the British CD Acts – and the Indian Contagious Diseases Act of 1868. The former authorised the direct supervision of the prostitute women of the *chaklas* or *lal bazaars* within or adjacent to the military cantonments, whilst the latter, first proposed in 1860, allowed sanitary supervision in the civilian towns. In these Acts, the lock hospital once again assumed its privileged position; it became the central node, 'the site where the contrapuntal forces of colonial social hygiene and military discipline were brought to bear on the diseased bodies of women inmates'.[15] As the repeal campaigner Henry Wilson put it, 'The term is used in India, not merely for a hospital in which venereal diseases are treated, but it stands for and includes the whole Regulation system.'[16]

The influence of colonial medicine on contagious diseases legislation in India has been widely recognised, and not merely for its practical but also for its symbolic effects. The paradigm of tropical medicine played a particularly important role in pathologising places and peoples, detaching disease from the individual body and embedding it in the physical and cultural environment, and the fight against venereal disease in many of the overseas colonies can be placed in this epistemological context.[17] Whilst Levine argues that tropical medicine had no interest in venereal diseases *per se*, since these were 'in no way specific to certain climates or environments', syphilis was in fact widely considered to assume a more threatening form in the tropics.[18] In the colonies the considered scientific view was in any case years or decades behind the most advanced European thinking, with the older 'topographical' or 'environmentalist' tradition stubbornly

---

[15] S. Hodges, '"Looting" the lock hospital in colonial Madras during the famine years of the 1870s', *Social History of Medicine*, 18 (2005), 379–98, p. 381.

[16] H. J. Wilson, *The history of a sanitary failure* (Sheffield, 1898), reprinted in I. Sharp (ed.), *Josephine Butler and the prostitution campaigns: diseases of the body politic, volume I: the moral reclaimability of prostitutes* (London, 2003), p. 441.

[17] See D. Arnold, *Colonizing the body: state medicine and epidemic disease in nineteenth-century India* (Berkeley, 1993), M. Harrison, 'Tropical medicine in nineteenth-century India', *British Journal for the History of Science*, 25 (1992), 299–318, M. Harrison, *Public health in British India: Anglo-Indian preventive medicine 1859–1914* (Cambridge, 1994).

[18] Levine, *Prostitution, race, and politics*, p. 5; but see Banerjee, *Under the Raj*, p. 181.

persistent in colonial medicine. In these circumstances, the biological and physical realities of venereal disease themselves called for appropriate treatment, the colonial medical paradigm inevitably taking on cultural particularities as well. Judy Whitehead has vigorously argued for instance that Indian contagious diseases legislation 'introduced a new form of bodily regulation, in which the moral division between unrespectable and respectable women in India began to be detached from a sacred social hierarchy and became, instead, expressed through Western medical metaphors of health and disease'.[19] This expanded 'environmentalist' concern acted as a form of Orientalist condescension, 'embodying and projecting Western ideas of how India was intrinsically different from the West, even in the nature of its diseases and the therapeutics appropriate for their treatment and cure'.[20] One of the most significant elements of this 'orientalist twist' to colonial medicine and sanitary science was the emphasis on the *normality* of prostitution within non-Western societies. The 'native' prostitute was deviant because she was normalised within her society and culture, and at the same time normal because she was deviant. As Peers notes for British India:

> The Indian prostitute, like India herself, was objectified and problematized in a way that would have been inconceivable had not colonial rule produced the types of cultural and scientific discourses that legitimated the belief in an inherent difference between India and Europe and between Indian prostitutes and European prostitutes.[21]

The colonial medical discourse and practice that subsumed the regulationist project thus placed special stress on the difference between East and West, 'white' and 'black', or, more generally, between Europe and its others. Venereal disease was raced as well as gendered and sexed; the fight against it demanded that the difference of race be recognised.

One associated element of this 'colonising epistemology' was the emphasis on the separation and segregation of colonisers and colonised. David Arnold has bluntly asserted, again with India in mind, that '[m]edicine served as an agency of social control: it helped to define the spatial and social distance between the European troops and the Indians with whom they came in contact'; and Philippa Levine has similarly stressed the role of 'the cordoning-off of racially and functionally segregated areas' in the paradigm of colonial medical modernity.[22] The influence of Anglo-Indian medical theory on the principles and theories of segregation has long been demonstrated. Segregation from the natives was promoted as the first law of hygiene for Europeans in the tropics.[23] Parallels were drawn

---

[19] Whitehead, 'Bodies clean and unclean', p. 41.
[20] Arnold, *Colonizing the body*, p. 59.   [21] Peers, 'Soldiers, surgeons', p. 160.
[22] D. Arnold, 'Medical priorities and practice in nineteenth-century British India', *South Asia Research*, 5 (1985), 167–83, p. 168; Levine, *Prostitution, race, and politics*, p. 89.
[23] See J. W. Cell, 'Anglo-Indian medical theory and the origins of segregation in West Africa', *American Historical Review*, 91 (1986), 307–35, p. 308.

between venereal and other diseases in promoting the utility and necessity of *cordons sanitaires* separating not only the healthy from the infectious, but also the orderly from the disorderly, the clean from the dirty. A defined spatial and social distance between Europeans and natives served a political as well as a physiological purpose: 'segregation did not simply mean isolating European rank and file from possible physical contagion; segregation was also put forward as a means of forestalling moral infection.'[24] This was always an unattainable ideal. The Indian cantonments may have been sanitary enclaves, but they could never be completely isolated, as medical and military authorities quite understood; segregation was never official policy. Acceptance of the inevitability of servicemen patronising prostitutes both in the cantonments and in the bazaars immediately conceded the point; and we should note that the principles that lay behind regulationism are quite distinct from those of quarantine; surveillance and supervision, not a model of isolation *per se*, are the guiding principles. Even the most apparently stringent segregation, such as the proposals for ring-fencing the prostitutes' district in Calcutta in the early 1880s, should be recognised as utopian and ultimately futile.[25] All the same, recognition of the controlled porosity of the cantonment and its associated institutions has not deterred commentators such as Radhika Ramasubban from proposing 'a colonial mode of health and sanitation based on the principle of social and physical segregation'.[26] This understanding also fits very well with the general models proposed for the 'colonial city'.

The Indian experience of colonial regulation is salutary, but whether it should be taken as *exemplary* is at least debatable. Some colonies – above all, India, 'the linchpin of imperial security and the symbol of Britain's imperial strength and achievement in the world' – were clearly more important in the imperial scheme than others, but it is invidious to relegate the latter to an even more marginal position than they presently obtain; and certainly, as Antoinette Burton reminds us, the temptation to conflate India with the colonial *tout court* should be vigorously resisted.[27] A glance at the range of prostitution legislation in the overseas colonies certainly suggests caution in the general characterisation of colonial regulationism. The Indian measures, including Burma, Ceylon and the North West Provinces, certainly had ready counterparts in many of the other

---

[24] Peers, 'Imperial vice', p. 31.   [25] Banerjee, *Under the Raj*, pp. 158–9.
[26] R. Ramasubban, 'Imperial health in British India, 1857–1900', in R. Macleod and M. Lewis (eds.), *Disease, medicine, and empire: perspectives on Western medicine and the experience of European expansion* (London, 1998), pp. 38–60, p. 41. For the cantonment and the lock hospital as porous social and economic organisms, see Hodges, '"Looting" the lock hospital', pp. 388, 389.
[27] A. Burton, *Burdens of history: British feminists, Indian women, and imperial culture, 1865–1915* (Chapel Hill, 1994), p. 142; A. Burton, 'Introduction: on the inadequacy and indispensability of the nation', in A. Burton (ed.), *After the imperial turn: thinking with and through the nation* (Durham, NC, 2003), p.11.

British overseas colonies. In Southeast Asia, Hong Kong had the priority, its 1857 ordinance notable for being the earliest specific contagious diseases legislation in the Empire; ordinances in the Straits Settlements, by contrast, arrived some time after the institution of the domestic Acts, in 1870 in the case of Singapore, and in 1872 and 1873 for Penang and Malacca respectively. Legislation in the Caribbean was coterminous with the British CD Acts, as was the first of the laws introduced into the Cape Colony in 1868.[28] In other regions, however, contagious diseases legislation had a rather more hesitant introduction: in Australia and the South Seas, Queensland and New Zealand were covered by statutes in 1868 and 1869, but Victoria and Tasmania not until 1878 and 1879, and Fiji had to wait until 1882, by which time the domestic Acts were more or less defunct. This is a complicated picture, therefore, and one that should not lend itself to easy review. Quite apart from the fact that many of Britain's imperial possessions *never* had contagious diseases legislation – where laws were either never proposed, or the suggestions and blandishments of the imperial and colonial authorities were successfully resisted – the nature of the legislation varied greatly, as well as the degree to which measures were implemented. In Canada, for example – that is, in Ontario and Quebec – CD laws were introduced for a limited period of five years, and even then were apparently barely enforced. John McClaren calls them a 'pale shadow' even of the less coercive metropolitan Acts; Constance Backhouse goes further, stating that the Acts were a dead letter, unenacted and unenforceable without the provision of certifiable hospitals.[29] Contagious diseases legislation in the Caribbean was also markedly less vigorous.[30] In a somewhat different register, Elizabeth van Heyningen has noted that the first of the contagious diseases laws in the Cape 'was an exotic with only shallow roots in the Colony', and, although it was replaced with a new Act in 1885, this is another indication that the differences in social and political contexts must be emphasised as much as any model of empire-wide sexuality politics.[31] Richard Phillips has with good reason placed a strong emphasis on the 'located-ness' of sexuality politics: on the role of colonial and local administrators, in concert with local colonial societies, in setting

---

[28] See B. L. Moore and M. A. Johnson, '"Fallen sisters"? Attitudes to female prostitution in Jamaica at the turn of the twentieth century', *Journal of Caribbean History*, 34 (2000), 46–70; van Heyningen, 'The social evil in the Cape Colony'; K. Jochelson, 'From paupers to pass laws: control of VD in the Cape and Transvaal, South Africa, 1880–1910', in *Comparative perspectives on the history of sexually transmitted diseases, volume I, being proceedings of a conference held on 26–28 April 1996* (London, 1996).

[29] McClaren cited by R. Phillips, *Sex, politics and empire: a postcolonial geography* (Manchester, 2006), p. 112, C. Backhouse, 'Nineteenth-century Canadian prostitution law: reflection of a discriminatory society', *Histoire Sociale – Social History*, 18 (1985), 387–423, p. 392.

[30] Levine, 'Rereading the 1890s', p. 588, n. 6.

[31] Van Heyningen, 'The social evil in the Cape Colony', p. 176.

the agenda for such experiments in sexuality politics.[32] The map of regulationism, as a result of these place-specific political histories, is much more heterogeneous than historians have tended to suggest. Even to refer to 'India' as a homogeneous entity of course begs the question of the implementation of laws at the level of the presidencies and the localities and beyond. It should be noted that the Indian Contagious Diseases Act of 1868 merely allowed the introduction of registration, examination and detention in places specified by local authorities with prior sanction by the government of India. Bombay, for example, was authorised as early as 1870, but the refusal of the Bench of Justices to contribute to the expenses of the Act led to its winding up two years later; the Act was reintroduced in 1880, but suspended once again in 1888.[33] Legislation in itself did not mean the imposition of the sort of sanitary surveillance that is associated with regulationist regimes; simply providing a gazette of legislation is clearly inadequate, without detailed reference to their actual operation.

Most pertinently, however, whether we should see *race* as the defining factor in the colonial regulation of prostitution needs much more questioning. Levine's influential study of British regulationism rightly states that everywhere, without exception, colonial ordinances *differed* from the domestic Acts; but this is emphatically not the same as arguing that it was *race* that was the crucial factor separating the 'colonial' from the 'domestic', however important are its political contours for the operation of legislation in the four colonial sites Levine compares.[34] For few of the characteristics of colonial regulationism noted above were *exclusive* to the overseas colonies in which racial differences were institutionalised, though they were inevitably more pronounced where this was the case. In this regard, Gibraltar and the Mediterranean colonies may be taken to constitute something of a middle ground, demonstrating that stringent regulationist regimes could be instituted in conditions where race – at least in the modern, conventional sense – was not a major factor. Race was clearly a central element in many of the overseas colonies, written into the colonial organisation of society, and installed at the heart of regulationist ordinances, and this is amply demonstrated later with Hong Kong in mind. But it is better to posit a continuum of regulationist practices rather than a unitary, purportedly 'colonial' management of race and sexuality for which contagious diseases legislation was central. Levine's early assertion, that 'prostitution became a racially definable category when moved to a colonising context', should at least be complemented by an emphasis on the heterogeneity of both the colonial world *and* the conceptions of race it promoted.[35] Sarah Hodges,

---

[32] Phillips, *Sex, politics and empire*, p. 136.
[33] Ramanna, 'Control and resistance: the working of the Contagious Diseases Acts in Bombay City', *Economic and Political Weekly*, April (2000), 1470–6, p. 1470.
[34] Levine, *Prostitution, race, and politics*, p. 52.
[35] P. Levine, 'Venereal disease, prostitution, and the politics of empire: the case of British India', *Journal of the History of Sexuality*, 4 (1994), 579–602, p. 590.

writing recently on the machinery of contagious diseases legislation in Madras, is surely right to argue that general studies of the colonial medicine of which it was a part need to be especially wary of 'invoking an explanatory colonial rule of racial difference'.[36]

So, as with the other studies in this book, it is the specificities and particularities of Hong Kong's experiences that are to the fore in the rest of this chapter. Contagious diseases legislation was introduced early on in the colony's history, in the context not only of pronounced venereal infection amongst the military, but also of a crisis of government prompted by racial fears and political antagonism between the British authorities and the Chinese community. This chapter focuses on the centrality of race to this regulation of prostitution; but it proposes that the 'racialised sexuality' that resulted was tied to the particular elaboration of that system in Hong Kong, rather than simply representing in yet another form the colonial rule of difference. To give but one example of the importance of context, we should note that in India Philippa Levine has emphasised the importance of an orientalising and racialist insistence that 'native' women lacked the sensibilities even of degraded 'white' prostitutes: 'A common theme, constantly contradicted by complaints and petitions for exemption from unhappy women, was that the internal genital examination, which lay at the heart of all the contagious diseases acts and ordinances, was regarded with nonchalance in India.'[37] In Hong Kong, however, in complete contrast, it became axiomatic for the colonial authorities that Chinese women regarded the examination with unmitigated and unjustifiable abhorrence. This was a Chinese 'prejudice' that, as we shall see, structured the entire approach to the control of prostitution and disease. The political significance of racial and cultural peculiarities was therefore always specific, located, differentiated. To put this another way, rather than seeing race as *the* consistent factor amongst colonial regimes, as part of the cultural and environmental conditions that necessitated an even more authoritarian form of regulationism – which would in any case be to accept rather too much of the British imperial apologia – race is better seen as the discursive and material product of the located politics of regulation and colonial government. A politics of race emerged, this chapter argues, within the elaboration of a 'colonial governmentality' that was localised and specific rather than universal and general. Sexual and sanitary discipline in Hong Kong was enmeshed in what was perceived to be a struggle between British values and Chinese prejudices, with regulationism the product of negotiation between the two rather than a simple imposition.

The resulting landscape of prostitution in Hong Kong was, accordingly, the product of a political process, not of unchecked imperial power or some general mechanics of colonial rule, and not of racial or regulationist discourse considered in the general and the abstract. This is brought out with especial force in relation

[36] Hodges, '"Looting" the lock hospital', p. 381.
[37] Levine, 'Venereal disease', p. 586.

to the question of social and sexual segregation, which rather than being the very icon of colonial rule is presented here as in part the outcome of specific political concessions, representing the limits to and limitations of imperial authority. This local geography of prostitution can be used to refine our understanding of the nature of colonial governance in Hong Kong.[38] It qualifies recent assessments of the place of sex and race in the colonial landscape, particularly the emphasis on segregation and collective isolation. Ultimately, this chapter contributes to the historical geography of colonial sexualities and the colonial city through a rethinking of the nature of colonial disciplinary power.

Venereal disease and medical policing in Hong Kong

The Crown Colony of Hong Kong was of considerable military importance to the British authorities, but its imperial significance also rested upon its status as a mercantile metropolis, as a centre of colonial capitalism in Southeast Asia. The dream of 'Anglo-China' was punctuated and punctured by political crises, however, amounting in Christopher Munn's words to a full-scale 'crisis of government' in the colony.[39] The position of the 'subject races' was the most intractable problem for the British authorities, with a long history of suspicion – described as 'mutual sullen consent' – developing between the Chinese population and the British colonists.[40] The Chinese were the great majority, Hong Kong being subject to large-scale immigration from China, impelled both by the collapse of the imperial regime and by the concurrent expansion of European colonial economies. The Chinese population grew very rapidly, to some 83,000 in 1865, set against the 4,000 or so non-Chinese. Four-fifths of these 'coolies' were male, and two-thirds adult men, a measure of the colony's domination by a migrant proletariat sourced overwhelmingly from the mainland. Such Chinese were both relied upon and reviled, the conditions under which their labour was exploited generating ominous sanitary and social problems. Prostitution, an inevitable accompaniment of this 'coolie capitalism', was one of the pre-eminent colonial concerns, Hong Kong having quickly acquired notoriety as a hub or 'clearing house' for prostitute women, the most characteristic of colonial 'urban pioneers'.[41] The associated

---

[38] For negotiation and resistance: C. W. Kwan, *The making of Hong Kong society: three studies of class formation in early Hong Kong* (Oxford, 1991), J.-F. Tsai, *Hong Kong in Chinese history: community and social unrest in the British colony 1842–1913* (New York, 1993).

[39] Munn, *Anglo-China*.

[40] The phrase 'mutual sullen consent' is taken from the *Report of the commissioners appointed to inquire into the working of the Contagious Disease Ordinance, 1867, in Hong Kong* (Hong Kong, 1879), p. 6.

[41] J. F. Warren, *Ah ku and karayuki-san: prostitution in Singapore 1870–1940* (Singapore, 1993), p. 74, notes Hong Kong's importance as a 'redistributive depot' for prostituted

threat of venereal diseases, here as elsewhere, posed serious challenges to the security and efficiency of the colonial state, particularly where the health of the military and naval forces was considered. The venereal problem in Hong Kong was said in the 1850s to have decimated the crew of every ship that entered the harbour, and Rear Admiral Stirling in 1854, in the missive that prompted the passing of the first contagious diseases ordinance, described Hong Kong as a 'Pest House' with the potential to infect the whole population of China.[42] Hong Kong being a microbial as well as a human clearing-house, venereal disease legislation had a clear 'biopolitical' rationale for the colonial state.

Unwilling to accept any complicity in creating the conditions under which prostitution and venereal disease flourished, however, the response of the British colonial power was stringent sanitary surveillance and coercive regulation. The introduction of regulated prostitution in Hong Kong was wholly consistent with the authoritarian nature of British government in a colony where the governing elite remained constantly on the alert for the dangers posed by the Chinese population, their habits, environments and political aspirations. Social and political unrest had already been countered there by draconian responses, and the colonial authorities continued to regard the maintenance of racial privileges as vital to the colony's security. For the colonial authorities, there was no great separation between social and political threats, and the concerns of sanitation and security, health and order, imperial hygiene and imperial authority, were characteristically united. As in British Malaya, where the problem of 'bodies out-of-control' was countered by the attempt to impose order onto colonial space, the attempt to discipline sexuality was much more than a matter of medical pragmatism: it was also a political programme, 'part of the exercise to know, claim and control'.[43]

The first attempt to control the spread of venereal disease was introduced in 1857 by the idiosyncratic but influential Governor Sir John Bowring, at the behest of naval officers on the China Station. An avowed Benthamite, Bowring's assertively utilitarian solution to the problem of prostitution was to introduce a straightforward system of brothel licensing, and to provide regular inspection and treatment of their inmates. The resulting 'Ordinance for Checking the Spread of Venereal Diseases' required brothel owners to register with the Registrar General, in a new capacity as Licenser of Brothels, and made prostitute women liable to removal to hospital if considered infectious. Bowring, we may note, was a friend

women. For 'urban pioneers', see L. White, *The comforts of home: prostitution in colonial Nairobi* (Chicago, 1990), p. 34.

[42] *Report of the commissioners appointed to inquire into the working of the Contagious Disease Ordinance, 1867, in Hong Kong* (Hong Kong, 1879), Macpherson, 'Conspiracy of silence', p. 88.

[43] L. Manderson, *Sickness and the state: health and illness in colonial Malaya, 1870–1940* (Cambridge, 1987), pp. 235, 237.

and biographer of Jeremy Bentham, a man whose philosophical radicalism could be made consistent with a fervent advocacy of a colonial discipline spreading from the space of the barracks to 'the whole surface of society'.[44] Bowring's energetic administration in Hong Kong must also be seen in the context of the rapid deterioration of relations between the British and Chinese communities, his introduction of emergency measures producing what has been called with little exaggeration a 'reign of terror' in the colony.[45] The strict measures that Bowring proposed for the control of disease had the more or less enthusiastic support of the Colonial Office, Colonial Secretary Henry Labouchere fighting down some lingering unease at the tenor of the legislation by emphasising the gravity of the problem and looking forward to the beneficial effect it would have on those he represented as the first victims of prostitution, namely, those prostitute women who had been sold into 'brothel slavery'. Regulationism could be presented, in these terms, as entirely consistent with the unimpeachable British mission to eradicate the stain of slavery; Labouchere envisaged that under a new system of registration such un-English practices would swiftly be brought to an end.[46]

The effect of the ordinances on venereal disease transmission in Hong Kong is at best debatable. The system of regulated brothels was nevertheless quickly regarded as a model of its kind, as a Royal Navy surgeon later noted in his evidence to the Skey Committee of 1864–5:

We had a good example of prevention at Hong Kong; it is one of those places in which there are excellent sanitary regulations. All the prostitutes are registered, the brothel keepers have licences, and are under government superintendence; the colonial surgeon examines the women periodically, and if a woman is found to be diseased she is immediately signed to the Lock Hospital, and kept there till she is cured.[47]

The only difficulty, this witness went on to add, in comments that are entirely characteristic, arose from the fact that the possibilities for surveillance and discipline were limited by the geographic and cultural situation of Hong Kong:

Hong Kong is a peculiar place. Opposite Hong Kong is the main land [sic] of China, quite out of our control, and those people passed backwards and forwards without let or hindrance. If the whole country, as Malta, were under English Government, I think that a registration and passport system, conjoined with other regulations, would be effectual.[48]

---

[44] T. Mitchell, *Colonising Egypt* (Cambridge, 1988), pp. 40, 42–3.
[45] Munn, *Anglo-China*, pp. 280–9.
[46] See correspondence between Labouchere and Bowring, 27 August 1856, NA CO 403/8, No. 103.
[47] *Report of the committee appointed to enquire into the pathology and treatment of the venereal disease, with the view to diminish its injurious effects on the men of the army and navy, with appendices, and the evidence taken before the committee*, P.P. 1867–8 (425) XXXVII, p. 67.
[48] *Ibid.*, p. 69.

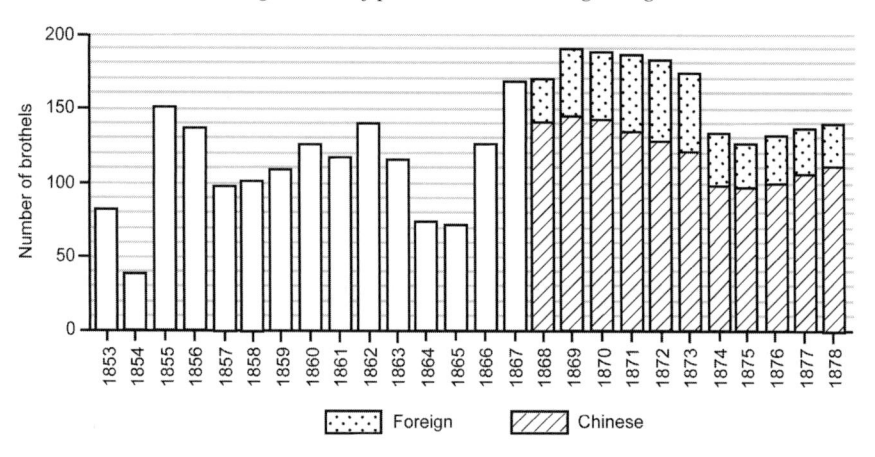

Figure 6.1 Recognised and licensed brothels in central Hong Kong, 1853–78. Source: *Report of the commissioners appointed to inquire into the workings of the Contagious Diseases Ordinance* (Hong Kong, 1879).

Given the fact that the whole country of China could not of course be brought under British jurisdiction and control, that Hong Kong could not be made another Malta, nor even a Gibraltar, these geographical limitations were inscribed into the colony's regulation of prostitution. The authoritarian ambition of this early system of medical surveillance is notable, however, and amply confirms the fact that colonial ordinances like these were more far-reaching than their domestic counterparts. Most obviously, the Hong Kong ordinances licensed brothels as well as registered prostituted women: Figure 6.1 shows the numbers of brothel houses that were recognised by the colonial government through this period, with no fewer than 70, and as many as 150 through the late 1850s and early 1860s. It is the explicitness of the 'brothel system' that made it easy for later critics to claim that prostitution was legalised in Hong Kong, however much regulationists demurred. The Bishop of Victoria, Charles Alford, complained in 1869 that the colony's brothel houses were numbered over their doors 'exactly in imitation of the French system'; and indeed the increasing severity and strictness of the law contributed to its characterisation by repealers as a formal regulationist regime:

The law in Hong Kong was at first experimental, little coercion being employed, but as the wretched women to whom it was applied became more and more averse to its degrading provisions, it was made increasingly stringent, until it became a complete counterpart of the French system.[49]

---

[49] 'Licensing prostitution'; reprinted (with permission) from the *Report for 1869 of the Rescue Society, London*, by the National Anti-Contagious Diseases' Act Association (London, c.1870), p. 24.

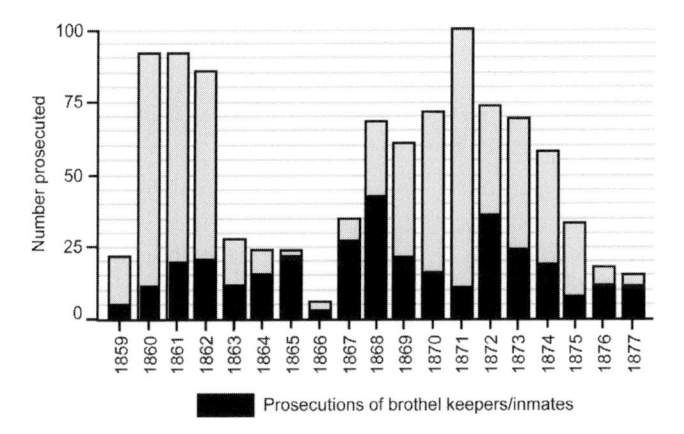

Venereal disease and medical policing in Hong Kong 203

Figure 6.2 Prosecutions under Hong Kong Contagious Diseases Ordinances, 1859–77.
Source: *Report of the commissioners appointed to inquire into the workings of the Contagious Diseases Ordinance* (Hong Kong, 1879).

The unparalleled severity of the regulations in Hong Kong noted by metropolitan repealers is also attributable to the revision of the colonial statutes in 1867, when 'a more vigorous policy of coercion' was essayed by the colonial legislature.[50] Bowring's original Ordinance 12 of 1857 was repealed by the new Governor, Sir Richard MacDonnell, and replaced with the '*necessarily* almost *despotic* powers' of Ordinance 10.[51] The impact of the new ordinance on the numbers of licensed brothels (Figure 6.1) and also its stimulus to police prosecutions (Figure 6.2) is perfectly plain. The old system, which was said to have fallen into 'paralysis', was clearly succeeded by an extensive and energetically prosecuted regulationist regime. This second ordinance put the system of licensing firmly in the hands of the Registrar General, and allowed the police, under an Inspectorate of Brothels, even greater powers in rooting out unregulated sexual commerce. Particularly significant was the removal of the requirement that prostitution cases were to be heard in open court, a liberal nicety whose continuance was urged by the Hong Kong Attorney General, Julian Pauncefote, but which Governor MacDonnell blamed for the calcification of the old system:

I fail to see much of the applicability of the Attorney-General's argument to the question ... At all events the experiment of dealing with brothels and their inmates through the magistrates in open Court has been tried and *failed*. Why should we try it again? Experience has shown that the evidence which is necessary for arriving at conclusions

[50] *Report of the commissioners*, p. 9.
[51] J. Stansfeld, *Lord Kimberley's defence of the government brothel system at Hong Kong* (London, 1882), p. 54, emphasis in original.

in points connected with the 'Social Evil' here, *cannot be produced in open Court*. The whole machinery was at a standstill. I have had indubitable evidence of malpractices, but could not obtain convictions, because I could not get the evidence into open Court, and yet the Attorney-General wishes to sacrifice *the object of the projected legislation*, to some DREAM OF THE NECESSITY FOR MAINTAINING A MAGNA CHARTA PALLADIUM OF LIBERTY for people who do not understand it.[52]

The terms expressed here so forcefully are representative of the emphasis on racial, cultural and political differences that characterised so many aspects of colonial policy, and which contrast so markedly with the supposed balance between liberalism and discipline that legitimated the CD Acts at home. A more coercive version of regulationism was considered by the likes of MacDonnell as indispensable where such a question of 'race' was involved; the limits of liberalism were here made quite explicit.

This was the system that would come under direct attack by repealers and sympathisers in the late 1870s, after the maverick Sir John Pope Hennessy, a man of a wholly different stripe to Bowring or MacDonnell, became Governor (Figure 6.3). Pope Hennessy's attention was drawn to this elaborate system a few months after his inauguration in 1877, following the deaths of two Chinese women who had fallen to their deaths whilst being pursued over rooftops by policemen sent to search out unregistered prostitutes.[53] The 'Irish, Catholic, reform-minded, "pro-native"' Pope Hennessy had already stirred up trouble with his liberal race-relations policies, and the deaths of the Chinese women acted as a further spur to his outrage at the colony's treatment of the subject races.[54] Pope Hennessy threw himself into the history and operation of prostitution policy in the colony since its foundation, and whatever enthusiasm he had had in England for the CD Acts evaporated on discovering that the promised eradication of venereal disease had yet to occur. Nor had anything seriously been done to combat brothel slavery, as Labouchere had recommended and promised in 1856. In fact, powers to protect brothel inmates were treated by colonial officials such as Lord Kimberley as quite separate from powers to treat disease. In the subsequent inquest into the deaths, a number of other troubling features of the case were revealed. It was not just the system of licensed brothels that was a matter for concern. More damningly, Pope Hennessy learned of the fact

[52] Quoted in Stansfeld, *Lord Kimberley's defence*, p. 8, emphasis in original.
[53] See the Hong Kong *Report of the commissioners*. See also P.P. 1880 (118) XLIX.69, *Report of the commissioners appointed to inquire into the workings of the Contagious Diseases Ordinance, 1867, in Hong Kong* and P.P. 1881 (C.3093) LXV.673, *Correspondence relating to the workings of the Contagious Diseases Ordinances of the colony of Hong Kong*.
[54] K. Lowe and E. McLaughlin, 'Sir John Pope-Hennessy and the "native race craze": colonial government in Hong Kong, 1877–1882', *Journal of Imperial and Commonwealth History*, 20 (1992), 223–47, p. 224.

Figure 6.3 Sir John Pope Hennessy and family, 1889. From J. Pope-Hennessy, *Verandah: some episodes in the crown colonies 1867–1889* (London, 1964).

that no licensed brothels were exempt from paying fees to the government; and that, since brothels exclusive to Chinese clients received no medical intervention whatsoever, he could only conclude that the colony was guilty of profiting from the business of prostitution (perhaps to the tune of a hundred thousand dollars over the years of the policy's operation). Some of this considerable amount of money, and the fines levied upon unlicensed women, was paid into funds used to pay informers, raising the spectre of widespread corruption as well as complicity.

Most worrying of all, though, was the suggestion that the colonial state turned a blind eye not just to immorality but also to slavery. One of the dead women was said to have had to sell one of her children into slavery in order to pay off a previous fine of $100. The implications of this allegation could be added to the general notion that brothels housed numbers of women who had been sold into slavery and who lived more or less in slavery. These elements of the system of regulated prostitution meant, to humanitarian and feminist critics, that the colonial state in Hong Kong was both pimp and slave master.

These facts came to light from the commission that Pope Hennessy appointed in 1877 to inquire into the scandal. The Governor seems to have given the commission both its direction and conclusions. One of the three commissioners was his protégé, the eminent sinologist Ernest Eitel. Another, often absent from the proceedings, subsequently dissented from the recommendations of the committee, after returning to England and conversing with pro-regulationist doctors in the services. Nevertheless, the remaining commissioners, in coming to the conclusion that the ordinances were despotic, ineffective and more or less illegal, did highlight serious irregularities and inconsistencies that not even the most wholehearted ideologues of contagious diseases legislation could defend. In Whitehall, Colonial Secretary Lord Carnarvon successfully resisted these calls for abolition, having been convinced of the wisdom of regulation by the private briefings of the regulationist apologist William Henry Sloggett. Sloggett, a naval surgeon at the time of the Skey Committee but later an Inspector of Hospitals under the CD Acts, mounted a strong defence of the Hong Kong ordinances. He accepted that the principles of the Hong Kong system could be construed as objectionable, and that they were 'entirely at variance' with the British Acts, but he insisted that the commissioners had ignored the necessity for regulatory measures in a colony where, he argued, three-quarters of the adult Chinese women were prostitutes in fact if not in name.[55] Sloggett argued that in denouncing regulation the Hong Kong commission had simply pandered to the interests of the unregistered Chinese prostitutes and brothel owners: 'One cannot but remark the extreme tenderness shown by the Commissioners to the feelings and prejudices of the Chinese brothel-keepers and prostitutes.'[56] In blatant contradiction to his evidence before the Skey Committee a decade earlier, the older and wiser, or perhaps just more diplomatic, Sloggett now argued that brothels in Hong Kong should continue to be inspected in the ways that they had been since 1857, but not licensed: a rather fine distinction that betrayed the defensiveness of regulationists in the late 1870s and early 1880s as opposed to the confidence of the 1860s:

Prostitution and its attendant results in the spread of venereal diseases is the fact so recognised and regulated, and all common prostitutes no matter where, or with whom they may be resident, are equally subject to the provisions of the Ordinance. Prostitution is not

---

[55] P.P. 1881 (C.3093) LXV.673, p. 700.   [56] *Ibid.*, p. 703.

legalised by such recognition, any more than brothels became legalised in England by enactments under which the keepers of such houses are liable to punishment.[57]

The system continued in force for many years, long outlasting the domestic CD Acts, despite the Commission's recommendations and despite being regularly reviled by British repeal activists. James Stansfeld made hay, for instance, with Colonial Secretary Lord Kimberley's defence of what Stansfeld called the 'government brothel system at Hong Kong'; he noted that 'the Government has reserved to itself the right to levy a duty on the bodies of women in Hong Kong, precisely as it has reserved to itself the right to levy duties upon brandy, tobacco and other profitable articles of consumption'.[58] On the operation of the system, he added that:

> the arrest of the women enabled the officials to store those whose bodies were to be offered for sale, in the Government warehouses – the lawful, licensed brothels – and thereby to secure that the articles offered by them to the public should be periodically inspected and medicated by the surgeons hired by the Government for that purpose; it being held to be obvious that every male person whose custom it was to commit prostitution, would prefer that the bodies of the females purchased by him should be cleansed, licensed and warranted by the state, rather than by a private dealer.[59]

Orientalising regulation

Central to the defence of regulated prostitution in Hong Kong was the argument that the measures were necessary given the specific conditions that the British found in Hong Kong. This was a characteristic justification of colonial regulation, but it was made particularly forcefully in the Southeast Asian dominions, where a cultural and political justification of prostitution policy was both casually assumed and carefully elaborated. In contrast to the virtually complete avoidance in colonial discourse of the role of colonialism in promoting sex work and the ravages of sexually transmitted diseases amongst both the colonising and colonised populations, colonial authorities turned instead to a model of a timeless Chinese culture of prostitution that justified special measures. Rather than acknowledge the imperial conscription of indigenous bodies in the circuits of colonial capitalism, colonial sexual discourse put forward the bluntest of contrasts between 'East' and 'West', between European people and cultures and their Chinese 'other'. As Philippa Levine has noted, this stance followed an orientalist logic: 'The idea of the libertine east allowed prostitution to be defined as regional, with the colonies depicted as a giant brothel … Since accepted forms of prostitution could hardly be dismantled in a short space of time, they argued, and since outlets for colonial male desire were necessary, local immorality was a convenience that could be

---

[57] *Ibid.*, p. 704.   [58] Stansfeld, *Lord Kimberley's defence*, p. 4.   [59] *Ibid.*, p. 4.

censured even while it was sampled.'[60] Regulationist ideologues took it as read, as Sloggett had argued, that the very low state of morality in the colony justified special measures. But the nature of this 'orientalist sociology' went much further than casual ascriptions of racial depravity, or even the normalisation of prostitution that as we have seen many colonial historians have recognised.[61] What has not been hitherto acknowledged is that, in Hong Kong at least, it was not just prostitution that was normalised as an indigenous cultural reality, but the political project of *regulation* itself.

The most revealing of the British accounts in this respect is a paper on the 'Chinese Social Evil' prepared by an officer of the Imperial Maritime Customs, apparently in conjunction with the inquiry instituted by Pope Hennessy. This characteristic digest of colonial expertise begins in classical 'regulationist' fashion, insisting on prostitution as a necessary evil, an inevitable concomitant of modern civilisation. But the author, a Mr Stent, went on to sketch out the history of the 'social evil' in China, arguing that it was Chinese ministers who 'originated and developed the practice of prostitution as a masterpiece of political economy, making it a source of revenue to the country'.[62] Tracing the development of state-organised prostitution down to the present day, dynasty by dynasty, Stent focused on the manner in which Chinese administrations were convinced of the benefits of 'encouraging rather than repressing prostitution'.[63] 'Regulationism' appears therefore in a double guise: essentially 'Chinese', but also necessitated by 'Chinese' conditions. Colonial pragmatism required its adoption, even though such methods might be regarded as culturally alien and abhorrent. The fact that this view was commended by the commissioners appointed by Pope Hennessy in 1877 to inquire into the operation of the Contagious Diseases Ordinances is telling, given the Governor's essentially 'liberal' views on colonial racial policy and the eventual recommendations of the commissioners. However much they disapproved of the regulation of prostitution, Pope Hennessy and his commissioners appear to have accepted much of Stent's culturally relativist argument. Regulation was, even for the most convinced opponents, a *Chinese* institution, embedded in Chinese history and culture, rather than being introduced by Britain to its colonial possession. It was 'naturally' diffused to the colony from the mainland, in the very culture and racial 'character' of its Chinese immigrants:

Whatever vices the Chinese of Hongkong may have learned from foreigners, whatever evils the intercourse between foreigner and Chinese may have created, prostitution, brothels and the system of licensing brothels with a view to raise a revenue, legally or illegally, were indigenous institutions in China centuries before the present nations of Europe emerged from barbarism. When the Colony of Hongkong was first established, in 1842, it

[60] Levine, *Prostitution, race, and politics*, p. 180.
[61] P. Levine, 'Orientalist sociologies and the creation of colonial sexualities', *Feminist Review*, 65 (2000), 5–21.
[62] *Report of the Commissioners*, p. 56.   [63] *Ibid.*, p. 57.

was forthwith invaded by brothel keepers and prostitutes from the adjoining districts of the mainland of China, who brought with them the national Chinese system of prostitution, and have ever since laboured to carry it into effect in all its details.[64]

Rather than considering the British colonisers' role in promoting prostitution, Pope Hennessy's commissioners were satisfied with listing the proximate or 'natural' causes which 'almost necessitate prostitution' – namely, overpopulation in the cities, the national system of polygamy, the law of inheritance which neglects daughters in favour of sons, and 'the universal practice of buying and selling females combined with the system of domestic slavery'.[65] Alfred Lister, the colony's Acting Registrar General in 1869, had recourse to this same appreciation of the Chinese context of Hong Kong's prostitution problem, and the same blindness about the colonial power's complicity and culpability:

> It is impossible for the Government to look upon prostitutes as other than people who have deliberately chosen their mode of life, and generally mean to adhere to it. The peculiar social position of Chinese women, the way in which the Empire is overstocked with them, their uselessness, according to Chinese ideas, for any other purpose, our proximity to mainland, whence fresh supplies are always to be obtained, and the very small amount of shame which attaches to the calling, all make the work of diminishing the evil, otherwise than by regulating it, one which at any rate at present seems hopeless.[66]

In terms of colonial 'biopower' then, it is important to underline the fact that for colonial projects administration was inevitably a kind of ethnography.[67] In Hong Kong, combating venereal disease by regulating prostitution necessitated a quasi-ethnographical appreciation of racial and cultural 'realities'. The geopolitics of disease in the colonies was built on the essentialising of race as well as sexuality. In this regard, regulationist discourse in Hong Kong differed but little from comparable colonial sites in Asia. In Shanghai, for instance, colonial medical authorities treated prostitutes not only as 'an ignorant but menacing conduit of infection to the white population' but also as a distinctive product of both unsanitary 'Chinese' conditions and a backward 'Chinese' culture.[68] This stance also signals, however, something of the limits to colonial state intervention – a theme that deserves more emphasis than it has received from historians of colonialism. Colonial government, in the conditions portrayed by its representatives and agents, required the careful management of racial 'others', not simply the imposition of 'English' standards of law, morality and discipline. In the 1860s, Governor Bowring's unease about the abrogation of English law gave way to Sir

---

[64] *Report of the Commissioners*, p. 3. [65] *Ibid.*, p. 5. [66] *Ibid.*, pp. 255–6.

[67] See A. L. Stoler, *Race and the education of desire: Foucault's History of Sexuality and the colonial order of things* (Durham, NC, 1996), p. 39.

[68] G. Hershatter, *Dangerous pleasures: prostitution and modernity in twentieth-century Shanghai* (Berkeley, 1997), p. 241; see also C. Henriot, *Prostitution and sexuality in Shanghai: a social history 1849–1949* (Cambridge, 2001).

Richard MacDonnell's round ridicule of those who attempted to ascribe English rights to the Chinese population. Colonial discipline was required to define the limits of its ambition through an orientalist discourse that blamed the Chinese for the very measures required to police them.

In Hong Kong, as in the Far East more generally, the overriding aim of this discursive work was thus to position the non-European 'other' as wholly distinctive from the European colonial population. This was not a matter of drawing lines within a population, defining and labelling particular individuals as deviant and abnormal, separated by a gulf from respectable peoples and mores; rather, in the colonies, it is the elaboration of native 'normality' which is at stake. As Megan Vaughan notes in relation to Foucault's analyses of power/knowledge complexes, 'in general the need to objectify and distance the "Other" in the form of the madman or the leper, was less urgent in a situation in which every colonial person was in some sense, already "Other"'.[69] Every effort was expended in pathologising the 'normal' nature of the colonised, first in terms of environments (as the tropes of 'tropicality' confirm) but later with the pathologising of races and cultures. There is certainly nothing monolithic here, and there are important differences between the ways in which, say, Africans, Indians and Chinese were characterised, but the point remains that the collectivities of non-European 'others' were targeted, rather than aberrant individuals.

In Hong Kong, the pathologising of the Chinese population was vigorously argued, in both environmental and cultural terms. Commentators on the question could not only speak disparagingly about the general state of female morality in the colony, asserting that no more than one-quarter of Chinese women in the colony were chaste. The European medico-moral discourse of prostitution also gave way to a culturally and geographically specific variant that indicted *Chinese* women and *Chinese* morality. The problem was the racial peculiarities of the Chinese, not the aberrant sexuality of a small number of prostituted women. We have already seen that Pope Hennessy's commissioners of 1877 insisted on the need to recognise that 'the radical difference which distinguishes the personal character, the life and surroundings of Chinese prostitutes from all that is characteristic of the prostitutes of Europe': so that 'the system of prostitution which obtains in Hongkong is essentially Chinese and radically un-English'.[70] But in a most revealing passage the commissioners defined this difference as follows:

Chinese prostitution is essentially a bargain for money and based on a national system of female slavery, whilst European prostitution is more or less a matter of passion, based on the national respect for the liberty of the subject.[71]

This statement parallels the famous dictum of the 1871 Royal Commission on the Contagious Diseases Acts in Britain, made in defence of the double standard

---

[69] Vaughan, *Curing their ills: colonial power and African illness* (Stanford, 1991), p. 10.
[70] *Report of the commissioners*, p. 3.   [71] *Ibid.*, p. 5.

of sexual morality, to the effect that 'With the one sex the offence is committed as a matter of gain; with the other it is an irregular indulgence of a natural impulse.'[72] Whilst in European discourse aberrant women were 'othered' and gender differences essentialised, in Hong Kong it is the 'Chinese' who were distanced and objectified, characterised not as individuals but as a culture of sexual mercenaries.

By portraying the Chinese as a racial, 'national' and cultural 'other' the way was opened to insisting that colonial policies take account of the peculiar situation in which the British administration was embedded. Colonial authority required active recognition of, engagement in, and negotiation with, what it took to be indigenous realities. The greatest single factor here was the universally acknowledged observation that Chinese women regarded internal medical examination by foreigners with utter revulsion. Conceding to their feelings as far as they allowed led to the colonial state restricting examination to those Chinese women who catered only to Western clients. Women who worked in exclusively Chinese brothels were to be spared such horrors, as were European and American prostitutes, who were only required to attend on the colonial medical officers from 1874. Once again, we see here a discourse of racial and cultural difference at work:

> It was a wise recognition of the natural laws at work in this mass of corruption called prostitution, when the Government of Hongkong confined the application of the principal provisions of the Contagious Diseases Ordinance, viz., compulsory medical examination, to the licensed prostitutes in houses for foreigners only, and exempted from the same law the great mass of prostitutes for Chinese.[73]

There were some who opposed such sensitivity to Chinese wishes and 'prejudices', for bringing the European down to the level of the Chinaman. But these were isolated voices, for medical discourse and colonial authority by now typically accepted the 'fact' of cultural difference, once more setting certain crucial limits to government intervention. Expertise concerning 'the Chinese character' was held to dictate that the provisions of the contagious disease ordinance could apply only to brothels frequented by 'foreigners'. For this reason, Ordinance 10 of 1867 directed attention to the prostitute women themselves rather than to brothel owners, for the intention was to police an unregulated prostitution threatening to disseminate venereal disease from Chinese-only brothels to those catering to Westerners.

All this reinforces the point, candidly conceded by Alfred Lister, that 'We were not trying to save the Chinese from syphilis.'[74] The ambitions of colonial regulationism extended only to the protection of British interests. But it is clear too that the control of venereal disease in Hong Kong was limited by the Chinese

---

[72] P.P. 1871 (C.108) XIX, *Report from the Royal Commission on the administration and operation of the Contagious Diseases Acts 1866–9*, p. 17.
[73] *Report of the commissioners*, p. 6.   [74] *Ibid.*, p. 5.

community and by its representatives, who were keen to develop their political influence through the promotion of individuals and institutions. Resistance to colonial medical surveillance meant that the regulation of prostitution was only ever extended to brothels patronised by 'foreign' clients. The inmates of these 'foreign' brothels received regular medical examination, and were required to attend the government-run lock hospital if found to be in a contagious state, whilst the 'Chinese' brothels, apparently right from the start, were granted wholesale immunity from these requirements. It might have been desirable from a purely prophylactic view to medically examine all brothels and their residents, but this was regarded as simply impossible given the social, cultural and political conditions. The geopolitics of colonial disease established limits to the authority and ambition of the biopolitical state.

Race, space and prostitution

Limits have so far been treated in a rather abstract sense, as defining cultural boundaries. But this was never separate from an insistently material geography. The emphasis on cultural difference necessarily had profound consequences for the management of colonial space, for its immediate analogue was geographical segregation. The geography of licensed brothels might be taken superficially as a textbook example of the segregated spatiality of colonial urbanism. The majority of brothels for 'foreign' clients were to be found in the 'Central' district of the city, along with the most important landmarks of the British and European presence (Figure 6.4). The Chinese-only brothels were located in the western district of the city of Victoria, as was the Tung Wah hospital – the premier institution of the Chinese political community – and also the lock hospital for diseased women.[75] There is a neat and ready symbolism at work in the opposition of these eastern and western districts. It is clear too from the pattern of prosecutions of unlicensed brothels that government effort was disproportionately expended on clearing the Central district of unauthorised houses (Figure 6.5). There was little point in policing the unlicensed Chinese houses, given that the government relied on their proscription of non-Chinese clients. The 1867 Ordinance was a crucial development, however, because the older Ordinance of 1857 had excluded registered brothels from the Central district, and restricted them particularly to the densely packed and homogeneously Chinese district of Tai Ping Shan.[76] Ordinance 10

---

[75] E. Sinn, *Power and charity: the early history of the Tung Wah Hospital, Hong Kong* (Hong Kong, 1989).

[76] In the 1857 Ordinance, registered brothels were confined 'within one or other of the following districts or portions of districts, namely, – Ha-wan, from Spring Gardens, eastward, – Sei-ping-poon, from the junction of Hollywood Road and Queen's Road West, westward, and Tai-ping-shan, except such parts of such districts or portions of districts as face the Queen's Road': see Hong Kong Acts, NA CO 130/2. Ordinance 10

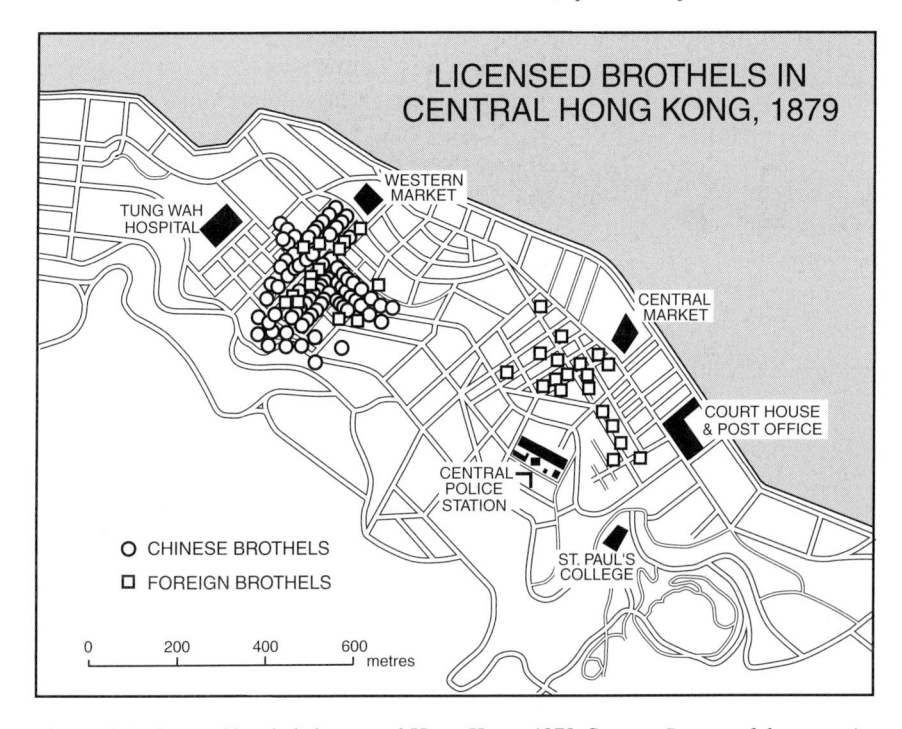

Figure 6.4 Licensed brothels in central Hong Kong, 1879. Source: *Report of the commissioners appointed to inquire into the workings of the Contagious Diseases Ordinance* (Hong Kong, 1879).

of 1867 relaxed this restriction by allowing for government authority to license brothels in the formerly proscribed eastern or 'Central' district of Victoria. This movement from a confinement of *all* brothels (whether they be visited by Chinese or 'foreigners') to a strict spatial separation of the two sexual clienteles has never been remarked, but it is highly significant in terms of race relations in the colony. This development must be viewed above all in connection with MacDonnell's turn to Chinese community leaders for support in policing Hong Kong and promoting public order. The alliance between colonial government and the Chinese elite is at the heart of MacDonnell's 'social revolution', and it is a natural outgrowth of the orientalist rhetoric of Chinese cultural difference.[77] The Tung Wah hospital was the key institution, being the effective voice of the Chinese community; but it was to be complemented by its offshoot, the Po Leung Kuk, established in 1878

of 1867 simply stipulated that 'the Registrar General may grant to any person to whom he shall think fit to keep a brothel in such district or other locality as the Governor in Council may from time to time appoint': see NA CO 130/3.

[77] Munn, *Anglo-China*, pp. 341–57.

214 *Race and the regulation of prostitution in Hong Kong*

UNLICENSED BROTHELS IN CENTRAL HONG KONG, 1866

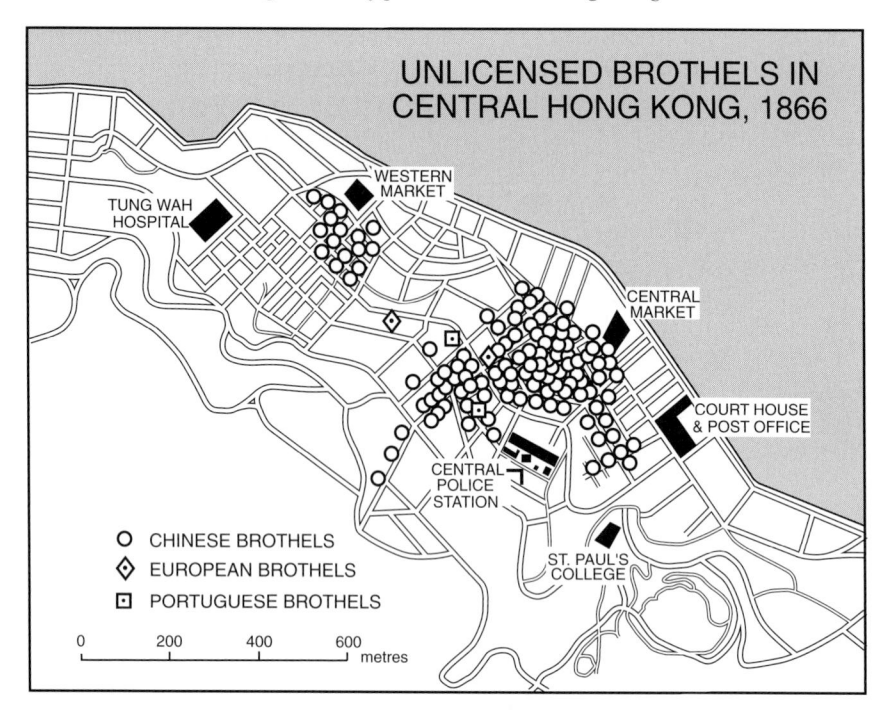

[Map showing locations of Tung Wah Hospital, Western Market, Central Market, Central Police Station, Court House & Post Office, and St. Paul's College, with symbols indicating Chinese brothels (○), European brothels (◇), and Portuguese brothels (▣). Scale: 0–600 metres.]

Figure 6.5 Unlicensed brothels in central Hong Kong, 1872. Source: *Report of the commissioners appointed to inquire into the workings of the Contagious Diseases Ordinance* (Hong Kong, 1879).

to combat the traffic in women and children.[78] These two institutions were effective in defending Chinese customs and maintaining the ability of the Chinese community to police itself, and were politically recognised by MacDonnell and his successor, Pope Hennessy. The Tung Wah hospital and the Po Leung Kuk embodied the fact that government in Hong Kong was re-established in terms of separate development and the legitimacy of Chinese aspirations to cultural autonomy and self-policing.

The segregation of brothel clienteles in Hong Kong was a geographical expression of this turn to policies of conscription, collaboration and concession. It has not been recognised that the new ordinance of 1867 went hand in hand with the *relaxation* of regulations restricting the Chinese population as a whole, one that produced in the Central district a 'marginal cosmopolitan neighbourhood', neither exclusively European nor Chinese: 'a mixed and polyglot group composed

---

[78] *History of the Po Leung Kuk Hong Kong 1878–1968* (Hong Kong Public Records Office, n.d.), H. J. Lethbridge, 'The evolution of a Chinese voluntary association in Hong Kong: the Po Leung Kuk', *Journal of Oriental Studies*, 10 (1972), 33–50.

of middle-class or wealthy Chinese, Chinese prostitutes serving non-Chinese, European prostitutes, Indian, Parsee and Muslim merchants and shopkeepers, a few scattered Portuguese and Macanese, and protected women.'[79] The mixed nature of this district alerts us to the fact that racial segregation was more of an ideal than an achievable reality in Hong Kong. Social and racial segregation was relaxed, rather than compounded, by the overhaul of the contagious diseases legislation in 1867. Cecil Clementi Smith, Registrar General of Hong Kong immediately prior to the introduction of Ordinance 10, declared to the 1879 committee that he had opposed the permitting of licensed brothels in the Central part of the city, adding that: 'As a rule I would only license houses in a street where Chinese only are living. I have never known a Chinaman object to a licensed brothel being in his neighbourhood'; Smith moreover stated that: 'As to the location of brothels, the general principle is to keep them out of sight, where they shall not offend the respectable portion of the community.'[80] This view was comprehensively altered by the introduction of the 1867 legislation. This is borne out by the comments of a succeeding Acting Registrar General. H. E. Wodehouse commented that: 'With a view to keeping down the number of unlicensed brothels it would also be desirable that the licensed brothels should be as centralised, as accessible and as well-known as possible.'[81] The 1867 Ordinance brought in a much more completely regulated landscape of sexual commerce, one quite distinct from the commitment to isolating brothels that marked the earlier legislation.

The new geography of regulated prostitution attempted to introduce a firmer spatial separation between the 'foreign' and Chinese brothels, but at the same time explicitly accepted that there were distinctions in the nature of their clienteles. Both Chinese and 'foreign' houses were divided into first-class, middle-class and lower-class brothels, though the most privileged Chinese brothels had no direct parallel amongst those for foreigners, as the elite of the European community were more likely to patronise kept women. The Chinese houses contained on average twice the number of inmates to those catering to non-Chinese (in 1877, thirteen women as opposed to six for the foreign brothels), with the best Chinese houses on Hollywood Road located only a few streets away from the third-class houses (Figure 6.6). 'Foreign' brothels were notably more spatially segregated by clientele. The Chief Inspector of Brothels declared that the lowest class of women were to be found in East Street and West Street in the far west of Victoria, in Tai Ping Shan, and in Wanchai, and that the better class of women were to be found first in the Central districts.[82] Discussion of the class and status of brothels is confused not only by the nature of such evaluations, but also by the fundamental racial distinction between brothel clienteles, by the presence of European and American prostituted women in Hong Kong, and also by the willingness of foreign brothel owners not only to cater to European men but also to

---

[79] *Report of the commissioners*, pp. 226–7. [80] *Ibid.*, p. 2. [81] *Ibid.*, p. 8.
[82] *Ibid.*, p. 13.

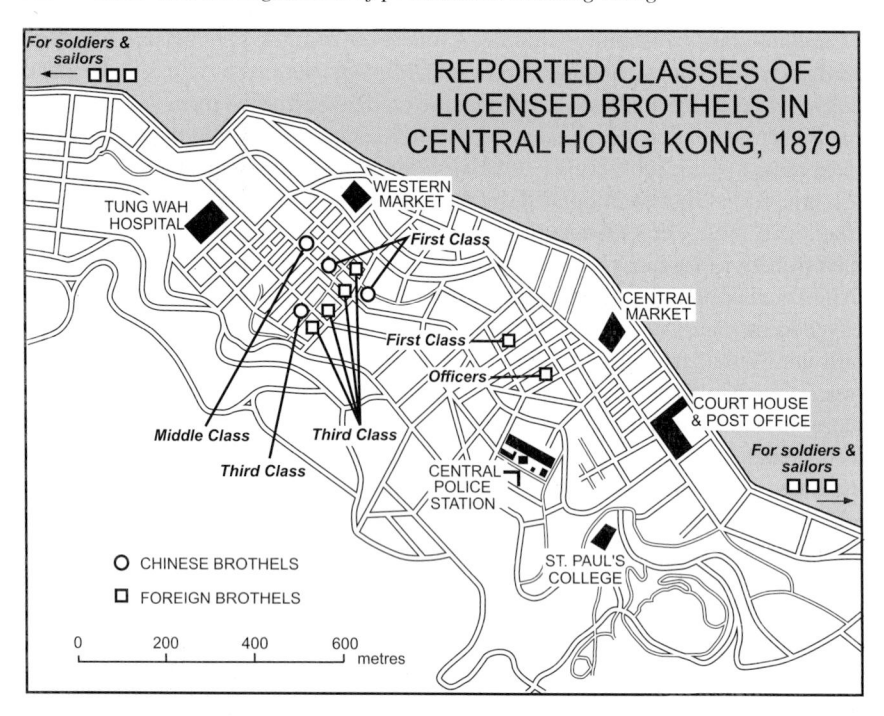

Figure 6.6 Reported classes of licensed brothels in central Hong Kong, 1879. Source: *Report of the commissioners appointed to inquire into the workings of the Contagious Diseases Ordinance* (Hong Kong, 1879).

Indian troops and Malay coolies. Nevertheless, it is possible from the witnesses to the 1879 enquiry to confirm Wanchai as the least privileged class of brothels and inmates, with the brothels in Ship Street, the most frequented by common soldiers and sailors. In 1873, there were said to be four brothels in Ship Street, with about seven girls in each. The brothels in the far west of Victoria were also of lowly status. Brothels Nos. 8 and 76, on East Street, for instance, catered to soldiers and sailors, Malays, 'and sometimes coloured men'.[83] But the highest rank of foreign brothels was concentrated in the Central district. The owner of No. 6 brothel on Peel Street claimed for instance that: 'My brothel is a first class one. No Europeans of inferior class go to my brothel; no soldiers or common sailors, and very rarely a Policeman': instead, the brothel accommodated seafaring men, captains and officers, and charged $2 a night, a rate comparable to the best Chinese institutions.[84] Not far away, at least three licensed brothels on Cochrane Street were charging similar rates, with brothel No. 65 serving ships' officers, military officers and clerks.

[83] *Ibid.*, pp. 27, 33.   [84] *Ibid.*, p. 28.

Brothels for Europeans and other non-Chinese were spatially separated then by class as well as by race, and their geography contrasts markedly with the concentration of the Chinese brothels. Most intriguingly, however, and in a manner that unsettles the seemingly strict segregation of Chinese and foreign brothels, is the concentration of licensed brothels for foreigners in Tai Ping Shan itself. Here there existed several houses catering to European soldiers and sailors and to Malays. These seem to have been small but thriving businesses of long-standing, relicts of the time when Chinese and non-Chinese brothels alike were confined to Tai Ping Shan. Lee-A-Oi, for instance, keeper of brothel No. 84 on Upper Lascar Row, was formerly a seamstress in a Chinese brothel, and had bought the business as a going concern a few years previously. Lee-Tai-Shing, owner of No. 72, on Ladder Street, had also bought her house, with funds supplied by friends. One more owner, U-A-Mui, at brothel No. 139 on Ladder Street, was a third woman from a respectable background who had relied on family income to help her into the business.[85] Together these women ran brothels catering to the lower class, if not the lowest class, of non-Chinese clients.

The spatial ordering of prostitutional space in Hong Kong was rather more complex than the historiography of the 'colonial city' – with its too-neat emphasis on racial segregation – allows. The earlier ordinance enacted a brothel quarter to which all prostitutes' clients could repair, containing commercial sexuality within a distinct native space. The later legislation abandoned this strict racial residential segregation for a more overtly racialised sexual economy. This was a geography shaped by economic, social and ethnic prerogatives, with the Chinese houses clustered in Tai Ping Shan, whilst the foreign institutions occupied a series of more or less differentiated spaces ranging from the slums of Wanchai to the first-class houses of the Central district. Class and caste distinctions within the non-Chinese clientele produced a distinctively managed sexual economy, a spatial order constructed through both cultural ascription and socio-political negotiation. It combined blatant racist abjection with a culturally relativist condescension, disciplinary power with sanitary and moral reticence, ambition with inhibition. It indicates the limits as well as the reach of the colonial biopolitical state.

To see the elaboration of regulationist policing in Hong Kong as a matter simply of the imposition of colonial order and discipline is too crude, therefore. Recognising the starkly coercive nature of colonial rule does not entail accepting the unrelieved picture of wholesale colonial disciplinary transformation that some cultural historians have promoted. Scholars like Timothy Mitchell have influentially but unfortunately argued, for instance, that colonial rule had to 'change the tastes and habits of an entire people'.[86] Brenda Yeoh, writing on Singapore, stresses resistance as well as domination, but she too portrays an overweening disciplinary ambition limited only by the response and resistance of the native population, a 'dialectic of power' between municipal attempts 'at imposing social

---

[85] *Ibid.*, pp. 25–7.   [86] Mitchell, *Colonising Egypt*, p. 75.

and spatial control to create a city after the colonial image – orderly, sanitized, racially divided, hierarchical – and on the other, Asian agency in wresting concessions and asserting its own view of urban life'.[87] We might consider, however, the construction of colonial projects in which the resistance of the colonised is matched by a reluctance to attempt a thoroughgoing application of disciplinary power. Colonial administration of prostitution in Hong Kong seems to illustrate both the ambition and the inhibition of the colonisers, a colonial pragmatism whose impress can be recognised time and again in the colonial world.

A more subtle reading of the record of Hong Kong's government suggests more than just a military-medical paradigm. What is clear is the priority not of social and sexual discipline *per se* but rather a problematic of government in which disciplinary ambition is at least matched by governmental inhibition. Concerns about venereal disease revealed in this situation a critical unease about prostitution and promiscuity, about miscegenation and the proliferation of mixed-race children, and a general blurring of the racial boundaries, which threatened the overwhelming of the colony by 'oriental' influences. The venereal problem was symbolic of what Christopher Munn has identified as 'the decay of the vision of Anglo-China', and spelled the *end* of a colonial project, not its further elaboration and extension.[88] The key problem here was the breakdown of English 'liberal' rule, the necessity of suspending its protection of liberties and turning to arbitrary and despotic powers that were long identified with the 'Orient'. On the one hand, the Chinese were blamed for sabotaging the colony's good government, contaminating it not just venereally but also governmentally. On the other, the only solution was to adopt disturbingly 'Chinese' methods. This was, in other words, not merely the extension of colonial discipline, but a full-blown crisis of government.

Prostitution, anti-slavery and the limits of liberty

The notion of limits can be taken one further step, however. I have argued above that the nature of the regulationist ordinances in Hong Kong, and the landscape they produced, depended less upon some one-size-fits-all colonial ideology than upon a specific politics of prostitution, a locally articulated colonial governmentality which articulated the boundaries of rule. But the limits of legitimate intervention were also problematised through the activities of anti-regulationist repealers working in and through international and transnational humanitarian networks. Political geographies of prostitution were also created through the activity of repeal agents determined to combat the iniquity of regulated prostitution whether at home or abroad. The campaign against regulated prostitution in Hong

---

[87] B. S. A. Yeoh, *Contesting space: power relations and the urban built environment in colonial Singapore* (Kuala Lumpur, 1996), p. 67.
[88] Munn, *Anglo-China*, p. 325.

Kong can be placed in this context, Pope Hennessy being a notable proponent of a humanitarian imperialism that would both prevent the worst abuses of imperial power and incorporate the subject races within the scheme of colonial government. There was nothing in the denunciation of 'brothel slavery' to challenge Pope Hennessy's humanitarian and political ideals. Indeed, Pope Hennessy's reactions to the system of regulated prostitution in Hong Kong were entirely predictable, and not only in hindsight. In his *Times* obituary, it was said that he was ill-suited to be placed in charge of colonies 'where the pretensions of the natives threatened to make trouble'.[89] In his previous postings Pope Hennessy had shown himself to be scornful of colonial arrogance and an opponent of the most blatantly coercive aspects of colonial rule; he was a humanitarian, an opponent of slavery and a supporter of aborigines' protection; he was already well known for his 'pro-native' views, and committed to encouraging the political representation of the 'subject races' in colonial government. For the bureaucrats at the Colonial Office, already resigned to trouble even before his assumption of power, Pope Hennessy's pathologically enlarged sympathy for the 'native races' could in Hong Kong only express itself as a 'Chinomania', a prospect they looked forward to with weary fatalism:

To my mind the history of all this trouble is a simple one. Mr Hennessy observes on arriving that long residence among Chinese, & familiarity with the Chinese character, has led the residents in Hong Kong to believe that a Chinaman is not to be dealt with as an Englishman, or even as an Indian or a Malay, might be. He thinks this inhuman, and determines to set to work vigorously to reform what he believes to be a grave abuse. But, having no political wisdom, he proceeds in such a manner as to alienate from him all public sympathy & support, & ultimately to cause a sort of panic as to his intentions & their probable results ... It is very unfortunate that with ambition, ability, & many good intentions, he cannot ever gain the confidence of those over whom he is placed.[90]

It was entirely foreseeable that the Governor would become straightaway embroiled in a series of disputes that more or less paralysed colonial government. He moved to reform the more glaring abuses of power such as the widespread recourse to public flogging, and he returned to his common themes of gaol reform and prisoner amnesties.[91] Always quick to condemn his predecessors' political records, and to praise his own efforts, Pope Hennessy represented himself as having constantly to combat the retrograde 'anti-native' views of the Colonial Office's officials and bureaucrats. Whilst the claims of humanity, justice and economy all pointed in the direction of promoting indigenous self-government, Pope Hennessy

---

[89] *The Times*, 8 October 1891, p. 11, quoted in J. Hammond and B. Hammond, *James Stansfeld: a Victorian champion of sex equality* (London, 1932), p. 214.
[90] NA CO 129/189, HK 14124, Herbert briefing Michael Hicks Beach, 19 November 1878.
[91] See for instance NA CO 882/4/11, 'Papers relating to the flogging of prisoners in Hong Kong', Hennessy to Carnarvon, August 1877.

argued that what he called the 'pro slavery view of the case' amounted to nothing but prejudice, viciousness and unnecessary expense. What was wanted, he ventured, 'was a man who could gain the confidence of the natives by strict justice & by sympathy for them. The "rod of iron" policy is a very expensive one & in truth very Anti English.'[92] Of course, Pope Hennessy saw himself in just such a role, picturing himself at the forefront of the campaign against the 'pro-slavery' party whether they were to be found in the Colonial Office or in the colonies.[93] Making common cause with the anti-slavery and aborigines' protection movements, Pope Hennessy understood his reforms in Hong Kong as directed at the eradication of slavery in all its guises. Pope Hennessy saw cruelly confirmed in Hong Kong all the evils of racial arrogance, and the heinous abuses of power to which they led. The British administration and the white residents of Hong Kong were complicit not only in the subjugation of the native races but also their subjection to real slavery. Opposition to his crusading measures merely demonstrated the entrenchment of white colonial power, and the reluctance to accept that the native residents would need to be encouraged to participate in their own government, no longer subject races but partners.

The powerful association of prostitution with slavery encompassed both humanitarian and political objections. For liberal feminist opponents of the Contagious Diseases Acts – significantly named 'abolitionists' of course – prostitution was directly linked to slavery, making state-regulated prostitution all the more obscene. This link was always evident to those who were quick to condemn the abhorrent practices of non-Western peoples, and in Hong Kong the Chinese were routinely vilified for the buying and selling of women for sex: 'The most infamous traffic that has ever disgraced mankind, and the one that has brought most intense misery to its victims is the slave-trade. But a lower deep is reached when it exists to supply women and girls for the purposes of prostitution.'[94] It was satisfying to assert British moral superiority by trumpeting Britain's role in the demise of chattel slavery and denouncing other races' continuing complicity in slavery slave trading. However, the notion that sexual slavery might exist in colonies like Hong Kong, and not merely winked at but sponsored by the British government, was an extraordinarily powerful accusation. It is one that Pope Hennessy, entirely characteristically, had no hesitation in making. The Governor quickly concluded that the government-licensed brothels were quite simply a 'means of keeping Chinese girls in a state of slavery'.[95] Pope Hennessy moreover dismissed with scorn the claims made by the original proponents of prostitution regulation that these measures would act to eliminate slavery by preventing the

[92] Rhodes House Library, MSS British Empire, Anti-Slavery Papers, s.18, c.137/236, Pope Hennessy to Chesson, 1 April 1879.
[93] *Ibid.*, c.137/240 and 241, Pope Hennessy to Chesson, 8 June 1884.
[94] *Hong Kong Daily Press*, 16 January 1875, p. 8.
[95] NA CO 129/205, HK 12623, Correspondence of Pope Hennessy, n.d.

trafficking in women. Pope Hennessy had had proved to his own satisfaction that no genuine attempts had ever been made to investigate and eliminate the sale of women into prostitution. In his prominent campaign against the contagious diseases ordinances, Pope Hennessy resolutely maintained that 'the brothel laws had created and intensified slavery in Hong Kong'.[96]

There was another issue, however, related to the phenomenon of prostitution and its policing in Hong Kong, which proved much more unsettling to the likes of Pope Hennessy. As David Lambert and I have previously demonstrated, the complementarity of humanitarian and political aims disappeared when it came to the issue of *mui tsai*.[97] This was the name – literally, 'little sisters' – given to the Chinese practice by which poor parents sold their children into the homes of the wealthy; such 'adopted' children were most often put to work as domestic servants, but sometimes more sinister uses were implied. The question of *mui tsai* merged in part with that of prostitution since it was frequently argued that female children were sold in this way into 'brothel slavery'. The practice could hardly be condoned by British officials and, as we have seen, Labouchere's recommendation of prostitution regulation was at least in part supposed to eradicate such iniquities. As Sir Michael Hicks Beach at the Colonial Office once remarked to Pope Hennessy: 'there is nothing on which the feelings of the English people & the House of Commons are so sensitive as on this question of slavery.'[98] Slavery was simply incompatible with British jurisdiction and with the extension of civilisation that the British brought to the world.

A great deal therefore hung on the word and the concept of 'slavery'. If the custom of 'adopting' *mui tsai* was indeed a form of 'domestic slavery', then it was of course the duty of any Governor to eradicate it. For an anti-slavery advocate such as Pope Hennessy, this might have appeared as another expression of the universally acknowledged evil of slavery. But 'domestic slavery' was different from the legacy of chattel slavery in Barbados or state-sponsored 'brothel slavery' in Hong Kong, for in this case the evil could be traced not to white colonial exploitation of subject races, but to one of those subject races themselves. This was unequivocally a *Chinese* social evil, not a colonial one, as the advocates of the British

---

[96] NA CO 882/5/1, *Correspondence relating to an inquiry held by the Right Hon. Sir Hercules Robinson, GCMG, as Royal Commissioner into the condition of affairs in Mauritius*, Pope Hennessy to Edward Stanhope MP, 18 January 1887.

[97] P. Howell and D. Lambert, 'Sir John Pope Hennessy and colonial government: humanitarianism and the translation of slavery in the imperial network', in D. Lambert and A. Lester (eds.), *Colonial lives: imperial careering in the long nineteenth century* (Cambridge, 2006). For general discussion of *mui tsai*, see M. Jaschok and S. Miers, 'Women in the Chinese patriarchal system: submission, servitude, escape and collusion', in M. Jaschok and S. Miers (eds.), *Women and Chinese patriarchy: submission, servitude and escape* (London, 1994).

[98] Rhodes House Library, MSS British Empire, Pope Hennessy Papers, s.409, Michael Hicks Beach to Pope Hennessy, n.d.

civilising mission were quick to point out. To act against it meant condemning the failings of Chinese society, and directly intervening in the lives and customs of the Chinese community. Unlike the campaign against 'brothel slavery', then, the claims of humanity and the policy of 'localisation' pulled in opposite directions. Pope Hennessy's 'pro-native' sympathies were here at loggerheads with a humanitarian discourse guided to such a great extent by antipathy to slavery.

Nothing that Pope Hennessy had encountered before could have prepared him for this particular dilemma. Whilst it was his custom to surround himself with like-minded allies – 'cronies', of course, to his opponents – in this case his appointees differed in their interpretation of the status of the *mui tsai*. On the one hand, as Pope Hennessy's Chief Justice, Sir John Smale, argued, the issue was unequivocal: the Chinese custom of buying children for adoption was nothing less than 'real slavery'. Holding forth on one of the common placards offering rewards for the return of runaway servants, Smale declared that slavery in every form in Hong Kong was illegal and must be put down. He dared his listeners to deny the existence of slavery in Hong Kong:

Has Cuba or has Peru ever exhibited more palpable, more public evidence of the existence of generally recognised slavery in these hotbeds of slavery, than such placards as the one I now hold in my hand, to prove that slavery exists in this Colony?[99]

Within the wider humanitarian discourse of anti-slavery, this kind of domestic servitude was comparable with the very worst exemplars of slavery. Sir John Smale went on to note that: 'The more I penetrate below the polished surface of our civilization [in Hong Kong] the more convinced am I that the broad undercurrent of life here is more like that in the Southern States of America when slavery was dominant than it resembles the all-pervading civilization of England.' Smale's comparison dismissed observations of the differences between chattel slavery and other forms of forced labour as merely a species of sophism: for 'all slavery, domestic, agrarian, or for immoral purposes, comes within one and the same category.'[100]

On the other hand, however, stood those who were prepared to emphasise the distinctiveness of Chinese culture and the inappropriateness of judging the Chinese by Western standards. Here, Pope Hennessy's Orientalist protégé, Ernest Eitel, was called upon to draw upon the wealth of his sinological expertise. In Eitel's academic counter-argument to Smale, he claimed that it was quite useless to use such words as slavery to characterise Chinese domestic customs, this demonstrating only the linguistic and analytical indiscipline of the non-expert mind. Endorsing the kinds of cultural relativism quite characteristic of 'orientalist sociology', Eitel proceeded in his judgement to distinguish between Western forms of

[99] *Correspondence respecting the alleged existence of Chinese Slavery in Hong Kong*, P.P. 1882 (C.3185) XLV.645, p. 5.
[100] *Ibid.*, pp. 234, 2, 6.

slavery, whose ideal type was the plantations of the southern United States, and Chinese customs:

the term 'slavery' is bound up with the peculiar development of the social life and the legal theories of the progressive societies of the West. It has, indeed, such a peculiar meaning attached to it that one ought to hesitate before applying the term rashly to the corresponding relation of a social organism like that of China, which had an entirely different history, and has hitherto been socially unconnected with those highly developed societies.[101]

Eitel argued moreover that '[s]lavery in China is not an incident of race as in the West, but an accident of misfortune' so that there was 'really little in the position of a Chinese family-slave which allows a close comparison with the condition of a slave under the Roman Law, or of a negro in the hands of his West Indian or American master'. Comparison with Caribbean or American chattel slavery was simply a case of sloppy thinking. Western conceptions of property, freedom, law, the role of women, the family and the individual were not directly applicable to Chinese society, and, in any case, exploitation of racial differences simply did not enter into the question of the *mui tsai*. Thus the practice could not be 'real slavery'. The most Eitel was prepared to concede was that this was a 'Chinese analogue of slavery'. In a tellingly nominalist peroration, Eitel argued that: 'To deal justly with the slavery of China we ought to invent a new name for it.'[102]

Behind the obvious war of words lay an argument about the demarcation of discourse and the field of legitimate humanitarian intervention. The history and geography of slavery, not just the name, was central to the argument: for Smale, impatient with relativist distinctions, slavery was a stain on humanity of urgent and universal importance; for Eitel, the claims of cultural difference were paramount. In the latter formulation, a kind of discourse of differentiation is set in play, one that set limits to the applicability not just of concepts but also of political projects developed in different places, times and conditions. Although Eitel accepted and celebrated the development of the universalising moral spirit expressed in Western humanitarianism, saying that '[t]he natural law of reaction was set in motion by that humanitarianism which, since the end of the last century, began to permeate, like an electric current, *the whole of the western world*', he quickly followed up this observation by endowing this humanitarianism with a distinctive geography, a mapping of the limits of its legitimate application.[103] Failing or refusing to recognise this geography was to give way to sentimentalism and incoherence. As Eitel insisted when directly considering Smale's pronouncements:

I observe that in these papers the term 'slavery' is indiscriminately used, – now in a strictly legal sense, and then again in its ethical or sentimental sense. As in the latter sense

[101] *Ibid.*, p. 50.   [102] *Ibid.*, pp. 52, 53.
[103] *Ibid.*, p. 50, emphasis added. For discussion of the discourse of differentiation and the registers of racism, see S. Hall, 'The multi-cultural question', in B. Hesse (ed.), *Un/settled multiculturalisms: diasporas, entanglements, disruptions* (London, 2001), pp. 209–41.

the word 'slavery' can idiomatically be applied to any irksome form of drudgery people in many ranks of society have to submit to in all countries, the indiscriminate use of the terms 'slavery' or 'genuine slavery' is a source of confusion and error.[104]

This is a problem therefore of translation: again not just a matter of words or of discourse, conceived in the sense of semantic coherence, rather a matter of geography. The contrast drawn here between British legal and humanitarian universalism on the one side and an ethnographically informed, pragmatic cultural relativism on the other is highly significant, and worthy of conclusive emphasis. What might have seemed, to both contemporaries and historians, merely the natural advance of anti-slavery principles, an expanding social and political geography of moral and humanitarian concern, is revealed in Eitel's construction to have an historical and cultural geography, and thus to have its own limits.

As Governor, Pope Hennessy's reaction to these arguments was crucial. Government 'brothel slavery' could be condemned without difficulty, but the *mui tsai* problem cut to the heart of Pope Hennessy's philosophy of government. For all his anti-slavery sympathies, it is the politics of 'localisation' – very different from the earlier policies of this name that we have considered – that, informed by Eitel's argument for cultural particularism, emerged victorious in his mind and in his actions. In the end, Pope Hennessy came down on the side of Eitel, rejecting Smale's argument and his call for the repression of 'domestic slavery' in Hong Kong. Pope Hennessy accepted the argument that a practice could not actually be called slavery 'where the individuals concerned go about our streets with a knowledge that they are free'. He contended that the existing law against slavery was enough, if properly enforced, to 'secure the real freedom of these women', and he accepted that 'since Chinese domestic servitude differed so widely from negro slavery, police prosecution of the former under any law with reference to the latter would constitute an act of very doubtful legality'.[105]

In coming to this decision, Pope Hennessy clearly deferred to the increasingly assertive Chinese political community, whose ambitions he supported. Chinese community leaders willingly agreed to help police the traffic in prostituted women but argued robustly for special protection of the practice of adopting *mui tsai*. The leading Chinese, anxious to protect an established social institution and faced with the possibility that the *mui tsai* might be caught up in the British philanthropic net, set out to carefully distinguish legitimate and benign custom from the undoubted evil of brothel trafficking. Representatives of the Chinese merchant community petitioned Pope Hennessy to be allowed to found an institution, the Po Leung Kuk, dedicated to putting down the kidnapping and traffic in human beings, particularly for purposes of prostitution, but made it quite clear

---

[104] *Correspondence respecting the alleged existence of Chinese slavery*, p. 109.
[105] E. Sinn, 'Chinese patriarchy and the protection of women in nineteenth-century Hong Kong', in M. Jaschok and S. Miers (eds.), *Women and Chinese patriarchy*, p. 148.

that the traditional custom of purchasing boys and girls for domestic servitude must be respected. The political implications of this move are clear: as Elizabeth Sinn has noted, 'In the final analysis, different views on kidnapping rested on different ideas about individual freedom and bondage. The Chinese, threatened by Hennessy's attitude, may have felt compelled at this point to stem the intrusion of English law into their patriarchal system.'[106] In ultimately referring to *mui tsai* as merely 'so-called slavery', Pope Hennessy followed not only the opinion of Eitel, but also that of the Po Leung Kuk petitioners and that of Ng Choy, the Acting Police Magistrate whom he had appointed as a crucial element in his project of incorporating the Chinese community into Hong Kong's government system. With the blessing of the Governor, then, the Chinese patriarchal system was bolstered and politically protected from accusations of slavery, at least until its reappearance as an international humanitarian issue in the early twentieth century, when the League of Nations took a dimmer view of the practice.[107]

Although supported by Eitel and the local Chinese elite, Pope Hennessy was nevertheless put on the defensive in his dealings with the Colonial Office. The latter, so long on the end of his criticisms of government complicity in humanitarian abuses, could hardly conceal their satisfaction at the fact that Pope Hennessy was forced finally to choose between siding with the indigenous community and siding with metropolitan humanitarianism. The Earl of Kimberley took the opportunity, for instance, to chide Pope Hennessy for previously having put down the system of licensing and inspection of prostitutes – on the grounds that it was 'a police measure intended to give to the Hong Kong Government some hold upon the brothels, in the hope of improving the condition of the inmates, and of checking the odious species of slavery to which they are at present subjected'.[108] Even Kimberley would in the end come round to Pope Hennessy's accommodation with Chinese custom, however. Sir John Smale, initially encouraged by the reputation Pope Hennessy had gained in Barbados and by his crusade against 'brothel slavery' in Hong Kong, was left to bemoan the Governor's actions and take whatever comfort he could from the judgement of posterity on plantation slavery.[109] For the time being, the humanitarian campaign against slavery had

---

[106] Sinn, 'Chinese patriarchy', p. 146. See also Sinn, *Power and charity*; Anonymous, *History of the Po Leung Kuk Hong Kong 1878–1968* (Hong Kong: Po Leung Kuk, n.d.); Lethbridge, 'The evolution of a Chinese voluntary association'.
[107] *Correspondence respecting the alleged existence of Chinese slavery*, pp. 4, 79, 82. For the twentieth-century, see N. Miners, 'The abolition of the *mui tsai* system, 1925 to 1941', in N. Miners, *Hong Kong under imperial rule*, S. Pedersen, 'The maternalist moment in British colonial policy: the controversy over "child slavery" in Hong Kong, 1917–1941', *Past and Present*, 171 (2001), 161–202.
[108] *Correspondence respecting the alleged existence of Chinese slavery*, p. 81, Earl of Kimberley to Pope Hennessy, 29 September 1880.
[109] *Correspondence respecting the alleged existence of Chinese slavery*, p. 96.

run up against impassable discursive and political barriers. Pope Hennessy's commitment to 'localisation', Eitel's argument for cultural relativism, and the demands of political pragmatism in the face of a newly assertive Chinese leadership ensured that any strict, legalistic adherence to anti-slavery principles remained a dead letter.

Conclusions

Regulation of prostitution in Hong Kong followed the 'biopolitical' rationale of a colony dependent on a migrant Chinese labour force for its prosperity, but menaced by the twin 'evils' of prostitution and venereal disease. Prostituted women were readily identified as threats to the colonial state, and being at the front line of colonial sexual discipline experienced its most intrusive surveillance. The 'normalising' discourse of colonial 'regulationism' proceeded by pathologising the Chinese racial 'other', holding up the Chinese as the ultimate authors of 'regulationist' policy at the same time as deploring them as the reason for its implementation. Yet the recognition in Hong Kong that it was unwise and unnecessary to bring medico-moral prophylaxis to the Chinese community in general betrays the limits of this colonial 'medicalisation' of power. The question of medical examination of Chinese sex workers catering exclusively to Chinese clients was, as Alfred Lister remarked in 1877, 'settled': 'With ordinary vigilance such examination is uncalled for, it would also involve the Government in a very perplexing and endless strife with Chinese prejudice.'[110] In Hong Kong, such 'othering' meant setting limits to state intervention and colonial disciplinary ambition, and the geography of the regulation of prostitution demonstrates both the power of the discourse and practice of racial objectification, so characteristic of colonial 'biopolitical' regimes, and also the fact that this did not lend itself to a straightforward racial segregation. The landscape of regulated sexuality in Hong Kong was the product of both a repressive racial pathology and the subsequent relaxation of restrictions on the Chinese community, the result not only of the objectification of the Chinese 'other' but also a recognition of its cultural power and legitimacy.

This must all be taken in the context of the crisis of government in Hong Kong persuasively identified by Christopher Munn.[111] The agenda of 'regulationism' in the colony reflects the contested and negotiated nature of colonial power, and the reliance both on a thoroughly repressive disciplinary apparatus and on the awareness of the difficulty of disciplining the colony's sexual subjects. Ultimately, the construction of colonial sexualities meant the management – or regulation – of sexuality, in both discursive and practical terms, rather than any simple repression and domination of indigenous peoples and practices. If Foucauldian terms are allowed, however, it is better to talk not of colonial 'discipline' but of

[110] *Ibid.*, pp. 31, 256–7.   [111] Munn, *Anglo-China*.

'governmentality'.[112] That is, a calculatedly tactical deployment of management and regulatory interventions, bound up with the discovery of the new 'realities' of economy and population – in this case those of 'Chinese' culture and 'prejudice'. Although this kind of power may be linked with modern Western liberalism and neo-liberalism, there is no reason why colonial societies should not be subject to forms of 'governmentality' that are cruder, more coercive and authoritarian. Governmentality meant 'the different ways in which the activity of government was made thinkable and practicable', and the imagination and institution of race must be fitted to this political imagination of the boundaries of rule, rather than the other way round; as Sarah Hodges has recently written, '"race" was not only constituted in large part *by* colonial power, race was a key sign *through* which colonial power operated'.[113] Such a colonial governmentality was concerned with crisis management rather than the consistency and the smooth operation of colonial discourse.

Hong Kong under the brothel ordinances of 1857 and 1867 fits this picture, concerned as it was with the 'biopolitical' threat that venereal diseases posed to colonial capitalism and imperial security, but increasingly disposed to work through the social 'realities' constructed by colonial ethno-cultural discourse. The government of sexuality was concerned with the setting of limits, with a restrained and circumscribed policy that intervened only where necessary to protect British citizens and British interests. As Alison Bashford has rightly argued, 'Lines of hygiene *were* boundaries of rule in many colonial and national contexts. Conversely ... many boundaries of colonial rule manifested as and through lines of hygiene, as spaces of public health.'[114] And it was not only the committed regulationists who traced the limits of government, the boundaries of rule. Although the humanitarian campaign against brothel slavery envisaged a liberal moral interventionism consistent with imperial responsibilities, even those of a repeal temper were exposed to the contradictions of liberal humanitarianism. Whilst prostitution regulation could be condemned as an outrageous abuse of power, the related issue of *mui tsai* had the potential to bring humanitarian ideals into conflict with political commitments. In these circumstances, even committed reformers found themselves relying upon an oriental sociology that conceded the

---

[112] See M. Foucault, 'Governmentality', in G. Burchell, C. Gordon and P. Miller (eds.), *The Foucault effect: studies in governmentality* (London, 1991). For colonial and authoritarian variants, see M. Dean, *Governmentality: power and rule in modern society* (London, 1999), M. Dean, 'Liberal government and authoritarianism', *Economy and Society*, 31 (2002), 37–61, U. Kalpagan, 'Colonial governmentality and the public sphere in India', *Journal of Historical Sociology*, 15 (2002), 35–58, U. Kalpagan, 'Colonial governmentality and the "economy"', *Economy and Society*, 29 (2000), 418–38, D. Scott, 'Colonial governmentality', *Social Text*, 43 (1995), 191–220.
[113] Hodges, '"Looting" the lock hospital', pp. 380, 381.
[114] Bashford, *Imperial hygiene*, p. 1.

cultural legitimacy of indigenous institutions. 'Race', as it was produced in these circumstances, was less of a biological category than the product of a spatialised political epistemology that laid down the limits to liberty and the legitimacy of British moral intervention. This is a theme to which I turn in the conclusions to this book.

7
Conclusions: mapping the politics of regulation

This book has argued that, for all its considerable diversity, the British experience with regulating prostitution in the nineteenth and early twentieth centuries amounts to a distinctive enterprise, one that should be placed alongside some of the better-known exemplars of the philosophy, policy and practice of regulationism. I have proposed the management of commercial sexuality as a contribution to a British tradition of modernity, marked by a number of culturally and politically characteristic features, chief of which is its indelibly military and imperial rationale. Regulation was not restricted to the military stations under the CD Acts and to those colonies where contagious diseases legislation was passed, and I have considered in some detail the important examples of institutionalised tolerance in the University towns and in the city of Liverpool. However, regulationist regimes were typically promoted by the British as a matter of security, this conceived of primarily in military and imperial terms, and as unfortunate but necessary departures from the national traditions of liberty and liberalism. In this regard, it is notable that the idiosyncratic example of regulation in Cambridge was mobilised politically in terms of the precedent that it gave to the extension of the military regulationism represented by the CD Acts, whilst the great port city of Liverpool was canvassed as the most likely beachhead for that experiment. That this extensionist project ultimately proved abortive, abhorrent as it was to civilian critics, only points up how reliant British regulationism was on the doctrine of necessity propounded by the military and imperial authorities. Only in these critical circumstances was it possible to argue that the cherished liberty of the subject, so central to the British political imagination, should be set aside.

There was, nevertheless, always a certain discretion, embarrassment even, combined with a politic rejection of European continental forms. Even when formal regulation was regarded as unavoidable – most prominently in the colonial regimes – the politics of discretion were still very much to the fore. This discretion was necessary because even the most stringent forms of regulationism found in these colonies could not operate in complete isolation from the mother country. They existed in ever more blatant contradistinction to the metropolitan arena, where outright regulationist practices were difficult or impossible to justify, being increasingly subject to scrutiny from critics whose liberalism regarded all forms of regulation as morally and politically indefensible. It was in these geopolitical circumstances that the political career of British regulationism was played out.

In this last chapter, and in lieu of a conventional summary, I want to turn from the experiences of particular places to the politics of prostitution that encompassed these regimes of regulated prostitution and ultimately governed their fate. I want to explore, through a consideration of the political geographies of regulation and repeal, the disappearance of regulationism not only from the statute books but also from the political terrain of Britishness itself – the production that is of Britain as the 'odd land out' in terms of the history of European regulationism. The focus here is on three interrelated discourses about the geographies of regulation and in particular on the place of the empire, three modes of understanding the spaces of regulated prostitution and mobilising them as part of a political argument. The first is the tension between pro-regulationists' tendency to portray the various sites of managed sexuality as essentially *local* accommodations to particular social, cultural and political conditions, more or less disparate and disconnected, and the repeal movement's invocation by contrast of an *empire-wide system* of state-regulated vice. Both amounted to powerful geographical imaginations, but it was the repeal argument that was ultimately successful in portraying regulation as a practice that flourished both at home and abroad as the distinctive product of an imperial polity. The efforts of the repealers, impelled by this vision of imperial moral corruption, contributed to the demise of contagious diseases legislation both at home and abroad in the late nineteenth and early twentieth centuries. This was a victory – of sorts – for late Victorian and Edwardian liberalism, humanitarianism and feminism.

The second geographical tension, though, and it is distinct from the first, stems from the contrast between *metropolitan* and *colonial* regimes of prostitution regulation, differences that had always existed but which emerged with special force after the repeal of domestic legislation in 1886, leaving British colonial regulationism specially visible and vulnerable to criticism. I ask to what extent our contemporary preoccupation with the specifics of *colonial* regulationism matched those of the imperial politics of regulation and repeal, particularly insofar as questions of racial difference were concerned. Although historians and post-colonial scholars tend to emphasise the fundamental importance of these differences, I suggest here instead that their significance was not a geographical given but was rather contingent upon political discourses that invoked a wider, more protean and ambiguous range of spaces and contexts. I argue that in this sense our understanding of the historical geography of prostitution regulation is well served neither by the currently dominant metropole/colony binary nor by our overarching conception of racialised imperial rule.

This criticism links directly into the third area of concern here, namely, the relationship between the geographical imaginations of *nation* and *empire*. Because empire and nation were – unlike metropolis and colonies in contemporary terminology – potentially overlapping rather than clearly distinct spaces, it was easier I contend to avoid the charge that regulationism bore down most heavily in the overseas colonies, on the non-white subjected races, and in the straightforward service of British imperial power. In the political discourse of repeal – and in the geographical imagination of what has been called 'imperial liberalism' – the emphasis was more prominently on Britain's national duties and its imperial mission than on any more trenchant critique of empire and of the practices of racial rule that might be found there.[1] The ultimate inability of the repeal movement to mount a resistance to imperialism itself stems from what we can see as its politics of patriotism, whose interest in cultural particularities was largely limited to a self-regarding concern for the British national character. This political and moral discourse was able to portray regulationism as an aberration merely, as an alien import, and also increasingly as an anachronism. By locating its origins both outside of the nation and outside the time of British modernity, regulationism could be almost wholly written out of Britain's island story.

Local and imperial

In this book, I have only considered a small number of places and episodes drawn from the nineteenth-century British experience of attempting to manage prostitution. No systematic comparison has been made between these sites, and no attempt either to aggregate local experiences into some composite history. These places are best considered as instances of British regulationist ambition, and in many ways I hesitate to make any grander claim than that. I have certainly not tried to produce a general survey, even the possibility of which may in any case be called into question. I have preferred to focus on relatively small sites with discrete histories, places whose irreducibly unique experiences cannot be taken as entirely representative of British attempts to manage and police prostitution, let alone the broader regulation of sexuality. I also share with the geographer Richard Phillips the concern that regulationism should not be seen as the imperial or colonial norm.[2] It was certainly the most high-profile intervention into the policing of sexual relations, and it can be fairly claimed that it was a critical prop for imperial rule, but it was not in fact empire-wide, it operated in many places briefly or intermittently, and its practices could only directly affect small numbers of people. It operated moreover in and through very local, closely circumscribed regimes. This so to speak *pointillist* portrayal of British regulationism offers a

---

[1] The phrase is taken from J. Pitts, *A turn to empire: the rise of imperial liberalism in Britain and France* (Princeton, 2005). See also J. Morefield, *Covenants without swords: idealist liberalism and the spirit of empire* (Princeton, 2005).

[2] R. Phillips, *Sex, politics and empire: a postcolonial geography* (Manchester, 2006), pp. 112–13.

clear contrast with the more familiar and misleading imperial chorography that paints the world in blocks of red, in that crude and misleading shorthand for British dominion, rule and authority. Committed instead to the particularities of place, I have tried to show in the preceding chapters how regulationist policing produced distinctive *local* landscapes, microgeographies of managed sexuality characteristically dependent on micro-tactics of localisation, containment and segregation.

As a practice, the regulation of prostitution operated in and through these landscapes. Philippa Levine has rightly noted that for the British colonial regulation of prostitution 'attention to spatial detail was more than incidental', and this is a conclusion fully supportable for regulationism in general.[3] The most visible element of this management was the formalisation of zones of tolerated prostitution – what in the informal but quite deliberate policies to be found in later nineteenth-century Liverpool was termed 'localisation'. This localisation, or containment, has its analogues in all of the regimes that I have considered here: not only in the Blandford Street district of Liverpool but also in the corralling of houses of assignation in the Cambridge district of Barnwell, in the installation of Serruya's Lane as the centre of the economy of prostitution in Gibraltar, and in the formation and transformation of specified brothel districts in colonial Hong Kong. Indeed, what is striking is the extent to which a seemingly ever greater insistence on the direction of commercial sexuality to such 'vice' districts seems to be characteristic of the modern era. We do need to insist that such districts are not exclusively the products of regulationist policing, formal or otherwise, and that some regulationist regimes seem to have worked well enough with a pattern of dispersed houses; but, nevertheless, containment and localisation are the hallmarks of the regimes that we have encountered here. It is at this very local scale that regulationist outcomes were obtained.

The sustained attention to the specific sites in which regulation was practised is a marker of my interest in and commitment to the particularities of place. But the local scale of these sites does not and should not preclude a wider view. I have attempted to place these in their most appropriate contexts, so that they make claims beyond their own localities. But it would be wrong, beyond this, to see these various regimes as purely the product of separate and isolated local circumstances, for this would be to accept the characteristic British apologia for regulationism, and to buy into a stance that is politically committed and compromised from the start. For the British authorities, avoidance of suggestions of system and centralism was almost second nature: in the imperial arena, localism was as much of a watchword as in domestic policy. Vulnerable in any case to charges that regulationism was a French or continental system illegitimately imported into Britain and to its possessions abroad, regulationists more or less consistently put

---

[3] P. Levine, *Prostitution, race, and politics: policing venereal disease in the British Empire* (New York, 2003), p. 297.

the stress on local pragmatism and the relative autonomy of colonial authorities to decide for themselves which measures were appropriate for their particular circumstances. Thus imperial lawmakers, instead of prescribing universally applicable legislation, settled for encouraging and enabling colonies to pass their own local statutes and ordinances, including those for the control and management of prostitution. In these ways, the British government could maintain that such practices did not amount to formal 'regulationism' at all. There was, at least in the terms of plausible denial, no such thing as an imperial system of sexual regulation. So in Gibraltar, as we have seen, colonial officials insisted on the local necessity for the regulation of prostitution, special rules being deemed appropriate for 'a place apart', with Whitehall firmly rejecting calls for the integration of domestic and colonial legislation. In Hong Kong, too, regulationism could be justified most forcefully as a response to particular, that is to say, 'Chinese' conditions; instead of being a British or French or European policy, it could be asserted without being disingenuous that prostitution regulation was essentially a Chinese institution, imperial, but only in the sense of the celestial empire, and developed in accordance with Chinese cultural sensitivities. Nor was this an exclusively colonial stance. Even at home this same doctrine of local necessity was consistently invoked, for places like Cambridge, Liverpool and the garrison towns, with their floating populations of young, unmarried men; for these 'favoured places', as we have seen, 'partial' and 'privileged' legislation was at least the first order of the day, even if a more extensive regulation was envisaged and implied.[4] This view may be characterised as official discourse, and its image or projection, bearing in mind the sanitary ideal of the small island, might be said to be an *archipelago* – a metaphorical island chain of regulationist sites held together by British sovereign authority but held apart by their local and particular situations.

No history or experience is ever truly local, however, as opposed to located and localised; these regimes were inevitably enmeshed in, and even constituted by, complex 'geographies of connection' that included the political networks of imperial authority and humanitarian advocacy.[5] As far as the former are concerned, we have seen that regulationist regimes such as Malta and Hong Kong were taken up as models for contagious diseases legislation elsewhere, both at home and in other parts of the Empire. The British Colonial Office was keen to encourage colonial governments to take advantage of the digest of expertise accumulated elsewhere, though always seeking to guide rather than to dictate – reluctant to cajole, let alone

---

[4] 'Favoured places' was the terminology of the Royal Commissions on the Contagious Diseases Acts: for a specimen of the repealers' sardonic commentary, see *The Shield*, 131, 21 September 1872, p. 1083.

[5] A. Lester, *Imperial networks: creating identities in nineteenth-century South Africa and Britain* (London, 2001), p. 5. For an earlier appeal to consider the connections between Britain and its empire, see S. Marks, 'History, the nation, and empire: sniping from the periphery', *History Workshop Journal*, 29 (1990), 111–19.

coerce. Moreover, some of the personnel who advocated regulationist solutions to the problems of prostitution and disease moved within the imperial network, developing their experience and strengthening their regulationist convictions: we have met functionaries like William Henry Sloggett, for instance, who began his career as a ship's surgeon working on the China station and later became an inspector under the CD Acts at home, and also more prominent individuals like Sir Henry Storks, whose governorship of Malta and the Ionian Islands prepared him for War Office appointments under a government that presided over regulation of prostitution in Britain. The career of British regulationism was dependent upon the shared assumptions and long-standing prejudices of such men, and their accumulation of knowledge and experience within the imperial network. The isolation and autonomy of regulated places was always therefore a convenient imperial fiction.

The *connections* between these islands of regulated prostitution were most tellingly brought out by the work of anti-regulationist or repeal activists, working in the wider imperial public sphere rather than in the private, cameral spaces of the bureaux, the barracks, the club and the academy.[6] Those who made the running in portraying regulationism as an inherently and characteristically *imperial* project were these men and women who had, since the late 1860s, increasingly put the British military and the British government firmly on the defensive. For these repealers, the regulation of prostitution simply licensed vice, entrenching the despised double standard, and riding roughshod over the cherished liberty of the subject. They identified regulationism with continental tyrannies and moral laxity, but, for all the British government's protestations, regarded British practice as a more or less domesticated variant of essentially the *same* policy. They kept a watchful, weather eye on the colonies, which they regarded as specially vulnerable, since British authorities could there introduce systems for the regulation of prostitution with little regard for either colonial subjects' liberties or for metropolitan opinion. As James Stansfeld put it in 1882, with the revelations about the system at Hong Kong in mind, such ordinances simply showed 'how far our rulers are prepared to go – when they dare'.[7] They posed a danger not just to faraway peoples with differently coloured skins but to each and every British citizen and subject. Stansfeld's fellow abolitionist James Stuart argued in corresponding terms that:

to get repeal in England alone is like taking a pitcherful of water out of the middle of the sea, and fancying you will leave a permanent hole there. You cannot do it; the water flows in from all sides, and England is so much in contact with the rest of the world, in spite of

---

[6] For 'imperial public sphere', see I. C. Fletcher, 'Double meanings: nation and empire in the Edwardian era', in A. Burton (ed.), *After the imperial turn: thinking with and through the nation* (Durham, NC, 2003), p. 246.

[7] J. Stansfeld, *Lord Kimberley's defence of the government brothel system at Hong Kong* (London, 1882), p. 40.

our insularity, that the opinions that influence the rest of the world, influence England in the long run. The whole civilised world moves now-a-days more or less together.[8]

Furthermore, in a neat appropriation of the discourse of contagion and prophylaxis, equating regulation with chattel slavery, the repealer Charles Bell Taylor quoted Lord Chatham's observation that 'slavery is a disease that spreads by contact, and if we once permit it in the extremities of the body politic, the time cannot be far distant when it will lay its paralysing influence upon the very heart of this nation'.[9] In such forbidding terms the regulationists' own discourse could be mobilised to invoke the interconnectedness of empire, the vulnerability of the imperial social body, and the danger of regulation to Britain's citizens as well as its subjects.

For these veteran campaigners, the invocation of local necessity, the emphasis on the need to let the bureaucrats, the *soi-disant* experts and the proconsular 'men on the spot' determine what measures should be employed in each colonial site, was anathema. In the Commons debate over the future of the Indian CD Acts, Sir Roper Lethbridge might insist that most MPs 'would be voting with an imperfect knowledge of the peculiar sanitary conditions of India', and should therefore leave the question to the experts in the Indian Medical Service.[10] But repealers were never going to be mollified by such arguments, Sir Robert Fowler replying that: 'It might be said that the conditions of India were different to those of England, but every argument that applied to England applied with equal force to India.'[11] In the same session, James Stuart claimed 'that that which was now the settled policy of England should be extended through the responsibility of the Ministers of the Crown to every portion of Her Majesty's dominions over which they had direct control'.[12] For such men, any temporising objection to a single moral standard throughout the empire was inherently political and inherently threatening.

These men and women did not just reveal the system of imperial regulation practised by the British from at least the beginnings of the nineteenth century; they also helped, in their humanitarian work, to construct it.[13] Their image, in contrast to the official discourse of an imperial archipelago, we might portray as a network or a web, to use the terms in which some have represented the British world. They achieved this in several ways. Repealers focused attention, for example, on the likes of Henry Storks, and campaigned against him when he stood for Parliament in the by-election of 1870; as one of the subjected districts under the CD Acts, Colchester offered repealers a chance to campaign against domestic regulationism, but, in making the link with the experiences of Malta

---

[8] Ladies' National Association, *24th Annual Report*, 1894–5, pp. 86–7.
[9] C. B. Taylor, *Speech on the second reading of a bill for the repeal of the Contagious Diseases Acts, 1866–1869* (London, 1883), p. 38.
[10] *Hansard*, 5 June 1888, c. 1204. [11] *Ibid.*, c. 1191. [12] *Ibid.*, c. 1202.
[13] For an acute discussion of purity activity and the mobilising of geographical networks and imaginations, see Phillips, *Sex, politics and empire*, pp. 26–56.

and Corfu, campaigners were able to present domestic parliamentary concerns as also necessarily connected to colonial, military ones. Even the relatively obscure William Sloggett was singled out for opprobrium and suspicion, being dubbed by Josephine Butler 'the secret "Minister of State for Prostitution" (for this is what he virtually is)'.[14]

Repealers tracked the movements not just of individuals, but also of policies, practices and prejudices. They disproved, in their discourse and political practice, the general line that held the colonial sites in isolation from each other and from the metropolis. Not only was the movement for repeal an international campaign, therefore – an international 'humanitarian network' – it also invested heavily in portraying British regulationism effectively as an imperial conspiracy.[15] Activists like Stansfeld were at pains to show that the British Colonial Office was wholly complicit in the 'government brothel system' in Hong Kong and elsewhere: there was in these terms no political distance at all between the metropolis and the periphery. Josephine Butler, the great champion of the repeal cause, similarly condemned what she called a 'network of deceit', linking domestic and colonial officials, that was responsible for the evil of British regulationism:

> We must endeavour to expose and get rid of this network of bureaucracy beneath which these crimes have been fostered, and those secret officials at home and abroad, who self-satisfied, irresponsible, and in deadly harmony, have industriously worked for their evil ends, guiding the hands of successive Governments, nominally over them.[16]

Others produced comparative surveys that repeatedly drew attention to both imperial and international systems for the regulation of prostitution.[17] The repeal house-journals, like the *Shield* and the *Sentinel*, were particularly important in focusing attention not just on individual cases but also on the system in which they were but elements. Repeal organisations also sponsored investigative tours, of which the Indian exposés of Elizabeth Andrew and Katharine Bushnell are

---

[14] J. E. Butler, *The revival and extension of the abolitionist cause: a letter to the members of the Ladies' National Association* (London, 1887), reprinted in I. Sharp (ed.), *Josephine Butler and the prostitution campaigns: diseases of the body politic, volume V: the Queen's daughters in India* (London, 2003), p. 24.

[15] For discussion of 'humanitarian networks', see D. Lambert and A. Lester, 'Geographies of colonial philanthropy', *Progress in Human Geography*, 28 (2004), 320–41.

[16] Butler, *The revival and extension of the abolitionist cause*, p. 19.

[17] For example: S. Amos, *A comparative survey of laws in force for the prohibition, regulation, and licensing of vice in England and other countries* (London, 1877); A. S. Dyer, *Slavery under the British flag: iniquities of British rule in India and in our crown colonies and dependencies* (London, 1886); H. J. Wilson, *Copy of a rough record of events and incidents connected with the repeal of the 'Contagious Diseases Acts, 1864–6–9,' in the United Kingdom, and of the movement against state regulation of vice, in India and the colonies, 1858–1906* (Sheffield, 1907).

the best known.[18] In all of this work, anti-regulationist campaigners constantly represented local regulationist ordinances as part of a wider, morally and politically corrupted imperial system:

> I beg you to take a map of the world, and mark in the two hemispheres every place where this abominable system has been established by England. It will give you an extent of the tyranny ... In conclusion; – let us try for a moment to take in at a glance all the portions of the globe in which the evil I have been recording is eating the heart out of humanity, and sapping the life of peoples ...[19]

Not content with rhetorically invoking this map of tyranny and iniquity, repealers made a point of demonstrating the empire-wide geography of state-regulated vice over which the British presided. At the 1887 meeting at Exeter Hall, for instance, when the campaign against colonial regulationist statutes was launched,

> Three great maps were stretched along the walls. That immediately behind the speakers showed the regulationists' map of the Empire, every colony where the system is in force being marked with a red cross. Crown Colonies were marked with a double cross, red and blue, as being under the direct control of Sir Henry Holland and the Colonial Office. An examination of the map shows the following results:

Red and blue cross	Red cross suspended	Red cross	
Jamaica	Canada	Gibraltar	Yokohama
Barbadoes	St Helena	Cape of Good Hope	(Introduced and carried on by British influence)
Trinidad		Tasmania	
Malta		Victoria	
Hong Kong		Queensland	
Labuan		Auckland	
Fiji		India	
Straits Settlements		Burmah	
		Ceylon	

> ... Here was Exeter Hall, which for well-nigh a century has rung with loud-voiced declaration of our duty to save the heathen, and there on the walls, blazoning our scarlet shame in scarlet letters, hung the map of the missionary establishment of the infernal order which in the Queen's reign has been established in the midst of the heathen aforesaid.[20]

---

[18] E. W. Andrew and K. C. Bushnell, *The Queen's daughters in India*, revised edition (London, 1898); see A. Burton, *Burdens of history: British feminists, Indian women, and imperial culture, 1865–1915* (Chapel Hill, 1994), pp. 157–66.

[19] Butler, *The revival and extension of the abolitionist cause*, pp. 23, 66.

[20] *Pall Mall Gazette*, 21 May 1887, p. 11. The meeting was held on the previous day, 20 May 1887.

Through such exemplary activities it was never possible in the imperial public sphere to consistently portray British regulationist practice as only a series of isolated, local ordinances, however much the British authorities would have preferred this.

The repealers' vision came out of this contest as the most powerful geographical imagination and discourse. The difficulties that they faced, in their long struggle with British and continental regulationism, should not be downplayed, but many of their immediate aims were met. The CD Acts were suspended and repealed in the 1880s, and the contemporaneous passing of the Criminal Law Amendment Act promised and promoted a new era of moral regulation. Vigilance societies set about 'purifying the public world', attacking the double standard and promoting a moralised model of masculinity.[21] We have seen that in Oxford and Cambridge, those symbols and bastions of the older culture of moral laxity, regulationist sexual policing had become an evident embarrassment and anachronism; by the early 1890s the old proctorial systems had been wholly dismantled. In Liverpool, though a vigorous resistance to the new regime of repression was mounted, here again by the early 1890s, institutionalised tolerance was in full retreat. In the colonies, regulationism was under sustained assault, repeal activists having persuaded the mandarins in Whitehall at least that the licensing of brothels could not be publicly sanctioned. The Indian CD Act was suspended in 1883, at the same time as the domestic legislation, and, after repeal had been secured at home in 1886, the Colonial Office shortly instructed the other colonies to comply.[22] In 1890, the Colonial Office directed the reluctant authorities in Hong Kong to wind up the system of licensed brothels. As Peter Baldwin puts it in his general survey of contagious diseases laws, 'by century's end regulationism was under attack from without while being hollowed out internally'.[23]

When domestic repeal was finally achieved, in 1886, it is telling that one Surgeon-Major, Blair Brown, could argue in these terms against the retention of contagious diseases ordinances in India: 'Surely the legislature of the English Parliament on such a subject is good enough for India? We hear of the unity of the Empire; in this there is little.'[24] The repeal-minded were in the end the ones who presented the most strongly unified vision of the empire. They not only helped construct the idea and reality of an imperial network; in so doing, they were at the forefront of those who aspired to a humanitarianism that transcended the artificial

---

[21] L. Bland, *Banishing the beast: English feminism and sexual morality 1885–1914* (Harmondsworth, 1995), pp. 95–123, A. Hunt, *Governing morals: a social history of moral regulation* (Cambridge, 1999), p. 154.

[22] See Levine, *Prostitution, race, and politics*, chapter 4.

[23] P. Baldwin, *Contagion and the state in Europe, 1830–1930* (Cambridge, 2005), p. 374.

[24] D. B. Brown, 'The pros and cons of the Contagious Diseases Acts, as applied in India', *Transactions of the Medical and Physical Society of Bombay*, 11 (1888), 80–97, p. 80.

moral frontier that separated the British metropolis from its colonies. This universalising humanitarian discourse endorsed the view that regulationist ordinances in colonial territories were more than just the sum of their parts. In contrast to what I have termed the official view – which, if it transcended the local at all, emphasised the difference that operating in the colonies made – for the repealers, regulationism was the same, imperial, legislation – the same outrage – wherever it took place and whomever it touched. Colonial and metropolitan forms of regulation were certainly distinctive, but they were not in principle separable.

Metropolitan and colonial

We cannot accept the humanitarian network on its own terms, however, and few would now want uncritically to valorise the ideology of British humanitarianism, feminism and social purity activism. Such quintessentially Victorian projects inevitably recapitulated characteristic colonial attitudes. Antoinette Burton has even gone so far as to say that, 'in the political culture of late-nineteenth century British feminism, reform work and imperial authority might be read as practically one and the same'.[25] Early British feminism was quite as imperial a cultural formation as anything that it opposed, for all that it counterposed a moral or ethical imperialism to the debased masculine and materialist imperialism represented by regulationist policies.

It would be wrong also to infer from the powerful repeal portrayal of an imperial system of regulated prostitution that *no* difference existed or was perceived between the worlds of colonial and metropolitan regulation. That these regimes were connected does not mean that a distinction could not be drawn between sanitary policing applied to women at home and that applied to, for instance, women of colour in the overseas colonies. In many ways, emphasis on connection and on the consistency of the regulationist evil served only to emphasise the importance of colonialism, empire and racial difference. It is striking for instance that the very first report of the Ladies' National Association insisted that the struggle at home was *already* a struggle for India and its indigenous peoples, and a struggle that was necessary to avert impending imperial disaster:

The Ladies' Association feels that in taking up its present position, it is not only contending against these laws amongst ourselves, and not only advocating their repeal and opposing their extension in our own country, but that it is opposing a gigantic evil which exists in many European countries and in our own colonies – chiefly in India, whence there are continually coming to us, not only expressions of native and European sympathy with our efforts, but cries of complaints of the bitter operation of these laws which have begun to eat into the heart of that country. We are assured by correspondents in India, who observe the signs of the times, that unless this military despotism exercised over the native women

[25] Burton, *Burdens of history*, p. 165. I have corrected a small typographical mistake in this quotation.

be removed, it threatens to bring about some appalling resistance to the power which has imposed it, reminding it of the horrors of Cawnpore.[26]

The campaign for justice contained in this manifesto was entirely consistent with the ultimate aims of the repeal movement, and there was always a strong emphasis not merely on colonial regimes but also on the mistreatment of the 'heathen' and 'subjected' races. This emerged most strongly as a political theme once the domestic CD Acts had been buried, however, as stringent forms of regulation continued in many colonies for many decades after the victory of the repeal movement in Britain in the 1880s. Many of the same pressures had been brought to bear on these regimes, and repealers like Butler were extremely vigorous in highlighting the colonial ordinances, yet authorities often managed successfully to recast their regimes in a more discreet and defensible form. In her study of India, E. M. Collingham notes of the survival of contagious diseases statutes in India that: 'It was not in the interests of the British government to worry about racial mixing, social purity or the moral reputation of Anglo-India when the health of soldiers was at stake.'[27] Venereal disease remained a paramount concern for imperial security, particularly at a time when the Empire was considered to be again under serious threat; even the introduction of Salvarsan and other advances in venereology in the early twentieth century did not immediately or decisively displace the traditional reliance on controlling disease by disciplining prostitution. In India, where the earlier proscription of regulation had in any case been routinely ignored and evaded, new cantonment acts ingeniously disguised the continuance of compulsory treatment. In Singapore, although contagious diseases legislation was left unenforced after 1887 and abolished in 1894, brothel medical clubs clandestinely continued a system of inspection of women, and an extra-legal system of publicly recognised houses was introduced in 1899.[28] In Hong Kong too, 'an elaborate if semiofficial system of regulation' had emerged by the early 1900s.[29] Nearer to home in Gibraltar, the authorities there not only continued the practice of regulating prostitution, but appear to have taken steps to make it stricter still in the first two decades of the twentieth century. In many of the colonies that had relied on regulation, and even in a few that had never even been

---

[26] *First annual report of the Ladies' National Association for the Repeal of the Contagious Diseases Acts* (Manchester, 1870), p. 17.
[27] E. M. Collingham, *Imperial bodies: the physical experience of the Raj c.1800–1947* (Cambridge, 2001), p. 184.
[28] See J. F. Warren, *Ah ku and karayuki-san: prostitution in Singapore 1870–1940* (Singapore, 1993), B. S. A. Yeoh, 'Sexually transmitted diseases in late nineteenth- and twentieth-century Singapore', in M. Lewis, S. Bamber and M. Waugh (eds.), *Sex, disease, and society: a comparative history of sexually transmitted diseases and HIV/AIDS in Asia and the Pacific* (Westport, 1997), pp. 180–3.
[29] Levine, *Prostitution, race, and politics*, p. 126.

so policed, regulationist regimes were instituted, to the horror of metropolitan repealers and to the satisfaction of the colonial authorities at home and abroad.

One of the most important political outcomes of the long struggle between regulationists and repealers was thus the emergence of a gulf between what was happening in Britain and what was happening in its colonial possessions, suggesting at first glance that the metropolitan and the colonial decisively diverged at this point. In the 1860s, when the CD Acts were introduced in Britain, they had been measures that grew out of and contributed to colonial legislation for the regulation of prostitution. The British metropolis learned from the colonies, both near and far, and the colonies in turn took their cue from metropolitan experience. By the late 1890s, however, when regulationism was officially abrogated at home, some forms of colonial regulation continued or re-emerged, and were met by the Colonial Office with either a blind eye or careful endorsement. Only in the inter-war years would these colonial systems be eliminated, and a degree of harmony between colonial and metropolitan practices restored. For most of the colonies, the decisive period for the demise of regulation was not the 1880s and 1890s but the 1920s and 1930s, when British practice came under the scrutiny and influence of the League of Nations and an international moral regime that challenged 'the principle of national sovereignty by recommending the abolition of the state regulation of prostitution'.[30] Under the influence of League of Nations surveillance, it was impossible to continue in the official or informal regulationist vein. In 1931, for example, colonial officials in Hong Kong admitted that there could be no 'window-dressing' now: 'we live in an age of League of Nations Commissions and are always in danger of being called to order if we fall short, in any part of the Empire, of Geneva standards.'[31] The League's methods – the use of confidential agents, for instance, on the ground, and of questionnaires distributed to metropolitan and colonial officials to ascertain the progress made in the campaigns against slavery and trafficking – echo those of the earlier repeal movements, but comprehensively transcended them in their ability to influence colonial governance. Under the aegis of what we might call an international 'meta-imperial network', the British system of regulated prostitution was exposed, condemned and finally dismantled.

If it is tempting to conclude that the colonial and the domestic policing of prostitution went their own ways for these fifty years or so, we must still be critically circumspect about the emergence and perception of this metropolitan/colonial distinction. For, even after the demise of the British legislation, there was never an *absolute* distinction between regulationist policies in the colonies and their

---

[30] B. Metzger, 'Towards an international human rights regime during the inter-war years: the League of Nations' combat of traffic in women and children', in K. Grant, P. Levine and F. Trentmann (eds.), *Beyond sovereignty: Britain, empire and transnationalism, c.1880–1950* (Basingstoke, 2007), p. 74.

[31] Memorandum, 10 June 1931, NA CO 129/533/10..

absence at home. The practices associated with regulationism in Britain did not simply disappear, nor everywhere at the same time. Regulation was certainly not replaced overnight by a *laissez-faire* approach to the policing of prostitution; compulsion was not replaced with voluntarism in the treatment of venereal disease; nor was a double standard replaced with a single standard of morality. Even in a city like Liverpool, the defeat of informal regulationism may have been only temporary, with municipal policies replicating certain aspects of regulationism. This is not the place to consider the history of what has been called neo-regulationism, but it can be asserted that regulationist practices continued to exist in the twentieth century, albeit with a certain reticence and a disavowal of the name of 'regulationism'. As Timothy Gilfoyle puts it in a general review, 'In the end, the language changed, but regulation remained.'[32] That these kinds of practices could persist in Britain, whilst not all of the colonies were characterised by regulationist policies, makes it difficult to endorse the essentialist colonial/metropolitan divide suggested by some historians of the British regulation of prostitution.

These difficulties in generalising about the *historical geography* of regulationism have been one of the central themes of this book. I have, however, also been reluctant to accept uncritically the notion that race and racial ideology was the basis for the differences between colonial and metropolitan regimes. Race was certainly the most powerful inscription of difference between rulers and ruled, colonisers and colonised. But it was not the only one, and its inflections are intermingled with other markers of difference such as gender, sexuality, class, environment, politics and culture. Race is arguably better seen as a 'sliding signifier', whose valences are far from synonymous with 'the colonial'.[33] It is better to suggest that the divergence between 'domestic' and 'colonial' emerged not at the level of a regulationist *praxis* dictated by some foundational rule of racial difference, but rather within the terms of a political discourse that encompassed race, cultural and political differences, rather than the other way round. Frederick Cooper notes helpfully here that 'It might be more useful to emphasize the *politics* of difference, for the meanings of difference were always contested and rarely stable.'[34] To put it another way, we might see the 'domestic' and the 'colonial' as dynamic and recursive geographical imaginations or geopolitical discourses, for which 'race' was a provocatively and usefully ambiguous theme.

The preoccupation with race should not be identified without qualification with the subject peoples of the overseas colonies. Even Philippa Levine, who has most strongly advocated the importance of race to the colonial regulation

---

[32] T. J. Gilfoyle, 'Prostitutes in history: from parables of pornography to metaphors of modernity', *American Historical Review*, 104 (1999), 117–41, p. 122.

[33] L. McWhorter, 'Sex, race and biopower: a Foucauldian genealogy', *Hypatia: A Journal of Feminist Philosophy*, 19 (2004), 38–62, p. 52.

[34] F. Cooper, *Colonialism in question: theory, knowledge, history* (Berkeley, 2005), p. 23.

of prostitution, accepts that 'It was not, however, only against the colonized that the British asserted racial and civilizational superiority. British pride centered as much on a perceived distance from continental European mores as it did on separation from nonwhite peoples. A constant unease with European decadence runs through this period.'[35] This is an important recognition, and it takes on extra significance in terms of Jonathan Parry's recent argument that in the high Victorian age empire was subordinate to Europe for Britain's foreign policy and political imagination.[36] There is an obvious sense in which Europe was indeed more central and imperialism more marginal to the politics of prostitution in our period, for repealers emphasised the continental, rather than the imperial, origins of regulationist policy. There were some who traced the iniquity of state-regulated vice to a British imperial system, but it was much more common to argue that the system of regulation was 'foreign' to Britain because of its origins on the *continent*, its genealogy being traced to Napoleonic France in particular.[37] Josephine Butler referred to regulation as 'a spurious and anti-Christian benevolence of Continental growth', and elsewhere she insisted quite unequivocally:

Now let me ask whence did this horrible invention of State Regulation of vice come to us? It did not come from America – from India – nor from any of the distant Colonies; it came from Paris, only some seven hours journey from London. And now we are assembled here today to consider the growth and poisonous fruits of this horrible Upas tree, which cost us so many years to eradicate from England, and which has spread to far-distant India.[38]

The continent was associated of course with any number of ills and evils, amongst them atheism and materialism, militarism and despotism, centralisation and statism, caesarism and Bonapartism.[39] The state regulation of prostitution, for the repeal-minded, exhibited most or all of these features, supposedly so alien to

---

[35] Levine, *Prostitution, race, and politics*, p. 6.
[36] J. Parry, *The politics of patriotism: English Liberalism, national identity and Europe, 1830–1886* (Cambridge, 2006), pp. 3, 20. See also A. Summers, 'Which women? What Europe? Josephine Butler and the International Abolitionist Federation', *History Workshop Journal*, 62 (2006), 215–31, for a critique of post-colonial neglect and distortion of 'European' issues in the repeal movement.
[37] Burton, *Burdens of history*, p. 153.
[38] J. Butler, 'The lovers of the lost', *Contemporary Review*, 13 (1870), 16–40, reprinted in I. Sharp (ed.), *Josephine Butler and the prostitution campaigns: diseases of the body politic, volume I: the moral reclaimability of prostitutes* (London, 2003), p. 100, J. E. Butler, *Mrs Butler's plea for an interest in the abolitionist work on the continent of Europe* (London, 1893), reprinted in I. Sharp (ed.), *Josephine Butler and the prostitution campaigns: diseases of the body politic, volume V: the Queen's daughters in India* (London, 2003), p. 234.
[39] Parry, *The politics of patriotism*, p. 44; for the critique of continental illiberalism, see B. Porter, '"Bureau and barrack": early Victorian attitudes towards the continent', *Victorian Studies*, 27 (1984), 407–33.

the national temper. Because the CD Acts were – or at least could be portrayed as – inspired by France, Prussia and the other illiberal continental polities, political Liberalism – which largely encompassed the repeal party – found itself a house divided on regulationist legislation. For, although many liberals had supported contagious diseases acts as proactive, scientific and modern – and they were prepared to take instruction from continental progressives – others condemned them as inherently vicious and illiberal.[40] The project of Liberal ethical statism fell foul of the notion that statism itself was un-English and materialist, never mind the moral violations that the CD Acts represented. But it was really the spectre of continental despotism that loomed largest in most liberals' objections to the Acts and their agents:

> They should have no arbitrary or undefined discretion. Least of all should they have a power outside of the Law; such a power cannot be, by any free people, permitted to any one, not even the Head of State, whether he is called, King, or Emperor, or President. Such a power as that of the 'Police des Moeurs' in France, is lawless oppression; it is founded on the ruins of law, justice, and right; it is profoundly, alarmingly, inevitably immoral.[41]

In this political geography, the focus on empire implied in the distinction between the metropolis and its colonies is overshadowed by a contrast between Britishness and the rest of Europe and the world. Inevitably, too, *British* imperial responsibility for the elaboration of systems of regulationism was largely sidelined in this critique of continental iniquity. Indeed, when empire and imperialism *were* condemned, it was as likely to be Napoleonic France – the France of Bonaparte himself or that of his nephew Louis-Napoléon – that critics had in mind. Parry has again noted that, in liberal and radical circles, 'there was a critique of "imperialism", though this was defined mainly in constitutional terms, to mean a Napoleonic perversion of political liberties for the pursuit of glory; it was not a refusal to accept imperial responsibilities'.[42]

It is misleading to suggest therefore that either the practice or the politics of British regulationism divided on a straightforward fault-line separating the metropolis from its (overseas) colonies. The emphasis on the overseas empire remained, even after the 1880s, submerged and subordinate in a more protean political geography, one that was in many ways more preoccupied with Europe than empire, and anti-imperialist either predominantly or exclusively in its condemnation of 'Napoleonic' imperial tyranny. We are drawn to the conclusion that, for the repeal movement at least, the distinction between the metropolis and the colonies was a political artefact as much as it was a measure of practical

---

[40] For Liberalism divided on the issue of the CD Acts, see Goldman, *Science, reform and politics*, pp. 127–42.

[41] W. Shaen, *Suggestions on the limits of legitimate legislation on the subject of prostitution* (London, c.1877), p. 6.

[42] Parry, *The politics of patriotism*, p. 9.

differences. It was a mapping of difference that was not, somehow, always already there. It was part of a series of overlapping and ambiguous ways of articulating difference and establishing the boundaries of legitimate rule. Although we have become accustomed to associating the metropolitan/colonial divide with the distinction between Britain and its overseas colonies, with the rule of racial difference, and with the oppression of subject races, these categories were not – or not yet at least – *fixed*: the British 'colonial' world included places rather nearer to 'home'; empire and imperialism could be invoked in order to contrast British liberties with continental tyranny; race was a powerful signifier, but it was not yet unambiguously the 'racialist' category that it would later become; and some of the older civilisational, cultural and constitutional meanings may have survived for much longer than some have accepted.[43] In short, the historical geography of British prostitution regulation is not best served by analyses of imperialism that see the distinction between the metropolitan and the colonial as essential.

Nation and empire

This is not to suggest that 'empire' was absent in the politics of British regulationism, nor is it an endorsement of those apologists for imperialism who marginalise its racial supremacism. But we are more likely to remark on the relative absence of decisive references to Britain's role in the racial and sexual subjugation of its colonial subjects. When we do find in the politics of regulation and repeal those who draw attention directly to the brute facts of colonial racial discrimination, in ways that chime in most closely with our contemporary sensibilities, the recognition has the power to shock precisely because of its relative rarity. Here is, for instance, Walter MacLaren's extraordinary and intemperate charge in the House of Commons, made in the 1888 debate over the future of the cantonment acts in India, which resonates all too clearly with contemporary assessments of the role of racial and sexual privilege in imperial rule:

The logical system is for the Government to send out English women to meet the demand. That is an extreme statement to make, and I should be sorry to see it carried out. You maintain that the Acts are for the benefit of English men and English women, and you sacrifice Indian women for them. You would not dare to send English women. Why? The reason is, because Indian women are black, and English women are white, and because they are a subject and inferior race, therefore you think they may be trodden upon.[44]

---

[43] P. Mandler, '"Race" and "nation" in mid-Victorian thought', in S. Collini, R. Whatmore and B. Young (eds.), *History, religion, and culture: British intellectual history 1750–1950* (Cambridge, 2000), p. 244.

[44] *The CD Acts in India: official report of Mr McLaren's speech in the House of Commons, on June the 5th, 1888. Reprinted from the Crewe & Nantwich Chronicle, of Saturday, June 16th 1888* (London, 1889), pp. 21–2.

Or, alternatively, consider the comments of an anonymous correspondent to the *Pall Mall Gazette* a year earlier, strikingly contemporary in their restriction of the term 'empire' to 'India and the scattered body of so-called Crown Colonies, peopled by men of inferior race, and practising a different form of morality and usually a different religion from the English people at home', and delineating an imperial contest between the realities of colonial administration and the demands of conventional bourgeois morality.[45] This 'public servant' noted the British political classes' commitment to the high standards of Puritan Christianity, particularly for those of the Liberal party, and in contrast to an earlier generation:

> I can remember the time when Liberalism was essentially Continental in its ideas of morality as also of religion – when the passing of the Contagious Diseases Acts, for example, was hailed in Radical circles as a triumph for the modern spirit over obscurantism – a good knock-down blow to the powers of darkness as we conceived of them.[46]

But he went on to doubt the possibility – even for the most high-minded – of a crusade to enforce these standards of morality on the 'uncleanly millions' of the inferior subject races. If this was inevitable, however, rather more to be regretted was the unwillingness even to hold British soldiers, seamen, civil servants and others to domestic moral account. 'Public servant' pictured the latter as men who adapt themselves to the habits of the heathen, and who come to consider that morals are matters merely 'of local and racial convention':

> Morality – as the stay-at-home English understands it – they come to regard as a local English institution, which is to be left behind in quitting England, like Crosse and Blackwell's pickles or Keen's mustard, the corresponding substitutes abroad being better adapted to local conditions.[47]

Moreover, if England had not intention or power to Christianise her heathen empire, the empire had yet the potential, in the immoral education of such men, to heathenise England. A contest between two Englands therefore emerges:

> To those who have eyes to see there is nothing more marked than the diversity of the two Englands – the Imperial England and the stay-at-home England – the one heathen, scoffing, ribald, cynical, sensual, and cultured, absolutely unbound by religious or national convention – the other modest in word and thought, devout, timid, chaste, uncultured, the slave of inherited precept, seeking only the beauty of holiness as it is to be found in obedience to Biblical precepts – one England Greek in spirit, the other Hebrew.[48]

This is a remarkable recognition of the limits of imperial morality campaigns, wrapped up in a condemnation of the realities and the contradictions of British rule over other races.

---

[45] 'Is the Empire consistent with morality? "No!"', *Pall Mall Gazette*, 19 May 1887, p. 2, reprinted in I. Sharp (ed.), *Josephine Butler and the prostitution campaigns: diseases of the body politic, volume V: the Queen's daughters in India* (London, 2003), p. 89.
[46] *Ibid.*, p. 2.   [47] *Ibid.*, p. 3.   [48] *Ibid.*, p. 3.

Finally, we might cite Josephine Butler's ranging of herself with all of the peoples who had suffered over the centuries from the depredations of their colonial masters:

> Let us not speak of the unbroken maintenance of our Empire as a blessing, when we have before us the facts of our Government's imposition of the drink and opium traffic, and of legalised vice, to the destruction of the bodies and souls of conquered races wherever we have planted our flag.[49]

> Is it not to be feared that India may one day herself answer her rulers, and cut through the heart of the problem in her own manner? for the natives of India, superstitious and ignorant, and for the present apparently submissive, have yet enough of the man in them not to endure for ever that the women of their people, – a conquered people, – should be taken and bound to the service of the vices of the troops of their conquerors.[50]

These kinds of statements are, however, and for all their acuity and resonance, unusual in their insistence on the brute facts of racial and cultural difference and the ignoble history of European violence towards the colonised races. Walter MacLaren seems to have stepped close to the bounds of legitimate debate, and it is telling that this statement did not make it into the official Parliamentary record.[51] The anonymous contributor to the *Pall Mall Gazette* is clearly aiming to shock, and even so predicts the eventual success of the purity party, the party of the agitation against the CD Acts and of 'stay-at-home' morality. His editor, the crusading journalist William Stead, was also quick to refute the argument, answering his own rhetorical question – 'Does the Empire or does it not tend in the direction of exalting or abasing woman?' – by arguing that:

> There can be little doubt that it operates steadily, and on the whole – notwithstanding some frightful occasional aberrations, such as the CD Acts – in favour of the recognition of the individuality and of the rights of woman. That being the case, we cannot regard it as a Moloch, nor can we lend a hand to demolish a system under which for many dark-skinned millions the sweet domesticities of home life, with all the resulting virtues, are rendered possible.[52]

Further, for all her animus against the colonial powers, Josephine Butler considered that Indian women were 'subjected' not only by Britain but also by their own menfolk and by their culture's superstitions and prejudices; she also notably included the Irish amongst Britain's 'conquered races'. Moreover, Butler looked forward to the empire's legitimate moral mission, to what she called its 'greater and nobler conquests', and defended British rule in South Africa on the basis of that empire's potential for protecting the native races:

> It is my deep conviction that Great Britain will in future be judged, condemned or justified, according to her treatment of those innumerable coloured races, heathen or partly

---

[49] J. E. Butler, *Our Christianity tested by the Irish question* (London, 1887), p. 29.
[50] J. E. Butler, *Truth before everything* (London, 1897), p. 355.
[51] See *Hansard*, 5 June 1888. Hansard has M'Laren.
[52] 'Is the Empire a Moloch?', p. 1.

Christianized, over whom her rule extends, or who, beyond the sphere of her rule, claim her sympathy and help as a Christian and civilizing power to whom a great trust has been committed.[53]

The repeal movement's denunciation of the sexual double standard should not then, even in the context of the campaign against colonial forms of regulationism, be seen as a straightforward critique of racial superiority and cultural inferiority. The language of race is in every case ambiguous and unstable, as even the strongest advocates of the development of racial and imperial consciousness in Victorian Britain tend to concede. Catherine Hall, for instance, whilst noting the emergence in the 1860s of 'a harsher racial vocabulary of fixed differences', and the consensus that race was a critical mark of distinction between peoples, also notes the fact that the emphasis on the superiority of Anglo-Saxons continued to play an important role.[54] Here, the notion of the superiority of the Anglo-Saxon 'race' was a statement that the providential history of English institutions placed them at the top of the (eminently climbable, albeit with difficulty) ladder of civilisation, in advance not only of the 'primitive races' but also of other less favoured nations and peoples ranged on a continuum of progress and modernity. Similarly, Antoinette Burton specifically recognises that '[t]he eagerness of repealers to stress the un-Englishness of regulation and the Englishness of the reform impulse reflected racial pride' as well as aversion to continental traditions, though she is unwontedly surprised by this inward emphasis, suggesting simply that it was some 'perversity of imperial ideology' that 'made the fulfilment of imperial rule a duty to the Anglo-Saxon race as much as to the "lower" races'.[55]

There is something characteristically inward-looking about the repealers' attention to the character of the Anglo-Saxon peoples, however, and to the virtues of British traditions that were inseparable from this 'racial' heritage. The fact that 'race' was for the Victorians a singularly self-regarding concept may take us one step further into the nature of British liberalism's connections with empire and the imperial mission. Perhaps we might say, following Uday Singh Mehta, that the movement for the repeal of contagious diseases legislation 'operates in the malleable and concealed space behind the starkness of blood and color to reproduce the familiar, even if somatically refracted, category of being English'.[56] From this route we may return to Parry's stress on the location of repeal within British liberal traditions, but recognise more strongly than he allows the distinctive imperial mission that pervades these political, philosophical, religious and humanitarian sentiments. The fact that the regulation of prostitution could be

---

[53] See Burton, *Burdens of history*, pp. 150, 153.
[54] C. Hall, *Civilising subjects: metropole and colony in the English imagination, 1830–1867* (Cambridge, 2002), pp. 440, 368; also see Stocking, *Victorian anthropology*, p. 62.
[55] Burton, *Burdens of history*, p. 153.
[56] U. S. Mehta, *Liberalism and empire: a study in nineteenth-century British liberal thought* (Chicago, 1999), p. 15.

found in England, Ireland and the Mediterranean, as well as in the overseas colonies, had the effect of turning political attention away from the cruder racial narratives and realities of empire, and towards this inward-looking theme of *national* 'racial' responsibility. Josephine Butler and other repealers do invoke the plight of the dependent, subjected and conquered races, as we have seen, but this seems to be defined in terms of political conditions as much as biological ones, and with implications as much for the fate of the British themselves as for native peoples. For repeal-minded activists, the question of the regulation of prostitution was nothing less than a question of the soul and destiny of Britain. William Stead thus argued that 'The responsibility rests on us all. The crime is national. It calls for national reparation ... It is the duty of all who wish to cleanse England's name, and England's fame from this foulest of blots.'[57]

The colonial possessions (in all their diversity) become in this vision a distinctly undifferentiated 'other' against which Britain's moral character and mission is defined. The politics of prostitution revolved in this sense around 'home', defined in relation to an empire in which it was both included *and* kept separate. The preoccupation with national identity, with 'the status, honour and role of Britain', may be seen as a development of the conjoint cultural work of nationalism and imperialism.[58] The seemingly solipsistic emphasis on the nation was not a marker of the irrelevance of empire: quite the opposite. The political geography of regulationism was an artefact of an imperial polity, not because it was distinctively a colonial phenomenon, but because its operations were projected across British imperialism's 'spatialized terrain of power', a terrain that both encompassed and transcended Britain itself.[59]

We may conclude that by tying the opposition to contagious diseases legislation so closely to the moral, ethical and religious duties of the *British* people and their governors, much of the imperial responsibility for regulation could be *displaced*. By tracing regulationism to the abhorrent influence of continental statism, or, in a much more minor register, to 'the most corrupt of corrupt officialism', the wirepullers at the War Office, the Admiralty, the Colonial Office and the colonial administrations, the central involvement of the British in regulating the sexuality of their imperial subjects could be sidestepped.[60] It could be excised and

---

[57] *Pall Mall Gazette*, 27 January 1887, quoted in Butler, *The revival and extension of the abolitionist cause*, pp. 35–6.

[58] Parry, *The politics of patriotism*, p. 388. See also C. Hall and S. O. Rose (eds.), *At home with the empire: metropolitan culture and the imperial world* (Cambridge, 2007), A. Burton, 'Introduction: on the inadequacy and indispensability of the nation', in A. Burton (ed.), *After the imperial turn: thinking with and through the nation* (Durham, NC, 2003).

[59] Burton, *After the imperial turn*, p. 5.

[60] J. E. Butler, 'A call to battle: a letter to my friends', *The Dawn*, April 1890, reprinted in I. Sharp (ed.), *Josephine Butler and the prostitution campaigns: diseases of the body politic, volume V: the Queen's daughters in India* (London, 2003), p. 164.

exorcised from the national story, in a signal instance of liberalism's strategies of exclusion.[61] Regulationists, particularly after 1886, could argue that contagious diseases legislation was appropriate in *other* places and *other* conditions, where the essential British qualities of understanding and respect for the liberties of the subject were not present; it could thus be displaced to the colonies where it was necessary to safeguard British security. Repealers had to reject this line, but insisted instead that regulationism was fundamentally *un-English*, a detestable import from the police-states of the continent, bearing the distinctive stamp of tyranny and despotism. Charles Newdegate stated in Parliament that 'the sooner the House gets quit of this noisome piece of legislation, of this aping of foreign police espionage, of this unconstitutional system of foreign police, the better for the country and the better for the reputation of this House'.[62] Francis Close also argued in a related register that the CD Acts 'have sprung exclusively from military and naval men, who have long introduced many of their provisions into foreign stations, as in China, India, Malta, Gibraltar, and other garrisons, where military absolutism reigned supreme, and civil liberty and rights were disregarded'.[63] As Levine has noted, for these repealers, 'It was *misplaced* imperial policy that endangered Britain's stability and the imperial idea; there was no intention on the part of antiregulationist campaigners to undermine the very edifice upon which empire was built.'[64] The movement for repeal was able to mobilise historical and geographical arguments – the displacement of regulation from the space of the nation, and also its relegation from the time of the modern; but this, because of its conjoining of national character and progressive universalism, could never be translated into a thoroughgoing critique of imperial institutions.

Conclusions

I have used this final chapter to explore some of the overlapping, inconsistent and perhaps also ultimately incoherent and impossible spatialities that underwrote the politics of prostitution in the era of state regulation and the most prominent attempts in Britain and its dependencies to formally manage prostitution and the problem of venereal disease. This is by no means a neat picture, and the politics of prostitution that I have presented here corresponds with the argument of the rest of this book that there is no straightforward mapping of projects, practices and policies. The political geographies of regulation and repeal are just as messy

---

[61] See U. S. Mehta, 'Liberal strategies of exclusion', in F. Cooper and A. L. Stoler (eds.), *Tensions of empire: colonial cultures in a bourgeois world* (Berkeley, 1997).
[62] *Hansard*, 24 May 1870, c. 1344.
[63] F. Close, *An examination of the witnesses, and their evidence, given before a Royal Commission upon the administration and operation of the 'Contagious Diseases Acts, 1871'* (London, 1872), p. 42.
[64] Levine, 'Rereading the 1890s', p. 605, emphasis added.

as was their practical elaboration, and as resistant to our contemporary categories as much as to those imposed by the Victorians themselves. There was, and is, no ready demarcation between the regulation of prostitution in some places and in others, no *a priori* geography of formal and informal policing, domestic and foreign, national and imperial, metropolitan and colonial. British regulationism was undoubtedly an imperial institution, but the place and space of the empire is an artefact of political discourse as well as a concrete landscape of power and authority. In emphasising the construction of a geopolitics of prostitution through a series of spatial narratives I have tried to attend to this complexity, with the repeal movement and its imperial liberal commitments to the fore in this analysis. Although anti-regulationists understood state regulation of prostitution as the product of interested medical and military parties within an imperial polity, I have argued that they largely avoided a direct engagement with British imperial complicity with the management of sex. Instead, the contemporary repeal politics of dislocation and displacement increasingly came to portray regulated prostitution as both out of place and out of the time of the true, ethical nation, as essentially 'un-English' and anachronistic. For all of their insistence on the connectedness of empire, their revelation of a corrupted imperial network, theirs was not in the end a political movement that decisively demarcated Britain from its imperial possessions, still less identifying British imperial power over its colonial subjects as illegitimate. Paradoxically, the attention to Britain's connections with an empire that encompassed the home country led to a solipsistic concentration on national purification, one that effectively contributed to the writing out of the experience of prostitution regulation from Britain's history. It is this *alibi* – the displacement of a history of managed and policed sexuality to other traditions, cultures and circumstances – which this book has sought to challenge.

Sources and bibliography

Archival sources

Cambridge, Cambridge University Archives (CUA)

CUR 40, Vice-Chancellor's Court.
CUR 41.1, Guard Book, 1548–1900.
Min.VI.6, Proctorial syndicate (1849–1900), flyleaf.
T.VIII.1–3, Spinning House committals books.
T.XI.1, Award of Sir J. Patteson, 1855 (1837–98).
VCCt/I/21, Acta Curiae 1846–61.
CUR 41.2 and 3, Proctorial suit, Kemp v. Neville.

Cambridge, Cambridgeshire Record Office (CRO)

PS/C/R/1–3, Cambridge Petty Sessions Court Registers, 1867–72.
R.60.27.1–2, Cambridge Female Refuge, inmate books.

Corfu, Corfu Archives (TIAK)

EA 22³, *Registro delle meretrici esistenti a Corfu*, 1814.
EA 22⁸, *Registro delle donne di publico piacere*, 1824.
EA 23/793, 1169, *Libro meretrici*, 1834–41.
EA 23/793, 1301, *Elenco delle meretric soggette alla medica explorazione*, 1844–51.

Cork, Cork City and County Archives

BG 69, Gaol records.

Gibraltar, Gibraltar Government Archives (GGA)

Gibraltar census.
AP1/2/2 Police Correspondence Book 1869–1875.
Box: VENEREAL DISEASE and other contagious diseases.
Boxes: Venereal Disease (1) and (2).

Box: ORDINANCES. Ordinances, draft ordinances and Orders in Council, 1832, 1867, 1869 and 1894–1895.

Hong Kong, Public Records Office

Hong Kong censuses.
Hong Kong Government Gazette.
HKRS 58-1-24-61, proposals to remove brothels in Possession Street, Hollywood Road, West Street, Lower Lascar Row, 1904–7
Report of commission of the National Council for Combating Venereal Diseases as to conditions affecting the prevention and cure of venereal disease in Hong Kong, January, 1921.
History of the Po Leung Kuk Hong Kong 1878–1968.

Liverpool, Liverpool University Special Collections and Archives

Josephine Butler correspondence.

Liverpool, Liverpool Record Office

352MIN/WAT, Liverpool Watch Committee minutes.
352POL 1/11, Watch Committee Order Book, 1870.
352POL 2/1, Head Constable's reports to the Watch Committee, 1857–61.
352POL 2/4–13, Head Constable's Special Report Books, 1866–94.
352POL 2/14, Head Constable's reports to the Watch Committee, 1894–7.

Liverpool, Merseyside Police Records Centre

Reports on the police establishment and the state of crime, with tabular returns, 1853–95.
Liverpool City Police: brothels 1915–1964.

London, British Library

Oriental and India Office Collections, F/4 series, Government of India, lock hospital administration.

London, National Archives

ASSI 36/21, Depositions in the case of Robert Browning, Norfolk Assizes.
CO 91, Gibraltar, original correspondence.
CO 129, Hong Kong, original correspondence.
CO 882, Confidential print, Eastern.
WO 33/12/188, Report of the committee upon venereal disease in the Army and Navy [1863].
WO 33/17A/274, Report of the committee, appointed October 18th, 1864, to enquire into the treatment of venereal disease in the Army and Navy [1866].

WO 33/27, Summary of replies and observations in reference to certain statements of the grounds on which the Contagious Diseases Acts are opposed [1875].

Oxford, Oxford University Archives (OUA)

MS NW4/8, Case for the opinion of Mr Serg.t Bosanquet, 1824.
NEP/A/7, Papers relative to a payment made to the city for the support of prostitutes confined in the city gaol by the authorities of the University.
WP.γ.7. (6), Senior Proctor's book, 1902–3.
WP.γ.8. (2), Senior Proctor's manual, 1837.
WP.γ.8. (19), Junior Proctor's manual, 1830–.
WP.γ.8. (21), Henry Pritchard, procuratorial experiences and observations, 1852–1853.
WP.γ.87/5, Senior Proctor's manual, 1897.
23/3, *Liber niger sine registrum nebulosum* [Black Book].
2.3.5., Vice-Chancellor's Court, register of proceedings against prostitutes, 1870–98.

Oxford, Centre for Oxfordshire Studies, Oxford Central Library

OXFU.24, University Police, general instructions, 1850.

Oxford, Rhodes House Library

MSS British Empire, anti-slavery papers.
Pope-Hennessy papers.

Unpublished theses and papers

Bartley, P. A., 'Seeking and saving: the reform of prostitutes and the prevention of prostitution in Birmingham 1860–1914' (PhD, Wolverhampton University, 1995).
Deslandes, P. R., 'Masculinity, identity and culture: male undergraduate life at Oxford and Cambridge' (PhD, University of Toronto, 1996).
Gamble, J. G., 'The origins, administration, and impact of the Contagious Diseases Acts from a military perspective' (PhD, University of Southern Mississippi, 1983).
Kitchingman, D., 'A study of the effects of the Criminal Law Amendment Act, 1885, on prostitution in Liverpool, 1885–1895' (MA, University of Liverpool, 2001).
Moore, F., 'Beyond the ideal: motherhood in industrial Lancashire 1860–1937' (PhD, University of Cambridge, 2008).
Mynott, E., 'Purity, prostitution and politics: social purity in Manchester 1880–1900' (PhD, University of Manchester, 1995).
Ogborn, M. J., 'Discipline, government and law: the response to crime, poverty and prostitution in nineteenth century Portsmouth' (PhD, University of Cambridge, 1990).
Taithe, B. O., 'From danger to scandal: debating sexuality in Victorian England: the Contagious Diseases Acts (1864–1869) and the morbid landscape of Victorian Britain' (PhD, University of Manchester, 1992).
Ware, H., 'The recruitment, regulation and role of prostitution in Britain from the middle of the nineteenth century to the present day' (PhD, University of London, 1969).

Annual reports

Association for Promoting the Extension of the Contagious Diseases Act, 1866, to the Civilian Population of the United Kingdom, Annual reports, 1868–75.
Cambridge Barnwell Mission, Report, 1878.
Cambridge Female Refuge, Annual reports, 1839–99.
Cambridge Mission for the Prevention of Vice in Young Women and the Restoration of Those Who Have Fallen, Annual reports, 1855–1906.
Cambridge Town Missionary Society, Annual report, 1876.
Ladies' National Association for the Repeal of the Contagious Diseases Acts, 1870–96.

Newspapers and periodicals

British Medical Journal.
Cambridge Chronicle and University Journal.
Cambridge Independent Press.
Cambridge Review.
Cork Examiner.
Friend of China and Hong Kong Gazette.
Granta.
Guardian.
Hansard.
Hong Kong Daily Press.
Jackson's Oxford Journal.
Journal of the Statistical Society of London.
Lancet.
Liverpool Citizen.
Liverpool Daily Post.
Liverpool Review.
Magdalen's Friend.
Medical Enquirer.
Meliora.
Morning Chronicle.
Observer.
Oxford University Herald.
Pall Mall Gazette.
Record.
Reformatory and Refuge Journal.
Shield.
Times.

Public documents

Judicial statistics, England and Wales.
Report of the Commissioners appointed in pursuance of Acts of Parliament, 58 Geo. III.c.91; 59 Geo.III.c.81; and continued by 5 Geo.IV.c.58; 10 Geo.IV.c.59; 1 & 2 Will.

IV.c.34; and 5 & 6 Will.IV.c.71; to inquire concerning charities and education of the poor in England and Wales, volume VI, Cambridge, 1839.
Royal Commission on the Sanitary State of the Army in India. P.P. 1863 [3184] XIX, Part I.
Copy of a Memorial to the Lord President of the Council from the President of the Royal College of Physicians, and others, respecting the extension of the 'Contagious Diseases Act, 1866'. P.P. 1867–68 [266] LV.421.
Report of the Committee appointed to enquire into the pathology and treatment of the venereal disease, with the view to diminish its injurious effects on the men of the Army and Navy, with appendices, and the evidence taken before the Committee. P.P. 1867–68 [4031] XXXVII.425.
Report from the Select Committee on Contagious Diseases Act (1866); together with the proceedings of the Committee, minutes of evidence, and appendix. P.P. 1868–69 [306] VII.1.
Copy of Official letters addressed to the First Lord of the Treasury from the Honorary Secretaries of the Association for the Extension of the Contagious Diseases Acts, dated the 8th and 14th days of March last, with the answers thereto; and, of the official letter from the Chairman of the National Association for the Repeal of the Contagious Diseases Acts, dated the 24th day of March, to the First Lord of the Treasury, with his answer thereto. P.P. 1871 [184] LVI.625.
Copy of Correspondence between the War Office and the Reverend Mr Dacre, late chaplain of the Colchester Lock Hospital, Respecting the efforts required to be made for the reclamation of women confined in the hospital under the operation of the Contagious Diseases Acts. P.P. 1871 [260] LVI.631.
Returns of the number of women summoned before magistrates in the various districts where the Contagious Diseases Acts are in force. P.P. 1871 [388] LVI.637.
Report of Royal Commission upon the administration and operation of the Contagious Diseases Acts. P.P. 1871 [C.408] XIX.1.
Copy of the Memorial presented to the Secretary of State for the Home Department in favour of Contagious Diseases Acts, signed by members of the medical profession resident in London. P.P. 1872 [80] XLVII.489.
Copy of Memorials presented to the Secretary of State for the Home Department from 2,500 medical men, praying that the principles of the Contagious Diseases Acts may be maintained. P.P. 1872 [245] XLVII.495.
Copy of Replies of the Reverend Mr Grant to the questions addressed by Convocation to the clergy as to the operation of the Contagious Diseases Acts. P.P. 1878 [306] LXI.97.
Report of the commissioners appointed to inquire into the working of the Contagious Diseases Ordinance, 1867, in Hong Kong. P.P. 1880 [118] XLIX.69.
Correspondence relating to the working of the Contagious Diseases Ordinances of the colony of Hong Kong. P.P. 1881 [C.3093] LXV.673.
Select Committee on the administration and operation of the Contagious Diseases Acts, P.P. 1881 [351] VIII.193.
Report from the Select Committee on Contagious Diseases Acts. P.P. 1882 [340] IX.1.
Extract from introduction to judicial statistics, 1893, P.P. 1895 [300] CVIII.271.
Report on criminal statistics for England and Wales, 1898, P.P. [Cd. 123] CIII.1.

Printed sources published before 1918

Acton, W., *Prostitution, considered in its moral, social & sanitary aspects, in London and other large cities. With proposals for the mitigation and prevention of its attendant evils* (London, 1857).
Prostitution, considered in its moral, social, and sanitary aspects, in London and other large cities and garrison towns. With proposals for the control and prevention of its attendant evils (London, 1870).
'Alumnus', *Letter to R. M. Beverley, Esq. in defence of his strictures on the University of Cambridge, by an undergraduate* (Cambridge, 1834).
Amos, S., *The policy of the Contagious Diseases Acts 1866 and 1869 tested by the principles of ethical and political science* (London, 1870).
A comparative survey of laws in force for the prohibition, regulation, and licensing of vice in England and other countries (London, 1877).
Andrew, E.W. and Bushnell, K.C., *The Queen's daughters in India*, revised edition (London, 1898).
An Anglo-Sapphic ode, dedicated (with French leave) to Robert Mackintosh Beverley, Esq., entitled the friend of veracity versus the lie grinder (Cambridge, 1833).
'Anthropos', *The Contagious Diseases Acts and the Contagious Diseases Preventive Bill* (London, 1872).
Armstrong, R.A., *The deadly shame of Liverpool. An appeal to the municipal voters* (London, 1890).
Two years ago and now. An appeal to the municipal electors (London, 1892).
Atchinson, T., *Letters to 'The Times' on small-pox encampments. And a word on the Contagious Diseases Acts* (London, 1871).
Balfour, T.G., 'Comparative health of seamen and soldiers, as shown by the naval and military statistical reports', *Journal of the Royal Statistical Society of London*, 35 (1872), 1–24.
Barrett, R.M., *Ellice Hopkins: a memoir* (London, 1907).
Barton, J.K., *Purity of life. The laws of nature and of scripture* (Dublin, 1887).
Beggs, T., 'The proposed extension of the Contagious Diseases Act in its moral and economical aspects', *Sessional Proceedings of the National Association for the Promotion of Social Science for the Year 1869–70* (London, 1870).
Bell, R., *The Beverlëid, an epic* (Cambridge, 1833).
[Bertram, J.G.], *The whole truth and nothing but the truth about the social evil: being deeper glimpses of the business of prostitution in Edinburgh, &c. By the Editor of the 'North Briton'* (Edinburgh, 1866).
Bevan, W., *Prostitution in the borough of Liverpool. A lecture, delivered in the Music Hall, June, 3, 1843* (Liverpool, 1843).
Beverley, R.M., *A letter to His Royal Highness the Duke of Gloucester, Chancellor, on the present corrupt state of the University of Cambridge* (London, 1833).
Reply to Professor Sedgwick's letter in the 'Leeds Mercury,' concerning the present corrupt state of the University of Cambridge (London, 1834).
Bird, J., *The laws of epidemic and contagious diseases and the importance of preventive medicine: an introductory address to the Epidemiological Society* (London, 1854).

258 *Sources and bibliography*

Blake, H.J.C., *The Cantab, or, a few adventures and misadventures in after life* (Chichester, 1845).

[Bowen, G.F.], *The Ionian Islands under British protection* (London, 1851).

Bright, J., *The Contagious Diseases Acts: speech delivered in the House of Commons (with closed doors) July 20, 1870* (Manchester, 1870).

Bristed, C. A., *Five years in an English university* (New York, 1852).

Brooke, R., *Liverpool as it was during the last quarter of the eighteenth century, 1775 to 1800* (Liverpool, 1853).

Brown, D.B., 'The pros and cons of the Contagious Diseases Acts, as applied in India', *Transactions of the Medical and Physical Society of Bombay*, 11 (1888), 80–97.

Brown, J., *Sixty years' gleanings from life's harvest* (Cambridge, 1858).

Browne, G.F., *The recollections of a bishop* (London, 1915).

Bunce, J.T., 'On the statistics of crime in Birmingham, as compared with other large towns', *Journal of the Statistical Society*, 28 (1865), 518–26.

Burne, P., *The teetotaler's companion; or, a plea for temperance* (London, 1847).

Butler, J.E., 'The lovers of the lost', *Contemporary Review*, 13 (1870), 16–40.

Social purity: an address (London, 1879).

The principles of the abolitionists (London, 1885).

A grave question that needs answering by the churches of Great Britain (London, 1886).

Our Christianity tested by the Irish question (London, 1887).

The revival and extension of the abolitionist cause: a letter to the members of the Ladies' National Association (London, 1887).

Mrs Butler's plea for an interest in the abolitionist work on the continent of Europe (London, 1893).

Personal reminiscences of a great crusade (London, 1896).

Truth before everything (London, 1897).

An autobiographical memoir, 2nd edition (Bristol, 1911).

'Cantabrigiensis' [or 'A. H.'], 'The regrets of a Cantab', *London Magazine and Review*, 4 (1825), 437–66.

The CD Acts in India: Official report of Mr McLaren's speech in the House of Commons, on June the 5th, 1888. Reprinted from the 'Crewe & Nantwich Chronicle,' of Saturday, June 16th 1888 (London, Moral Reform Union, 1889).

The chronicle of Convocation. Being a record of the proceedings of the Convocation of Canterbury the tenth Victoria regnante, sessions, February 8, 9, 10, 11, 1881 (London, 1881).

City of Liverpool. Report of the special committee of magistrates on the state of the laws affecting houses of ill-fame within the city, and to consider the best mode of putting the laws in force (Liverpool, 1889).

Clark, J.W., and Hughes, T.M., *The life and letters of the Reverend Adam Sedgwick* (Cambridge, 1890).

Close, F., *An examination of the witnesses, and their evidence, given before a Royal Commission upon the Administration and Operation of the 'Contagious Diseases Acts, 1871'* (London, 1872).

Compston, H.F.B., *The Magdalen Hospital: the story of a great charity* (London, 1917).

Curgenven, J.B., *The Contagious Diseases Act of 1866, and its extension to the civil population of the United Kingdom* (London, 1868).

Deakin, C. W. S., *The Contagious Diseases Acts: the Contagious Acts '64, '66, '68 (Ireland), '69. From a sanitary and economic point of view* (London, 1872).
Deane, A. C., 'The religion of the undergraduate', *The Nineteenth Century*, 38 (1895).
Dyer, A. S., *Slavery under the British flag: iniquities of British rule in India and in our crown colonies and dependencies* (London, 1886).
Edmondson, J., *The moral forces which defeat the hygienic regulation of social vice* (London, 1882).
 By stealthy steps: regulation in Gibraltar (London, 190[?]).
Farrar, F. W., *Julian Home: a tale of college life* (London, 1905).
Fowler, W., *Speech in the House of Commons, on May 24th, 1870, on the Contagious Diseases Acts, with notes* (London, 1870).
Garrett, E., *An enquiry into the character of the Contagious Diseases Acts of 1866–1869* (London, 1870).
Gordon, C. A., 'Notes on the early history of Contagious Diseases Acts in India', *The Medical Press and Circular* (1890).
Gradus ad Cantabrigiam: or, a dictionary of terms, academical and colloquial, or cant, which are used at the University of Cambridge (Cambridge, 1803).
Gradus ad Cantabrigiam: or, new university guide to the academical customs, and colloquial or cant terms, peculiar to the University of Cambridge (Cambridge, 1824).
Hall, F. R., *A letter to R. M. Beverley, Esq., containing strictures on his letter to His Royal Highness the Duke of Gloucester, Chancellor of the University of Cambridge, on the present corrupt state of the university* (Cambridge, 1834).
Hammick, J. T., 'On the judicial statistics of England and Wales, with special reference to the recent returns relating to crime', *Journal of the Statistical Society*, 30 (1867), 375–426.
Hill, B., 'Illustrations of the working of the Contagious Diseases Act. I – Chatham and Portsmouth', *British Medical Journal*, 28 December 1867, pp. 583–5.
 'Illustrations of the working of the Contagious Diseases Act. II – Plymouth and Devonport', *British Medical Journal*, 11 January 1868, pp. 21–2.
 'Illustrations of the working of the Contagious Diseases Act. III – Aldershot, Winchester, and Windsor', *British Medical Journal*, 1 February 1868, pp. 94–5.
 'Illustrations of the working of the Contagious Diseases Act. IV – The venereal disease among prostitutes in London', *British Medical Journal*, 23 May 1867, pp. 505–6.
 'Should the principle of the Contagious Diseases' Act be applied to the civil population?', *Transactions of the National Association for the Promotion of Social Science* (1869), 428–38.
 'Statistical results of the Contagious Diseases Acts', *Journal of the Statistical Society of London*, 33 (1870), 463–85.
History of the social evil from the remotest antiquity to the present time (London, 1862).
Hopkins, E., *A plea for the wider action of the Church of England in the prevention of the degradation of women, as submitted to a committee of Convocation on July 3, 1879* (London, 1879).
 The power of womanhood; or mothers and sons: a book for parents and those in loco parentis (London, 1899).
Hughes, T., *Tom Brown at Oxford* (London, 1861).
Hume, A., *Dr Hume's four maps of Liverpool, ecclesiastical, historical, municipal, moral & social* (Liverpool, 1858).

Condition of Liverpool, religious and social; including notices of the state of education, morals, pauperism, and crime, 2nd edition (Liverpool, 1858).

Important testimonies of eminent divines and of religious conferences and synods; in support of the entire repeal of the Contagious Diseases Acts, 1866–69 (London, n.d.).

'An Ionian', *The Ionian Islands; what they have lost and suffered under the thirty-five years' administration of the Lord High Commissioners sent to govern them. In reply to a pamphlet entitled 'The Ionian Islands under British Protection'* (London, 1851).

Jacob, A. H., 'The working of the Contagious Diseases Acts', *The Medical Press and Circular*, 96 (1886), 445–8.

Joyce, J., *Licensing of sin in India: facts about the legalization of impurity by British authority* (London, c.1887).

Lawson, R., 'The operation of the Contagious Diseases Acts among the troops in the United Kingdom, and men of the Royal Navy on the Home Station, from their introduction in 1864 to their ultimate repeal in 1884', *Journal of the Royal Statistical Society*, 54 (1891), 31–69.

Legge, H., 'The religion of the undergraduate II: A reply from Oxford', *The Nineteenth Century*, 38 (1895).

Levi, L., 'A survey of indictable and summary jurisdiction offences in England and Wales, from 1857 to 1876, in quinquennial periods, and in 1877 and 1878', *Journal of the Statistical Society*, 43 (1880), 423–56.

Lewis, J. D. [John Smith], *Sketches of Cantabs* (London, 1849).

'Licensing prostitution'; reprinted (with permission) from the Report for 1869 of the Rescue Society, London, by the National Anti-Contagious Diseases' Act Association (London, c.1870).

List, A. C. C., *The two phases of the social evil* (Edinburgh, 1861).

Little, T., *Confessions of an Oxonian* (London, 1826).

Logan, W., *An exposure, from personal observation, of female prostitution in London, Leeds, and Rochdale, and especially in the city of Glasgow; with remarks on the cause, extent, results, and remedy of the evil* (Glasgow, 1843).

The great social evil: its causes, extent, results, and remedies (London, 1871).

Lowndes, F. W., *Prostitution and syphilis in Liverpool, and the working of the Contagious Diseases Acts, at Aldershot, Chatham, Plymouth, and Devonport* (London, 1876).

Lock hospitals and lock wards in general hospitals (London, 1882).

Prostitution and venereal diseases in Liverpool (London, 1886).

'The reopening of the Liverpool Lock Hospital – the study and treatment of syphilitic diseases', *Liverpool Medico-Chirurgical Journal*, 22 (1892), 104–12.

McLaren, D., *Facts respecting the Contagious Diseases Acts: substance of a speech by Duncan McLaren, Esq., MP, at a public meeting, in the Music Hall, Newcastle, September 27th, 1870 – Revised. with an appendix, containing a summary of the government tables; and the report* (Manchester, 1870).

Mayhew, H., and Hemying, B., 'Prostitutes', in *London labour and the London poor*, volume IV, pp. 35–272, reprint of 1861 original (New York, 1968).

'A member of the University', 'The sins of our cities', *The Modern Review* (1893), 329–39.

'A member of Trinity College', *Remarks upon Mr Beverley's letter to the Duke of Gloucester, coupled with a few statements in contradiction of the charges therein*

contained, and illustrative of the present state of the University of Cambridge (Cambridge, 1833).
Miller, J., *Prostitution considered in relation to its cause and cure* (Edinburgh, 1859).
Milton, J., *The social good versus the social evil: a new version of an old story* (London, 1860).
Morgan, W., *Contagious diseases: their history, anatomy, pathology, and treatment, with comments on the Contagious Diseases Acts* (London, 1877).
'Mr anti-reform high church orthodox', *Beverley unmaskt, a canino-Greek poem, written for the instruction of R. M. Beverley, liar* (Cambridge, 1833).
Nevins, J.B., *Statement of the grounds upon which the Contagious Diseases' Acts are opposed* (London, 1874).
   The health of the Navy: an analysis of the Official Report for 1876, and of the special return relating to five ports under and five ports not under the Contagious Diseases Acts, which was ordered to be laid before the House of Commons, on the 4th July, 1877 (London, 1878).
Nightingale, F., *Army sanitary administration and its reform under the late Lord Herbert* (London, 1862).
Nott-Bower, J.W., *Houses of ill-fame, &c. Report of the Head Constable* (Liverpool, 1890).
'Oxford: its morals and its politics', *The Ecclesiastic*, 168 (1866), 543–51.
'Oxford University extension', *The North British Review*, 91 (1867), 223–41.
Parent-Duchâtelet, A.J.B., *De la prostitution dans la ville de Paris* (Paris, 1836).
'A public servant', 'Is the Empire consistent with morality? "No!"', *Pall Mall Gazette*, 45 (1887), 2–3.
Regulations and instructions for the guidance of the Cambridge Police Force, by order of the Watch Committee (Cambridge, 1862).
Richardson, B.W., 'The medical history of Cambridge', excerpted from *The medical history of England, The Medical Times and Gazette: A Journal of Medical Science, Literature, Criticism, and News, Volume II* (1864), pp. 559–601, 628–32, 657–61.
Rumsey, H.W., *Essays on state medicine* (London, 1856).
   On state medicine in Great Britain and Ireland (London, 1867).
Russell, J.F., *A letter to the Rt Hon. Henry Goulburn, MP on the morals & religion of the University of Cambridge with reference to a recent letter from R. M. Beverley, Esq. to His Royal Highness the Duke of Gloucester* (Cambridge, 1833).
Ryan, M., *Prostitution in London, with a comparative view of that of Paris and New York, as illustration of the capitals and large towns of all countries; and proving moral depravation to be the most fertile source of crime, and of personal and social misery; with an account of the nature and treatment of the various diseases, caused by the abuses of the reproductive function* (London, 1839).
[Scholefield, H.], *Memoir of the late Rev. James Scholefield, MA* (London, 1855).
Sedgwick, A., *Four letters to the editors of the Leeds Mercury in reply to R. M. Beverley, Esq.* (Cambridge, 1836).
'A Senior Wrangler', 'Struggles of a poor student through Cambridge', *London Magazine and Review*, 4 (1825), 491–510.
   'Continuation of the struggles of a senior wrangler', *London Magazine and Review*, 4 (1825), 161–82.

Shaen, W., 'Contagious Diseases Acts': aid and defence operations. Paper read by W. Shaen, Esq., MA, at the conference of delegates from the associations and committees formed in various towns for promoting the repeal of the Contagious Diseases Acts, held at the Freemasons' Tavern, 5th and 6th May, 1870 (London, 1870).
   Suggestions on the limits of legitimate legislation on the subject of prostitution (London, c.1878).
Simon, J., Report on the Contagious Diseases Act shewing the expense, impolicy, and general inutility of its proposed extension to the civil population. Reprinted from the Blue Book, containing the eleventh annual report of the Medical Officer to the Lords of Her Majesty's most Honourable Privy Council, by the National Anti-Contagious Diseases Act Association (Nottingham, n.d.).
Social versus political reform: The sin of great cities; or, the great social evil a national sin. Illustrated by a brief enquiry into its extent, causes, effects, and existing remedies (London, 1859).
'Socius', The Cambridge tart: epigrammatic and satiric-poetical effusions; &c. &c. Dainty morsels served up by Cantabs, on various occasions (London, 1823).
Soldiers and the social evil. A letter addressed by permission to the Right Hon. Sidney Herbert, MD, Secretary of State for War, by a chaplain to the forces (London, 1860).
The Spinning House abomination, from the Special Commissioner of the Morning Chronicle (Cambridge, 1851).
Stansfeld, J., Substance of the speeches of the Rt Hon. James Stansfeld, MP, on the Contagious Diseases Acts (London, 1875).
   'On the validity of the annual government statistics of the operation of the Contagious Diseases Acts', Journal of the Statistical Society of London, 39 (1876), 540–72.
   Lord Kimberley's defence of the government brothel system at Hong Kong, 'Correspondence relating to the Contagious Diseases Ordinances in Hong Kong.' (Presented to both Houses of Parliament in August, 1881.) With an introduction by the Rt Hon. James Stansfeld, MP (London, 1882).
Stuart, J., 'Social purity', Cambridge Review, 1 (1879), 84–5.
   Reminiscences (London, 1912).
The student's guide to the University of Cambridge (Cambridge, 1862).
Tait, W., Magdalenism: an inquiry into the extent, causes, and consequences, of prostitution in Edinburgh, 2nd edition (Edinburgh, 1842).
Talbot, J.B., The miseries of prostitution (London, 1844).
Taylor, C.B., Observations on the Contagious Diseases Act, (women, not animals), showing how the new law debases women, debauches men, destroys the liberty of the subject, and tends to increase disease; being a reply to Mr W. Paul Swain's paper on the working of the act at Devonport (Nottingham, n.d.).
   Speech on the second reading of a bill for the repeal of the Contagious Diseases Acts, 1866–1869 (London, 1883).
[Thomas, E.W., et al.], An exposure of the false statistics of the Contagious Diseases Acts (Women) contained in Parliamentary Paper No. 149, on the return of the Assistant Commissioner of Metropolitan Police, by the managers of metropolitan female reformatories (London, 1873).

Tuckniss, W., 'The agencies at present in operation within the metropolis, for the suppression of vice and crime', in H. Mayhew, *London labour and the London poor*, Volume IV, pp. xi–xl, reprint of 1861 original (New York, 1968).

'Undergraduate', *A letter to His Royal Highness Frederick Duke of Gloucester, DCL Chancellor, in vindication of the University of Cambridge from the calumnious attacks of R. M. Beverley, Esq.* (Cambridge, 1833).

'An undergraduate of the University of Cambridge' [W. Forsyth], *A letter to R. M. Beverley, esq.* (Cambridge, 1833).

'Venereal disease in the Army and Navy', *The Lancet*, 19 March 1864, pp. 327–9.

Vintras, A., *On the repressive measures adopted in Paris compared with the uncontrolled prostitution of London and New York* (London, 1867).

[Walker, J.], *Curia oxoniensis: or, observations on the statutes which relate to the University Court; on the illegality of searching houses; on the procuratorial office; and on the University Police Act* (Oxford, 1825).

Wardlaw, R., *Lectures on female prostitution: its nature, extent, effects, guilt, causes, and remedy* (Glasgow, 1842).

Weldon, G. W., 'Seven years' personal recollections of parochial work in Cambridge', *The Churchman*, August 1883.

'The Western Harem'. Reprinted from the 'Westminster Review', July 1884 (London, 1885).

Wilson, H. J., *The history of a sanitary failure* (Sheffield, 1898).

 Copy of a rough record of events and incidents connected with the repeal of the 'Contagious Diseases Acts, 1864–6–9,' in the United Kingdom, and of the movement against state regulation of vice, in India and the colonies, 1858–1906 (Sheffield, 1907).

Wilson, J. M., *An address to the Cambridge University Association for the Promotion of Purity of Life* (Cambridge, 1883).

Wood, J. S., *The following remarks on the bearing of the proposed statute 'de electione procuratorum et vice-procuratorum', on that part of the proctors' office which concerns the maintenance of discipline and supervision of morals, are submitted to the consideration of members of the Senate* (Cambridge, 1857).

Worth, T., *A second letter to the Right Hon. W. Ewart Gladstone, First Lord of the Treasury, opposing the attempt under the title of the 'Contagious Diseases Bill,' to introduce into this country the continental system of licensed prostitution, with its attendant evils* (Nottingham, 1870).

Printed sources published after 1918

Agamben, G., *Homo sacer: sovereign power and bare life* (Stanford, 1998).
 State of exception (Chicago, 2005).
Aisenberg, A., 'Syphilis and prostitution: a regulatory couplet in nineteenth-century France', in R. Davidson and L. A. Hall (eds.), *Sex, sin and suffering: venereal disease and European society since 1870* (London, 2001), pp. 15–28.
Alberti, J., *Gender and the historian* (Harlow, 2002).
Amey, L., 'A plethora of public houses', *Cambridgeshire Local History Society Bulletin*, 41 (1986), 1–5.

Anderson, A., *Tainted souls and painted faces: the rhetoric of fallenness in Victorian culture* (Ithaca, 1993).
Anderson, R., *British universities: past and present* (London, 2006).
Armstrong, D., 'Public health spaces and the fabrication of identity', *Sociology*, 27 (1993), 393–410.
Arnold, D., 'Medical priorities and practice in nineteenth-century British India', *South Asia Research*, 5 (1985), 167–83.
  Colonizing the body: state medicine and epidemic disease in nineteenth-century India (Berkeley, 1993).
  'Syphilis', in K.F. Kible (ed.), *The Cambridge world history of human disease* (Cambridge, 1990), pp. 1025–33.
  'Sexually transmitted diseases in nineteenth and twentieth century India', *Genitourinary Medicine*, 69 (1993), 3–8.
  The problem with nature: environment, culture and European expansion (Oxford, 1996).
  'Sex, state, and society: sexually transmitted diseases and HIV/AIDS in modern India', in M. Lewis, S. Bamber and M. Waugh (eds.), *Sex, disease, and society: a comparative history of sexually transmitted diseases and HIV/AIDS in Asia and the Pacific* (Westport, 1997), pp. 19–36.
  'Introduction: disease, medicine and empire', in D. Arnold (ed.), *Imperial medicine and indigenous societies* (Manchester, 1998), pp. 1–26.
  (ed.), *Imperial medicine and indigenous societies* (Manchester, 1998).
  The new Cambridge history of India III, 5: science, technology and medicine in colonial India (Cambridge, 2000).
  The tropics and the traveling gaze: India, landscape and science, 1800–1856 (Seattle, 2006).
Arrizabalaga, J., Henderson, J. and French, R., *The great pox: the French disease in Renaissance Europe* (New Haven, 1997).
Ashworth, G.J., White, P.E. and Winchester, H.P.M., 'The red-light district in the West European city: a neglected aspect of the urban landscape', *Geoforum*, 19 (1988), 201–12.
Aughton, P., *Liverpool: a people's history* (Preston, 1990).
Backhouse, C., 'Nineteenth-century Canadian prostitution law: reflection of a discriminatory society', *Histoire Sociale – Social History*, 18 (1985), 387–423.
Bala, P., *Imperialism and medicine in Bengal: a socio-historical perspective* (New Delhi, 1991).
Baldwin, P., *Contagion and the state in Europe, 1830–1930* (Cambridge, 1999).
Ballhatchet, K., *Race, sex and class under the Raj: imperial attitudes and policies and their critics, 1793–1905* (London, 1980).
Banarjee, S., *Under the Raj: prostitution in colonial Bengal* (New York, 1998).
Banks, O., *Faces of feminism: a study of feminism as a social movement* (Oxford, 1981).
Barker-Benfield, G.J., *The horrors of the half-known life: male attitudes toward women and sexuality in nineteenth-century America* (New York, 1976).
  The culture of sensibility: sex and society in eighteenth-century Britain (Chicago, 1992).
Barlow, T.E., 'Introduction: on "colonial modernity"', in T.E. Barlow (ed.), *Formations of colonial modernity in east Asia* (Durham, NC, 1997), pp. 1–20.

Barret-Ducrocq, F., *Love in the time of Victoria: sexuality and desire among working-class men and women in nineteenth-century London* (London, 1991).
Bartley, P., 'Preventing prostitution: the Ladies' Association for the Care and Protection of Young Girls in Birmingham, 1887–1914', *Women's History Review*, 7 (1998), 37–60.
  Prostitution: prevention and reform in England, 1860–1914 (London, 2000).
Bashford, A., *Purity and pollution: gender, embodiment and Victorian medicine* (Basingstoke, 1998).
  Imperial hygiene: a critical history of colonialism, nationalism and public health (Basingstoke, 2004).
Bashford, A. and Hooker, C., 'Introduction: contagion, modernity and postmodernity', in A. Bashford and C. Hooker (eds.), *Contagion: historical and cultural studies* (London, 2001), pp. 1–14.
  (eds.), *Contagion: historical and cultural studies* (London, 2001).
Batson, J., *Oxford in fiction: an annotated bibliography* (New York, 1989).
Beckingham, D., 'Geographies of drink culture in Liverpool: lessons from the drink capital of nineteenth-century England', *Drugs: Education, Prevention and Policy*, 15 (2008), 305–13.
Beisel, N., *Imperiled innocents: Anthony Comstock and family reproduction in Victorian America* (Princeton, 1997).
Belchem, J., *Merseypride: essays in Liverpool exceptionalism* (Liverpool, 2000).
Bell, S., *Reading, writing and rewriting the prostitute body* (Bloomington, 1994).
Bell, V., 'The promise of liberalism and the performance of freedom', in A. Barry, T. Osborne and N. Rose (eds.), *Foucault and political reason: liberalism, neoliberalism and rationalities of government* (London, 1996), pp. 81–97.
Bennett, G. V., 'University, society and church 1688–1714', in L. S. Sutherland and L. G. Mitchell (eds.), *The history of the University of Oxford, volume V: the eighteenth century* (Oxford, 1986), pp. 359–400.
Benton, L., *Law and colonial cultures: legal regimes in world history* (Cambridge, 2002).
Berger, M. T., 'Imperialism and sexual exploitation: a response to Ronald Hyam's "Empire and sexual opportunity"', *Journal of Imperial and Commonwealth History*, 17 (1988), 83–9.
Bernheimer, C., *Figures of ill repute: representing prostitution in nineteenth-century France* (Cambridge, MA, 1989).
Bernstein, L., *Sonia's daughters: prostitutes and their regulation in imperial Russia* (Berkeley, 1995).
Bickerton, T. H., *A medical history of Liverpool from the earliest days to the year 1920* (London, 1936).
Birken, L., *Consuming desire: sexual science and the emergence of a culture of abundance, 1871–1914* (Ithaca, 1988).
Blanco, R. L., 'The attempted control of venereal disease in the Army of mid-Victorian England', *Journal of the Society for Army Historical Research*, 45 (1967), 234–41.
Bland, L., '"Guardians of the race," or "vampires upon the nation's health"?: female sexuality and its regulation in early twentieth-century Britain', in E. Whitelegg *et al.* (eds.), *The changing experience of women* (Oxford, 1982), pp. 373–88.

'"Cleansing the portals of life": the venereal disease campaign in the early twentieth century', in M. Langan and B. Schwarz (eds.), *Crises in the British state 1880–1930* (London, 1985), pp. 192–208.

'In the name of protection: the policing of women in the First World War', in J. Brophy and C. Smart (eds.), *Women-in-law: explorations in law, family and sexuality* (London, 1985), pp. 23–49.

Banishing the beast: English feminism and sexual morality 1885–1914 (Harmondsworth, 1995).

Blunt, A., *Domicile and diaspora: Anglo-Indian women and the spatial politics of home* (Oxford, 2005).

Boehrer, B. T., 'Early modern syphilis', in J. C. Fout (ed.), *Forbidden history: the state, society, and the regulation of sexuality in modern Europe* (Chicago, 1992), pp. 11–28.

Boyd, N., *Josephine Butler, Octavia Hill, Florence Nightingale: three Victorian women who changed their world* (London, 1982).

Boyle, F. M., Glennon, S., Najman, J. M., et al., *The sex industry: a survey of sex workers in Queensland, Australia* (Aldershot, 1997).

Brand, J. L., *Doctors and the state: the British medical profession and government action in public health, 1870–1912* (Baltimore, 1965).

Brandt, A. M., *No magic bullet: a social history of venereal disease in the United States since 1880*, expanded edition (Oxford, 1987).

Bremner, G. A. and Lung, D. P. Y., 'Spaces of exclusion: the significance of cultural identity in the formation of European residential districts in British Hong Kong', *Environment and Planning D: Society and Space*, 21 (2003), 223–52.

Bristow, E. J., *Vice and vigilance: purity movements in Britain since 1700* (Dublin, 1977).

Bristow, J., *Sexuality* (London, 1997).

Brock, M. G., 'A "plastic structure"', in M. G. Brock and M. C. Curtoys (eds.), *The history of the University of Oxford, volume VII: nineteenth-century Oxford, Part II* (Oxford, 2000), pp. 3–66.

Brooke, R., *Liverpool as it was: 1775 to 1800* (Liverpool, 2003).

Brooks, P., *Reading for the plot: design and intention in narrative* (New York, 1984).

Bryder, L., 'Sex, race, and colonialism: an historiographical review', *International History Review*, 20 (1998), 791–822.

Bullough, V. and Bullough, B., *Women and prostitution: a social history* (Buffalo, 1987).

Burford, E. J. and Wotton, J., *Private vices – public virtues: bawdry in London from Elizabethan times to the Regency* (London, 1995).

Burke, S. D. A. and Sawchuk, L. A., 'Alien encounters: the jus soli and reproductive politics in the 19th-century fortress and colony of Gibraltar', *History of the Family*, 6 (2001), 531–61.

Burton, A., *Burdens of history: British feminists, Indian women, and imperial culture, 1865–1915* (Chapel Hill, 1994).

At the heart of the empire: Indians and the colonial encounter in late Victorian Britain (Berkeley, 1998).

'Introduction: the unfinished business of colonial modernities', in A. Burton (ed.), *Gender, sexuality and colonial modernities* (London, 1999), pp. 1–16.

'"States of injury": Josephine Butler on slavery, citizenship and the Boer War', in I. C. Fletcher, L. E. N. Mayhall and P. Levine (eds.), *Women's suffrage in the British empire: citizenship, nation, and race* (London, 2000), pp. 18–32.

'Introduction: on the inadequacy and indispensability of the nation', in A. Burton (ed.), *After the imperial turn: thinking with and through the nation* (Durham, NC, 2003).

Bynum, W. F., Hardy, A., Jacyna, S., et al. (eds.), *The Western medical tradition 1800–2000* (Cambridge, 2006).

Caine, B., *Victorian feminists* (Oxford, 1992).

'When did the Victorian period end? Questions of gender and generation', *Journal of Victorian Culture*, 11 (2006), 317–25.

Cairoli, A., Chiaberto, G. and Engel, S., *Le déclin des Maisons Closes: la prostitution à Genève à la fin du XIXe siècle* (Geneva, 1987).

Cantlie, N., *A history of the Army Medical Department, volume 2* (Edinburgh, 1974).

Carroll, P., 'Science, power, bodies: the mobilization of nature as state formation', *Journal of Historical Sociology*, 9 (1996), 139–67.

Cassar, P., *Medical history of Malta* (London, 1965).

Cassel, J., *The secret plague: venereal disease in Canada, 1838–1939* (Toronto, 1987).

Cell, J. W., 'Anglo-Indian medical theory and the origins of segregation in West Africa', *American Historical Review*, 91 (1986), 307–35.

Chakravorty, S., 'From colonial city to global city: the far-from-complete spatial transformation of Calcutta', in P. Marcuse and R. van Kempen (eds.), *Globalizing cities: a new spatial order?* (Oxford, 2000), pp. 56–77.

Chatterjee, P., *The nation and its fragments: colonial and postcolonial histories* (New Delhi, 1993).

Chatterjee, R., 'Prostitution in nineteenth century Bengal: construction of class and gender', *Social Scientist*, 21 (1993), 159–72.

Chiu, F. Y. L., 'Politics and the body social in colonial Hong Kong', in T. E. Barlow (ed.), *Formations of colonial modernity in East Asia* (Durham, NC, 1997), pp. 295–322.

Clayson, H., *Painted love: prostitution in French art of the Impressionist era* (New Haven, 1991).

Clement, E., 'Prostitution', in H. G. Cocks and M. Houlbrook (eds.), *The modern history of sexuality* (Basingstoke, 2006), pp. 206–30.

Cliff, A. D., Haggett, P. and Smallman-Raynor, M., *Island epidemics* (Oxford, 2000).

Cobban, A. B., *The medieval English universities: Oxford and Cambridge to c.1500* (Aldershot, 1988).

Cockcroft, W. R., 'The Liverpool police force, 1836–1902', in S. P. Bell (ed.), *Victorian Lancashire* (Newton Abbot, 1974), pp. 150–68.

Cocks, H. G. and Houlbrook, M. (eds.), *The modern history of sexuality* (Basingstoke, 2006).

Cohen, P. C., *The murder of Helen Jewett* (New York, 1998).

Cohen, S., *The evolution of women's asylums since 1500: from refuges for ex-prostitutes to shelters for battered women* (Oxford, 1992).

Cohn, S. K., *Women in the streets: essays on sex and power in Renaissance Italy* (Baltimore, 1996).

Collingham, E. M., *Imperial bodies: the physical experience of the Raj, c.1800–1947* (Cambridge, 2001).

Collins, N., *Politics and elections in nineteenth-century Liverpool* (Aldershot, 1994).
Conner, S. P., 'Politics, prostitution and the pox in Revolutionary Paris, 1789–1799', *Journal of Social History*, 22 (1989), 713–34.
  'Public virtue and public women: prostitution in Revolutionary Paris, 1793–1794', *Eighteenth-Century Studies*, 28 (1994), 221–40.
Cook, H., *The long sexual revolution: English women, sex, and contraception 1800–1975* (Oxford, 2004).
Cooper, F., 'Race, ideology and the perils of comparative history', *American Historical Review*, 101 (1996), 1122–38.
  'Empire multiplied: a review essay', *Comparative Studies in Society and History*, 46 (2004), 247–72.
  Colonialism in question: theory, knowledge, history (Berkeley, 2005).
Cooper, F. and Stoler, A. L., 'Between metropole and colony: rethinking a research agenda', in F. Cooper and A. L. Stoler (eds.), *Tensions of empire: colonial cultures in a bourgeois world* (Berkeley, 1997), pp. 1–56.
Cooper, R., 'Imperial liberalism', *The National Interest*, 79 (2005), 25–34.
Cooter, R. and Sturdy, S., 'Of war, medicine and modernity: introduction', in R. Cooter, M. Harrison and S. Sturdy (eds.), *War, medicine and modernity* (Stroud, 1998), pp. 1–21.
Corbin, A., *Prèsentation, Alexandre Parent-Duchâtelet, la prostitution à Paris au XIXe siècle* (Paris, 1981), pp. 9–47.
  'Commercial sexuality in nineteenth-century France: a system of images and regulations', *Representations*, 14 (1986), 209–19.
  Women for hire: prostitution and sexuality in France after 1850 (Cambridge, MA, 1990).
  Time, desire and horror: towards a history of the senses (Cambridge, 1995).
Costello, C., *A most delightful station: the British Army on the Curragh of Kildare, Ireland, 1855–1922* (Cork, 1996).
Cox, P., 'Compulsion, voluntarism, and venereal disease: governing sexual health in England after the Contagious Diseases Acts', *Journal of British Studies*, 46 (2007), 91–115.
Craddock, S., *City of plagues: disease, poverty and deviance in San Francisco* (Minneapolis, 2000).
Crossley, A. (ed.), *Victorian history of the counties of England: a history of the county of Oxford, volume IV: the city of Oxford* (Oxford, 1979).
Crozier, I., 'William Acton and the history of sexuality: the medical and professional context', *Journal of Victorian Culture*, 5 (2000), 1–27.
Curthoys, M. C. and Day, C. J., 'The Oxford of Mr Verdant Green', in M. G. Brock and M. C. Curthoys (eds.), *The history of the University of Oxford, volume VI: nineteenth-century Oxford, Part I* (Oxford, 1997), pp. 268–86.
Curtis, L. P., *Apes and angels: Irishmen in Victorian caricature*, 2nd revised edition (Washington, 1996).
D'Amico, S., 'Shameful mother: poverty and prostitution in seventeenth-century Milan', *Journal of Family History*, 30 (2005), 109–20.
Dang, K., 'Prostitutes, patrons and the state: nineteenth century Awadh', *Social Scientist*, 21 (1993), 173–96.
Darwin, J., 'Hong Kong in British decolonisation', in J. M. Brown and R. Foot (eds.), *Hong Kong's transitions, 1842–1997* (London, 1997), pp. 16–32.

Daunton, M. and Rieger, B., 'Introduction', in M. Daunton and B. Rieger (eds.), *Meanings of modernity: Britain from the late-Victorian era to World War II* (Oxford, 2001), pp. 1–21.
Davenport-Hines, R., *Sex, death and punishment: attitudes to sex and sexuality in Britain since the Renaissance* (London, 1990).
Davidson, R., *Dangerous liaisons: a social history of venereal disease in twentieth-century Scotland* (Amsterdam, 2000).
Davidson, R. and Hall, L. A. (eds,), *Sex, sin and suffering: venereal disease and European society since 1870* (London, 2001).
Day, C. J., 'The University and the city', in M. G. Brock and M. C. Curthoys (eds.), *The history of the University of Oxford, volume VI: nineteenth-century Oxford, Part I* (Oxford, 1997), pp. 441–76.
Dean, M., *Governmentality: power and rule in modern society* (London, 1999).
  'Liberal government and authoritarianism', *Economy and Society*, 31 (2002), 37–61.
Dennis, R., *Cities in modernity: representations and productions of metropolitan space, 1840–1930* (Cambridge, 2008).
Deslandes, P. R., ' "The foreign element": newcomers and the rhetoric of race, nation, and empire in "Oxbridge" undergraduate culture, 1850–1920', *Journal of British Studies*, 37 (1998), 54–90.
  Oxbridge men: British masculinity and the undergraduate experience, 1850–1920 (Bloomington, 2005).
Desmond, A. and Moore, J., *Darwin* (London, 1991).
Diduck, A. and Wilson, W., 'Prostitutes and persons', *Journal of Law and Society*, 24 (1997), 504–25.
Dietz, P., 'Gibraltar', in P. Dietz (ed.), *Garrison: ten British military towns* (London, 1986), pp. 177–200.
  The British in the Mediterranean (London, 1994).
Dossal, M., *Imperial designs and Indian realities: the planning of Bombay city, 1845–1875* (Bombay, 1991).
Drenth, A. van, and de Haan, F., *The rise of caring power: Elizabeth Fry and Josephine Butler in Britain and the Netherlands* (Amsterdam, 1999).
Driver, F. and Martins, L. (eds.), *Tropical visions in an age of empire* (Chicago, 2005).
Duffy, M. 'World-wide war, 1793–1815', in P. J. Marshall (ed.), *The Oxford history of the British Empire, volume II: the eighteenth century* (Oxford, 1998), pp. 184–207.
Dunsford, D., 'Principle versus expediency: a rejoinder to F. B. Smith', *Social History of Medicine*, 5 (1992), 505–13.
Durbach, N., *Bodily matters: the anti-vaccination movement in England, 1853–1907* (Durham, 2005).
Eagleton, T., 'Afterword: Ireland and colonialism', in T. McDonough (ed.), *Was Ireland a colony? Economics, politics and culture in nineteenth-century Ireland* (Dublin, 2005), pp. 326–33.
  Holy terror (Oxford, 2005).
Eitel, E. J., *Europe in China* (Hong Kong, 1983).
Elden, S. *Mapping the present: Heidegger, Foucault and the project of a spatial history* (London, 2001).
Elias, T. O., 'Form and content of colonial law', *International and Comparative Law Quarterly*, 3 (1954), 645–51.

'Form and content of colonial law – II', *International and Comparative Law Quarterly*, 4 (1955), 533–41.
Engel, A.J., '"Immoral intentions": the University of Oxford and the problem of prostitution, 1827–1914', *Victorian Studies*, 23 (1979), 79–107.
  From clergyman to don: the rise of the academic profession in nineteenth-century Oxford (Oxford, 1983).
Engelstein, L., 'Syphilis, historical and actual: cultural geography of a disease', *Reviews of Infectious Diseases*, 8 (1986), 1036–48.
  The keys to happiness: sex and the search for modernity in fin-de-siècle Russia (Ithaca, 1992).
  'Combined underdevelopment: discipline and the law in imperial and Soviet Russia', *American Historical Review*, 98 (1993), 338–53.
  'Combined underdevelopment: discipline and the law in imperial and Soviet Russia: reply', *American Historical Review*, 98 (1993), 376–81.
Evans, R.J., 'Prostitution, state and society in imperial Germany', *Past and Present*, 70 (1976), 106–29.
  Tales from the German underworld: crime and punishment in the nineteenth century (New Haven, 1998).
Fagan, T., *Monto: madams, murder and black coddle* (Dublin, 1978).
Finnegan, F., *Poverty and prostitution: a study of Victorian prostitutes in York* (Cambridge, 1979).
Finnegan, J., *The story of Monto: an account of Dublin's notorious red-light district* (Cork, 1978).
Fisher, T., *Prostitution and the Victorians* (Stroud, 1997).
Fletcher, A., *Gender, sex and subordination in England 1500–1800* (New Haven, 1995).
Fletcher, I.C., 'Double meanings: nation and empire in the Edwardian era', in A. Burton (ed.), *After the imperial turn: thinking with and through the nation* (Durham, NC, 2003), pp. 246–59.
Forbes, G., *The new Cambridge history of India, volume IV.2: women in modern India* (Cambridge, 1996).
Ford, R.T., 'Law's territory (a history of jurisdiction)', in N. Blomley, D. Delaney and R.T. Ford (eds.), *The legal geographies reader: law, power, and space* (Oxford, 2001), pp. 200–17.
Foucault, M., *Discipline and punish: the birth of the prison* (New York, 1979).
  The history of sexuality, volume I: an introduction (New York, 1980).
  The history of sexuality, volume II: the use of pleasure (Harmondsworth, 1987).
  The history of sexuality, volume III: the care of the self (Harmondsworth, 1990).
  'Governmentality', in B. Burchell, C. Gordon and P. Miller (eds.), *The Foucault effect: studies in governmentality* (London, 1991), pp. 85–103.
  'Space, knowledge, and power', in P. Rabinow (ed.), *The Foucault reader* (London, 1991), pp. 239–56.
  'Society must be defended': lectures at the Collège de France 1975–1976 (New York, 2003).
Fout, J.C. (ed.), *Forbidden history: the state, society, and the regulation of sexuality in modern Europe* (Chicago, 1992).
Frazer, W.M., *A history of English public health 1834–1939* (London, 1950).

Frost, G. S., *Promises broken: courtship, class, and gender in Victorian England* (Charlottesville, 1995).
Gallant, T. W., *Experiencing dominion: culture, identity, and power in the British Mediterranean* (Notre Dame, 2002).
Garon, S., 'The world's oldest debate? Prostitution and the state in imperial Japan, 1900–1945', *American Historical Review*, 98 (1993), 710–32.
Gattrell, V. A. C., 'The decline of theft and violence in Victorian and Edwardian England and Wales', in V. A. C. Gattrell, B. Lenman and G. Parker (eds.), *Crime and the law: the social history of crime in western Europe since 1500* (London, 1980), pp. 238–70.
  'Crime, authority and the policeman-state', in F. M. L. Thompson (ed.), *The Cambridge social history of Britain, 1750–1950* (Cambridge, 1990), pp. 243–310.
Gattrell, V. A. C. and Haddon, T. B., 'Nineteenth-century criminal statistics and their interpretation', in E. A. Wrigley (ed.), *Nineteenth-century society: essays in the use of quantitative methods for the study of social data* (Cambridge, 1972), pp. 336–96.
Ghirardo, D. Y., 'The topography of prostitution in Renaissance Ferrara', *Journal of the Society of Architectural Historians*, 60 (2001), 402–31.
Gibson, M., *Prostitution and the state in Italy, 1860–1915* (New Brunswick, 1986).
  'Prostitution laws after Italian unification: the role of "regulationist" and "abolitionist" elites', *Criminal Justice History*, 11 (1990), 105–17.
Gilbert, P. K., *Mapping the Victorian social body* (Albany, 2004).
Gilfoyle, T., *City of eros: New York city, prostitution and the commercialization of sex, 1790–1920* (New York, 1992).
  'Prostitutes in history: from parables of pornography to metaphors of modernity', *American Historical Review*, 104 (1999), 117–41.
Gillis, J. R. 'Servants, sexual relations, and the risks of illegitimacy in London, 1801–1900', *Feminist Studies*, 5, 1 (1979), 142–73.
  Youth and history: tradition and change in European age relations, 1770–present, expanded student edition (New York, 1981).
Gilman, S., 'The Hottentot and the prostitute: toward an iconography of female sexuality', in *Difference and pathology: stereotypes of sexuality, race, and madness* (Ithaca, 1985), pp. 77–108.
Goldman, L., *Science, reform, and politics in Victorian Britain: the Social Science Association 1857–1886* (Cambridge, 2002).
Gorham, D., 'The "Maiden Tribute of Modern Babylon" re-examined: child prostitution and the idea of childhood in late-Victorian England', *Victorian Studies*, 21 (1978), 353–79.
Green, V. H. H., *The universities* (Harmondsworth, 1969).
Grewal, I., *Home and harem: nation, gender, empire, and the cultures of travel* (London, 1996).
Groot, J. de, '"Sex" and "race": the construction of language and image in the nineteenth century', in S. Mendus and J. Rendall (eds.), *Sexuality and subordination: interdisciplinary studies of gender in the nineteenth century* (London, 1989), pp. 89–128.
Guy, D. J., *Sex and danger in Buenos Aires: prostitution, family, and nation in Argentina* (Lincoln, NE, 1991).
Hall, C., *Civilising subjects: metropole and colony in the English imagination, 1830–1867* (Cambridge, 2002).

Hall, C. and Rose, S. O. (eds.), *At home with the empire: metropolitan culture and the imperial world* (Cambridge, 2007).

Hall, L., '"War always brings it on": war, STDs, the military and the civil population in Britain, 1850–1950', in *Comparative perspectives on the history of sexually transmitted diseases, volume I, being proceedings of a conference held on 26–28 April 1996* (London, 1996).

 'Hauling down the double standard: feminism, social purity and sexual science in late nineteenth-century Britain', *Gender and History*, 16 (2004), 36–56.

Hall, S., 'The multi-cultural question', in B. Hesse (ed.), *Un/settled multiculturalisms: diasporas, entanglements, disruptions* (London, 2001), pp. 209–41.

Hamilton, M., 'Opposition to the Contagious Diseases Acts, 1864–1886', *Albion*, 10 (1978), 14–27.

Hammond, J. L. and Hammond, B., *James Stansfeld: a Victorian champion of sex equality* (London, 1932).

Hardy, A., *The epidemic streets: infectious disease and the rise of preventive medicine, 1856–1900* (Oxford, 1993).

Harling, P., 'The state', in C. Williams (ed.), *A companion to nineteenth-century Britain* (Oxford, 2007), pp. 110–24.

Harris, J., *Private lives, public spirit: Britain 1870–1914* (London, 1994).

Harrison, B., 'Underneath the Victorians', *Victorian Studies*, 10 (1967), 239–62.

Harrison, M., 'Tropical medicine in nineteenth-century India', *British Journal for the History of Science*, 25 (1992), 299–318.

 Public health in British India: Anglo-Indian preventive medicine 1859–1914 (Cambridge, 1994).

 Review of P. Levine, *Prostitution, Race and Politics: Policing Venereal Disease in the British Empire*, *American Historical Review*, 109 (2004), 483–4.

Harsin, J. *Policing prostitution in nineteenth-century Paris* (Princeton, 1985).

Hart, A., '(Re)constructing a Spanish red-light district: prostitution, space and power', in D. Bell and G. Valentine (eds.), *Mapping desire: geographies of sexualities* (London, 1995), pp. 214–28.

Haslewood, H. L. and Haslewood, C., *Child slavery in Hong Kong: the mui tsai system* (London, 1930).

Headrick, D. R., *The tools of empire: technology and European imperialism in the nineteenth century* (Oxford, 1981).

Henderson, T., *Disorderly women in eighteenth-century London: prostitution and control in the metropolis, 1730–1830* (London, 1999).

Hendrickson, K., 'A kinder, gentler British Army: mid-Victorian experiments in the management of army vice at Gibraltar and Aldershot', *War and Society*, 14 (1996), 21–33.

Henriot, C., *Prostitution and sexuality in Shanghai: a social history 1849–1949* (Cambridge, 2001).

Hershatter, G., 'Modernizing sex, sexing modernity: prostitution in early twentieth-century Shanghai', in C. K. Gilmartin, G. Hershatter, L. Rofel and T. White (eds.), *Engendering China: women, culture, and the state* (Cambridge, MA, 1994), pp. 147–74.

 Dangerous pleasures: prostitution and modernity in twentieth-century Shanghai (Berkeley, 1997).

Herzog, D. (ed.), *Sexuality and German fascism* (New York, 2005).
Heyningen, E. B. van, 'The social evil in the Cape Colony 1868–1902: prostitution and the Contagious Diseases Acts', *Journal of Southern African Studies*, 10 (1984), 170–97.
Hicks, G., *The comfort women: Japan's brutal regime of enforced prostitution in the Second World War* (New York, 1995).
Higgs, E., *The information state in England: the central collection of information on citizens since 1500* (London, 2003).
Hill, M. W., *Their sisters' keepers: prostitution in New York City, 1830–1870* (Berkeley, 1993).
Hills, G., *Rock of contention: a history of Gibraltar* (London, 1974).
Hilton, B., 'Continuity or change in nineteenth-century moral attitudes', *Journal of Victorian Culture*, 1 (1996), 130–6.
Hitchcock, T., *English sexualities, 1700–1800* (London, 1997).
Hobson, B. 'Prostitution', in M. K. Cayton, E. J. Gorn and P. W. Williams (eds.), *Encyclopedia of American social history, volume III* (New York, 1993), pp. 2157–65.
Hodges, S., '"Looting" the lock hospital in colonial Madras during the Famine years of the 1870s', *Social History of Medicine*, 18 (2005), 379–98.
Holcombe, L., *Wives and property: reform of the married women's property law in nineteenth-century England* (Toronto, 1983).
Hopkins, A. G., 'Back to the future: from national history to imperial history', *Past and Present*, 164, 1 (1999), 198–243.
Howarth, J., '"In Oxford but ... not of Oxford": the women's colleges', in M. G. Brock and M. C. Curthoys (eds.), *The history of the University of Oxford, volume VII: nineteenth-century Oxford, Part II* (Oxford, 2000), pp. 237–307.
Howe, A., 'Intellect and civic responsibility: dons and citizens in nineteenth-century Oxford', in R. C. Whiting (ed.), *Oxford: studies in the history of a university town since 1800* (Manchester, 1993), pp. 12–52.
Howe, S., *Ireland and empire: colonial legacies in Irish history and culture* (Oxford, 2000).
Howell, P., 'Prostitution and racialised sexuality: the regulation of prostitution in Britain and the British Empire before the Contagious Diseases Acts', *Environment and Planning D: Society and Space*, 18 (2000), 321–39.
  'A private Contagious Diseases Act: prostitution and public space in Victorian Cambridge', *Journal of Historical Geography*, 26 (2000), 376–402.
  'Prostitutional space in the nineteenth-century European city', in I. S. Black and R. A. Butlin (eds.), *Place, culture and identity: essays in historical geography in honour of Alan R. H. Baker* (Quebec, 2001), pp. 181–202.
  'Sex and the city of bachelors: popular masculinity and public space in nineteenth-century England and America', *Ecumene*, 8 (2001), 20–50.
  'Venereal disease and the politics of prostitution in the Irish Free State', *Irish Historical Studies*, 33 (2003), 320–41.
  'Colonial law and legal historical geography: an argument from Gibraltar', in A. R. H. Baker and I. S. Black (eds.), *Home and colonial: essays on landscape, Ireland, environment and empire in celebration of Robin Butlin's contribution to historical geography*, RGS-IBG Historical Geography Research Series 39 (London, 2004), pp. 113–24.

'Prostitution and the place of empire: regulation and repeal in Hong Kong and the British imperial network', in L. J. Proudfoot and M. M. Roche (eds.), *(Dis)placing empire: renegotiating British colonial geographies* (Aldershot, 2005), pp. 175–97.

'Foucault, sexuality, geography', in J. W. Crampton and S. Elden (eds.), *Space, knowledge and power: Foucault and geography* (Aldershot, 2006), pp. 291–315.

Howell, P. and Lambert, D., 'Sir John Pope Hennessy and colonial government: humanitarianism and the translation of slavery in the imperial network', in D. Lambert and A. Lester (eds.), *Colonial lives: imperial careering in the long nineteenth century* (Cambridge, 2006), pp. 228–56.

Hubbard, P., *Sex and the city: geographies of prostitution in the urban West* (Aldershot, 1999).

'Desire/disgust: mapping the moral contours of heterosexuality', *Progress in Human Geography*, 24 (2000), 191–217.

'Sexing the self: geographies of engagement and encounter', *Social and Cultural Geography*, 3 (2002), 365–81.

Hull, I. V., *Sexuality, state, and civil society in Germany, 1700–1815* (Ithaca, 1996).

Hunt, A., *Governing morals: a social history of moral regulation* (Cambridge, 1999).

'Regulating heterosocial space: sexual politics in the early twentieth century', *Journal of Historical Sociology*, 15 (2002), 1–34.

Hunt, A. and Wickham, G., *Foucault and law: towards a sociology of law as governance* (London, 1994).

Hyam, R., '"Imperialism and sexual exploitation": a reply', *Journal of Imperial and Commonwealth History*, 17 (1988), 90–8.

Empire and sexuality: the British experience (Manchester, 1990).

Inwood, S., 'Policing London's morals: the Metropolitan Police and popular culture, 1829–1850', *London Journal*, 15 (1990), 129–46.

Israel, K., 'French vices and British liberties: gender, class and narrative competition in a late Victorian sex scandal', *Social History*, 22 (1997), 1–26.

Jackson, L. A., *Child sexual abuse in Victorian England* (London, 2000).

Jackson, S., and Scott, S. (eds.), *Feminism and sexuality: a reader* (Edinburgh, 1996).

Jackson, W. G. F., *The Rock of the Gibraltarians: a history of Gibraltar* (London, 1987).

JanMohamed, A. R., 'Sexuality on/of the racial border: Foucault, Wright, and the articulation of "racialized sexuality"', in D. Stanton (ed.), *Discourses of sexuality: from Aristotle to AIDS* (Ann Arbor, 1992), pp. 94–116.

Jaschok, M. and Miers, S. (eds.), *Women and Chinese patriarchy: submission, servitude and escape* (Hong Kong, 1994).

Jeffreys, S., *The spinster and her enemies: feminism and sexuality 1880–1930* (North Melbourne, 1997).

The idea of prostitution (North Melbourne, 1997).

Jochelson, J., 'From paupers to pass laws: control of VD in the Cape and Transvaal, South Africa, 1880–1910', in *Comparative perspectives on the history of sexually transmitted diseases, volume I, being proceedings of a conference held on 26–28 April 1996* (London, 1996).

Jones, C., 'Prostitution and the ruling class in eighteenth-century Montpellier', *History Workshop Journal*, 6 (1978), 7–28.

Jones, M., 'Tuberculosis, housing and the colonial state: Hong Kong, 1900–1950', *Modern Asian Studies*, 37 (2003), 653–82.

Jordan, J., *Josephine Butler* (London, 2001).
  (ed.), *Josephine Butler and the prostitution campaigns: diseases of the body politic, volume II: the Ladies' appeal and protest* (London, 2003).
  (ed.), *Josephine Butler and the prostitution campaigns: diseases of the body politic, volume III: the constitution violated: the Parliamentary campaign* (London, 2003).
Joyce, B., *The Chatham scandal: a history of Medway's prostitution in the late 19th century* (Rochester, 1999).
Kalpagan, U., 'Colonial governmentality and the "economy"', *Economy and Society*, 29 (2000), 418–38.
  'Colonial governmentality and the public sphere in India', *Journal of Historical Sociology*, 15 (2002), 35–58.
Kamen, H., *Empire: how Spain became a world power 1492–1763* (New York, 2003).
Kaminsky, A. P., 'Morality legislation and British troops in late nineteenth-century India', *Military Affairs*, 43 (1979), 78–83.
Karras, R. M., *Common women: prostitution and sexuality in medieval England* (New York, 1996).
  'Sex, money, and prostitution in medieval English culture', in J. Murray and K. Eisenbichler (eds.), *Desire and discipline: sex and sexuality in the premodern West* (Toronto, 1996), pp. 201–16.
  'Women's labours: reproduction and sex work in medieval Europe', *Journal of Women's History*, 15 (2004), 153–8.
  Sexuality in medieval Europe: doing unto others (London, 2005).
Kearns, K., *Dublin tenement life: an oral history* (Dublin, 1994).
Kennedy, D., 'Imperial history and post-colonial theory', *Journal of Imperial and Commonwealth History*, 34 (1996), 345–63.
Kenny, K. (ed.), *Ireland and the British Empire* (Oxford, 2005).
Kent, S. K., *Gender and power in Britain, 1640–1990* (London, 1999).
Kibre, P., *Scholarly privileges in the Middle Ages: the rights, privileges, and immunities of scholars and universities at Bologna, Padua, Paris, and Oxford* (London, 1961).
Knox, B., 'British policy and the Ionian Islands, 1847–1864: nationalism and imperial administration', *English Historical Review*, 49 (1984), 503–29.
Koven, S., *Slumming: sexual and social politics in Victorian London* (Princeton, 2004).
Kumar, M. S., '"Oriental sore" or "public nuisance": the regulation of prostitution in colonial India, 1805–1889', in L. J. Proudfoot and M. M. Roche (eds.), *(Dis)placing empire: renegotiating British colonial geographies* (Aldershot, 2005), pp. 155–73.
Kwan, C. W., *The making of Hong Kong society: three studies of class formation in early Hong Kong* (Oxford, 1991).
Laite, J., 'Taking Nellie Johnson's fingerprints: prostitutes and legal identity in early twentieth-century London', *History Workshop Journal*, 65 (2008), 96–116.
Lambert, D., '"As solid as the Rock": place, belonging and the local appropriation of imperial discourse in Gibraltar', *Transactions of the Institute of British Geographers*, 30 (2005), 206–20.
Lambert, D. and Howell, P., 'John Pope Hennessy and the translation of "slavery" between late nineteenth-century Barbados and Hong Kong', *History Workshop Journal*, 55 (2003), 1–24.
Lambert, D. and Lester, A., 'Geographies of colonial philanthropy', *Progress in Human Geography*, 28 (2004), 320–41.

(eds.), *Colonial lives across the British Empire: imperial careering in the long nineteenth century* (Cambridge, 2006).

Lansbury, C., *The old brown dog: women, workers, and vivisection in Edwardian England* (Madison, 1985).

Laqueur, T., *Making sex: body and gender from the Greeks to Freud* (Cambridge, MA, 1990).

'Sexual desire and the market economy during the industrial revolution', in D. Stanton (ed.), *Discourses of sexuality: from Aristotle to AIDS* (Ann Arbor, 1992), pp. 185–215.

Lawrence, P. K., *Modernity and war: the creed of absolute violence* (Basingstoke, 1997).

Lee, A. C. W. and So, K. T. 'Child slavery in Hong Kong: case report and historical review', *Hong Kong Medical Journal*, 12, 6 (2006), 463–6.

Legg, S., 'Foucault's population geographies: classifications, biopolitics and governmental spaces', *Population, Space and Place*, 11 (2005), 137–56.

Spaces of colonialism: Delhi's urban governmentalities (Oxford, 2007).

Lester, A., *Imperial networks in nineteenth century South Africa and Britain* (London, 2001).

Lethbridge, H. J., 'The evolution of a Chinese voluntary association in Hong Kong: the Po Leung Kuk', *Journal of Oriental Studies*, 10 (1972), 33–50.

Levine, P., 'Rough usage: prostitution, law and the social historian', in A. Wilson (ed.), *Rethinking social history: English society 1570–1920 and its interpretation* (Manchester, 1993), pp. 266–92.

'"Walking the streets in a way no decent woman should": women police in World War I', *Journal of Modern History*, 66 (1994), 34–78.

'Consistent contradictions: prostitution and protective labour legislation in nineteenth-century England', *Social History*, 19 (1994), 17–35.

'Venereal disease, prostitution, and the politics of empire: the case of British India', *Journal of the History of Sexuality*, 4 (1994), 579–602.

'Rereading the 1890s: venereal disease as "constitutional crisis" in Britain and British India', *Journal of Asian Studies*, 55 (1996), 585–612.

'Battle colors: race, sex, and colonial soldiery in World War I', *Journal of Women's History*, 9 (1998), 104–30.

'Modernity, medicine, and colonialism: the Contagious Diseases Ordinances in Hong Kong and the Straits Settlements', *Positions*, 6 (1998), 675–705.

'Modernity, medicine, and colonialism: the Contagious Diseases Ordinances in Hong Kong and the Straits Settlements', in A. Burton (ed.), *Gender, sexuality and colonial modernities* (London, 1999), pp. 35–48.

'Orientalist sociologies and the creation of colonial sexualities', *Feminist Review*, 65 (2000), 5–21.

'Public health, venereal disease and colonial medicine in the later nineteenth century', in R. Davidson and L. A. Hall (eds.), *Sex, sin and suffering: venereal disease and European society since 1870* (London, 2001), pp. 160–72.

Prostitution, race, and politics: policing venereal disease in the British Empire (London, 2003).

'Sexuality, gender and empire', in P. Levine (ed.), *Gender and empire* (Oxford, 2004), pp. 134–55.

'Sexuality and empire', in C. Hall and S. O. Rose (eds.), *At home with the empire: metropolitan culture and the imperial world* (Cambridge, 2006), pp. 122–42.

Lewis, M., Bamber, S., and Waugh, M. (eds.), *Sex, disease, and society: a comparative history of sexually transmitted diseases and HIV/AIDS in Asia and the Pacific* (Westport, 1997).

Lieven, D., *Empire: the Russian Empire and its rivals* (London, 2000).

Littlewood, B. and Mahood, L., 'Prostitutes, magdalenes, and wayward girls: dangerous sexualities of working class women in Victorian Scotland', *Gender and History*, 3 (1991), 168–75.

Lloyd, S., '"Pleasure's golden bait": prostitution, poverty and the Magdalen Hospital in eighteenth-century London', *History Workshop Journal*, 41 (1996), 51–70.

Lowe, K. and McLaughlin, E., 'Sir John Pope-Hennessy and the "native race craze": colonial government in Hong Kong, 1877–1882', *Journal of Imperial and Commonwealth History*, 20 (1992), 223–47.

Luddy, M., 'Prostitution and rescue work in nineteenth-century Ireland', in M. Luddy and C. Murphy (eds.), *Women surviving: studies in Irish women's history in the 19th and 20th centuries* (Dublin, 1990), pp. 51–84.

'An outcast community: the "wrens" of the Curragh', *Women's History Review*, 1 (1992), 341–55.

'Women and the Contagious Diseases Acts 1864–1886', *History Ireland*, 1 (1993), 32–4.

Women and philanthropy in nineteenth-century Ireland (Cambridge, 1995).

'"Abandoned women and bad characters": prostitution in nineteenth-century Ireland', *Women's History Review*, 6 (1997), 485–503.

Prostitution and Irish society 1800–1940 (Cambridge, 2007).

Luker, K., 'Sex, social hygiene, and the state: the double-edged sword of social reform', *Theory and Society*, 27 (1998), 601–34.

McCalman, I., 'Unrespectable radicalism: infidels and pornographers in early nineteenth-century London', *Past and Present*, 104 (1984), 74–110.

Radical underworld: prophets, revolutionaries and pornographers in London, 1795–1840 (Cambridge, 1988).

McClintock, A., *Imperial leather: race, gender and sexuality in the colonial contest* (London, 1995).

McCracken, S., 'Male sexuality and the gender industry', *Gender and History*, 7 (1995), 106–12.

McDonough, T. (ed.), *Was Ireland a colony? Economics, politics and culture in nineteenth-century Ireland* (Dublin, 2005).

McGinn, T. A. J., *Prostitution, sexuality and the law in ancient Rome* (New York, 1998).

McHugh, P., *Prostitution and Victorian social reform* (London, 1980).

'James Stuart: engineering, philanthropy and radical politics', in R. Mason (ed.), *Cambridge minds* (Cambridge, 1994), pp. 100–9.

MacKinnon, C. A., 'Does sexuality have a history?', in D. Stanton (ed.), *Discourses of sexuality: from Aristotle to AIDS* (Ann Arbor, 1992), pp. 117–36.

McLaren, A., *The trials of masculinity: policing sexual boundaries 1870–1930* (Chicago, 1997).

Twentieth-century sexuality: a history (Oxford, 1999).

Macleod, R. and Lewis, M. (eds.), *Disease, medicine, and empire: perspectives on Western medicine and the experience of European expansion* (London, 1988).

MacPherson, K. L., *A wilderness of marshes: the origins of public health in Shanghai, 1843–1893* (Hong Kong, 1987).

'Caveat emptor! Attempts to control the venereals in nineteenth century Hong Kong', in L. Bryder and D. A. Dow (eds.), *New countries and old medicine: proceedings of an international conference on the history of medicine and health. Auckland, New Zealand, 1994* (Auckland, 1995), pp. 72–8.
'Conspiracy of silence: a history of sexually transmitted diseases and HIV/AIDS in Hong Kong', in M. Lewis, S. Bamber and M. Waugh (eds.), *Sex, disease, and society: a comparative history of sexually transmitted diseases and HIV/AIDS in Asia and the Pacific* (Westport, 1997), pp. 85–112.
McWhorter, L., 'Sex, race and biopower: a Foucauldian genealogy', *Hypatia: A Journal of Feminist Philosophy*, 19 (2004), 38–62.
Madden, F. and Fieldhouse, D. (eds.), *The dependent empire and Ireland, 1840–1900: advance and retreat in representative self-government* (New York, 1991).
Mahood, L., *The magdalenes: prostitution in the nineteenth century* (London, 1990).
Policing gender, class and family: Britain, 1850–1940 (London, 1995).
Malcolm, E., '"Troops of largely diseased women": VD, the Contagious Diseases Acts and moral policing in late nineteenth-century Ireland', *Irish Economic and Social History*, 26 (1999), 1–14.
Malleson, H. (ed.), *Elizabeth Malleson 1828–1916: autobiographical notes and letters* (printed for private circulation, 1926).
Manderson, L., *Sickness and the state: health and illness in colonial Malaya, 1870–1940* (Cambridge, 1987).
'Colonial desires: sexuality, race, and gender in British Malaya', *Journal of the History of Sexuality*, 7 (1997), 372–88.
'Migration, prostitution and medical surveillance in early twentieth-century Malaya', in L. Marks and M. Worboys (eds.), *Migrants, minorities and health: historical and contemporary studies* (London, 1997), pp. 49–69.
Mandler, P., '"Race" and "nation" in mid-Victorian thought', in S. Collini, R. Whatmore and B. Young (eds.), *History, religion, and culture: British intellectual history 1750–1950* (Cambridge, 2000), pp. 224–44.
Mann, G., 'Locating colonial history: between France and West Africa', *American Historical Review*, 110 (2005), 409–34.
Mann, M., *The sources of social power, volume 1: a history of power from the beginning to AD 1760* (Cambridge, 1986).
Mansfield, N., 'Grads and snobs: John Brown, town and gown in early nineteenth-century Cambridge', *History Workshop Journal*, 35 (1993), 184–98.
Marcus, S., *The other Victorians: a study of sexuality and pornography in mid-nineteenth-century England* (London, 1966).
Marks, S., 'History, the nation, and empire: sniping from the periphery', *History Workshop Journal*, 29 (1990), 111–19.
Mason, M., *The making of Victorian sexuality* (Oxford, 1994).
The making of Victorian sexual attitudes (Oxford, 1994).
'Response', *Journal of Victorian Culture*, 1 (1996), 150–2.
Mathers, H., 'The evangelical spirituality of a Victorian feminist: Josephine Butler, 1828–1906', *Journal of Ecclesiastical History*, 52 (2001), 282–312.
Matlock, J., *Scenes of seduction: prostitution, hysteria, and reading difference in nineteenth-century France* (New York, 1994).
'Liberal strategies of exclusion', in F. Cooper and A. L. Stoler (eds.), *Tensions of empire: colonial cultures in a bourgeois world* (Berkeley, 1997), pp. 59–86.

Mehta, U. S., *Liberalism and empire: a study in nineteenth-century British liberal thought* (Chicago, 1999).
Metzger, B., 'Towards an international human rights regime during the inter-war years: the League of Nations' combat of traffic in women and children', in K. Grant, P. Levine and F. Trentmann (eds.), *Beyond sovereignty: Britain, empire and transnationalism, c.1880–1950* (Basingstoke, 2007), pp. 54–79.
Michie, E. B., *Outside the pale: cultural exclusion, gender difference, and the Victorian woman writer* (Ithaca, 1993).
Midgley, G., *University life in eighteenth-century Oxford* (New Haven, 1996).
Miller, A. H. and Adams, J. E. (eds.), *Sexualities in Victorian Britain* (Bloomington, 1996).
Mills, S., *Gender and colonial space* (Manchester, 2005).
Miners, N., *Hong Kong under imperial rule, 1912–1941* (Hong Kong, 1997).
Mitchell, J. C., 'The political demography of Cambridge 1832–1868', *Albion*, 9 (1977), 242–71.
Mitchell, T., *Colonising Egypt* (Cambridge, 1988).
Mitterauer, M., *A history of youth* (Oxford, 1992).
Moore, B. L. and Johnson, M. A., '"Fallen sisters"? Attitudes to female prostitution in Jamaica at the turn of the twentieth century', *Journal of Caribbean History*, 34 (2000), 46–70.
Moore, J., 'The art of philanthropy? The formation and development of the Walker Art Gallery in Liverpool', *Museum and Society*, 2 (2004), 68–83.
Morefield, J., *Covenants without swords: idealist liberalism and the spirit of empire* (Princeton, 2005).
Morgan, S., '"Wild oats or acorns?" Social purity, sexual politics and the response of the late-Victorian Church', *Journal of Religious History*, 31 (2007), 151–68.
Mort, F., 'Purity, feminism and the state: sexuality and moral politics, 1880–1914', in M. Langan and B. Schwarz (eds.), *Crises in the British state 1880–1930* (London, 1985), pp. 209–25.
  Dangerous sexualities: medico-moral politics in England since 1830 (London, 1987).
  'Archaeologies of city life: commercial culture, masculinity, and spatial relations in 1980s London', *Environment and Planning D: Society and Space*, 13 (1995), 573–90.
Mort, F. and Nead, L., 'Sexuality, modernity and the Victorians', *Journal of Victorian Culture*, 1 (1996), 118–30.
Moscucci, O., *The science of woman: gynaecology and gender in England, 1800–1929* (Cambridge, 1990).
Mosse, G. L., *Nationalism and sexuality: middle-class morality and sexual norms in modern Europe* (Madison, 1985).
Muirhead, I. A., 'Churchmen and the problem of prostitution in nineteenth-century Scotland', *Records of the Scottish Church History Society*, 18 (1974), 223–43.
Mumm, S., '"Not worse than other girls": the convent-based rehabilitation of fallen women in Victorian Britain', *Journal of Social History*, 29 (1996), 527–46.
Munn, C., *Anglo-China: Chinese people and British rule in Hong Kong* (London, 2001).
Murdoch, N. H., 'From militancy to social mission: the Salvation Army and street disturbances in Liverpool, 1879–1887', in J. Belchem (ed.), *Popular politics, riot and labour: essays in Liverpool history 1790–1940* (Liverpool, 1992), pp. 160–72.
Naphy, W., *Sex crimes from Renaissance to Enlightenment* (Stroud, 2002).

Nash, S.D., *Prostitution in Great Britain 1485–1901: an annotated bibliography* (Metuchen, NJ, 1994).
Nead, L., *Myths of sexuality: representations of women in Victorian Britain* (Oxford, 1988).
— *Victorian Babylon: people, streets and images in nineteenth-century London* (New Haven, 2000).
Neal, A.W., 'Cutting off the king's head: Foucault's *Society Must Be Defended* and the problem of sovereignty', *Alternatives*, 29 (2004), 373–98.
Neal, F., 'A criminal profile of the Liverpool Irish', *Transactions of the Historical Society of Lancashire and Cheshire*, 140 (1999), 161–99.
Nield, K., *Prostitution in the Victorian age: debates on the issue from 19th century critical journals* (Westmead, 1973).
Norberg, K., 'From courtesan to prostitute: mercenary sex and venereal disease, 1730–1802', in L.E. Merians (ed.), *The secret malady: venereal disease in eighteenth-century Britain and France* (Lexington, 1996), pp. 34–50.
Nord, D.E., 'The urban peripatetic: spectator, streetwalker, woman writer', *Nineteenth-Century Literature*, 46 (1991), 351–75.
— *Walking the city streets: women, representation, and the city* (Ithaca, 1995).
— '"Vitiated air": the polluted city and female sexuality in *Dombey and Son* and *Bleak House*', in A.H. Miller and J.E. Adams (eds.), *Sexualities in Victorian Britain* (Bloomington, 1996), pp. 38–69.
Nott-Bower, J.W., *Fifty-two years a policeman* (London, 1926).
Ogborn, M., 'Love – state – ego: "centres" and "margins" in 19th-century Britain', *Environment and Planning D: Society and Space*, 10 (1992), 287–305.
— 'Law and discipline in nineteenth century English state formation: the Contagious Diseases Acts of 1864, 1866 and 1869', *Journal of Historical Sociology*, 6 (1993), 28–55.
— 'Ordering the city: surveillance, public space and the reform of urban policing in England 1835–56', *Political Geography*, 12 (1993), 505–21.
— *Spaces of modernity: London's geographies, 1680–1780* (London, 1998).
Ogborn, M. and Philo, C., 'Soldiers, sailors and moral locations in nineteenth-century Portsmouth', *Area*, 26 (1994), 221–31.
Oldenburg, V.T., *The making of colonial Lucknow 1856–1877* (Princeton, 1984).
Oriel, J.D., *The scars of Venus: a history of venereology* (London, 1994).
Osborne, T. and Rose, N., 'Governing cities: notes on the spatialisation of virtue', *Environment and Planning D: Society and Space*, 17 (1999), 737–60.
Otis, L.L., *Prostitution in medieval society: the history of an urban institution in Languedoc* (Chicago, 1985).
Owen, R., *Lord Cromer: Victorian imperialist, Edwardian proconsul* (Oxford, 2004).
Padgug, R.A., 'Sexual matters: on conceptualizing sexuality in history', *Radical History Review*, 20 (1979), 3–23.
Palmer, J. and Pearce, F., 'Legal discourse and state power: Foucault and the juridical relation', *International Journal for the Sociology of Law*, 11 (1983), 361–83.
Parker, R., *Town and gown: the 700 years' war in Cambridge* (Cambridge, 1983).
Parry, J., *The politics of patriotism: English Liberalism, national identity, and Europe, 1830–1886* (Cambridge, 2006).
Parsons, D.L., *Streetwalking the metropolis: women, the city, and modernity* (Oxford, 2000).

Pateman, C., *The sexual contract* (Cambridge, 1988).
Peatling, G., 'Race and empire in nineteenth-century British intellectual life: James Fitzjames Stephen, James Anthony Froude, Ireland, and India', *Eire-Ireland*, 42 (2007), 157–79.
Pedersen, S. 'The maternalist moment in British colonial policy: the controversy over "child slavery" in Hong Kong, 1917–1941', *Past and Present*, 171 (2001), 161–202.
Peers, D. M., 'Soldiers, surgeons and the campaigns to combat sexually transmitted diseases in colonial India, 1805–1860', *Medical History*, 42 (1998), 137–60.
  'Imperial vice: sex, drink and the health of British troops in North Indian cantonments, 1800–1858', in D. Killingray and D. Omissi (eds.), *Guardians of empire: the armed forces of the colonial powers c.1700–1964* (Manchester, 1999), pp. 25–52.
  'The Raj's other great game: policing the sexual frontiers of the Indian Army in the first half of the nineteenth century', in S. Pierce and A. Rao (eds.), *Discipline and the other body: correction, corporeality, colonialism* (Durham, NC, 2006), pp. 115–50.
Pemble, J., *The Mediterranean passion: Victorians and Edwardians in the south* (Oxford, 1987).
Perry, M. E., 'Deviant insiders: legalized prostitutes and a consciousness of women in early modern Seville', *Comparative Studies in Society and History*, 27, 1 (1985), 138–58.
  Gender and disorder in early modern Seville (Princeton, 1990).
Peterson, M. J., *The medical profession in mid-Victorian London* (Berkeley, 1978).
  'Dr Acton's enemy: medicine, sex, and society in Victorian England', *Victorian Studies*, 29 (1986), 569–90.
Petrow, S., *Policing morals: the Metropolitan Police and the Home Office 1870–1914* (Oxford, 1994).
Phillips, K. M. and Reay, B. (eds.), *Sexualities in history: a reader* (London, 2002).
Phillips, M., *The ascent of woman: a history of the suffragette movement and the ideas behind it* (London, 2003).
Phillips, R., 'Imagined geographies and sexuality politics: the city, the country and the age of consent', in R. Phillips, D. Watt and D. Shuttleton (eds.), *De-centring sexualities: politics and representations beyond the metropolis* (London, 2000), pp. 102–24.
  Sex, politics and empire: a postcolonial geography (Manchester, 2006).
  'Histories of sexuality and imperialism: what's the use?', *History Workshop Journal*, 63 (2007), 136–53.
Phillips, R., Watt, D. and Shuttleton, D. (eds.), *De-centring sexualities: politics and representations beyond the metropolis* (London, 2000).
Pitts, J., *A turn to empire: the rise of imperial liberalism in Britain and France* (Princeton, 2005).
Pivar, D. J., *Purity crusade: sexual morality and social control, 1868–1900* (Westport, 1973).
Pooley, C. G., 'The residential segregation of migrant communities in mid-Victorian Liverpool', *Transactions of the Institute of British Geographers*, 2 (1977), 363–82.
Poovey, M., *Uneven developments: the ideological work of gender in mid-Victorian England* (Chicago, 1988).
  Making a social body: British cultural formation 1830–1864 (Chicago, 1995).
Pope-Hennessy, J., *Verandah: some episodes in the crown colonies 1867–1889* (London, 1964).

Porter, B., '"Bureau and barrack": early Victorian attitudes towards the continent', *Victorian Studies*, 27 (1984), 407–33.
　The absent-minded imperialists: empire, society, and culture in Britain (Oxford, 2004).
Porter, D., *Health, civilization and the state: a history of public health from ancient to modern times* (London, 1999).
Porter, D. and Porter, R., 'The politics of prevention: anti-vaccinationism and public health in nineteenth-century England', *Medical History*, 32 (1988), 231–52.
Porter, E., 'For unruly and stubborn rogues', *East Anglian Magazine*, 18 (1958), 72–7.
　'The proctors fight against prostitution in the 18th and 19th century', *Cambridgeshire, Huntingdon and Peterborough Life*, June (1968), 21–3.
Porter, R. and Hall, L., *The facts of life: the creation of sexual knowledge in Britain 1650–1950* (New Haven, 1995).
Post, J. B., 'A Foreign Office survey of venereal disease and prostitution control, 1869–70', *Medical History*, 22 (1978), 327–34.
Pratt, M., *Britain's Greek empire: reflections on the history of the Ionian Islands from the fall of Byzantium* (London, 1978).
Pratt, M. L., *Imperial eyes: studies in travel writing and transculturation* (London, 1992).
Price, R., *British society 1680–1880* (Cambridge, 1999).
Prochaska, F. K., *Women and philanthropy in nineteenth-century England* (Oxford, 1980).
Proudfoot, L. J. and Roche, M. M. (eds.), *(Dis)placing empire: renegotiating British colonial geographies* (Aldershot, 2005).
Prunty, J., *Dublin slums, 1800–1925: a study in urban geography* (Dublin, 1999).
Puccio, P. M., 'Victorian sexuality', *Dickens Quarterly*, 14 (1997), 178–84.
Quètel, C., *History of syphilis* (Oxford, 1990).
Ramanna, M., 'Control and resistance: the working of the Contagious Diseases Acts in Bombay City', *Economic and Political Weekly*, April (2000), 1470–6.
Ramasubban, R., 'Imperial health in British India, 1857–1900', in R. Macleod and M. Lewis (eds.), *Disease, medicine, and empire: perspectives on Western medicine and the experience of European expansion* (London, 1988), pp. 38–60.
Rendell, J., *The pursuit of pleasure: gender, space and architecture in Regency London* (London, 2002).
Richards, J., *Sex, dissidence and damnation: minority groups in the Middle Ages* (London, 1990).
Ringdal, N., *Love for sale: a global history of prostitution* (London, 2004).
Roach, J. P. C., 'Victorian universities and the national intelligentsia', *Victorian Studies*, 3 (1959), 131–50.
Roos, J., 'Backlash against prostitutes' rights: origins and dynamics of Nazi prostitution policies', *Journal of the History of Sexuality*, 11 (2002), 67–94.
Roper, L., 'Discipline and respectability: prostitution and the Reformation in Augsburg', *History Workshop Journal*, 19 (1985), 3–28.
　The holy household: women and morals in Reformation Augsburg (Oxford, 1989).
Roper, M., and Tosh, J. (eds.), *Manful assertions: masculinities in Britain since 1800* (London, 1991).
Rose-Redwood, R. S., 'Governmentality, geography, and the geo-coded world', *Progress in Human Geography*, 30 (2006), 469–86.

Rosen, G., *From medical police to social medicine: essays on the history of health care* (New York, 1974).
Rosen, R., *The lost sisterhood: prostitution in America, 1900–1918* (Baltimore, 1980).
Rossiaud, J., *Medieval prostitution* (Oxford, 1995).
Roston, M., *Victorian contexts: literature and the visual arts* (London, 1996).
Rothblatt, S., 'The student sub-culture and the examination system in early 19th century Oxbridge', in L. Stone (ed.), *The university in society, volume I: Oxford and Cambridge from the 14th to the early 19th century* (Princeton, 1975), pp. 247–303.
 The revolution of the dons: Cambridge and society in Victorian England (Cambridge, 1981).
Rotundo, E. A., *American manhood: transformations in masculinity from the Revolution to the modern era* (New York, 1993).
Ruggiero, G. *The boundaries of eros: sex, crime and sexuality in Renaissance Venice* (Oxford, 1985).
Russett, C.E., *Sexual science: the Victorian construction of womanhood* (Cambridge, 1989).
Said, E., 'Secular interpretation, the geographical element, and the methodology of imperialism', in G. Prakash (ed.), *After colonialism: imperial histories and post-colonial displacements* (Princeton, 1995), pp. 21–39.
Sauerteig, L. D. H., 'Sex, medicine and morality during the First World War', in R. Cooter, M. Harrison and S. Sturdy (eds.), *War, medicine and modernity* (Stroud, 1998), pp. 167–88.
Scaff, L. A., *Fleeing the iron cage: culture, politics, and modernity in the thought of Max Weber* (Berkeley, 1989).
Scott, A.L., 'Physical purity feminism and state medicine in late nineteenth-century England', *Women's History Review*, 8 (1999), 625–53.
Scott, D., 'Colonial governmentality', *Social Text*, 43 (1995), 191–220.
Scott, J.W., *Gender and the politics of history*, revised edition (New York, 1999).
Searby, P. *A history of the University of Cambridge, volume III: 1750–1870* (Cambridge, 1997).
Self, H.J., *Prostitution, women and misuse of the law: the fallen daughters of Eve* (London, 2003).
Sennett, R., *Flesh and stone: the body and city in Western civilization* (London, 1994).
Shahar, S., *The fourth estate: a history of women in the Middle Ages* (London, 1990).
Shapiro, A.-L., *Breaking the codes: female criminality in fin-de-siècle Paris* (Stanford, 1996).
Sharp, I. (ed.), *Josephine Butler and the prostitution campaigns: diseases of the body politic, volume I: the moral reclaimability of prostitutes* (London, 2003).
 (ed.), *Josephine Butler and the prostitution campaigns: diseases of the body politic, volume V: the Queen's daughters in India* (London, 2003).
Shemek, D., *Ladies errant: wayward women and social order in early modern Italy* (Durham, NC, 1998).
Shoemaker, R.B., *Gender in English society, 1650–1850: the emergence of separate spheres?* (London, 1998).
Shorter, E., *A history of women's bodies* (London, 1983).

Siena, K. P., *Venereal disease, hospitals, and the urban poor: London's 'foul wards', 1600–1800* (Rochester, 2004).
Sigsworth, E. M. and Wyke, T. J., 'A study of Victorian prostitution and venereal disease', in M. Vicinus (ed.), *Suffer and be still: women in the Victorian age* (Bloomington, 1972), pp. 77–99.
Sinha, M., *The 'manly Englishman' and the 'effeminate Bengali' in the late nineteenth century* (Manchester, 1995).
    'Britishness, clubbability, and the colonial public sphere: the genealogy of an imperial institution in colonial India', *Journal of British Studies*, 40 (2001), 489–521.
Sinn, E., *Power and charity: the early history of the Tung Wah Hospital, Hong Kong* (Hong Kong, 1989).
    'Chinese patriarchy and the protection of women in 19th-century Hong Kong', in M. Jaschok and S. Miers (eds.), *Women and Chinese patriarchy: submission, servitude and escape* (Hong Kong, 1994), pp. 141–70.
Smart, J., 'Sex, the state and the "scarlet scourge": gender, citizenship and venereal disease regulation in Australia during the Great War', *Women's History Review*, 7 (1998), 5–35.
Smith, F. B., 'Ethics and disease in the later nineteenth century: the Contagious Diseases Acts', *Historical Studies*, 15 (1971), 118–35.
    Florence Nightingale: reputation and power (London, 1982).
    'The Contagious Diseases Acts reconsidered', *Social History of Medicine*, 3 (1990), 197–215.
    The people's health 1830–1910 (London, 1990).
    '"Unprincipled expediency": a comment on Deborah Dunsford's paper', *Social History of Medicine*, 5 (1992), 515–16.
Smith-Dorrien, H., *Memories of forty-eight years' service* (London, 1925).
Soffer, R., *Discipline and power: the university, history and the making of an English elite, 1870–1930* (Stanford, 1994).
Spiegelhalter, D., 'The Contagious Diseases Acts: a controlled experiment in criminal justice', *Significance*, 1 (2004), 88–9.
Spiers, E. M., *The late Victorian army 1868–1902* (Manchester, 1992).
Spongberg, M., *Feminizing venereal disease: the body of the prostitute in nineteenth-century medical discourse* (New York, 1997).
Stansell, C., *City of women: sex and class in New York, 1789–1860* (New York, 1986).
Stearns, C. Z. and Stearns, P. N., 'Victorian sexuality: can historians do it better?', *Journal of Social History*, 18 (1985), 625–34.
Stepan, N. L., *The idea of race in science: Great Britain 1800–1960* (London, 1982).
    'Race, gender, science and citizenship', *Gender and History*, 10 (1998), 26–52.
Stewart, J. D., *Gibraltar the keystone* (London, 1967).
Stocking, G., *Victorian anthropology* (New York, 1987).
Stoler, A. L., *Race and the education of desire: Foucault's History of Sexuality and the colonial order of things* (Durham, NC, 1996).
    'Carnal knowledge and imperial power: gender, race, and morality in colonial Asia', in R. N. Lancaster and M. di Leonardo (eds.), *The gender/sexuality reader: culture, history, political economy* (London, 1997), pp. 13–36.
    'Making empire respectable: the politics of race and sexual morality in twentieth-century colonial cultures', in A. McClintock, A. Mufti and E. Shohat (eds.), *Dangerous*

liaisons: gender, nation, and postcolonial perspectives (Minneapolis, 1997), pp. 344–73.

Carnal knowledge and imperial power: race and the intimate in colonial rule (Berkeley, 2002).

Stone, L., 'The size and composition of the Oxford student body 1580–1910', in L. Stone (ed.), *The university in society, volume I: Oxford and Cambridge from the 14th to the early 19th century* (Princeton, 1975), pp. 3–110.

(ed.), *The university in society, volume I: Oxford and Cambridge from the 14th to the early 19th century* (Princeton, 1975).

Strasser, U., *State of virginity: gender, religion, and politics in an early modern Catholic state* (Ann Arbor, 2004).

Summers, A., 'The constitution violated: the female body and the female subject in the campaigns of Josephine Butler', *History Workshop Journal*, 48 (1999), 1–15.

'Which women? What Europe? Josephine Butler and the International Abolitionist Federation', *History Workshop Journal*, 62 (2006), 215–31.

Swenson, K., *Medical women and Victorian fiction* (Columbia, MO, 2005).

Symanski, R., *The immoral landscape: female prostitution in Western societies* (Toronto, 1981).

Szreter, S., 'Victorian Britain, 1831–1963: toward a social history of sexuality', *Journal of Victorian Culture*, 1 (1996), 136–49.

Tabili, L., 'Women "of a very low type": crossing racial boundaries in imperial Britain', in L. L. Frader and S. O. Rose (eds.), *Gender and class in modern Europe* (Ithaca, 1996), pp. 165–90.

Taithe, B., 'Working men, old Chartists and the Contagious Diseases Acts', in K. Laybourn (ed.), *Social conditions, status and community 1860–c.1920* (Stroud, 1997), pp. 184–203.

'Consuming desires: female prostitutes and "customers" at the margins of crime and perversion in France and Britain, c.1836–85', in M. L. Arnot and C. Usborne (eds.), *Gender and crime in modern Europe* (London, 1999), pp. 151–72.

'Morality is not a curable disease: probing the history of venereal diseases, morality and prostitution', *Social History of Medicine*, 14 (2001), 337–50.

Tanaka, Y., *Japan's comfort women: sexual slavery and prostitution during World War II and the US occupation* (London, 2002).

Taylor, H., 'Rationing crime: the political economy of criminal statistics since the 1850s', *Economic History Review*, 51 (1998), 569–90.

Thomas, K., 'The double standard', *Journal of the History of Ideas*, 20 (1959), 195–216.

Thomas, N., *Colonialism's culture: anthropology, travel and government* (Oxford, 1994).

Timm, A. F., 'Sex with a purpose: prostitution, venereal disease, and militarized masculinity', in D. Herzog (ed.), *Sexuality and German fascism* (New York, 2005), pp. 223–55.

Tosh, J., *A man's place: masculinity and the middle-class home in Victorian England* (New Haven, 1999).

Trexler, R., 'Florentine prostitution in the fifteenth century: patrons and clients', in R. Trexler (ed.), *Dependence in context in Renaissance Florence* (Binghamton, NY, 1994), pp. 373–414.

Trumbach, R., 'Sex, gender, and sexual identity in modern culture: male sodomy and female prostitution in Enlightenment London', in J.C. Fout (ed.), *Forbidden history: the state, society, and the regulation of sexuality in modern Europe* (Chicago, 1992), pp. 89–106.

Trustram, M., 'Distasteful and derogatory? Examining Victorian soldiers for venereal disease', in The London Feminist History Group (eds.), *The sexual dynamics of history: men's power, women's resistance* (London, 1983), pp. 154–64.

Women of the regiment: marriage and the Victorian army (Cambridge, 1984).

Tsai, J.-F., *Hong Kong in Chinese history: community and social unrest in the British colony 1842–1913* (New York, 1993).

Valverde, M, 'The love of finery: fashion and the fallen woman in nineteenth-century social discourse', *Victorian Studies*, 32 (1989), 169–88.

'"Despotism" and ethical liberal governance', *Economy and Society*, 25 (1996), 357–72.

Law's dream of a common knowledge (Princeton, 2003).

Van Doorninck, M., and Campbell, R. '"Zoning" street sex work: the way forward?', in R. Campbell and M. O'Neill (eds.), *Sex work now* (Cullompton, 2006), pp. 62–91.

Vaughan, M., *Curing their ills: colonial power and African illness* (Stanford, 1991).

Venn, J. A., *Alumni Cantabrigienses* (Cambridge, 1940).

Vicinus, M. (ed.), *Suffer and be still: women in the Victorian age* (Bloomington, 1972).

Voeltz, R. A., 'The British Empire, sexuality, feminism and Ronald Hyam', *European Review of History*, 3 (1996), 41–5.

Wagner, P., *A sociology of modernity: liberty and discipline* (London, 1994).

Waldron, J., 'Mill on liberty and on the Contagious Diseases Acts', in N. Urbinati and A. Zakaras (eds.), *J. S. Mill's political thought: a bicentennial reassessment* (Cambridge, 2007), pp. 11–42.

Walker, L., 'Home and away: the feminist remapping of public and private space in Victorian London', in R. Ainley (ed.), *New frontiers of space, bodies and gender* (London, 1998), pp. 65–75.

Walkowitz, J. R., 'The politics of prostitution', in C. R. Stimpson and E. S. Person (eds.), *Women: sex and sexuality* (Chicago, 1980), pp. 145–57.

Prostitution and Victorian society: women, class, and the state (Cambridge, 1980).

'Male vice and female virtue: feminism and the politics of prostitution in nineteenth-century Britain', in A. Snitow, C. Stansell and S. Thompson (eds.), *Desire: the politics of sexuality* (London, 1984), pp. 43–61.

City of dreadful delight: narratives of sexual danger in late-Victorian London (London, 1992).

'Going public: shopping, street harassment, and streetwalking in late Victorian London', *Representations*, 62 (1998), 1–30.

Walkowitz, J. R. and Walkowitz, D. J., ' "We are not beasts of the field": prostitution and the poor in Plymouth and Southampton under the Contagious Diseases Acts', *Feminist Studies*, 1 (1973), 73–106.

Waller, P. J., *Democracy and sectarianism: a political and social history of Liverpool 1868–1939* (Liverpool, 1981).

Ware, V., *Beyond the pale: white women, racism and history* (London, 1992).

Warren, J. F., 'Prostitution in Singapore society and the karayuki-san', in P. J. Rimmer and L. M. Allen (eds.), *The underside of Malaysian history: pullers, prostitutes, plantation workers ...* (Singapore, 1990), pp. 161–76.

Ah ku and karayuki-san: prostitution in Singapore 1870–1940 (Singapore, 1993).

Weeks, J., *Sex, politics and society: the regulation of sexuality since 1800*, 2nd edition (London, 1989).
'Inverts, perverts, and Mary-Annes: male prostitution and the regulation of homosexuality in England in the nineteenth and early twentieth centuries', in M.B. Duberman, M. Vicinus and G. Chauncey (eds.), *Hidden from history: reclaiming the gay and lesbian past* (London, 1991), pp. 195–211.
Welsh, F., *A history of Hong Kong*, revised edition (London, 1997).
Werth, P.W., 'Through the prism of prostitution: state, society and power', *Social History*, 19 (1994), 1–15.
White, B.M., 'Medical police. Politics and police: the fate of John Robertson', *Medical History*, 27 (1983), 407–22.
White, B.S. (ed.), *Hong Kong: between heaven and Earth* (Oxford, 1996).
White, K., *The first sexual revolution: the emergence of male heterosexuality in modern America* (New York, 1993).
White, L., 'Prostitutes, reformers, and historians', *Criminal Justice History*, 6 (1985), 201–27.
The comforts of home: prostitution in colonial Nairobi (Chicago, 1990).
Whitehead, J., 'Bodies clean and unclean: prostitution, sanitary legislation, and respectable femininity in colonial North India', *Gender and History*, 7 (1995), 41–63.
Wiener, M.J., *Reconstructing the criminal: culture, law, and policy in England, 1830–1914* (Cambridge, 1990).
Wilcox, P., 'Marriage, mobility, and domestic service in Victorian Cambridge', *Local Population Studies*, 29 (1982), 19–34.
Wills, C., 'Joyce, prostitution, and the colonial city', in J.P. Waters (ed.), *Ireland and Irish cultural studies, special issue of South Atlantic Quarterly*, 95 (1996), 79–95.
Winchester, H.P.M. and White, P.E., 'The location of marginalised groups in the inner city', *Environment and Planning D: Society and Space*, 8 (1988), 37–54.
Winstanley, D.A., *Early Victorian Cambridge* (Cambridge, 1955).
Wood, N., 'Prostitution and feminism in nineteenth-century Britain', *M/F: a feminist journal*, 7 (1982), 61–77.
Woods, A., 'The construction of an animal plague: foot and mouth disease in nineteenth-century Britain', *Social History of Medicine*, 17 (2004), 23–39.
Wyke, T.J., 'Hospital facilities for, and diagnosis and treatment of, venereal disease in England, 1800–1870', *British Journal of Venereal Disease*, 49 (1973), 78–85.
'The Manchester and Salford Lock Hospital', *Medical History*, 19 (1975), 73–86.
Yeoh, B.S.A., *Contesting space: power relations and the urban built environment in colonial Singapore* (Kuala Lumpur, 1996).
'Sexually transmitted diseases in late nineteenth- and twentieth-century Singapore', in M. Lewis, S. Bamber and M. Waugh (eds.), *Sex, disease, and society: a comparative history of sexually transmitted diseases and HIV/AIDS in Asia and the Pacific* (Westport, 1997), pp. 177–202.
Yoshimi, Y., *Comfort women: sexual slavery in the Japanese military during World War II* (New York, 2000).
Zatz, N.D., 'Sex work/sex act: law, labor, and desire in constructions of prostitution', *Signs*, 22 (1997), 277–308.
Zedner, L., *Women, crime, and custody in Victorian England* (Oxford, 1991).

Index

abolitionists, *see* repeal movement
Acton, William 14, 32, 36, 58, 67, 78, 81
  on Aldershot 48
  author of *Prostitution* 32
  on the geography of prostitution 82
  on prostitution in the University towns 114, 115, 116–17, 137
Admiralty 38, 169, 180, 249
Africa 19, 247, *see also* Cape Colony; South Africa
Agamben, Giorgio 186
Airey, Richard 169
Aisenberg, Andrew 165
Albania 160
Aldershot 31, 44, 45, 47, 48, 51, 52, 69
  alleged improvement under the CD Acts 48–9
  as scheduled district under the CD Acts 28, 39, 46, 50
  lock hospital accommodation 43
  public opinion in 48
  support for regulationist measures 35
Alford, Charles 202
Amos, Sheldon 62
Amsterdam 119
Andrew, Elizabeth 236
Argentina 7
Armstrong, Richard 93, 107
  author of *The Deadly Shame of Liverpool* 92
  campaign against drink and prostitution in Liverpool 92
  on brothel districts in Liverpool 99, 107, 108
Army, British
  Army Medical Department 33
  Army medical officers 36
  Army medical reports 33, 37, 51
  concerns over venereal disease 33, 182–5
  in Bombay 36
  in Gibraltar 155
  movement for reform 15
Arnold, David 194
Association for Promoting the Extension of the Contagious Diseases Acts 55, 56–9, *see also* Contagious Diseases (CD) Acts, campaign for extension of
Atchinson, Thomas 37
Athlone 50, 52
Auckland 237
Australia 19, 196, *see also* Queensland, Tasmania, Victoria
Aves, Jane 141

Backhouse, Constance 196
Baldwin, Peter 8, 14, 73, 238
Banks, F. C. 62
Barbados 221, 225, 237
Barnwell, *see* Cambridge, Barnwell
Bartley, Paula 80, 94, 105
Bashford, Alison 227

Battel, Eliza 143
Beach, Michael Hicks 221
Beadsworth, Mary Ann 141
Belfast 50, 52
Belgium 7
Bengal 191, 192
Bentham, Jeremy 200, 201
Berlin 108
Bevan, William 89
Beverley, Robert Mackenzie 127, 128, 129
biopolitics 9, 200, 209, 212, 217, 226, 227
Bird, James 36
Birmingham 94, 95, 104, 105, 109
Bland, Lucy 93
Bombay 36, 192, 197
Bowen, George Ferguson 159, 188
Bowler, Susanna 141
Bowring, John 200–1, 203, 204, 209
Bristol 63
Brooke, Richard 88
brothels 16, 17, 70, 77, 83, 116, 133, 144, 189, 232, 238
  brothel districts, *see* zoning of prostitution
  brothel keepers, *see below*
  brothel medical clubs in Singapore 240
  comparative police statistics of 76, 82, 87, 96–7
  in Aldershot: brothel keepers 35
  in Cambridge: as part of informal system of regulation 121, 122, 125, 126
  in Cambridge: brothel keepers 140
  in Cambridge: disorderly houses 115
  in Cambridge: geography of 122–4
  in Corfu (Kerkyra) 160
  in Cork 69
  in Gibraltar 25, 164, 169, 174–9, 182
  in Gibraltar: brothel keepers 174–6
  in Gibraltar: demise of 184
  in Gibraltar: existence of brothel system under challenge 183
  in Hong Kong 25, 189, 200, 201, 202, 203, 206
  in Hong Kong: attacked by repealers 236
  in Hong Kong: blamed on Chinese 208
  in Hong Kong: brothel keepers 200, 201, 206, 209, 211, 215, 217
  in Hong Kong: 'brothel slavery' 201, 204, 219, *see also* slavery
  in Hong Kong: investigated by Pope Hennessy 204–6
  in Hong Kong: racial and spatial segregation of 190, 212–17, 221–2, 224, 225, 227
  in La Linea, Spain 183
  in Liverpool: alleged connections with drinks trade 92
  in Liverpool: as part of system of toleration 77, 92–3, 95–7, 98
  in Liverpool: brothel keepers 93, 97
  in Liverpool: geography of 90–1, 97–102, 111–12
  in Liverpool: racialisation of 90
  in Liverpool: subject to campaign of repression 105–8
  in subjected districts of the CD Acts 29, 46, 49, 55, 68, 89
  in Zante (Zakinthos) 157
  legislated against by Criminal Law Amendment Act 104, 108
  licensed and inspected in regulationist regimes 3
  licensed in *ancien régime* France 7
  licensed in pre-Reformation Europe 6
  regulated in modern France 7, 10, 73
  repression of in Glasgow 93
  repression of in Manchester 94
  suppressed by vigilance groups 104, 106
  tolerated in Dublin 95
Brown, Blair 238
Browne, George Forrest 130
Browning, Robert 142
Bruce, Henry 30, 65
Bryder, Linda 190
Burke, Stacie 167, 169
Burma 195, 237

Burne, Peter 91
Burton, Antoinette 195, 239, 248
Bushnell, Katharine 236
Butler, Josephine 12, 62, 63, 69, 236, 243, 247
  campaign in Colchester 64–5
  experience in the University towns 149
  on Gibraltar 25
  on Malta 154
  on regulationism and the British Empire 240, 247, 249

Calcutta 195
Cambridge 2, 24, 25, 113–51, 155, 165, 172, 229, 232, 233, 238
  Barnwell 121–2, 126, 127, 128, 132, 135, 137, 232
  Cambridge Union 148
  Castle End 122
  example for regulationists 120–1, 229
  Female Refuge 127, 135, 140–2, 143
  geography of prostitution in 122–6
  morality of University debated 127–9, 144–8
  New Town 122, 132
  proctorial system in 24, 113, 114, 115–16, 119, 126, 127
  proctors 116–17, 119, 121, 122, 123, 125, 126, 127, 130, 135, 137, 139, 140, 143, 144–5, 147–8
  prostitution in 115, 135–43, 148
  Spinning House 117–19, 120, 127, 129, 140, 142, 151
  undergraduate sexuality in 130–5, 149–51
  see also undergraduates
Cambridge Chronicle 122
Cambridge University, *see* Cambridge
Canada 196, 237
Canterbury 28, 42, 44, 45, 46, 47, 50, 52
Cape Colony 196, 237
Caribbean 196, *see also* Barbados, Jamaica, Trinidad
Carnarvon, Lord 206
Cassar, Paul 156, 157
Catholic Church 49, 61, 69, 204
Cawnpore 240

Cephalonia 153
Ceylon 195, 237
Chadwick, Edwin 36
Chatham 44, 45, 47, 52
  alleged improvement under the CD Acts 49
  as scheduled district under the CD Acts 28, 46, 50
  lock hospital accommodation 43
  prostitution in 68, 69, 70
  support for regulationist measures 50
Chatham, Lord 235
Chatterjee, Partha 19
Cheshire 103
child abuse 72, 110
child prostitution 65
China 199, 200, 201, 202, 208, 209, 223, 234, 250
Choy, Ng 225
Christian, Elizabeth 143
Church of England 61, 63, 108
Clausewitz, Carl von 13
Close, Francis 192, 250
Cochrane, James 171
Colchester 44, 45, 47, 52, 141
  agitation against the CD Acts 50, 64–5, 235
  as scheduled district under the CD Acts 28, 39, 42, 46, 50
  lock hospital accommodation 43
Collin, Shilton 108
Collingham, E. M. 240
Colonial City model 195, 217
Colonial Office 170, 180, 201, 219, 220, 221, 225, 233, 236, 237, 238, 241, 249
colonialism, and regulation of prostitution 11–22, 37, 75, 152–87, 188–228, 229, 230, 232, 234, 241
Conservative Party 65, 92, 106–7, 108
Contagious Diseases Acts 4, 14, 15, 16, 22–3, 28–75, 76, 77, 93, 99, 108, 113, 120, 121, 144, 147, 148, 153–4, 155, 162, 166, 169, 172, 185, 189, 192, 193, 196, 204, 206, 207, 229, 234, 235, 241, 244, 246, 247, 250

campaign for extension of 54–62, 77, 89, 92, 154
differences between subjected districts 43–50
efficacy in combating venereal diseases 50–3
geography of 30, 39–41, 42–3
imperial nature and context 38, 75, 190–1
introduction of 30–1
justified in relation to colonial experience 36–8
medical rationale and promotion 32–3
militarisation of prostitution 14–15
military rationale and promotion 14, 33
operation of 38–53
opposition to, *see* repeal movement
origins of 15, 30–8
proctorial systems a precedent for 24
regulationist nature of 94
Royal Commission, 1871 210
significance of 66–73, 73–5
suspension and repeal 65–6, 73, 77, 90, 97, 104, 151, 169, 180, 181, 238, 240
contagious diseases legislation 1, 196, 229, 230, 233, 238, 244
Cook, Hera 86, 87
Cooper, Frederick 242
Cooter, Roger 13
Corbin, Alain 10, 98, 164
Corfu 153, 155, 158–61, 185, 236
   Kerkyra town 158, 160
   Kerkyra town, Jewish quarter 160
Cork 44, 47, 52
   as scheduled district under the CD Acts 28, 46, 50
   brothels and prostitution in 69, 71
   campaign against brothels in 47
   lock hospital accommodation 43,
   support for regulationist measures 49
Cork Examiner 69
Cox, Pamela 73
Crimean War 15, 36
Criminal Law Amendment Act 72, 77, 92, 98, 104, 105, 106, 108, 238

Crowe, Sarah 143
Curgenven, John Brendon 154
Curragh, the 44, 47, 52
   as scheduled district under the CD Acts 28, 46, 50
   lock hospital accommodation 43

Danson, J. T. 90
Dartmouth 28, 42, 46
Deakin, C. W. Shirley 154
Deal 28, 42, 45, 44, 46, 47
Defence of the Realm Act 73
Denmark 7
Deptford 42
Deslandes, Paul 151
Devonport 43, *see also* Plymouth and Devonport
disciplinary power 11, 12, 25, 38, 164–6, 186, 190, 199, 204, 217, 226
Dorrington, Charlotte 143
Dover 28, 42, 44, 45, 46, 47, 50, 52
drinking and drunkenness 83, 91–2, 107, 126, 131, 140, 151, 162, 179
Dublin 50, 51, 52, 61
   Monto district 95
Duncan, Clara 143
Durham, county 86

Eagleton, Terry 153
East India Company 191
Edinburgh 50, 52, 146
Edmondson, Joseph 54, 181
Eitel, Ernest J. 206, 222–4, 225, 226
Emergency Powers (Defence) Act 73
Emery, William 117
evangelicalism 63, 127, 144, 146
Exeter Hall 237,
extensionist campaign, *see* Contagious Diseases (CD) Acts, campaign for extension of

Farrar, Frederic 150–1
fascism 12
feminism 62, 63–4, 73, 104, 149, 220, 230, 239,
Fermoy 50, 52

292 Index

Fernandez, Dolores 174
Fiji 196, 237
Finnegan, Frances 68, 103
Flood, Frederick Solly 170–2
Folkestone 42
Fordham, Sarah 143
Foucault, Michel 7, 21, 190, 210, 226, *see also* biopolitics, disciplinary power, governmentality
   on discipline 11, 164
   on law and sovereign power 165–6, 186, 187
   on war and the military 13, 165
Fowler, Robert 235
France 3, 7–8, 9–10, 11, 14, 15, 16, 73, 103, 158, 165, 243, 244,
   see also regulationism, French system
French Revolution 7
Fuller, Elizabeth 141

Gallant, Thomas 157–8
Garrett, Elizabeth 154
Gattrell, Vic 79
gender roles 5–6, 13, *see also* masculinity
Geneva 241
Germany 6, 7, 12
Gibraltar 2, 152, 153, 155–6, 161, 162–4, 166–87, 188, 197, 202, 233, 237, 240, 250
   Aliens Order in Council, 1885 173, 181
   Aliens Order in Council, 1900 181
   attempt to frame contagious diseases legislation 169, 180
   brothels and prostitution in 162, 173, 182–5
   cited by regulationists 37, 154
   Civilian Hospital 168, 172
   dependence of regulationism upon law 184, 186–7
   immigration and overcrowding 162, 166–7
   informal system of regulation 24–5
   naturalisation problem 167, 170–1, 179–82
   permit system 164, 168–9, 170, 172–3
   problems of colonial law 171
   Sanitary Order Further Amendment Ordinance 180, 181
   Serruya's Lane 174–5, 177–8, 182, 184, 232
Gilbert, Pamela 88
Gilfoyle, Timothy J. 242
Gladstone, William Ewart 31
Glamorgan 83
Glasgow 23, 93–4, 95, 96, 105, 108
Gloucester 83
Gonzalez, Christina 174
governmentality 21–2, 25, 78, 186, 190, 198, 218, 227
Grant, Rhoda 140
Gravesend 28, 42, 44, 45, 46, 47, 50
Greece 152, 160
Greenwich 28, 42, 44, 45, 46, 47
Greg, William Rathbone 36
Grewal, Inderpal 18
Guardian, The 146

Hall, Catherine 248
Hall, Lesley 14
Hamburg 12
Hammick, James 81, 86, 87
Harsin, Jill 165
Hereford 83
Hernandez, Carmen 168, 187
Heyningen, Elizabeth van 196
Higgs, Edward 79
Hill, Berkeley 49, 56, 68, 70
Hodges, Sarah 197, 227
Holland, Henry 237
Home Office 39, 79
homosexuality 5, 65, 72, 97–102, 184
Hong Kong 2, 19, 25–6, 37, 188, 190, 197, 198–9, 199–228, 232, 233, 234, 237, 238, 240, 241
   brothel keepers in 206, 216, 217
   brothel system attacked by repeal activists 26, 207, 218, 236
   brothels investigated by Pope Hennessy 204–6
   Chinese political community 224–5
   cited by regulationists 37

concerns over venereal disease in 199–200, 218, 227
crisis in government in 199, 218, 226
geography of brothel prostitution in 212–17
introduction of regulationist measures 200–1
licensing of brothels in 202
lock hospital 212
mui tsai controversy in 221–5
Ordinance 10, 1867 203, 211, 212–13, 214, 215
Ordinance 12, 1857 196, 200, 203, 212
Orientalist discourse on prostitution 207–11
Po Leung Kuk institution 213, 214, 224, 225
prostitution associated with slavery in 206, 220–1, *see also* slavery
racialised sexuality in 25, 198, 210–11
regulationist system in 189–90
relations between British and Chinese 199, 201
Tai Ping Shan 212, 215, 217
Tung Wah hospital 212, 213, 214
Wanchai 215, 216, 217
Hopkins, Ellice 72, 150
hospitals 7, 10, 36, 120, 157, 161, 180
Inspectors of 38, 39, 41, 206
lock hospitals 3, 28, 34, 43, 45, 61, 94, 99, 120, 157, 169, 191–2, 193, 201, 212
visiting surgeons 28, 42, 46
Hounslow 50, 52
Hughes, John 92
Hull, Isabel 6
Hume, Abraham 99
Hunt, Aland 166
Hyam, Ronald 16, 17, 21

imperial networks 1, 21, 233, 234, 235, 238, 241
India 19, 36, 37, 152, 197, 198, 235, 236, 238, 239–40, 246, 250, 237
1857 rebellion 15, 192
Cantonment Act, 1864 193
cantonment regulations 180, 240, 245

cited by repeal activists 243, 245, 247
colonial medical tradition in 193–4
Contagious Diseases Act, 1868 193, 197
contagious diseases legislation 194, 235, 238, 240
introduction of regulationist measures 191–5
orientalist ideas of 194
India Office 35
Ionian Islands 64, 152, 153, 154, 158, 164, 234, 236
colonial identity 153
prostitution regulated in 24, 37, 154, 155, 156, 158, 159–61, 185
Ireland 23, 28, 43, 56, 75, 148, 169, 247, 249
prostitution offences in 79
support for repeal movement in 63
Irish immigrants to Britain 48, 103–4
Isle of Wight 50, 52
Ison, Elizabeth 143
Italy 7, 103

Jacob, Archibald 51
Jamaica 237
James, Edwin 147
Jameson, F. J. 145
Japan 12
Joyce, Brian 70

Karras, Ruth 4
Kent 41
Kildare 43
Kimberley, Lord 204, 207, 225
Kipling, Rudyard 21

La Linea, Spain 183, 184
Labouchere, Henry 201, 221
Labuan 237
Ladies' National Association for the Repeal of the Contagious Diseases Acts 62, 63, 239, *see also* repeal movement
Lambert, David 221–5
Lancashire 83–6, 103
Lancet, The 32, 54, 57, 61
Langley, J. Baxter 64

law, colonial 25, 164, 186
Lawrence, Philip 14
Lawson, Robert 41
League of Nations 225, 241
Leeds 63, 94
Legg, Stephen 2
Lethbridge, Roper 235
Letteridge, Sarah 143
Levi, Leone 86
Levine, Philippa 15, 17, 19, 22, 74, 185, 193, 194, 197, 198, 207, 232, 242, 250
Liber Niger, see Oxford, Oxford University 'Black Book'
Liberalism
  and empire 26, 231, 244, 251
  party political 64, 65, 107, 108, 147, 244, 246
  philosophical and political 6, 7, 16, 26, 204, 218, 220, 227, 229, 230, 248, 250, 251
Liddell, John 34, 120
Limerick 50, 52
Lister, Alfred 209, 211, 226
Liverpool 2, 25, 33, 43, 63, 76–110, 121, 122, 137, 155, 165, 229, 233, 238, 242
  Blandford Street 99–102, 111, 232
  drunkenness in 83, 91–2
  informal system of regulation 23, 77, 95–6, 109, 113
  overrepresentation in statistics of prostitution offences 82–8
  policy of localisation 23, 77, 98, 109–10, 232
  policy on prostitution contrasted with Manchester 94, 96–7
  prevalence of venereal disease 89
  prostitution associated with drink 91–2, 107
  prostitution associated with Irish immigrants 89–90, 91, 104
  prostitution in 88–9, 90–1
  prostitution policy challenged by reformers 93, 106–8, 110
  target for extension of CD legislation 61–2, 63, 76, 89, 92, 110
Liverpool Citizen 99
Liverpool Daily Post 107

Liverpool Review 108
Liverpool Vigilance Committee 106
localisation, *see* Liverpool, policy of localisation, zoning of prostitution
Logan, William 91
London 14, 18, 29, 30, 42, 43, 48, 50, 51, 56, 61, 62, 63, 68, 70, 72, 52, 81–2, 83, 93, 126, 141, 146, 243
London Labour and the London Poor 82, 83
Lowndes, Frederick 43, 80, 82, 88, 90, 91, 92–3, 98, 103, 104
Luker, Kristin 8
Lundie, Robert 107

MacDonnell, Richard 203, 204, 210, 213, 214
MacLaren, Walter 245, 247
Madras 191, 198
magdalens 94, 127, 141, *see also* Cambridge, Female Refuge
Mahood, Linda 93
Maidstone 28, 42, 44, 45, 46, 47, 50, 51, 52
Maitland, Thomas 158
Malacca 196
Malaya 200
Malta 24, 64, 152, 153, 155, 156–7, 158, 160, 161, 164, 170, 185, 201, 202, 233, 234, 250, 237
  cited by repealers 64, 154, 235
  cited by supporters of CD legislation 37, 154–5
  Knights of St John 156, 157
  Ordinance IV, 1861 5.75
Manchester 23, 50, 2.578, 85, 86, 87, 94, 95, 96–7, 104, 105, 108
Mann, Gregory 20, 21
Mann, Michael 22
Martin, William Fanshawe 154
masculinity 13, 130, 150–1
Mason, Michael 60, 86, 87, 88, 89, 131
Mayhew, Henry 82, 83, *see also London Labour and the London Poor*
McClintock, Anne 17
McHugh, Paul 31, 63

McLaren, John 196
medical police 8, 32, 36, 179, 192
Mehta, Uday Singh 248
Melville, Herman 88
Mexico 7
Middlesex 83
military, and British regulation of prostitution 33, 36, 229
Mitchell, Timothy 157, 217
Modern Review 151
modernity 4, 6, 11, 12, 14, 17, 165, 190, 229, 231
Monto, *see* Dublin, Monto district
Moreno, Benedeta 175
Morgan, William 37
Morning Chronicle 76, 89, 96
Morocco 174
Mort, Frank 14, 105
Mowlam, Catherine 135
mui tsai, *see* Hong Kong, *mui tsai* controversy in
Munn, Christopher 199, 218, 226
Mynott, Edward 94

Naples 160
Napoleon
  Bonapartism 243, 244
  Code Napoléon 7
  Louis-Napoléon 244
  Napoléon Bonaparte 244
  Napoleonic conquests 12, 158
  Napoleonic era 7, 9, 158
  Napoleonic France 12, 243
National Anti-Contagious Diseases Acts Association, *see* National Association for the Repeal of the Contagious Diseases Acts
National Association for the Repeal of the Contagious Diseases Acts 62–3
National Council for Combating Venereal Diseases 184
National Vigilance Association 94, 104
Navy, British 201
  concern over venereal disease 33, 183
  medical department 34
  navy medical reports 33, 37, 76

promotion of regulation of prostitution 35
  surgeons 180, 201, 206, 234
neo-regulationism 72
Nevins, John Birkbeck 33, 51, 53
New Zealand 196
Newcastle 63, 83, 91
Newdegate, Charles 250
Newman, Cardinal 131
Newmarket 121, 132
Nightingale, Florence 31, 33
Nonconformism 63
Norberg, Kathryn 8
North West Provinces, India 195
Nott-Bower, William 87, 92, 93, 95–6, 97, 98, 105, 106, 108
Nottingham 62,

Ogborn, Miles 39–41, 63, 166
Ontario 196
Orientalism, and discourses of sexuality 18, 194, 198, 207–12
Oxford 24, 172, 229, 238
  morality of University debated 129–30
  Oxford University 'Black Book' 132–4
  proctorial system in 113, 114, 116
  proctors 116, 132, 133, 134
  prostitution in 115
  undergraduate sexuality in 130–5, *see also* undergraduates
  University Police Act 116
Oxford Herald 116

Paget, Francis Bradley 135
Pall Mall Gazette 246, 247
Parent-Duchâtelet, Alexander 5, 9, 14, 78
  author of *De la prostitution dans la ville de Paris* 9
Paris 7, 9, 14, 108, 165, 243
Parry, Jonathan 243, 244, 248
Patteson, John 144,
Pauncefote, Julian 203
Peers, Douglas 192, 194
Pembroke Dock 50, 51, 52
Penang 196
Perry, Mary Elizabeth 156
Phillips, Richard 19, 196, 231

Playfair, Lyon 156
Plymouth and Devonport 30, 42, 44, 47, 50, 52
  alleged improvement under the CD Acts 89
  as scheduled district under the CD Acts 28, 42, 43, 46, 50
  prostitution in 68
  support for regulationist measures 49
police 4, 9, 34, 38, 39, 41, 49, 61, 65, 68, 77, 79, 81, 86, 87
  Cambridge 135, 140, 143
  Gibraltar 168, 170, 172, 173, 174, 177, 179, 180, 183
  Glasgow 94
  Hong Kong 203
  Ionian Islands 159
  Liverpool 87, 92–3, 95–7, 96–9, 104, 105–8, 122
  Manchester 87, 94
  Metropolitan 38, 39, 83
  Oxford 116
  Sheffield 96
  Zante 157
police des moeurs 3, 8, 29, 116, 126, 244
Poor Law 39
Pope Hennessy, John 26, 208, 209, 214, 219, 221, 222
  denunciation of 'brothel slavery' 220–1
  embroiled in *mui tsai* controversy 222, 224–6
  investigation into brothel system in Hong Kong 204–6
Portsmouth 44, 45, 46, 47, 52
  as subjected district under the CD Acts 28, 29, 43, 50
  lock hospital accommodation in 43
  support for regulationist measures 49
Portugal 7
Preston 50, 52
Price, Richard 72
prostitutes 1, 3, 5, 6, 7, 8, 10, 11, 16, 17, 18, 24, 25, 29, 32, 36, 39, 42, 50, 55, 56, 67, 68, 72, 73, 74, 75, 76, 80, 81, 82, 86, 87, 98, 110, 132, 148, 155, 161, 165, 166, 189, 191, 192

  age profile of 67–8, 70, 102–3, 137, 161, 176, 177
  claimed to be helped by CD Acts 54–5
  condition of, in subjected districts of CD Acts 48, 49
  examination under CD Acts 38, 41
  identification as 'common prostitutes' 28, 41
  in Cambridge 117, 119, 124–6, 127, 128, 135–43, 144, 150
  in Corfu 158–61
  in Gibraltar 162, 164, 166, 168–9, 169, 170, 172, 173–9, 180, 181, 183, 184, 185
  in Hong Kong 199, 200, 201, 202, 204, 206, 209, 210–11, 215, 217, 224, 225, 226
  in India 193–5, 198
  in Ionian Islands 153
  in Liverpool 88, 89, 90–1, 92, 97, 99, 102–4
  in Malta 153, 156–7
  in Manchester 94
  in Oxford 129, 133
  in York 103
  in Zante 157–8
  legal status of 186–7
  penalties for harbouring, under CD Acts 39, 42
  police statistics 79
  problems in definition and identification of 134, 135–7, 147
  proctorial powers over 115–16
  professionalisation of 67, 68, 71, 103, 138–40, 160–1, 164, 176
  recognition of in regulationist regimes 5, 70–1
  registered under CD Acts 28
  registration under regulationist regimes 3
  social investigation of 9–10
  statistics of, in subjected districts of CD Acts 46
Prussia 244
public health movement 8, 32, 33
Public Opinion (Malta) 157

Quebec 196
Queensland 19, 196, 237
Queenstown 28, 47, 50

race 2, 16, 17, 26, 90, 152, 189, 190, 231
　and colonial governmentality 190, 198, 227–8
　and geographical segregation of brothels in Hong Kong 189–90, 212–18, 226
　and regulation of prostitution 19, 197–9, 230, 242
　and politics of repeal movement 26, 239–40, 245–8
　and venereal disease 194
　Chinese culture of prostitution asserted 207, 208–9, 220
　humanitarian anti-racism 204, 219–20
　pathologisation of other races 210–11, 226
　political ambiguity of racial discourse 242, 245
　racial identification of the Irish 86, 153
　racial politics in Hong Kong 199, 204, 213–14, 224–5
　racialised sexuality 18, 25, 208–9
Ramasubban, Radhika 195
Record, The 146
Reformation 6
reglémentation, see regulationism, French system
regulationism 1
　and neo-regulationism 242
　British tradition of regulationism 1, 4, 14–16, 22, 73, 229
　French system 3, 7–8, 10, 12, 16, 55, 73, 107, 158, 165, 202, 232
　identified as indigenous Chinese policy 208
　nature and definition 3–16
　relationship to law 164–6, 186–7
　relationship to medical science 6, 8
　relationship to the state 6–8
　relationship to war and imperialism 6, 11–16
repeal movement 23, 24, 25, 26, 50, 54–66, 71–2, 76–7, 143, 181, 204, 218, 230, 239, 241, 244, 250–1
　and imperial rule 26–7, 230, 234–9, 240, 245–50
　complexity of racial politics 245–8
　connections to social purity campaigns 71
　linking of prostitution to slavery 220
　on Cambridge 148, 149
　on colonial regulation of prostitution 188, 192, 193, 240
　on efficacy of CD Acts 51–3
　on Hong Kong 203
　on introduction of CD Acts 30–1
　on the national character 248–9, 250
Richardson, B. W. 148
Ringdal, Nils 30
Robinson, Lavinia 141
Rochester 49, 50
Rolfe, Emma 142
Roos, Julia 12
Rumbelow, Ann 135
Rumsey, Henry Wyldbore 32, 36
Russell, Mary 141
Russia 6, 7, 103, 129

St Augustine 5
St Helena 237
St Paul 5
Saint-Lazare hospital 7
Salvarsan 240
sanitary discourse 38, 71
Sawchuk, Lawrence 167, 169
Scott, Anne 71
Scott, Joan 10
Sedgwick, Adam 117, 126, 128, 130, 145–6
Seed, William 169
Sentinel, The 236
Seville 156
sexuality, concepts of 4, 5–6, 17–19
sexually transmitted diseases, *see* venereal disease

Shaen, William 62
Shanghai 209
Sheerness 28, 43, 44, 45, 46, 47, 50, 52
Sheffield 50, 52, 62, 94, 96, 105
Shield, The 147, 236
Shorncliffe 44, 45, 47, 52
  as subjected district under CD Acts 28, 42, 46, 50
  lock hospital accommodation in 43
Sicily 160
Simon, John 33
Singapore 196, 217, 240
Sinn, Elizabeth 225
Skey Committee 154, 201, 206
slavery 219, 220, 235, 241
  associated with Chinese culture 210
  associated with prostitution 18
  controversy over application to *mui tsai* 220–6
  denunciation of 'brothel slavery' in Hong Kong 26, 201, 204, 206, 219
Sloggett, William Henry 206, 208, 234, 236
Smale, John 222, 223, 224, 225
Smith, Cecil Clementi 215
Smith, F. B. 38
Smith-Dorrien, Horace 184
Social Purity Alliance 105
social purity movement 17, 64, 65, 71, 72, 77, 92, 93, 94, 104–8, 110, 149–51, 239
Social Science Congress 62
Soldiers and the Social Evil 33, 37, 120
Somerset, Duke of 61
South Africa 237
Southampton 30, 43, 44, 45, 47, 68
  as subjected district under the CD Acts 28, 29, 42, 46, 50, 54
  repeal agitation in 50
Spain 7, 155, 162, 169, 172, 183, 184, 187
Sparrow, Amelia 141
Spiers, Edward 53
Spinhuis, Amsterdam 119

Stansfeld, James 51, 62, 192, 207, 234, 236
Stead, William 247, 249
Stent, Mr, customs officer 208
Stevens, Maria 140
Stevens, Martha 141
Stirling, Rear Admiral 200
Stittle, Hannah 141
Storks, Henry 64, 153, 154, 158, 170, 234, 235
Straits Settlements 19, 196, 237
Strood 49
Stuart, James 149, 234. 235
Sturdy, Steve 13
Sweden 7
Switzerland 7

Tait, William 114
Taithe, Bertrand 57, 63, 64, 71
Tasmania 196, 237
Taylor, Charles Bell 235
Taylor, Howard 86
Telegraph, The 147, 148
Thomas, Enriqueta 174, 179, 187
Thomas, Nicholas 157
Times, The 15, 35, 37, 119, 120, 126, 129, 219
Titcomb, J. H. 135
Tom Brown at Oxford 150
Townshend, Marquess 61
Trinidad 237
Tripoli 160
tropical medicine 193
Tyneside 83

undergraduates 24, 114, 119–20, 123, 124, 126, 127, 139, 148
  as targets of moral reform 149–51
  collegiate ethos of protection of 131
  sexual culture 132
  sexual experiences 114, 126, 132–5, 140, 141, 142
  sexual reputation of 114, 128, 132, 135, 150
United States 223, 243

Valletta 156, 157
Valverde, Mariana 2
Vaughan, Megan 210
venereal disease 1, 3, 7, 8, 10, 15, 24, 28, 36, 37, 38–9, 41, 54, 56, 72, 89, 91, 115, 119, 126, 153, 154, 155, 156, 157, 158, 161, 164, 168, 172, 173, 179, 180, 180, 181, 189, 191, 193, 195, 201, 204, 206, 207, 209, 211, 218, 226, 240, 242
  alleged prevalence amongst undergraduates 149
  amongst British troops 33, 35, 37, 52, 120, 154, 182, 184, 192, 198, 200, 240
  associated with women 6
  efficacy of CD Acts in combating 41, 51–3
  gonorrhoea 36, 142
  in colonial medical paradigm 193–4
  racialisation of 194
  syphilis 8, 10, 34, 36, 53, 76, 161, 193, 211
venereology 58, 73, 80, 88, 98, 240
Venice 158, 159, 160
Victoria, Australia 196, 237
Vienna 108
Vienna, Congress of 158
Vintras, Alex 54

Walker, John 116, 129
Walker and Cain brewers 92

Walkowitz, Daniel 50
Walkowitz, Judith 33, 50, 55, 63, 67, 68, 71, 72, 81
War Office 169, 180, 234, 249
Warley 50, 52
Weber, Max 10, 13
Westminster Review 18
Whitbread, Samuel 33
White Cross Army 105
white slavery 65, 72
Whitehead, Judy 194
Wickham, Gary 166
Williams, George 145
Wilson, Henry 62, 193
Winchester 28, 42, 44, 45, 46, 47, 50, 52
Windsor 28, 42, 44, 45, 46, 47, 49, 50, 52
Wodehouse, H. E. 215
Woolwich 28, 42, 44, 45, 46, 47, 50, 52
Worcester 83
World War I 15, 73, 173, 182, 183
World War II 15, 73

Yeoh, Brenda 217
Yokohama 237
York 63, 68, 103
Yorkshire 63

Zante 153, 157–8, 160, 187
zoning of prostitution 2, 3, 10, 69, 70, 97–104, 114, 121, 178, 212–18, 232